I0815866

"O'Donnell has produced a solid and thoughtful exposition of the book of Job by laying bare not only the meaning of each section of the book, including the speeches of Job and his 'friends,' but also the heart wrenching up-and-down journey of Job's thinking as he wrestles with his innocence through his experience of suffering. He also shows what we can learn from each passage of the book and gives good guidance on how the book relates to Christ. I highly recommend this clear presentation of the message of the book of Job."

—**Richard P. Belcher Jr.,** John D. and Frances M. Gwin Professor of Old Testament, Reformed Theological Seminary, Charlotte; Academic Dean (Atlanta, Dallas, and Houston), Reformed Theological Seminary

"With his usual astute theological insight and careful exegesis, Doug O'Donnell unfolds the book of Job, clarifying how to approach and apply this powerful Old Testament text. This volume will no doubt prove to be an invaluable resource for anyone who desires a greater grasp of this vital component of biblical wisdom literature."

—**Lydia Brownback,** author, Flourish Bible Study series; coeditor, Conversational Commentaries

"There is so much to like about this commentary. You have a fine scholar, an experienced pastor, and a faithful Christian showing you the way through a book of gripping beauty and heart-stopping challenge (in about equal measure!). The volume displays the writer's clear head, loving hand, and warm heart—and nice, approachable style. It is both an honor and a pleasure to commend this book to you."

—**C. John ("Jack") Collins,** Professor Emeritus of Old Testament, Covenant Theological Seminary

"Douglas O'Donnell has a special gift for building a bridge between the exegesis of the scriptural text and its exposition for God's people. In his commentary on Job, he combines careful research, insightful reflection, broad reading, and vivid language as he elucidates the message of this magisterial book of the Bible for life today. Few pastors are willing to take on the formidable challenge of preaching through Job, but O'Donnell skillfully shows us how it can be done."

—**Daniel J. Estes,** Distinguished Professor of Old Testament, Cedarville University

"I have always found Doug O'Donnell's exegesis of biblical books insightful, stimulating, and 'preachable'—and this commentary, on one of the hardest books of the Old Testament to preach, is no exception. Here the Monday-morning minister will find much relief for his stressed mind and troubled soul, with knowledgeable nuggets, quotable quotes, and preachable points readily available. Highly recommended!"

—**Jonny Gibson,** Professor of Biblical and Systematic Theology, Westminster Theological Seminary; author, *Lamentations*, ESV Expository Commentary Series

"A commentary that is intended to help the ordinary Christian reader understand a book of the Bible, rather than to summarize every scholarly point of view on that book, needs to achieve at least three goals. First, it should orient the reader to the book's context, structure, and genre. Second, it should clarify the meanings of words and sentences within the book's overall unity to reveal its theological content and relationship to the wider theology of the Bible. Third, particularly when dealing with a book from the Old Testament, it should show how the text testifies to Jesus Christ and, through him, instructs the believer. Doug O'Donnell's volume on the book of Job succeeds admirably on all three counts. While he does not neglect the wisdom of other writers on Job, the author writes with a style that is engaging and suitable for both the preacher and the less technically trained Bible reader. The pastoral concerns addressed are a refreshing change from those commentaries that do not see the need to extend exegesis to application. The serious Bible reader will gain much from this treatment of a challenging part of Scripture."

—**Graeme Goldsworthy,** Lecturer in Old Testament and Biblical Theology, Moore Theological College, Sydney

"Doug O'Donnell's commentary on Job is sensitive to the text as literature, as theology, and (refreshingly) as the basis for practical Christian sermons. For those who want to preach on the book of Job—or study it on their own—with attention to detail and in conversation with insightful thinkers past and present, O'Donnell's work will be splendidly useful and a delight to read."

—**Michael Graves,** Armerding Professor of Biblical Studies, Wheaton College

"These days, more people are turning to Job, Lamentations, and other Bible texts that deal with suffering and the possibility of hope. Those who open this volume will find that Douglas Sean O'Donnell provides a faithful and careful reading of Job that will aid preaching and teaching and reading of this great and difficult book. Writing in the tradition of Francis Andersen and John Hartley, O'Donnell highlights God's greatness, human suffering, the role of evil in the world, and the hope that comes through God the Father, Son, and Holy Spirit."

—**Paul R. House,** Professor Emeritus of Divinity Old Testament, Beeson Divinity School

"Crack open this commentary, read the first few pages, and you will realize that you have been invited to a feast. This commentary is chock-full of important questions and illuminating—indeed, sometimes arresting—insights, undergirded by O'Donnell's having read very widely among the other commentators, whom he quotes judiciously. It has often caused me to stop, look up from the page, and reflect. It will take its place near the top of my significant stack of commentaries on Job."

—**Mark R. Talbot,** Associate Professor of Philosophy Emeritus, Wheaton College

Job

Reformed Expository Commentary

A Series

Series Editors

Richard D. Phillips
Philip Graham Ryken

Testament Editors

Iain M. Duguid, Old Testament
Daniel M. Doriani, New Testament

Job

Douglas Sean O'Donnell

P&R
PUBLISHING
P.O. BOX 817 • PHILLIPSBURG • NEW JERSEY 08865-0817

Italics within Scripture quotations indicate emphasis added.

Printed in the United States of America

Library of Congress Cataloging-in-Publication Data

Names: O'Donnell, Douglas Sean, 1972- author
Title: Job / Douglas Sean O'Donnell.
Description: Phillipsburg, New Jersey : P&R Publishing, [2025] | Series: Reformed expository commentaries | Includes bibliographical references and index. | Summary: "The man Job both prefigures Christ and illustrates our deep need of him. In this redemptive-historical commentary, Douglas O'Donnell applies the teaching of this ancient book to our lives today"-- Provided by publisher.
Identifiers: LCCN 2025017071 | ISBN 9781629954523 hardcover | ISBN 9781629954530 epub
Subjects: LCSH: Bible. Job--Commentaries | LCGFT: Commentaries
Classification: LCC BS1415.53 .O36 2025 | DDC 223/.107--dc23/eng/20250813
LC record available at https://lccn.loc.gov/2025017071

To Marc Davidson (1973–2022)

"Whatever you do, work heartily, as for the Lord and not for men."
(Col. 3:23)

Contents

Series Introduction

In every generation there is a fresh need for the faithful exposition of God's Word in the church. At the same time, the church must constantly do the work of theology: reflecting on the teaching of Scripture, confessing its doctrines of the Christian faith, and applying them to contemporary culture. We believe that these two tasks—the expositional and the theological—are interdependent. Our doctrine must derive from the biblical text, and our understanding of any particular passage of Scripture must arise from the doctrine taught in Scripture as a whole.

We further believe that these interdependent tasks of biblical exposition and theological reflection are best undertaken in the church, and most specifically in the pulpits of the church. This is all the more true since the study of Scripture properly results in doxology and praxis—that is, in praise to God and practical application in the lives of believers. In pursuit of these ends, we are pleased to present the Reformed Expository Commentary as a fresh exposition of Scripture for our generation in the church. We hope and pray that pastors, teachers, Bible study leaders, and many others will find this series to be a faithful, inspiring, and useful resource for the study of God's infallible, inerrant Word.

The Reformed Expository Commentary has four fundamental commitments. First, these commentaries aim to be *biblical*, presenting a comprehensive exposition characterized by careful attention to the details of the text. They are not exegetical commentaries—commenting word by word or even verse by verse—but integrated expositions of whole passages of Scripture. Each commentary will thus present a sequential, systematic treatment of an entire book of the Bible, passage by passage. Second, these commentaries are unashamedly *doctrinal*. We are committed to the Westminster Confession of Faith and Catechisms as containing the system of doctrine taught in the Scriptures of the Old and New Testaments. Each volume will teach, promote, and defend the doctrines of the Reformed faith as they are found in the Bible. Third, these commentaries are *redemptive-historical* in their orientation. We believe in the unity of the Bible and its central message of salvation in Christ. We are thus committed to a Christ-centered view of the Old Testament, in which its characters, events, regulations, and institutions are properly understood as pointing us to Christ and his gospel, as well as giving us examples to follow in living by faith. Fourth, these commentaries are *practical*, applying the text of Scripture to contemporary challenges of life—both public and private—with appropriate illustrations.

The contributors to the Reformed Expository Commentary are all pastor-scholars. As pastor, each author will first present his expositions in the pulpit ministry of his church. This means that these commentaries are rooted in the teaching of Scripture to real people in the church. While aiming to be scholarly, these expositions are not academic. Our intent is to be faithful, clear, and helpful to Christians who possess various levels of biblical and theological training—as should be true in any effective pulpit ministry. Inevitably this means that some issues of academic interest will not be covered. Nevertheless, we aim to achieve a responsible level of scholarship, seeking to promote and model this for pastors and other teachers in the church. Significant exegetical and theological difficulties, along with such historical and cultural background as is relevant to the text, will be treated with care.

We strive for a high standard of enduring excellence. This begins with the selection of the authors, all of whom have proved to be outstanding communicators of God's Word. But this pursuit of excellence is also reflected in a disciplined editorial process. Each volume is edited by both a series editor and a testament editor. The testament editors, Iain Duguid for the Old Testament and Daniel Doriani for the New Testament, are accomplished pastors and respected scholars who have taught at the seminary level. Their job is to ensure that each volume is sufficiently conversant with up-to-date scholarship and is faithful and accurate in its exposition of the text. As series editors, we oversee each volume to ensure its overall quality—including excellence of writing, soundness of teaching, and usefulness in application. Working together as an editorial team, along with the publisher, we are devoted to ensuring that these are the best commentaries that our gifted authors can provide, so that the church will be served with trustworthy and exemplary expositions of God's Word.

It is our goal and prayer that the Reformed Expository Commentary will serve the church by renewing confidence in the clarity and power of Scripture and by upholding the great doctrinal heritage of the Reformed faith. We hope that pastors who read these commentaries will be encouraged in their own expository preaching ministry, which we believe to be the best and most biblical pattern for teaching God's Word in the church. We hope that lay teachers will find these commentaries among the most useful resources they rely on for understanding and presenting the text of the Bible. And we hope that the devotional quality of these studies of Scripture will instruct and inspire each Christian who reads them in joyful, obedient discipleship to Jesus Christ.

May the Lord bless all who read the Reformed Expository Commentary. We commit these volumes to the Lord Jesus Christ, praying that the Holy Spirit will use them for the instruction and edification of the church, with thanksgiving to God the Father for his unceasing faithfulness in building his church through the ministry of his Word.

Richard D. Phillips
Philip Graham Ryken
Series Editors

Preface

The month before I began a sermon series on the book of Job, my friend Dr. Phil Ryken walked into my office on a Sunday morning as my church's guest preacher. He asked, "How are you doing?" My honest and direct response was "God is preparing me to preach Job." I am thankful to Phil because he then, before then, and since then has listened carefully and responded thoughtfully to some of my struggles. That day I faced the loss of three key staff members, the financial failure of the church's school, a letter of resignation from the head of school, who indirectly named me as the major reason he was moving on, opposition from a narcissist, a serious and frightening verbal-abuse issue within a marriage (I feared for my life!), and a friend's cancer diagnosis. Then, a few Sundays into opening the book of Job for my struggling community, the coronavirus pandemic hit. In God's providence, it was the perfect book for the imperfect times.

I dedicate this book to Marc Davidson, a friend lost to cancer on May 9, 2022. He was forty-nine and is survived by his wife, Lisa, and their seven children. Marc was an amazing Christian, husband, father, coach, and athlete. I first met him on the basketball court during my senior year of high school, and after I became a Christian the next year, he was the first person who encouraged me to read and study the Bible. I am eternally indebted to his faithful modeling of the Christian life, his bold testimony, and his help in pointing me in the right direction in the first few years of my Christian walk. You are loved and missed, brother!

I want to acknowledge other brothers and sisters who helped me, with this particular commentary, to exegete faithfully and communicate clearly. Davis Wetherell and Josh McQuaid read a number of the chapter drafts. Thank you! Phil Ryken and Iain Duguid, two of the editors for this series, read the final manuscript carefully, corrected mistakes, and offered suggestions for improvement. It was, once again, an honor to work with you both. I also thank the team at P&R, especially John Hughes and Karen Magnuson, for skillfully bringing this book into its finished form.

As you use this commentary, my hope is that I will provide an example of how to explain, illustrate, and apply biblical poetry, along with showing you various paths to journey from Job to Jesus. Moreover, I hope to heighten your appreciation for the book of Job as a literary masterwork—that you might echo the acclaim of Alfred, Lord Tennyson, who called it "the greatest poem of ancient and modern times";[1] Victor Hugo, who said that it is "perhaps the greatest masterpiece of the human mind";[2] and Thomas Carlyle, who stated, "There is nothing written, I think, in the Bible or out of it, of equal literary merit."[3] But whether you agree or not with such high commendations from these three literary giants, I hope you recognize something of Job's beauty. For where else in biblical literature can you experience together such awesome imagery ("my belly is like wine that has no vent," Job 32:19), sharp wit ("the bushes of the earth . . . will teach you . . . that the hand of the Lord has done this," 12:8–9), ironic prayers of personification ("O earth, cover not my blood," 16:18), dark humor (Job's digging for death "more than for hidden treasures," 3:21), clever turns of phrase ("eyes to the blind," 29:15a), biting sarcasm ("wisdom will die with you" 12:2b), acrostic closures (14:1 begins with the first letter of the Hebrew alphabet, while the last word of 14:22 begins with the alphabet's last letter), and eloquently structured prose (e.g., 1:13–19)? And in what other book of the Bible do you have a story of human tragedy and divine comedy that is enhanced by its realistic characters, its profound poetry, a courtroom scene, and a surprise ending? Enjoy!

1. Tennyson, quoted in Lawrence Boadt, *The Book of Job: Why Do the Innocent Suffer?*, Classic Bible Series (St. Martin's Press, 1997), 32.

2. Hugo, quoted in Henry H. Halley, *Pocket Bible Handbook* (H. H. Halley, 1946), 232.

3. Thomas Carlyle, *On Heroes, Hero-Worship, and the Heroic of History* (Chapman and Hall Limited, 1901), 49.

Abbreviations

CSB	Christian Standard Bible
ESV	English Standard Version
JSOT	Journal for the Study of the Old Testament
KJV	King James Version
LXX	Septuagint
MEV	Modern English Version
MSG	The Message
NASB	New American Standard Bible
NET	New English Translation
NICOT	New International Commentary on the Old Testament
NIDOTTE	*New International Dictionary of Old Testament Theology and Exegesis*, ed. Willem A. VanGemeren, 5 vols. (Zondervan, 1997)
NIV	New International Version
NIVAC	NIV Application Commentary
NKJV	New King James Version
NLT	New Living Translation
NRSV	New Revised Standard Version
PCA	Presbyterian Church in America
TLB	The Living Bible
YLT	Young's Literal Translation

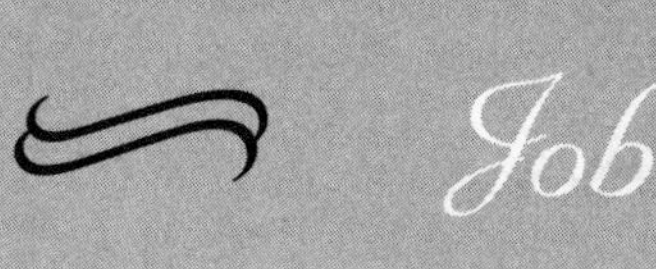

Job

Where Wisdom Is Found

Prologue

1

Job's Person, Possessions, and Priesthood

Job 1:1–5

There was a man in the land of Uz whose name was Job, and that man was blameless and upright, one who feared God and turned away from evil. (Job 1:1)

When the Cuban Missile Crisis played out for thirteen days in October 1962, it was the hottest moment of the Cold War. The two world superpowers—the Soviet Union and the United States—were on the brink of nuclear war. Thankfully, through tense but successful negotiations between Kennedy and Khrushchev, a peaceful agreement was reached. The United States agreed to dismantle missiles in Turkey and Italy and never to invade Cuba without direct provocation; the Soviet Union agreed to remove the missiles from Cuba. In July 2015, Cuba and the United States restored diplomatic relations. But from 1960 until that moment, Americans could not travel to Cuba, or Cubans to America, without a special visa.

Twice in the 1990s I traveled to Cuba with a group of American athletes to play several basketball games against the Cuban national team. The experience was extraordinary. We witnessed firsthand the effects of Castro's communism and Eisenhower's embargo. For example, we went to a restaurant where only four sandwiches were on the menu: ham and cheese, cheese and ham, ham with cheese, cheese with ham. I'm not kidding! Cuba's national team wore old uniforms and tattered shoes. When we gathered for a final meal together, we were served the worst steak I have ever seen or eaten, or tried to eat. The Americans cut the fat, pushed aside the bones, and tried to find the meat. The Cubans ate everything, the boiled bones and all. Also, at that meal we sat American-Cuban-American-Cuban around the table, which was a nice arrangement. The only problem was that no one on the Cuban team knew English, only one player on our team was fluent in Spanish, and the rest of us, like me, were desperately racking our brains for vocabulary words from our high school Spanish classes. Needless to say, holding a conversation was nearly impossible. What I entered in Cuba was a completely different world.

The opening lines of the book of Job offer a similar impression. Job 1:1 introduces us to the book's protagonist, who has an unusual name and lived in an unfamiliar place: "There was a man in the land of Uz whose name was Job." We might wonder, "Is Job a real person and the land of Uz a real place?" Other questions abound. If Job "was the greatest of all the people of the east" (Job 1:3), who are "the people of the east"—the Babylonians, the Persians, the Chinese? We are told that Job "feared God" (v. 1) and that he "would consecrate" his children and "offer burnt offerings" for them (v. 5), but who is the God (*'elohim*) that Job worships? Is Job a priest within some religious tradition? Whatever our answers are to these questions, we know that we have entered into a world very different from ours.

This affirmation does not mean, however, that we cannot find answers to our questions or that we cannot bridge the gap from Job's world to ours. In fact, my aim for this introductory chapter on these introductory verses is to do just that. Our path is straightforward: by looking at Job's person (Job 1:1), possessions (vv. 2–3), and priesthood (vv. 4–5) in *his* world, we will have the opportunity to return to our own world with fresh wisdom and insight. Along the way, we will learn more than a lesson on history and hermeneutics. We will learn about ourselves and our God and the wisdom he offers us.

Person

We start our journey with Job's person. Job 1:1 introduces us to a man ("There was a man . . . whose name was Job"). The formulaic start of the setting might remind us of how parables are often told in the Bible. For example, Nathan's parable to David begins, "There were two men in a certain city, the one rich and the other poor" (2 Sam. 12:1). Similarly, Jesus' parable of the rich fool starts, "There was a rich man" (Luke 16:19). Such a formulaic start, along with lengthy poetic monologues and dialogues[1] and the etymology of Job's name, has led some scholars to argue that the book of Job is a work of fiction.[2] It is certainly true that Job's name (a name found only here in all of ancient Hebrew literature but appearing frequently in other ancient texts) suggests symbolic value in that *'iyyob* (which means "Where is the Divine Father?")[3] could be an artistic expression used to suit Job's future dilemma, along with an ironic wordplay on the word "enemy" (*'yb*)[4]—a word that Job uses twice: "Why do you hide your face and count me as your enemy?" (Job 13:24) and "Behold, he [God] finds occasions against me, he counts me as his enemy" (33:10).

My view is that Job was a real person, not a fictional character—someone whose legendary sufferings were the historical ground on which the author of Job built his story, a story that features his magnificent literary embellishment and flair. Part of that literary flair might include using poetic speeches to capture the message of the actual dialogues—between Job and his friends—and renaming the historical sufferer *'iyyob* to "indicate the protagonist's experience of hostility,"[5] both with his accusatory friends and with his silent God.

One reason that I take Job, along with all the characters named (including Satan) and the details of the story told (including the unprecedented misfortunes), to be historically grounded is the referencing of Job in Ezekiel

1. Ninety-five percent of the book is poetry.

2. Who speaks in beautiful parallelisms when arguing or in imaginative imagery when scraping his wounds? (Indeed, who was there to record more than ten thousand words of elevated extemporaneous dialogue?)

3. "The name Job . . . was well-attested in the Near East in the second millennium B.C.E. and appears to have originally signified a quest for divine presence ('Where is the Divine Father?'). . . . If so, the name presages the content of the book, which is largely concerned with God as *Deus Absconditus*, a God whose face is hidden (Job 13:24; 34:29)." C. L. Seow, *Job 1–21: Interpretation and Commentary*, Illuminations (Eerdmans, 2013), 252–53. For a detailed discussion on Job's name, see David J. A. Clines, *Job 1–20*, Word Biblical Commentary 17 (Word, 1989), 10–11.

4. "To many of the rabbis, Job is not so much a historical figure as he is a *māšāl*, a symbolic figure (*b. B. Bat.* 15a; *y. Soṭah.* 5:8/20C; *Gen. Rab.* 57:4). . . . In fact, Eliezer argued that Job himself knew that he was a symbolic figure, for Job says in 17:6a, '[God] made me a *māšāl* for people.'" Seow, *Job 1–21*, 264.

5. "In this sense, early and medieval Christian commentators may have been right that Job represents anyone who suffers." Seow, 252–53.

14:14, 20 (Ezekiel names Job alongside Noah and Daniel) and in James 5:11 ("the steadfastness of Job"). Another reason is the location named in the setting. Job lived in "the land of Uz" (Job 1:1), on the border of Edom and Northern Arabia.[6] The author's focus, however, is not on Job's historical setting (he spends almost no time there!) but on his godly life.

Job is really righteous: "There was a man . . . , and that man was blameless and upright, one who feared God and turned away from evil" (Job 1:1). Four descriptions of holiness are provided. The first two have to do with Job's life in relation to people and the second two in relation to God. Both pairs are parallelisms. In relation to people, Job is "blameless and upright." The word "blameless" means not that he is sinless, but rather that he is a man of integrity. He has nothing to hide. His faithful and consistent goodness is evident to all. Job alone in the book of Job receives this designation,[7] and in the context of the book the word is used as simply synonymous with the person who is "just" (12:4) or "right" (9:20; "in the right," 22:3). The word "upright" is synonymous with "blameless," and it refers to the person who is "pure" or "innocent," in contrast with "evildoers," "the wicked," and "bloodthirsty men."[8] So Job is "blameless and upright" (1:1), or, to offer a spatial translation, he is "whole" and "straight." We might say, in the vocabulary of Jesus, that as Job walks down the *straight* and narrow way that leads to life, he treats others the same way that he wishes to be treated; his wholehearted submission to and reverence, respect, and love for God show themselves in his *whole* (or "perfect," Matt. 5:48) love for others. Because of this, other people—even his enemies—have nothing against him. He has treated them with fairness and equity and charity. He is "the man of peace [*shalom*]," namely, a "blameless" and "upright" man (Ps. 37:37).

In these ways, Christians should imitate Job. We should be known for teaching wisdom ("you have instructed many") and also for caring for and helping out the needy (his "soul grieved for the needy"): Job "strengthened the weak hands" and "delivered the poor who cried for help," including "the blind," "the lame," "the fatherless," and widows; he even invited orphans into his home to dine with him, clothed the cold with warm clothes, and

6. "Rejoice and be glad, O daughter of Edom, you who dwell in the land of Uz" (Lam. 4:21; cf. Jer. 25:20). Of course, some of Jesus' parables have real cities in the historical setting. But there are only a few examples of this in Old Testament narratives.

7. See Job 1:1, 8; 2:3; 8:20; 9:20, 21, 22.

8. See, in order of quotation above, Job 8:6; 17:8; 8:20; 9:24; Prov. 29:10.

brought justice to many. Moreover, like Job, we should treasure God's words and keep his commandments and thus avoid idolatry; flee the love of money; remain sexually pure; confess our sins and ask for forgiveness; be honest, fair, and responsible in business dealings; show hospitality; care for creation; love our enemies; and comfort mourners ("Did not I weep for him whose day was hard?").[9] Put simply, we should be salt and light in the world so that others see our "good works and give glory" to God (see Matt. 5:13–16). We should imitate Job! As the Puritan Thomas Brooks put it:

> Set the highest examples and patterns before your face of grace and godliness for your imitation. In the business of faith, set an Abraham before your eyes. In the business of courage, set a Joshua. In the business of uprightness, set a Job. . . . Next to Christ, set the pattern of the choicest saints before you.[10]

Job is in right relationship with his fellow man. He is also in right relationship with God, as seen in the two other descriptions of holiness. Job fears God and he turns away from evil (Job 1:1; cf. 28:28). With these phrases, we have another parallelism—a synthetic or focusing parallelism—in which the second half focuses on or expands on or even explains more fully the first. Throughout the Wisdom Literature of the Bible, to "fear God" takes on various qualities, such as the attitude of humble reverence and the action of totally dependent trust. Here in Job, fearing God encompasses those qualities, but it also flows into moral purity. Thus, Job demonstrates his reverence for God and trust in God by turning away from evil. The focus is on *actions* that stem from an *attitude* ("The fear of the Lord is hatred of evil," Prov. 8:13; "by the fear of the Lord one turns away from evil," 16:6) and include both turning from evil and turning to God and keeping his commandments (see Eccl. 12:13; or, in Job's case, what he knows of God's will).

Job is not holy, holy, holy like the Lord God (see Isa. 6:3), but this opening description highlights his unique holiness, as God himself will later state: "There is none like him on the earth, a blameless and upright man, who fears God and turns away from evil" (Job 1:8; 2:3). The phrase "There is none like him," which summarizes the descriptors of Job's character, is—as Eric

9. In the paragraph above, verses quoted from or alluded to that support Job's character include Job 4:3; 6:22; 23:11–12; 29:12–13, 15–17, 25; 30:25; 31:1, 9, 13, 19, 21, 24–30, 32–34, 38–40.

10. Thomas Brooks, "Appendix to Memoir," *Works of Thomas Brooks*, vol. 1 (Banner of Truth, 1980), lxiv.

Ortlund points out—"an amazing thing to say because it is most often said in praise of God himself and only occasionally to describe human beings."[11] The point of such language is plain: Job is quite out of the ordinary! He is "the most godly and virtuous man on earth."[12]

Possessions

As a result of his godly life, Job embodies Proverbs 22:4 ("The reward for humility and fear of the Lord is riches and honor and life") and Psalm 112:1b–3a ("Blessed is the man who fears the Lord. . . . His offspring will be mighty in the land. . . . Wealth and riches are in his house"). Perhaps that is why the author transitions from Job 1:1 into Job 1:2 with the unusual phrase "there were born to him" ten children. It leaves the reader wondering whether the pinnacles of Job's blessings—his offspring—are born as a result of Job's impeccable character and not merely his wife's reproductive system. Whatever the intention of the transitional phrase, the thought is clear: "Following the fourfold statement about Job's person, there is a fourfold build-up of evidence of Job's blessedness: his family, his livestock, his household, and his status (1:2–3)."[13]

We can umbrella those blessings under the term *possessions*,[14] as identified in Job 1:2–3: "There were born to him seven sons and three daughters. He *possessed* 7,000 sheep, 3,000 camels, 500 yoke of oxen, and 500 female donkeys, and [he *possessed*] very many servants, so that this man was the greatest of all the people of the east." The numerology here presents Job as

11. See 1 Kings 8:23; Pss. 35:10; 71:19; 86:8–9; Jer. 10:6–7; Mic. 7:18. Eric Ortlund, *Suffering Wisely and Well: The Grief of Job and the Grace of God* (Crossway, 2022), 40, citing Norman Habel, *The Book of Job: A Commentary*, Old Testament Library (Westminster, 1985), 40.

12. C. J. Williams, *The Shadow of Christ in the Book of Job* (Wipf & Stock, 2017), 27.

13. Seow, *Job 1–21*, 253.

14. In the ancient Near East, and as repeatedly recorded throughout Scripture, children are the patriarch's "possessions" in that he legally owns them and is responsible for them, along with other members of his household, including his wife and servants (see Ex. 20:17; Matt. 18:23–24). Contemporary readers are understandably uncomfortable with this ancient approach to property, especially when it extends to the apparent "possession" of humans—God's own image bearers. Nevertheless, we should not be surprised when ancient texts employ their own customary manners of speech, nor should we forget to interpret this verse in light of Scripture's clear teachings elsewhere that all humans are made in God's image and likeness (Gen. 1:26–27; 5:1; James 3:9), and that Israel's own practices on such matters were to reflect the character of the God "who brought you out of the land of Egypt, out of the house of slavery" (Ex. 20:2; cf. Lev. 25:38).

the "perfect" man in that he has ten children ("*seven* sons and *three* daughters," Job 1:2) and ten thousand animals (v. 3).[15] And the large numbers of animals and laborers indicate that he owns what we can label a successful fabric company (sheep's wool used for clothing), agricultural operations (oxen to plow the abundant acreage of his large estate and servants to harvest crops), travel and trade industries (donkeys and camels for transport of people and goods), and perhaps food distribution (mutton chops and donkey's milk). Job has deep pockets (made of wool, we assume); and he receives deep respect, for both his piety and his possessions—sheep, camels, oxen, donkeys, servants, and children—earn him the prestigious title "the greatest of all the people of the east" (v. 3), the indicator "east" designating the regions of Edom, Moab, and Ammon (Isa. 11:14) and "the nomadic groups that migrated about the Arabian desert, occasionally raiding the settled communities of the Transjordan and even Cisjordan itself."[16] Though he is not a Hebrew, he is the personification of the perfect son of Proverbs and the promised blessings of Deuteronomy come to life. He fears God and reaps the rewards of affluence, offspring, and honor.

Priesthood

Satan will slither onto the scene soon enough to test this whole paradigm, and we will turn to the texts about him in chapters 2 and 4 below. For now, all is well in the world. What an idyllic introduction! Standing atop the world's stage is the righteous man (*person*), surrounded by his servants and sons and donkeys and daughters (*possessions*); and his only action—perhaps a daily one—that our text focuses on is Job's *priesthood*, as detailed in Job 1:4–5:

> His sons used to go and hold a feast in the house of each one on his day, and they would send and invite their three sisters to eat and drink with them. And when the days of the feast had run their course, Job would send and consecrate them, and he would rise early in the morning and offer burnt offerings according to the number of them all. For Job said, "It may be that my children have sinned, and cursed God in their hearts." Thus Job did continually.

15. The numbers 3, 7, and together 10 are all symbolic of completion or perfection. On the round numbers as representing perfection, see David J. A. Clines, "False Naivety in the Prologue to Job," *Hebrew Annual Review* 9 (1985): 127–36.

16. Daniel I. Block, *The Book of Ezekiel, Chapters 25–48*, NICOT (Eerdmans, 1998), 17.

While Job might have lived at or near the same time as the patriarchs of Genesis, there is no clear indication that he is part of God's covenant people, even as a Gentile convert. He is a wise man from "the east" (cf. 1 Kings 4:30) who, like the magi in Matthew, has some revelation about God from God, and in light of that light, he seeks to know, serve, and worship him. In fact, Job twice addresses God as Yahweh (Job 1:21; 12:9), a title used by the author thirty-two times in total. And when God speaks in chapters 38–41, it is obvious that he is the Creator and Sustainer and Redeemer, the only true and living God, the covenant Lord of Israel.

Part of Job's dedication to God is demonstrated in his priestly sacrifices. After Job cleanses his children—perhaps "by means of a sanctification or purification ceremony"[17]—he offers burnt offerings by killing and scorching bulls and rams (see Job 42:8; cf. Lev. 1:5; 5:15–16) for each of his children (ten costly sacrifices!) on a regular basis ("continually," Job 1:5). Job barbecues all day most days. His robe must smell like the cook's apron at Pappy's Smokehouse in St. Louis. Again, since the likely historical setting for the characters in the narrative (not necessarily the author) is during the patriarchal period (roughly 2000–1700 B.C.)[18] and since there is no mention of a tabernacle and any of the specific garb and rituals associated with Israelite cultic practice, Job is not a priest from the line of Aaron. He more closely resembles Noah, Abraham, and Jacob, who, as the heads of their families, offered sacrifices on open-air altars and were called righteous before the law came into being.[19] Job might also resemble Abraham's contemporary, "Melchizedek, king of Salem, priest of the Most High God" (Heb. 7:1; cf. Gen. 14:18)—also called "king of righteousness" and "king of peace"—a man who was "without . . . genealogy" and who became "a priest, not on the basis of a legal requirement concerning bodily descent [like Aaron's sons], but by the power of an indestructible life" (Heb. 7:2, 3, 16). But there is some indica-

17. John Goldingay, *Job for Everyone*, Old Testament for Everyone (Westminster John Knox, 2013), 9.

18. The evidence for this era is that Job's wealth is measured in the number of animals and servants he possesses (Job 1:3), his service as a priest on behalf of his family (v. 5; cf. Gen. 12:7–8), and the longevity of his life and description of his death: "Job lived 140 years" (Job 42:16); "these are the days of the years of Abraham's life, 175 years" (Gen. 25:7); "Job died, an old man, and full of days" (Job 42:17); "Abraham . . . died in a good old age, an old man and full of years" (Gen. 25:8). See Richard P. Belcher Jr., *Job: The Mystery of Suffering and God's Sovereignty*, Focus on the Bible (Christian Focus, 2017), 13.

19. Or if we follow Martin Luther, we take Job to be a Gentile who received God's "irregular grace" because he was saved before the giving of the law of Moses. Martin Luther, *Luther's Works*, vol. 6, *Lectures on Genesis, Chapters 31–37*, ed. Jaroslav Pelikan and Hilton C. Oswald (Concordia, 1970), 380.

tion that the author of Job lived much later than the setting of the story he gives us.[20] It seems most likely that the book itself comes from a time when wisdom writing flourished in Israel (from Solomon in the tenth century B.C. to Hezekiah in the eighth). If so, then the book's author most likely took the well-known sufferings of Job, set the story in the patriarchal age (with authentic language and coloring), and retold the story for Israelites (Job is written in Hebrew), perhaps for the exiled people of Israel, who were then living not only east of Eden but east of Jerusalem.

Regarding the routine sacrifices, why does Job do what he does? Some commentators make much of his children's overindulging at their feasts ("His sons" would "hold a feast" and "their three sisters" would come "to eat and drink with them," Job 1:4). But as Francis Andersen rightly notes: "We need not suppose that they spent all their time in roistering and did no work. There is no hint of drunkenness or license or laziness."[21] Elsewhere in the Old Testament when the verbs "eat and drink" are used together, they symbolize joy ("And when Boaz had *eaten* and *drunk*, and his heart was merry," Ruth 3:7; "Judah and Israel were as many as the sand by the sea. They *ate* and *drank* and were happy," 1 Kings 4:20). Moreover, the sons' independence and successes are described (each of the seven has his own house and can afford routine feasts for a large group), and there is no sibling rivalry (they all attend the festivals) but only harmony. Job's household is harmonious and also happy. So these festivals, which might have been birthday parties ("his day," Job 1:4, equals "his birthday"), or more likely seven religious feasts throughout the year,[22] are celebrations of *pure* pleasure!

But within all this wholesomeness, harmony, and happiness, something is amiss. God's will in heaven is not yet done perfectly on earth. Satan is to come, but sin is already there. We are not in Eden; we are east of it. Job has to turn away from evil, and the reason he thinks it necessary to sanctify and sacrifice is rooted in his fear that his children might have sinned by cursing God in their hearts. It is difficult to know what is meant by "cursed God in their hearts" (Job 1:5). Part of the difficulty is that the word translated

20. For example, the reference to mined iron ("Iron is taken out of the earth," Job 28:2)—as opposed to meteoric iron—is quite significant for the dating of the book, since iron ore didn't start to be mined until the beginning of the Iron Age (toward the end of the first millennium B.C.).

21. Francis I. Andersen, *Job*, Tyndale Old Testament Commentaries 13 (InterVarsity Press, 1976), 80.

22. That last reading fits the idea of their "blessing" (*barak*) God at these events. See Seow, *Job 1–21*, 269.

"cursed" (*barak*) is usually rendered "blessed," as it is translated in Job 1:10, "You have *blessed* the work of his hands," and in 42:12, "And the LORD *blessed* the latter days of Job more than his beginning." The context determines the translation, and here in 1:5 "cursed" is the right sense. But we might say it this way: "While they praised Yahweh outwardly, they belittled him inwardly."

We aren't told why Job offers sacrifices. Perhaps it is due to the deceitfulness of riches (his children are quite wealthy), the lure of pagan idols (they live in "the east"), patriarchal fraternal pressure (their father's faith isn't always theirs, but they dare not rebel outwardly), or simply some unintentional attitude or action ("And the priest shall make atonement before the LORD for the person who makes a mistake, when he sins unintentionally, to make atonement for him, and he shall be forgiven," Num. 15:28). *Or*, as Job himself admits, their sin is just a possibility: "It *may* be that my children have sinned" (Job 1:5). This view fits with what Job will later admit, namely, that he might not have known the sins he should confess because they are too many to know: "How many are my iniquities and my sins?" And this is why he asks God to reveal how he might have offended him: "Make me know my transgression and my sin" (13:23).

Whatever the case, the description of Job's scrupulousness is not intended to come across as spiritually neurotic (like Martin Luther before his conversion climbing the stairs of the *Scala Sancta* on his knees or quivering the first time he officiated the Mass) but as sin-sensitive (humans can sin even when they worship) and God-honoring. Job cleanses his children and sacrifices for their sins because he cares for their souls. Job's fatherly priesthood—his protection and provision—is put forward as something quite positive. Job takes seriously his household's right standing before God. "He is," as Christopher Ash states, "watchful in prayer, ever concerned as his highest priority in life to keep himself and his family in right relationship with God."[23] Thus, we may take verses 1 and 5 of Job 1 as an inclusio of admiration!

The point of this practice for us, however, is not that of direct imitation, namely, that we should kill animals and set them on fire for our children's possible sins. Due to Jesus' atoning death, there is no need for us to offer such sacrifices. That is not to say, however, that we shouldn't pray for our children and do all we can to "consecrate" them, that is, set them apart

23. Christopher Ash, *Trusting God in the Darkness: A Guide to Understanding the Book of Job* (Crossway, 2021), 23.

from the world and wholly dedicate them to God. Most mornings, I pray the Lord's Prayer *by* myself *for* my whole family:

> *Our* Father in heaven, . . .
> forgive *us our* debts. (Matt. 6:9, 12)

Other times, I have used Daniel's "prayer and pleas for mercy" on behalf of Israel (see Dan. 9:3–18) as a model in praying for myself, wife, and children:

> O Lord, *our* great and awesome God, who keeps covenant and steadfast love with those who love him and keep his commandments, *we* acknowledge that *we* have sinned and done wrong and turned aside from your commandments. Forgive *us*, God of mercy, for all the times *we* have rebelled against you and have not obeyed your voice. God, please listen to *my* pleas for mercy, and for your own sake make your face to shine upon *us*. For *I* do not present *our* pleas before you because of *my* righteousness, but because of your great mercy. O Lord, hear; O Lord, forgive.

A Second Sacrifice

We can, to some extent, imitate Job's consecration of his children. But again, the point of Job's priesthood, as it is presented here, is not merely imitation in some form. The text also foreshadows a second sacrifice scene in Job 42:7–9, where Job offers blood sacrifices for his foolish friends:

> After the Lord had spoken these words to Job, the Lord said to Eliphaz the Temanite: "My anger burns against you and against your two friends, for you have not spoken of me what is right, as my servant Job has. Now therefore take seven bulls and seven rams and go to my servant Job and offer up a burnt offering for yourselves. And my servant Job shall pray for you, for I will accept his prayer not to deal with you according to your folly. For you have not spoken of me what is right, as my servant Job has." So Eliphaz the Temanite and Bildad the Shuhite and Zophar the Naamathite went and did what the Lord had told them, and *the Lord accepted Job's prayer.*

This final sacrifice scene (the only other sacrifice scene in Job) is both the key that unlocks the book's themes and thesis and also the lens through which we are to read the whole narrative. But it is more than a lens that helps us look backward; it also—like the lens on a telescope—helps us look forward to the ultimate scene of sacrifice in Scripture. As we will see, the book of Job in some ways prefigures the purposeful sufferings of Jesus Christ. That is, the story of God's servant Job (*a* suffering servant) prepares us for the story of Jesus (*the* Suffering Servant), who in his passion and death demonstrates how innocent suffering can show forth the justice and wisdom of God.

Our study of the drama of Job has just begun. We are only five verses into it. But by the end of the book (its *telos*), we will see a righteous sufferer vindicated, sinners atoned for through a costly blood sacrifice, and the sovereign freedom and justice of God upheld. In short, we will see what the New Testament calls the gospel. We will also see the Philippians 2 pattern of a man who starts with a blessed and exalted position, goes through undeserved sufferings and utter humiliation, and, in the end, receives "subsequent glories" (1 Peter 1:11); that is, Job (somehow!) receives greater blessings and an even more exalted position.

But for now, we pause. We are off to a good start. In the next chapter, we return to what Alfred, Lord Tennyson, called "the greatest poem of ancient and modern times"[24] and the greatest story ever told. Until then, let us be in awe of God, bow before his awesome providence, grasp something of his inexplicable wisdom, pray always and without ceasing, and claim his forgiveness through the sacrifice offered for our many sins.

24. Tennyson, quoted in Lawrence Boadt, *The Book of Job: Why Do the Innocent Suffer?*, Classic Bible Series (St. Martin's Press, 1997), 32.

2

God's Servant into Satan's Hands

Job 1:6–12

And the Lord said to Satan, "Behold, all that he has is in your hand. Only against him do not stretch out your hand." (Job 1:12)

The Great Courses are a series of recorded lectures on a variety of topics given by experts in the field. As I watched astrophysicist Neil deGrasse Tyson's course "The Inexplicable Universe," wherein everyone's favorite astrophysicist (as he is dubbed) lucidly explained what we know and don't know about the universe, two thoughts came to mind. First was an observation: as much as we have learned about the universe, we still know so little. Second was the question "How do we know anything about the Creator of this amazing universe?" I did not ask that question in ignorance. I have theological training and know that the Bible's answer is that God has revealed himself to us through creation, the incarnation, and written revelation. Reciting those realities strengthens my faith. But what the book of Job so often does is to take our faith to new heights. It helps us peer into the heavens!

What is recorded in Job 1:6–12 is unusual in this regard. There are so few places in the Bible where we get a front-row seat to the cosmic chamber room of God and get to listen in and learn something about who God is and how he works in this world—a revelation that might be different than we imagined or were likely taught in Sunday school or seminary.

Into the Heavens

We start with an obvious, but important, observation. The scene has shifted from earth (Job 1:1–5) to "heaven" or "the heavens" (e.g., 16:19; 22:12) and "the presence of the Lord" (1:12): "Now there was a day when the sons of God came to present themselves before the Lord, and Satan also came among them" (v. 6). Other observations may follow. The author moves from "[all] the days" (v. 5) to "a day" (v. 6) and from Job and his family to God and the "sons of God." Here we learn that Job's God is the covenant God of Israel, as the name Yahweh ("the Lord") is used here—the first of thirty-two times in the book total. We also learn that there are supernatural beings, here called "the sons of God," who are "heavenly beings"[1] (commonly translated "angels") and who serve on God's "divine council" (Ps. 82:1), or what could be labeled the parliament of the universe. Elsewhere in the Old Testament, such a gathering is called "the assembly" or "the council of the holy ones" (89:5, 7), and they gather to render judgments (82:1), give reports (Zech. 1:10), and receive orders to carry out (1 Kings 22:18–23).

Within this cosmic cabinet that enjoys access to God, has his ear, and helps him govern the world,[2] we are introduced to someone who is, or will become, the least honorable character in the Bible—the Satan. This Hebrew noun (*satan*), joined to the definite article (*ha*),[3] could be translated "the adversary," but he seems to function here not as a direct enemy but as an opposing ally. John Goldingay sees him in Job as functioning something like a prosecuting attorney or the political party in the British parliament

1. For example, the ESV renders the phrase "the sons of God" (*bene ha 'elohim*) as "heavenly beings" in Psalms 29:1 and 89:6.

2. It is also possible (likely!) that Satan is not a member, but an intruder. See Richard P. Belcher Jr., *Job: The Mystery of Suffering and God's Sovereignty*, Focus on the Bible (Christian Focus, 2017), 23.

3. The definite article used in Job is later dropped by biblical authors (e.g., 1 Chron. 21:1), and by the time of the New Testament, the title Satan becomes a proper name. Thus, following the ESV and other translations, and to make a connection to New Testament usage, I will call "the Satan" (*hassatan*) merely "Satan."

known as the monarch's "loyal opposition." Just as the prosecuting attorney is not an opponent of the judge and the loyal opposition is not set against the government, so Satan's role in "Yahweh's cabinet" (so to speak) is to serve Yahweh by making sure that his rule and law are properly upheld.[4]

This more positive view of the Satan of Job makes sense of the honest dialogue and contractual agreement between Satan and Yahweh in Job 1:7–12 in regard to Job. But this view disconnects the character of "Satan" from characterizations of him in Chronicles and Zechariah (see 1 Chron. 21:1; Zech. 3:1),[5] as well as throughout the New Testament (the title "Satan" is used thirty-six times in the New Testament) and interchangeably for "the devil": "he seized the dragon, that ancient serpent, who is the devil [*diabolos*] and Satan [*Satanas*]" (Rev. 20:2). Moreover, "the devil" (1 John 3:8) or "Beelzebul" (Matt. 12:24) or "the evil one" (Eph. 6:16) or "the accuser of our brothers" (Rev. 12:10), whose power and ploys are strikingly similar to Satan's activity in Job (Matt. 4:1–11; Acts 10:38; Rev. 12:10), is the ultimate enemy of God and his kingdom (Rev. 12:9; 20:2). And as we will see next in Job 1:7, this "Satan," who perfectly reflects the same tone as the serpent in the garden (Gen. 3:1–5), also walks (or "prowls") about the earth "like a roaring lion, seeking someone to devour" (1 Peter 5:8). Yet as powerful as this evil angel is, what is clear in what follows, as well as in the New Testament's view of Satan, is that he is subservient to God's will. This is what Martin Luther means when he says that the devil is God's devil.

With that said about Satan, we return to the story of Job, which means getting back to heaven in order to overhear one of the most curious conversations in the cosmos. What is curious is that the Lord seems limited in his knowledge ("The Lord said to Satan, 'From where have you come?'"), whereas Satan seems boundless in his abilities ("Satan answered the Lord and said, 'From going to and fro on the earth, and from walking up and down on it,'" Job 1:7). We shouldn't read God's question the wrong way, for the question here is of the same type as the one asked to Adam after the fall, "Where are you?" (Gen. 3:9). Just as God knew where Adam was hiding, he well knew where Satan had been. The point of such language is not to say

4. See John Goldingay, *Job for Everyone*, Old Testament for Everyone (Westminster John Knox, 2013), 12. Cf. Norman C. Habel, *The Book of Job: A Commentary*, Old Testament Library (Westminster, 1985), 89.

5. The Hebrew for "Satan" is rendered "devil" (*diabolos*) in the LXX.

that the limitless God of the universe is limited. Rather, it is to say that the transcendent God of the universe is personal. He listens to his creatures. He even clearly communicates to them, such as what he says to Satan in Job 1:8: "And the LORD *said* to Satan, 'Have you considered my servant Job, that there is none like him on the earth, a blameless and upright man, who fears God and turns away from evil?'" What is also curious is that God is impressed not by Satan's extraordinary abilities but rather by Job's character. Instead of praising Satan for his world speed-walking tour, he commends Job. Echoing the narrator's fourfold commendation (Job 1:1), the Lord agrees that Job is "a blameless and upright man, who fears God and turns away from evil" (v. 8). Moreover, in God's estimation, Job is more than merely "the greatest of all the people of the east" (v. 3); he is unlike any other ("there is none like him on the earth," v. 8). If anyone has traveled east, west, north, and south, as Satan has, he certainly knows the worth of this wise man. Just as "there is no God like you [Yahweh], in *heaven* or on earth" (2 Chron. 6:14), so there is no man like Job on *earth*.

Notice finally, from what God says in Job 1:8, the addition of the designation "servant." The LORD labels Job "my servant," with the sense being "Satan, have you taken a good look at my servant Job?" We will say more about the importance of this title when we come to Job 42. For now, we should not miss the fact that Job joins Abraham (Gen. 26:24), Moses (Ex. 14:31), David (2 Sam. 7:5), and Isaiah (Isa. 20:3) in receiving this rare and significant title.

So we might say, with the compliments God gives in Job 1:8, that Job receives the highest commendation that any human receives in the Bible—besides our Savior, of course, who received the honor of the Father's acclamation, "This is my beloved Son, with whom I am well pleased" (Matt. 3:17; 17:5). Yet Satan, as we see in Job 1:9–11, is not overly impressed with Job—or with Jesus, for that matter.

Two Interrogatives, an Indictment, and an Invitation

Satan believes that God's appraisal is an overstatement because he surmises that Job's faithfulness is shallow and superficial. In fact, he suggests that it is but a refined form of selfishness,[6] for he answers Yahweh's inter-

6. William Henry Green, *The Argument of the Book of Job Unfolded* (1873; repr., James & Klock, 1977), 74.

rogative invitation—"Have you considered my servant Job?" (Job 1:8)—with two interrogatives, an indictment, and an invitation of his own:

> Then Satan answered the Lord and said, "Does Job fear God for no reason [interrogative]? Have you not put a hedge around him and his house and all that he has, on every side [interrogative]? You have blessed the work of his hands, and his possessions have increased in the land [indictment]. But stretch out your hand and touch all that he has [invitation], and he will curse you to your face." (Job 1:9–11)

Of the many commendations that God offered in Job 1:8, Satan focuses only on the fear of the Lord: "Does Job fear God for no reason?" (Job 1:9). The sense of Satan's question is this: "Does Job respect, worship, honor, trust, obey, and love God because God is God or only because God bestows blessings?" Satan not only questions Job's heart religion; he also questions the Lord's overprotection and overindulgence: "Have *you* [emphatic] not put a hedge around him and his house and all that he has, on every side?" (v. 10). The hedge is an "image" that connotes "protection and safety from human and non-human marauders," such as the depiction of Israel as a vineyard with hedges around it (see Isa. 5:1–7, esp. v. 5).[7] Of course, Satan believes that God has and that Yahweh's protective hedge is made not of short shrubbery but of tall stone. He thus calls God to stop the providential pandering and to blow the trumpet, so that the walls of Job's mighty fortress might fall to the ground.

Then in the second half of Job 1:10, this so-called son of God uses the Word of God—the distinctly Deuteronomic phrase "You have blessed the work of his hands" (cf. Deut. 28:12; 33:11)—to further challenge God, even to attack God's character. The sense of the verse below is something like this: "Lord, you are not only an overprotective Father but also an overindulgent one."

> **You have blessed** *the work of his hands*, and
> *his possessions* **[you] have increased** in the land.

Satan thinks of God as a Father, but an overprotective and an overindulgent one, who has built a wall around Job and provided him, within that wall,

7. J. Gerald Janzen, *Job*, Interpretation: A Bible Commentary for Teaching and Preaching (John Knox, 1985), 39.

a plethora of paradisaic provisions. In such a situation, Satan surmises, it's easy to be righteous.

Satan's solution to God's overindulgence is simple: he dares God to smite his saint. In the language of Exodus,[8] he asks God to take away the land flowing with milk and honey and bring on some of Egypt's plagues—bestow boils, eliminate the animals, kill the firstborn son, and so much more. Or, in the language of Job 1:11: "But stretch out your hand and touch all that he has," he suggests, "and he will curse you to your face." What a bold, brazen, and blasphemous challenge from "the challenger."[9] The last picture we saw of Job was of his offering God sacrifices for his children's sins. He was loving God and loving others. Satan forces us to envision a very different scene. He wants us to see this blessed man eye-to-eye with God, cursing him to his face. To curse God is "the gravest sin of all,"[10] which according to Old Testament law rightly deserves the death penalty (see 1 Kings 21:10); to curse God "to [his] face" (Job 1:11) connotes a direct confrontation, rejection, and even hatred of God,[11] the greatest imaginable transgression.

Whatever we make of Satan's attitude and accusations, we should not make little of his challenge. We should reflect on why we trust and treasure God. Is it solely for his protection and provisions? Are we treating God as a cosmic Santa Claus—if he stops bestowing gifts, will we no longer believe in him? Will our faith waver if we face adversity? Will tribulation undermine us? Is our trust in God shallow like a seed sown on rocky ground? Are we in a contract with God based on the blessings he bestows, or are we in a covenant with God based on his sovereign calling of us, our genuine relationship of love, and our dutiful but delightful glorifying of him? However we understand this challenge of Satan, we ought not to underestimate its richness for matters of practical theology. Why do we trust and treasure God? Good question! Do we fear God for no reason?

In theological terms, this concept is called *disinterested love*. Jonathan Edwards defines *disinterested love* this way: "God is loved for himself and for his own sake; and men are loved not because of their relation to self,

8. See Ex. 3:20; cf. 9:15; Ps. 138:7.

9. John H. Walton suggests the translation "the challenger" for "the Satan." See *Job*, NIVAC (Zondervan, 2012), 20.

10. David J. A. Clines, *Job 1–20*, Word Biblical Commentary 17 (Word, 1989), 16.

11. "In contrast to the curse which Job's sons may have spoken 'in their hearts' (v. 5), Job's curse is expected to be a blatant public utterance in God's face." Habel, *Job*, 91.

but because of their relation to God, either because they are the children of God, or because they have either the spiritual or natural image of God."[12] So do we love God "for himself and for his own sake," or do we love him simply because God is intrinsically worthy to be loved? Such a question, if we take it at face value and face it directly, should cause tension in our own Christian lives. On the one hand, there is the reality that too many of God's blessings can (and such is the deceitfulness of the human heart!) turn us from loving our Creator to loving his gifts, or erase the need we have for him because we take such blessings for granted, or think they are self-generated rather than God-given. On the other hand, a lack of blessings or, worse, the persistence of trials and losses can turn us from fearing God. For example, reflecting on the blessing of family, and in the context of reflecting on Job 1:9, Eric Ortlund writes: "What if I had to bury a member of my family—or all of them? Would I give up on God? Would it be seen that what I really love was my family and was interested in God only as long as my family was safe? Would it turn out that all my years as a Christian had actually been a way of dishonoring God by treating a person of infinite worth as a means to some other end?"[13] Ortlund continues:

> Job loses every reason to be in a relationship with God outside of God himself—God gives Job every earthly reason to give up on him (1:12). A little reflection will help us see why God allows this instead of rebuking the accuser and sparing Job this agony. After all, the only kind of relationship with God that will save us is one where he is loved for who he is, for his own sake, irrespective of what secondary, earthly blessings we gain or lose because of our relationship with him. . . . Furthermore, although it is a good and healthy practice to affirm our love for God when our health is good and our family safe, some affirmations cannot remain theoretical forever. God occasionally proves the reality of our relationship with him by means of extreme suffering. When God allows these ordeals, he is not torturing us with pain when he already knows the outcome of the test. Job-like suffering is actually a matter of saving our souls by delivering us into and sealing us in the only kind of relationship with God that will make us happy in heaven, one in which we love God for no reason external to himself.[14]

12. Jonathan Edwards, *Ethical Writings*, ed. Paul Ramsey, vol. 8 of *The Works of Jonathan Edwards* (Yale University Press, 1989), 264.

13. Eric Ortlund, *Suffering Wisely and Well: The Grief of Job and the Grace of God* (Crossway, 2022), 42.

14. Ortlund, 45.

Doubtless part of the final point that Ortlund makes is true, and true of the testing of Job, and that "God put Job in a position in which he has every earthly reason to give up on God; the only reason left for Job to endure in a relationship with God is God."[15] This also is true: "If God loves us, he will at some point put us in a position where we must worship him for his own sake, in the midst of agony,"[16] and that "what God wants from us in Job-like suffering is neither repentance nor deeper spiritual discipline," but "for us to hold onto him—not to curse him and walk away from him, but just to maintain our relationship with him through tears and sackcloth."[17]

That admitted, we are saved not by our disinterested love in God, but through faith in Jesus and his perfect disinterested love toward his Father and perfect obedience to his will. And while there are times when God tests us to help us move toward the perfect disinterested love that we will obtain *in glory*, our love for him, as Gerald Janzen argues, progresses in stages. Thus, Janzen rejects the view that Job 1:6–12 teaches that "true piety . . . must be totally disinterested in causal considerations or in prospects of reward" and that "piety and uprightness must exist for their own sake, or purely for God's sake, or forfeit any claim to be called piety," or what the author of Job calls "fearing God." Janzen does so because he believes that "such a view . . . approaches issues of piety and morality in altogether too rational and intellectually abstractive a manner, divorced from the dynamics of human development." He uses the illustration of a child's relationship with a parent in different stages, arguing that a toddler's "devotion and loyalty" to his parent based on the benefits she receives are no less acts of genuine love than a college student's selfless sacrifice for others, with no benefit to self. Janzen favors instead the way that the medieval saint and scholar Bernard of Clairvaux illustrates the progress of our affections:

> According to Bernard, one begins by loving oneself for one's own sake. . . . Becoming aware that one is not sufficient unto oneself, but depends radically upon God, one begins to love God for one's own sake. This is the love of dependence and gratitude and expectation. . . . In the course of loving God for one's own sake, one may discover the intrinsic worthiness of God apart from all interested considerations; or, rather, the nature of one's interestedness

15. Ortlund, 48.
16. Eric Ortlund, *Job: A 12-Week Study*, Knowing the Bible (Crossway, 2017), 16.
17. Ortlund, *Suffering Wisely and Well*, 49.

> begins to shift, so that one begins to discover an interest in the love of God for God's own sake. . . . These modes of loving may arise developmentally; but they need not supersede one another, even though on a given occasion one or another may take the center of one's consciousness and intentionality. In such a view, not only can the earlier modes of piety be appreciated as praiseworthy or otherwise, within their own terms and relative to their own concrete circumstances, but they can and should persist alongside the latter modes. . . . A piety which has arrived at one or the other of the last two stages, therefore, may also contain within it appropriate motives of gratitude and of expectation.[18]

This perspective makes sense in light of both Christian experience and Job's experience. While Job's first responses to his inexplicable sufferings are remarkable and beautiful examples of disinterested love, he wavers, in various ways, on the ash heap. During his months of mourning, he complains to God and questions God. In the end, he will see afresh that God is God and that the Lord is to be feared simply for that fact, and yet one wonders why then God vindicates Job and bestows twice the blessings if the purpose of the whole ordeal was for Job to fear God purely for God's sake.

In Your Hand

As we return to Satan's questions of God's provision and protection of Job, we arrive at the final verse, where we read of God's immediate, and perhaps surprising, consent to Satan's suggestion: "And the Lord said to Satan, 'Behold, all that he has is in your hand. Only against him do not stretch out your hand.' So Satan went out from the presence of the Lord" (Job 1:12). This anticlimactic verse ("anticlimactic" in the sense that we might have hoped that God, the hero, would rescue chapter 1's hero, Job!) yields an observation, a surprise, and a final application.

The observation is to behold the "behold"—"*Behold*, all that he has is in your hand." It is hard to think of a time when we would use the word "behold" today. I doubt that I ever started a Sunday service, "Behold, the Lord's Day has arrived." But I'm glad that the ESV didn't erase this archaic word, for rendering the Hebrew particle *hinneh* as "behold" adds theological

18. Janzen, *Job*, 40–41. See Bernard of Clairvaux, *On Loving God*, with an Analytical Commentary by Emero Stiegman, Cistercian Fathers 13B (Cistercian, 1995).

stress. From Genesis ("and behold, it was very good," Gen. 1:31) to Revelation ("Behold, I am coming soon," Rev. 22:12) and from the incarnation announcement ("Behold, the virgin shall conceive and bear a son," Matt. 1:23) to the empty tomb ("And behold, . . . an angel of the Lord . . . came and rolled back the stone," 28:2), the "beholds" of the Bible are there to catch our attention. The "behold" in Job 1:12 is no different; it announces that something important is to follow: a surprising announcement.

We might expect God to follow his "behold" with a "be gone," as Jesus ordered after his final temptation in the wilderness: "Be gone, Satan!" (Matt. 4:10). Instead, the "behold" is followed by an unexpected bestowal of power: "Behold, all that he has is in your hand. Only against him do not stretch out your hand" (Job 1:12). It is not surprising that the brilliant author has used clever connecting metaphors:

- God has blessed the work of Job's *hands* (Job 1:10).
- Satan asks God to stretch out his *hand* against Job (1:11).
- God allows Satan to stretch out his *hand* against Job's possessions (1:12).[19]

What is surprising is his theology. Is God in the business of bargaining with Satan? Or, worse, is God in the business of giving authority to Satan? Worst still, is God in the business of giving Satan power to do evil to good people? Here we step over from the surprise into the application. The answer to those questions is yes. But the key to grasping why yes is the right answer is to understand and rightly apply the final phrase from our final verse, namely, "So Satan went out from the presence of the Lord" (Job 1:12b). This ending leaves little doubt who ultimately is in control of Satan, the world, and even what is soon to befall "a man in the land of Uz whose name was Job" (v. 1). As Christopher Ash summarizes, the book of Job makes it clear that the "Sovereign God who governs the world through the intermediate agency of a number of supernatural forces ('the sons of God'), some of whom are evil[,] . . . uses evil to work out his purpose ultimately to defeat evil," and that "Even Satan's will, which is distinct from and opposite of God's, is only part of a larger plan in which God's purposes are coming

19. Eric Ortlund, *Job: A 12-Week Study*, Knowing the Bible (Crossway, 2017), 16.

to pass. Job may be under Satan's power, but Satan is under God's power, and whatever comes to pass through evil intentions will ultimately suit the good purposes of God."[20]

If we do not understand or appreciate the sovereignty of God, the Wisdom Literature will help open our eyes. The book of Job will teach us that "the sovereignty of God is that golden scepter in his hand by which he will make all bow, either by his word or by his works, by his mercies or by his judgments,"[21] and that the world is the theater of God's sovereign glory, which is a concept that so few people (even Christians) understand.

God Sovereignly Loves Through Suffering

The Japanese artist Goro Kakei's sculpture *Job* exemplifies our confusion about God's sovereignty. The artwork depicts three clay figures—Job, Satan, and God.[22] Job and Satan are on one flat surface (presumably representing earth) and Yahweh is on another (presumably representing heaven). Or perhaps the two foundations simply represent distance. God will now be distant from Job, and Satan will be too close for comfort, literally any comfort. It's as if they are stuck on a little island together—Job and his challenger. God is depicted as tall but having small hands. This gives the impression that God is unable to reach out and help Job, even if he desired to do so. Satan, though, has one huge hand that is half the size of Job, who is the smallest character. This hand is coming toward Job and Job is leaning away from it, as if he is saying, "No!" Satan's hand is not merely a symbol of the hand of affliction to come, but also a sign that Satan has won the victory. Satan's hand is not only larger than God's hand; it is also straight out. God's hand is clenched. The artist thus depicts Satan as winning the cosmic rock-paper-scissors game. Satan's "paper" covers God's "rock."

Of course, this is not a fair representation of the biblical text. God hasn't lost to Satan by entering into some schoolyard game. Nor is the dialogue and decision recorded in Job 1:6–12 a "crude representation of a divinity

20. Christopher Ash, *Trusting God in the Darkness: A Guide to Understanding the Book of Job* (Crossway, 2021), 139–40, 36.

21. Thomas Brooks, in *The Westminster Collection of Christian Quotations*, comp. Martin H. Manser (Westminster John Knox, 2001), 142.

22. For a visual and comments, see C. L. Seow, *Job 1–21: Interpretation and Commentary*, Illuminations (Eerdmans, 2013), 257.

who cruelly permits the torture of his creation,"[23] as the psychoanalyst Carl Jung saw it. In fact, our text and the texts to follow present an image of a God who sovereignly rules but who also sovereignly loves through suffering. God allows the trials of Job not because he wants to *know* whether Job will continue to honor him (for God knows all things) but rather because God wants to *show* that Job will honor him despite his cataclysmic circumstances. God tests Job not to find out whether Job will succeed or fail but rather to reveal the essence of authentic faith and to demonstrate that his divine power is made perfect in human weakness. The Bible teaches that trials and testings can authenticate or refine faith and that divine love can show itself through suffering. It is a strange sovereignty, perhaps, but it is one that we see played out in the Bible over and over again—and ultimately in our Lord Jesus Christ.

In the thought-provoking folk song "Show the Way," songwriter David Wilcox sings of "someone" (a God-figure in the song) writing a play in which he would "glorify" what is "stronger than hate." He would do so through love—the power at work behind the scenes—and through a hero (a Christ-figure) who seems to arrive too late and is up against the impossible odds of winning against a dark and evil world. Yet when he comes, the victory is his! The darkness dissipates, and love and light prevail.

Similarly, Scripture teaches that God (who is love!) wrote the play. What is more, in this play, so vividly illustrated in the book of Job, divine love could (would!) be glorified within "the definite plan and foreknowledge of God" (Acts 2:23) when Jesus was "betrayed into the *hands* of sinners" (Matt. 26:45) and "delivered up" to be "crucified and killed by the *hands* of lawless men" (Acts 2:23). When Jesus calls out with a loud voice, "Father, into your *hands* [his big, grace-filled hands] I commit my spirit!" (Luke 23:46), we see the perfect picture of love triumphing through suffering and of Satan's power being crushed once and for all by the sovereign love of God. If we struggle to believe this, we must see afresh the story of Job and touch afresh our Savior's hands: "Put your finger here, and see my hands; and put out your hand, and place it in my side. Do not disbelieve, but believe" (John 20:27). The Son of Man suffered at the hands of sinful men to bring salvation through suffering.

23. See R. A. F. MacKenzie and Roland E. Murphy, "Job," in *New Jerome Biblical Commentary*, ed. Raymond E. Brown et al. (Prentice Hall, 1990), 467.

There is so little we know about the universe, and so little we know about God, the Creator of this amazing universe. But what we do know—indeed, what we are taught in this text—is that God can use even the schemes of Satan and the horrors of human suffering to show forth his sovereign love.

3

Blessed Be the Name of the Lord: Job's Godly Response to the Loss of His Wealth

Job 1:13–22

The Lord gave, and the Lord has taken away;
blessed be the name of the Lord. (Job 1:21b)

On September 24, 1757, Aaron Burr died unexpectedly. It was two days before what would have been his public commencement as the first president of the College of New Jersey (now Princeton University). During this tragic time, his wife, Esther, wrote a letter to a close family friend, which reads, in part:

> Your most kind letter of condolence gave me inexpressible delight, and at the same time set open afresh all the avenues of grief, and again probed the deep wound death has given me. My loss—Shall I attempt to say how great my loss is—God only can know—And to him alone would I carry my complaint. . . . Had not God supported me by these two considerations; first, by showing the right he has to his own creatures, to dispose of them when and in what manner he pleases; and secondly, by enabling me to [someday] follow [my husband] beyond the grave, into the eternal world, and there to view him in unspeakable

> glory and happiness, . . . I should not, long before this, have been sunk among the dead. . . . God has wise ends in all that he does. This thing did not come upon me by chance; and I rejoice that I am in the hands of such a God.[1]

Less than eight months after Aaron Burr's death, Esther's father, Jonathan Edwards, also died. On April 3, 1758, Jonathan's wife, Sarah, wrote to Esther: "My dear child, what shall I say? A holy and good God has covered us with a dark cloud. O that we may kiss the rod, and lay our hands on our mouths! The Lord has done it. . . . But my God lives; and he has my heart. . . . We are all given to God; and there I am, and love to be."[2]

What do we think of God in times of sorrow, sickness, suffering, and death? Have we ever thought of God in the way that these two widows wrote of him? Do we actually believe that God has "the right . . . to his own creatures, to dispose of them when and in what manner he pleases" and that "God has wise ends in all that he does"? Do we "kiss the rod," even rejoicing in such tragic times that we are "in the hands of such a God"?[3]

In our study of Job, we come to a book that will teach us that God's love for us is bigger and broader than sentimentality and sympathy and that his will for our lives is vaster and grander than our personal happiness and success. We come to a book that will renew our vows, so to speak, reminding us that we are to be faithful to God—for better or for worse, for richer or for poorer, in sickness and in health—that we are to love God, to cherish him as he does us, whether he gives or takes away.[4] That is what Job's response in Job 1:13–22 ought to teach us.

What Happened

Job 1:13 sets the celebratory scene: "Now there was a day when [Job's] sons and daughters were eating and drinking wine in their oldest brother's

1. Quoted in Jonathan Edwards, *The Works of Jonathan Edwards*, ed. Edward Hickman, 2 vols. (Banner of Truth, 1992), 1:clxxiii.

2. Quoted in Edwards, 1:clxxix.

3. Of historical interest, the Edwards family echoes the language of the Heidelberg Catechism. The answer to question 27 ("What do you understand by the providence of God?") speaks of God's providence as upholding heaven, earth, and all creatures "as with his hand" and that he "so governs" the world that "all things [including 'health and sickness'], come not by chance but by his fatherly hand."

4. Sections of this chapter were first published in Douglas Sean O'Donnell, *The Beginning and End of Wisdom: Preaching Christ from the First and Last Chapters of Proverbs, Ecclesiastes, and Job* (Crossway, 2011), 91–92, 99–103. Used by permission.

house." All is well in Job's world. We might imagine laughter and music mixed with questions such as: "Some more Cabernet, anyone? Are we out of brie?" Then, as Job's children are eating and drinking and enjoying one another's company, the unthinkable happens. Human savagery (the Sabeans and Chaldeans) and natural disasters (fire and wind) crash the party:

> Now there was a day when his sons and daughters were eating and drinking wine in their oldest brother's house, and there came a messenger to Job and said, "The oxen were plowing and the donkeys feeding beside them, and the Sabeans fell upon them and took them and struck down the servants with the edge of the sword, and I alone have escaped to tell you." While he was yet speaking, there came another and said, "The fire of God fell from heaven and burned up the sheep and the servants and consumed them, and I alone have escaped to tell you." While he was yet speaking, there came another and said, "The Chaldeans formed three groups and made a raid on the camels and took them and struck down the servants with the edge of the sword, and I alone have escaped to tell you." While he was yet speaking, there came another and said, "Your sons and daughters were eating and drinking wine in their oldest brother's house, and behold, a great wind came across the wilderness and struck the four corners of the house, and it fell upon the young people, and they are dead, and I alone have escaped to tell you." (Job 1:13–19)

The inspired author offers a structured account of a most unruly day (Job 1:13–19), a day in which Job loses all his possessions. The destruction happens in reverse order of the description of Job's possessions in Job 1:2–3—moving from least important (the animals) to the most (his children). First, some of Job's servants are massacred ("The Sabeans fell upon them and took them and struck down the servants with the edge of the sword," v. 15) and his oxen and donkeys are taken ("They stole all the animals," v. 15 NLT). Second, a lightning storm destroys more servants, along with his sheep ("The fire of God fell from heaven and burned up the sheep and the servants and consumed them," v. 16). Third, more servants are slaughtered, with his camels' being taken ("The Chaldeans . . . made a raid on the camels and took them and struck down the servants with the edge of the sword," v. 17). Fourth, "a great wind" (v. 19) blows down the walls of Job's oldest son's house, leaving all of Job's children dead ("The young people . . . are dead," 1:19). Their house of celebration (vv. 4, 13) has become their burial chamber. At the end of the day, all that is left is Job, four messengers, and, as we will see, Job's wife. He has almost lost it all. He has certainly lost enough. The refrain of Ecclesiastes is "vanity of vanities"; here we might label Job 1:13–19 "tragedy of tragedies."

In four waves of woe, Job loses his livestock, servants, and children. The structure of this destruction is clear: (1) a messenger speaks (2) about a catastrophe that happened, and (3) as the messenger is ending with the line "and I alone have escaped to tell you" (repeated four times), the cycle begins again (with the line "While he was yet speaking, there came another and said" repeated three times and "emphasizing the rapidity with which these disastrous events occur"[5]). It is also clear who is to blame. Human savagery is one enemy to credit with Job's calamities.

Two Arabian tribes ruthlessly steal Job's oxen and donkeys and destroy his servants through the sword—literally, by "the mouth of the sword." The image depicts "the sword as a monster devouring its victims."[6] The nomadic "Sabeans" trust in their military might when they "[fall] upon" Job's servants working the fields. The marauding "Chaldeans" focus on military strategy, overtaking Job's servants by dividing and conquering. Their three military units come from three different directions upon their unsuspecting targets. The record of their victory (Job 1:17) gives the sense of a big and bloody battle. Picture three thousand armed men against one thousand unarmed, or barely armed, slaves—a bloody mess.

Human savagery is one cause of calamity; the second is divine determination. While "fire" and "wind" are mentioned as *natural causes* in popular jargon, the language here points beyond the natural to the supernatural. The verb "fall" (*naphal*) is "repeatedly used to describe these disasters 'falling' upon Job, which highlight their divine origins. . . . It was obvious that this sudden, extreme, disastrous upheaval of Job's life was the doing of God."[7] Moreover, the phrase *'esh 'elohim*, which can be translated as "a fire of God," is obvious enough. The only "God" in Job is Yahweh. Moreover, the expression *'esh 'elohim* is used of God elsewhere, such as in 2 Kings 1:12, and its equivalent, but more precise, expression "Yahweh's fire" is used in Numbers 11:1–3 and 1 Kings 18:38. So we may envision a scenario similar to what occurs in 2 Kings 1, where Elijah calls on "the fire of God from heaven"

5. Gerald H. Wilson, *Job*, Understanding the Bible Commentary 10 (Baker, 2007), 26.

6. John Goldingay, *Job for Everyone*, Old Testament for Everyone (Westminster John Knox, 2013), 278.

7. C. J. Williams, *The Shadow of Christ in the Book of Job* (Wipf & Stock, 2017), 36.

three times to annihilate God's adversaries, although there are distinctions between the two situations.[8]

The destructive wilderness wind can also be attributed to coming from God's hand, both in the fact that storm metaphors are used in Job (see Job 38:1; 40:6) and other places in the Old Testament for God ("Behold, the storm of the LORD!," Jer. 23:19; cf. 30:23; Zech. 9:14) and in the language used: God "struck," or the God-sent wind merely "touch[ed]," the house and it immediately fell down—the very touch that Satan challenged God to give (Job 1:11).

God as the cause—the ultimate cause not only of the natural disasters but even of human actions—should not surprise us as readers because we have been privy to the cosmic chamber-room conversations and we know how Job will respond ("the LORD has taken away," Job 1:21; cf. Westminster Confession of Faith 5.4). Job doesn't mention the wind, the fire, and savage men! That said, if we are honest, for most of us that concept of God as the cause leaves a bad taste in our mouths, an aching in our souls, and burning questions in our minds. Is this what God is like? Is this how God rules the world? Is this how God treats his friends? Those are good questions, but they are not questions to which we get answers here. Instead of taking us into the mind of God, the author focuses on Job's response to God.

Job's Response

After the author details Job's terrible, horrible, no good, very bad day (Job 1:13–19), he records Job's remarkable response—unspeakable grief ("Then Job arose and tore his robe and shaved his head"), submissive faith ("fell on the ground and worshiped," v. 20), recognition of his own mortality and that all he had was a divine gift ("And he said, 'Naked I came from my mother's womb, and naked shall I return'"), and unwavering commitment to God's free and sovereign rule ("The LORD gave, and the LORD has taken away; blessed be the name of the LORD," v. 21). Let's explore each aspect in turn.

First, Job "arose." The last time Job arose was to offer sacrifices for his children ("he would *rise* early in the morning and offer burnt offerings," Job

8. Rabbinic exegesis first noted the wordplay (without the vowel markings, added later to the original) on the name "Job" (Hebrew: *'yb*, later *'oyeb*) and the word "enemy" (*'yb*, later *'iyyob*). Job (*'yb*) says to God, "Why do you hide your face and count me as your enemy [*'iyyob*]?" (Job 13:24).

1:5). Now he arises to mourn their deaths. He will never again sacrifice for them. Instead, he will cry out for them. He does this by tearing his robe (the second reaction) and shearing his head (the third), outward symbols of his inward sorrow.[9] It is as though his heart has been torn in two and his head severed from his body. Through the ripping of his robe and the shearing of his scalp, he weeps over his unimaginable loss.[10]

"Death is the Great Interruption," writes Tim Keller, "tearing loved ones away from us, or us from them. Death is the Great Schism, ripping apart material and immaterial parts of our being and sundering a whole person, who was never meant to be disembodied, even for a moment."[11] Job rips his robe and shaves his head. Note this: at this point he has so little left. He has lost his businesses—his supermarket (the oxen plowing the fields to farm), his clothing company (the sheep), and his transportation enterprise (the camels). Yet what does this once-rich man still have? His hair and his robe. And what does he do? He shaves off his likely long and well-kept hair and tears his outer garment. Maybe his hair isn't as dolled up as Queen Esther's or his robe as glamorous as Joseph's amazing technicolor dreamcoat, but Job is one of the richest guys on the planet! He would have taken care of his body and clothed himself in expensive and elegant attire. Job's shaving of his head and rending of his garment thus suggests more than mourning; it is an act of desperation. Instead of holding on to the few material things of value, he rids himself of them. He is perhaps now naked, as the artist Gonzalo Carrasco depicts him in his work *Job on the Dunghill* (1881), an image that would fit what the poor man says next.

Job's fourth response to the fourfold calamities follows: he "fell on the ground and worshiped. And he said, 'Naked I came from my mother's womb, and naked shall I return. The Lord gave, and the Lord has taken away; blessed be the name of the Lord'" (Job 1:20b–21). All the actions above—the falling down, worshiping, and short speech—can be placed under the category of *humble adoration*. Job's immediate reflex is one of both genuine sorrow

9. "Tearing the clothes was a common sign of grief and mourning (2 Sam. 1:11). Cutting the hair or shaving . . . the head (or forehead) was a mourning practice among the Canaanites and other Near Eastern peoples (Isa. 22:12; Jer. 7:29; Mic. 1:16), but Israelite law prohibited it (Lev. 19:27–28; Deut. 14:1). Job's practice is consistent with his presumed non-Israelite status." Wilson, *Job*, 28.

10. As the commentary for Job 1:20 in the 1560 Geneva Bible states, Job's tearing his robe "declares that the children of God are not insensible like blocks, but . . . they feel affliction and grief of mind" (spelling updated).

11. Timothy Keller, *On Death* (Penguin, 2020), 1–2.

and genuine praise. In wisdom, he admits his mortality ("Naked I came from my mother's womb, and naked shall I return") and God's sovereignty ("The Lord gave, and the Lord has taken away"). Indeed, his confession "blessed be the name of the Lord"—his inclusio of adoration—especially leaps off the page! For all of us can acknowledge that just as we were born without any clothes on, so when we are dead and buried, no matter what we are buried in, it will decay and we will be naked again (cf. 1 Tim. 6:7), as it were. Most pious people could acknowledge God's sovereignty even amid tragedies. Many Christians say when they experience loss, "The Lord gave, and the Lord has taken away." But in light of all this, to say "blessed be the name [the honor and reputation] of the Lord" is a very remarkable reaction indeed. Our familiarity with this famous response can desensitize us to the depths of devotion expressed here. There is nothing quite like this extraordinary response to the sovereign will of God in the whole Bible, other than that of our Lord Jesus Christ in Gethsemane: "My Father, . . . let this cup pass from me; nevertheless, not as I will, but as you will" (Matt. 26:39).

A Short Commentary on the Short Commentary

After Job's fourfold response to the fourfold calamities, Job's author offers a brief commentary: "In all this Job did not sin or charge God with wrong" (Job 1:22). My commentary follows. Job's godliness has been praised by God (v. 8). Job has also been praised by the narrator (v. 1). Now, for the third and final time in chapter 1, our author adds approval, as an inclusio (v. 22). He commends Job for his godly response to the horrific events of the day ("in all this"). The parallelism—"Job did not sin" and Job did not "charge God with wrong" (v. 22)—summarizes Job's resilient faith. Here Job is praised not for what he does but for what he does *not* do. Because this is a synthetic parallelism, the sense is that Job does not sin in that he does not charge God with wrong. This focus on what Job does not do perhaps heightens Job's unparalleled character, since the predictable human response would be to give in to the temptation to curse God and accuse him of evildoing.

Most people, as Job's wife later suggests, *would* sin by cursing God. That would be the top temptation for him, and for us in similar situations. If we were in Job's shoes (minus the shoes, I suppose), would we accuse God of wrongdoing, or blame him for letting evil strike the godly? Job lives up to the heavenly hype. He does not, as Habakkuk does after his first vision, complain (see Hab. 1:12–13). Nor does he draw his sword, as Peter does when God's plan of the wicked's destroying his holy Lord is playing out before his eyes (Matt. 26:51). Instead, despite this great tragedy, Job's immediate response is not to take it out on himself, others, or God (he doesn't question or curse his Creator), but rather, in sorrow and humility and faith, to prostrate himself on the earth and worship its sovereign Sustainer. Job bows his head, praises God, and accepts God's sovereign plan. "In all this Job did not sin or charge God with wrong" (Job 1:22) is not an anticlimactic answer; it is one of the climactic claims of the Scriptures.

Three Roots

Job's faith is so deeply rooted that it is not as easy for Satan to sift him as he thought it would be. Likewise, while we realize both that Job's sufferings exceed anything we have experienced or will experience and that his faith is deeper than ours will ever be, yet we must also realize that the substance of Job's strength can be ours. Like everything else in Scripture, the story of Job can make us wise unto salvation *and* train us in righteousness (see 2 Tim. 3:15–16). It can teach us what it means to stay grounded in God, what it means that "the righteous shall live by . . . faith" (Hab. 2:4). To this end, in the second half of this chapter, we will expose Job's roots. That is, we will uncover the under-the-surface theological foundations that help him hold up under duress.

Know That Suffering Isn't Always Evil

The first root of Job's faith is his knowledge that suffering isn't always evil. Or, put more positively, suffering can be good, or for one's spiritual benefit. That is why, when the commodities of Job's comfortable life are snatched away, he doesn't view it as something purely evil. He doesn't say, "What's the devil up to?" or "Why has this great evil come upon me?" In fact, nowhere in his reactions and replies do we have the remotest suggestion that Job sees suffering as abnormal or immoral (or satanic, although we know that Satan indeed has a role in it). Instead, Job realizes that material and spiritual prosperity are divine gifts and that as divine gifts they are freely given and can be freely taken away. He must know that peace, prosperity, self-security, and happiness can become perils that threaten to hinder or prohibit fallen human beings from undertaking and continuing the arduous journey of faith (as well described in John Bunyan's *Pilgrim's Progress*). He must believe that suffering possesses the strange but beautiful power of liberating one's soul from the seduction of safety and the love of temporal, perishable goods. In these ways, Job anticipates the Christian life—the necessity of cross-bearing (Luke 9:23), persecution for righteousness' sake (Matt. 5:10), learning obedience from hardships (Heb. 5:8), and sharing in the sufferings of Christ (Phil. 1:29).

Trust in God's Providence

The second root is Job's trust in God's providence. A century ago, the words *Providence* and *God* were used virtually interchangeably. In those days, many people took for granted the reality that God rules every aspect of the universe and every event of history. But since the rise of the scientific worldview, it seems now that only believers and some insurance companies recognize God's continuing activity in the world. The largest insurance companies in America still call unpreventable destructive occurrences of the natural world, such as earthquakes and cyclones, "acts of God." To them, at least on paper, God can be credited (or "blamed") as the architect and builder of both personal calamities and national catastrophes.

Most people today hold a progressive view of providence that is similar to what was advocated by H. G. Wells in *Undying Fire*. In that novel, the protagonist, Job (!) Huss, is an atheistic evolutionist, and as such he sees no benevolence, wisdom, or justice in the random ways of this world. He refuses to recognize faith in the ultimate providence of God as a valid or respectable answer to cosmic and human cruelty. Rather, he believes that only the "undying fire"—the subjective spirit of God in the human heart—can bring any meaning or significance to earthly affliction. If there is a God, he is silent in the midst of suffering. His eyes are closed, his hands are tied, and he has fallen asleep, or rolled over and died. All that remains to warm ourselves in this bitterly cold cosmos is human love for each other—that undying fire.

Needless to say, the biblical Job doesn't think this way. Call him prehistoric. Call him unscientific. Call him naive. Or call him correct! For why is it more historical, scientific, and sophisticated to reason that if God is all-loving, then the existence of suffering tells us that he must not be all-powerful; and if God is all-powerful and yet such affliction exists, then he must not be all-loving? People reach these unbiblical conclusions today, and then think they are so clever. They smugly wash their hands of God and Christianity. God-problem solved. Case closed. Debate won.

There are, however, at least two flaws in such logic. First, such a view refuses to fathom that human misery can in any way contain elements of divine love. Yet this is the message of our faith. At the center of the gospel is God's omnipotent love incarnate, a love that is pierced through the wood of an old rugged cross. A love that suffers, a love that dies!

Second, such a view assumes that if suffering appears to be pointless, then it must be pointless. Sometimes we are so arrogant and ignorant. While we know from experience that good can come from suffering (as we look back to times of suffering in our lives and see the benefits of such times), we still assume that if our finite "minds can't plumb the depths of the universe for good answers to suffering, well, then, there can't be any!"[12] The esteemed philosopher Alvin Plantinga illustrates this flawed attitude by speaking of the existence of an extremely small insect called a no-see-um. Plantinga's argument, as summarized by Keller, goes like this: "If you were out camping and you looked into your pup tent for a St. Bernard, and you don't see one, it is reasonable to conclude there is no St. Bernard in your tent. But if you look into your tent for a 'no-see-um' . . . and you don't see any of *um*, it is not reasonable to assume they aren't there. Because, after all, no one can see 'em." Keller concludes: "Many people assume that if there were good reasons for the existence of evil [or suffering], they would be accessible to our minds, more like St. Bernards than like no-see-ums, but . . . why should that be the case?"[13]

Job has no idea what is going on in the heavens. He is not privy to the chamber-room conversation. Yet he gives God the benefit of the doubt. He knows what the Bible calls *wisdom*. He knows who is the potter and who is the clay, and as the clay he does not say to the potter, "Do you know what you are doing?" Rather, he is able to be remolded and reshaped because he trusts that he is still in God's wise and just and loving hands. Job must agree with the sentiment expressed by Miroslav Volf that "much like all the dark shadows in the world 'harmonize' with patches of light and contribute to the

12. Timothy Keller, *The Reason for God: Belief in an Age of Skepticism* (Dutton, 2008), 23.
13. Keller, 23–24.

beauty of the world when the whole is seen from the ultimate perspective of the Creator, so also all the ugliness in [his] life contributes in some inexplicable way to its future beauty."[14] Job trusts in the purposeful *providence* of God. Do we trust God like that? We should. See-um or no-see-um, we should see *him* at work—certainly in our dog-sized dilemmas, but also in as many minuscule actions as we can notice. Following Job's lead, we should trust that God rules every aspect of the universe, every event of history, and every detail of our personal lives.

Believe in the Resurrection

The third root of Job's faith is to believe in the resurrection. This conviction is not directly apparent from Job 1, where we do not see Job testifying to life after death or to a day when all wrongs will be judged and made right. Yet as Job continues to speak with his friends, it becomes evident that he believes in (or at least hopes for) some sort of bodily resurrection. For example, in Job 14:13–14, he states:

> Oh that you would hide me in Sheol,
> that you would conceal me until your wrath be past,
> that you would appoint me a set time, and remember me!
> If a man dies, shall he live again?
> All the days of my service I would wait,
> till my renewal should come.

Here Job asks God to (1) hide him "in the grave" (Job 1:13 KJV), (2) forget about him until God's anger subsides, (3) set a day and time ("But mark your calendar to think of me again!," NLT), and (4) come and get him, renew him, and revive him. Eugene Peterson's paraphrase summarizes well the idea behind the Hebrew word *khalifah* (rendered "renewal" in v. 14 ESV):

> So mortals lie down and never get up,
> never wake up again—never.
> Why don't you just bury me alive,
> get me out of the way until your anger cools?
> But don't leave me there!

14. Miroslav Volf, *Exclusion and Embrace: A Theological Exploration of Identity, Otherness, and Reconciliation*, rev. and updated ed. (Abingdon, 2019), 137.

> Set a date when you'll see me again.
> If we humans die, will we live again? That's my question.
> All through these difficult days I keep hoping,
> waiting for the final change—for resurrection! (Job 1:13 MSG)

Job 14:13–14 offers more than a hint that Job might believe in a bodily resurrection; it declares his hope that he does. While Job's hope may not be as bold as the psalmists' ("I shall behold your face . . . when I awake," Ps. 17:15; cf. Pss. 16:10; 49:15) and prophets' ("Your dead shall live; their bodies shall rise. You who dwell in the dust, awake and sing for joy! For your dew is a dew of light, and the earth will give birth to the dead," Isa. 26:19; cf. Dan. 12:2),[15] he knows that the covenant God of Israel is the God of the living and not of the dead (see Luke 20:38).

Another example, perhaps the most evident, is in Job 19:25–26, where Job answers his friends' false accusations by declaring: "For I know that my Redeemer lives, and at the last [day] he will stand upon the earth. And after my skin has been thus destroyed, yet in my flesh [a new body!] I shall see God." Job holds the belief—or at least ponders the possibility—that there would be a bodily resurrection and that in that day there would also be retribution—final justice.[16] If we would look toward the afterlife and live in light of our future resurrection grounded in Christ's past resurrection (we know so much more than Job did!), then our troubles would be far more tolerable. The apparent tyrannies of providence would be more palatable, for we would remember that God still "has time," so to speak, to remedy all injustices of history, including our personal histories. By looking forward to a future vindication and the joy that will accompany it, we can affirm Paul's

15. There are other underlying concepts in the Old Testament itself of an afterlife. As Michael Graves, in *How Scripture Interprets Scripture: What Biblical Writers Can Teach Us About Reading the Bible* (Baker Academic, 2021), summarizes: "(1) Sheol as an inhabited netherworld, (2) spirits of the dead, and (3) burial customs" (146). The Old Testament does not have, as the New Testament does, "a fully formed theology of the afterlife but a vague assumption that people continue to exist in some way after they die" (149).

16. John Walton paraphrases Job 19:26–27 as "Despite my peeling skin, I expect to have enough left to come before God in my own flesh [to be restored to favor]." John H. Walton and Tremper Longman III, *How to Read Job* (IVP Academic, 2015), 108. I favor Graves' rendering (154): "And after my skin has been destroyed, then from my flesh. Whom I will see for myself; and my eyes will behold and not a stranger. My feelings (kidneys) are consumed inside of me," and his conclusion: "Job clearly believes that he will see God after his flesh has been destroyed. . . . He expects to see God after he dies." More will be said on this theme in chapter 16 below.

words in Romans 8:18: "For I consider that the sufferings of this present time are not worth comparing with the glory that is to be revealed to us."

His Question, Our Answer

When Jesus walked this earth, he called everyone—as he still calls us today—to put him and his kingdom above possessions, family, friends, and reputation. He also calls us to accept, if necessary, suffering, persecution, and the loss of home, job, money, and even life.

Remember Satan's question from Job 1:9 ("Does Job fear God for no reason?"). Satan wants to know whether Job would still trust God even if God were to take it all away. We know how Job answers that question. He trusts God through the trials. "Take away my possessions. Take away my children. Take it all away, and yet I will praise the Lord." But what about us? How do we answer Satan's question? Would we follow the Lord, trust in him, love him, and fear him no matter what? In times of sorrow, sickness, and suffering, would we, as the Edwards family did, "kiss the rod," rejoicing that we are "in the hands of such a God"? Let us hope so and pray so. May God help *us* to persevere in the faith—to find wisdom in the cross and wisdom in the resurrection and return of Jesus Christ, the very wisdom of God incarnate.

4

Sitting on the Ashes: Job's Godly Responses to the Loss of His Health

Job 2:1–13

Skin for skin! All that a man has he will give for his life.
(Job 2:4)

For this heavy text, we start on a lighter note. Many young Americans grew up watching *Sesame Street.* One of the games regularly featured on the show was called "One of These Things"—a game that helped children grasp the concept of *same* versus *different.* As the words "One of these things is not like the others; one of these things doesn't belong; can you tell which thing is not like the others by the time I finish this song?" played in the background, four things appeared on the screen. Three featured something the same and one was different. What was different, once discovered, was obvious. "Oh, there it is!"

Reading the first part of this text (Job 2:1–10) is a bit like watching that television segment, in that most of what we see looks like what we have seen: Job 2:1 repeats 1:6; 2:2 repeats 1:7; 2:3 repeats 1:8; and 2:5–7a is similar to 1:11–12. The purpose of such repetition is threefold. First, it reemphasizes the person and power of Job's accuser. Astonishingly, Satan has once again walked the world; importantly, he has access to God. Second, it reacknowledges God's sovereignty over the situation. Satan has to ask and be granted permission. Third, the repetition helps us notice what is different.

Two differences are obvious but important. First, after God repeats his praise of Job's extraordinary character ("Have you considered my servant Job, that there is none like him on the earth, a blameless and upright man, who fears God and turns away from evil?"), he adds a commendation of Job's resilience ("He still holds fast his integrity"), along with a censure on Satan ("although you incited me against him to destroy him without reason," Job 2:3). We might paraphrase this sentence, "I told you so!" It is the author's way of emphasizing the reality of Job's amazing perseverance.

The other difference is Satan's new and ingenious strategy. When we read Job 1:7–12 and then 2:1–7, what Satan says in 2:4 stands out like a sore thumb, or sore *everything*, as the case will be for Job: "Skin for skin!" Satan wants to touch Job's "flesh" (Job 2:5) because he believes that "all that a man has he will give for his life" (v. 4). In other words, since our natural disposition is to place an extremely high value on protecting and caring for our physical bodies ("No one ever hated his own flesh," Eph. 5:29), Satan's new angle of attack banks on Job's desire for self-preservation, aligned with self-love. Satan knows now that the losses of wealth, children, assets, and financial legacy have not moved Job from praising God to cursing him. So he surmises that if God allowed him to touch Job's body, then Job would pause in his praise and, more than that, "curse" God to his face (Job 2:5). Satan reckons that if God would just give him the green light to turn Job's body black and blue—and red (the sores)—then Job would surely turn yellow. He'd cower, and then he'd curse.

Well, the light turns green! God concedes to the challenger's challenge ("Behold, he is in your hand"), under one condition ("only spare his life," Job 2:6). An agreement is made, and soon the attack starts. Satan strikes Job "with loathsome sores from the sole of his foot to the crown of his head" (v. 7). His whole body is black and blue with bruises and red with sores. Will Job turn yellow? Will he cower and curse? In what follows, we will see his responses both to Satan's strike and to his helpmate's diabolical suggestion. We will witness his friends' remarkable responses as well. In doing so, we will learn God's wisdom on how and how not to respond to a personal tragedy, especially as it relates to physical calamities.

Job's Initial Response

We start with Job, whose response to his physical sufferings is both realistic and resilient. Job 2:8 describes his realistic reaction to his boil-plagued body: "he took a piece of broken pottery with which to scrape himself while he sat in the ashes." We are not told whether Job's house has been destroyed. If so, perhaps he sits in the ashes of his estate. The other option for "the ashes" is the garbage dump where people would burn their trash. The Septuagint takes it this way and renders the Hebrew "in the ashes" (*b^{e}tok-ha 'epher*) as "on the garbage pile outside the city" (*epi tes koprias exo tes poleos*). In the New Testament, this place is called "hell" (*genna*), or the "hell of fire" (*geenna tou puros*, Matt. 5:22; 18:9), as our Lord Jesus often referred to it.

Job has descended into this hell (or ascended onto the ash heap!) to symbolize his mortality (the cursed children of Adam will work until they "return to the ground," for they "are dust, and to dust [they] shall return," Gen. 3:19) and to embody his inner emotions. He makes clear in his suicidal soliloquy (Job 3) after seven days of silence (2:13) that he would be better off dead ("After this Job opened his mouth and cursed the day of his birth," 3:1). He wishes that his once-strong body was lying as lifeless ashes. He feels like "the damned in hell," in that he longs for death, but it eludes him (see 3:21).[1] Because death somehow evades him, he seeks to soothe himself from the itchiness of his awful and all-intrusive sores by taking from the pile of rubbish "a piece of broken pottery with which to scrape himself" (2:8), a measure so severe that his closest friends "did not recognize him" (v. 12) when they arrived on the scene. As we will learn, these "loathsome sores" (v. 7, likely boils that continually discharge pus) are only the surface of Satan's "touch" of Job's "bone and his flesh" (v. 5). Later, Job will describe a "fever with chills (21:6; 30:30), darkening and shriveling of the skin (30:30), red eyes swollen from weeping (16:16), diarrhea (30:27), sleeplessness and delirium (7:4, 13–14), bad breath (19:17), emaciation (19:20), and excruciating pain through the body (30:17)."[2]

1. See Joseph Caryl, "An Exposition upon Job," in *ESV Church History Study Bible: Voices from the Past, Wisdom for the Present* (Crossway, 2023), 707.

2. Richard P. Belcher Jr., *Job: The Mystery of Suffering and God's Sovereignty*, Focus on the Bible (Christian Focus, 2017), 26.

Job's Wife's Response

As realistic as Job's response is, it is also, and once again, amazingly resilient. Despite being on the verge of despair, he refrains from blaming others for his troubles, and most importantly, he does not curse God. Instead, he remains silent until his wife breaks the silence. When we read, "Then his wife said to him" (Job 2:9a), we may anticipate comforting words from his soulmate and source of solace to follow. But that's not what we get. Instead, she questions her husband's pigheaded piety ("Do you still hold fast [to] your integrity?") and offers a simple solution ("Curse God and die," v. 9b), a clear echo of Satan's hope for Job (cf. "he will curse you [God]," 1:11; 2:5) and a twist on God's commendation of Job's "integrity" (2:3). The title of this chapter is "Sitting on the Ashes." But this section, as Job's lament over his wife, could be called, humorously, "I Can't Eat by Day, I Can't Sleep by Night, and the Woman I Love Don't Treat Me Right."[3] Her solution makes sense from a human perspective. She wants her husband put out of his misery, an emotional misery in which she shares. Together they have lost ten children in one day. Imagine such a loss! Also imagine her and her husband burying each body, one after the other, from morning light till night. What she has had to go through is so awful that perhaps she has longed for death too.

From 2020–22, Pastor Tim Challies wrote extensively about the sudden loss of his twenty-year-old son, a project that culminated with his book *Seasons of Sorrow*. Thousands were blessed that Challies shared some of his private grief publicly. He begins with a blog post he wrote the day after his son Nick's death: "In all the years I've been writing, I have never had to type words more difficult, more devastating than these: Yesterday the Lord called my son to himself—my dear son, my kind son, my godly son, my only son," a day that caused Tim and his wife to cry "until there were no tears left to cry."[4]

Later, in chapter 5 ("From Grave to Glory"), Challies recalls his thoughts when Nick was laid into his grave:

> My life has known no moment harder than this. My heart has known no sorrow deeper than this. Nothing could be more final, nothing more sobering,

3. Charles R. Swindoll, *Job: A Man of Heroic Endurance* (Word, 2004), 5n3.
4. Tim Challies, *Seasons of Sorrow: The Pain of Loss and the Comfort of God* (Zondervan, 2022), xii.

nothing more shattering than watching my son's casket be lowered, inch by inch, foot by foot, until at last it comes to rest at the bottom of the grave. His grave. . . . I hear the pastor say the words, "Dust to dust." A piece of me is being buried. A piece of my heart. A piece of my soul. A piece of my very self.[5]

What Job and his wife have been through—in losing their possessions and *ten* children—is so awful. But that's not all. Her bald-headed husband, "the greatest of all the people of the east" (Job 1:3), is not sitting on a throne but perching on the garbage dump, wearing little or no clothing, scraping his wounds (2:8). Her lifestyle, her family, her marriage, *her everything* has changed in a day. And perhaps day after day for weeks or months she has visited this great man, a man who once went from good to great and who has now gone from great to grotesque. She believes in God; she does not doubt his existence and certainly not his power. So with her advice she is urging: "Get this over with. Take a break from being so virtuous and take control of the situation. Stop praising God and start cursing him. For once you curse him, he will destroy you, and death would be preferable, right?" Wrong. Very wrong. Satan may have slithered away from the scene, but this "devil's advocate" (*diabolic adjutrix*), as Augustine (perhaps too harshly!) calls her, or "tool of Satan" (*organum satani*), as John Calvin claims,[6] echoes his voice from Job 1:11. Satan's test was tough, but this test might be tougher.

Job's Next Response

We should not underestimate just how tempting the suggestion of Job's wife is. A man often feels most helpless when his helpmate fails to help. But Job does not eat from the fruit she offers. He replies, "You speak as one of the foolish women would speak" (Job 2:10). In other words, he says: "You are no fool! Why then are you speaking like one? Listen, we have lived through a lot of death and destruction. But we have also had times of great life and

5. Challies, 19.

6. Quoted, without reference, in Derek Thomas, *The Storm Breaks: Job Simply Explained*, Welwyn Commentary Series (repr., Evangelical Press, 2005), 54. Thomas also notes that "Thomas Aquinas theorized that Satan had spared her in his opening salvo against Job in order to use her against Job" (54). Earlier in church history, Gregory the Great, in his *Moralia*, says that as Satan "fixed his hold on the heart of the woman [Eve] and found in it a ladder by which he might mount up to the heart of the man [Adam]," so "he seized the mind of [Job's] wife, which was the ladder to the husband." Quoted in *ESV Church History Study Bible*, 706.

joy. 'Shall we [notice that he includes her] receive good from God [the gift of children], and shall we not receive evil [the death of children]?' (2:10)."[7] Put differently, Job counsels his wife to keep trusting God through these incomprehensible cruelties.

After this incredibly wise and pastoral response, we do not know directly how the wife responds. Does she nod in agreement and sit silently by Job through the coming storm? There is only a hint that she does. Though there are only two further explicit references to her (Job 19:17; 31:10) and one obvious allusion to her in the book ("Those whom I loved have turned against me," 19:19), God grants ten additional children (42:13) to Job through her and for them as a couple. So it can be safely assumed that they stay on talking terms and *touching* terms. It can also be said that his wife sticks with him through to the end. She doesn't abandon him and return to her clan.

Irrespective of how we interpret their relationship at this particular moment and throughout the unfolding drama, a valuable lesson emerges for all of us: a lot of love from a lover and a little help from a friend (or three friends) goes a long way. While it is not an absolute requirement for our endurance in faith to have others who encourage and support us, embarking on the Christian journey to the Celestial City all by ourselves proves nearly impossible. We all need help. Jesus called twelve men to follow him, eleven of whom persevered. Jesus has called us to follow him, and such discipleship involves walking with other disciples. So we must pray for healthy Christian marriages and for strong and supportive Christian communities.

Next, in Job 2:10, the narrator, instead of focusing on Job's wife's response and their relationship, returns our eyes to Job himself: "In all this Job did not sin with his lips." This comment is one of the great understatements of the Bible, right next to "And after fasting forty days and forty nights [from food in the wilderness, Jesus] was hungry" (Matt. 4:2). For Job not to sin with his lips was one of the hardest things to do in human history.

The point of this high commendation is for us to continue to applaud and emulate Job's faithful endurance. Here are two suggestions for emulation. First, like Job, we should have a high view of God's sovereignty. When God says to Satan, "Although you incited *me* against him to destroy him without reason"

7. The word *ra'* ("evil," ESV) is often translated as "adversity" (NKJV, NASB, CSB), "bad" (NRSV, NLT), or "trouble" (NIV). The ESV alternative is "disaster." "The best way to understand this word in 2:10 is in the sense of calamity or misfortune." Belcher, *Job*, 27–28.

(Job 2:3), the word "me" opens afresh the mystery of evil. It is clear that Satan is accountable for the attacks on Job's family and flesh. The blood is on his hands. Here, however, God acknowledges his sovereignty over all. Later, Job rightly speaks of receiving both "good" (wealth and health) and "evil" (troubles and tragedies) from God (v. 10). God is completely sovereign. Do we believe this?

Second, it really matters how we respond to our sovereign God in times of trouble. Like Job, we can trust and hope in God, or, like his wife, we can doubt and despair. We should trust. We should be hopeful. To illustrate, a few years ago, I gathered with other pastors to spend three days with renowned theologian Dr. Kevin Vanhoozer. At one point, Professor Vanhoozer shared with the group a story about his mother. She had suffered from the awful disease of dementia for over a decade. Vanhoozer said that sometimes his mother would just recite the first verse of Psalm 23. Also, she often hummed the tune for "Just a Closer Walk with Thee." And sometimes when she hummed that gospel song, he would feed her the lines, line by line, and she would repeat them back to him:

> I am weak but Thou art strong;
> Jesus, keep me from all wrong;
> I'll be satisfied as long
> As I walk, let me walk close to Thee.

Then follows the famous refrain:

> Just a closer walk with Thee,
> Grant it, Jesus, is my plea,
> Daily walking close to Thee,
> Let it be, dear Lord, let it be.

Followed by two more verses:

> Thro' this world of toil and snares,
> If I falter, Lord, who cares?
> Who with me my burden shares?
> None but Thee, dear Lord, none but Thee.
>
> When my feeble life is o'er,
> Time for me will be no more;

Guide me gently, safely o'er
To Thy kingdom's shore, to Thy shore.[8]

How beautiful! When we find ourselves sitting on the ash heap—in the struggles of life or at the end of our lives—can we say with Job, "We take the good days from God—why not also the bad days?" (Job 2:10 MSG), and can we hum with the hymn writer, "Keep me, Jesus, walk with me, Jesus," "guide me gently, safely o'er to Thy kingdom's shore"?

The Response of Job's Friends

Having looked at Job's initial response, his wife's response, and his subsequent response, we come to the response of Job's friends—a response that contrasts with the one that Job received from his wife. Georges de La Tour's artwork *Job and His Wife* (1630s) presents Job's wife in a favorable light, bringing illumination and compassion to the scene. She is standing over him as he sits on the ash heap. She is holding a candle in her right hand (which brings light to his face), eyeing him with a sympathetic glance, and touching his forehead with her other hand, as if patting a fever with a cold, wet cloth. If de La Tour intends to portray the moment of her arrival, he might be accurate in his depiction, since Scripture provides no prior context for her visit, unlike the detailed introduction of the three friends. The artist certainly errs, however, if he intends to capture their ensuing conversation, for there she surely fails to soothe Job's spirit or offer care for his body. Instead, she questions his sanity and offers devilish advice.

In contrast (for now!) is the sympathy and silence offered by Eliphaz, Bildad, and Zophar.[9] Job 2:11–13 records their idea, arrival, attitudes, and actions:

> Now when Job's three friends heard of all this evil that had come upon him, they came each from his own place, Eliphaz the Temanite, Bildad the Shuhite, and Zophar the Naamathite. They made an appointment together to come to show him sympathy and comfort him. And when they saw him from a distance, they did not recognize him. And they raised their voices

8. "Just a Closer Walk with Thee" (1942).

9. Of historical interest, the Septuagint labels them as royalty: Eliphaz and Zophar as kings (*basileus*) and Bildad as a sovereign or governor (*tyrannos*, see Esth. 9:3).

> and wept, and they tore their robes and sprinkled dust on their heads toward heaven. And they sat with him on the ground seven days and seven nights, and no one spoke a word to him, for they saw that his suffering was very great.

With the arrival of these friends, we might think that the testing is over. Job has made it. The protagonist has persevered, and help has finally arrived to support him through the storm. But alas, their arrival introduces a final test,[10] perhaps the toughest. Satan and Job's wife bow out of the drama (they make no further appearances), while Job's closest companions cozy up to him and speak to him at great length. As stated above, however, there is no hint of testing in this passage. Instead, we are introduced to Eliphaz, Bildad, and Zophar as "Job's three friends."

Like Job, these men are from the east (Teman, Shuah, and Naamah) and apparently considered wise. Their wisdom is shown in six ways, the first three in Job 2:11. First, after hearing of Job's demise (they "heard of all this evil that had come upon him"), they independently resolve to act. Second, they gather together to act collectively ("they came each from his own place"). Third, they agree to travel to him ("they made an appointment together to come").

Next, Job 2:12a describes what Job's friends see when they finally arrive. "They did not recognize" Job, likely because his head was shaved, his body emaciated, and his face scarred from and scabbed with sores. While Satan struck Job's flesh apparently in an instant (Job 2:7), Job must have been sitting on that ash heap, scraping himself with pottery pieces, for days, if not months (his "months of emptiness," 7:3),[11] before his friends arrive. He is not dressed like a rich man, if he has any clothes on at all (after rending his garments and speaking of his nakedness, 1:20–21).

Verses 12b–13 of Job 2 describe what Job's friends do, the fourth and fifth ways they show wisdom. Fourth, they mourn for Job, opening their mouths not to advise or admonish but to cry and cry out ("And they raised their

10. The verb (*nsh*) that starts Eliphaz's speech is *hanissâ* ("ventures," Job 4:2 ESV), which means "to test." He and the other friends are putting Job to the test!

11. "For the news to reach the friends in their several countries and for them to arrange for a meeting suggest that Job's suffering has extended over a considerable period of time." Robert Gordis, *The Book of Job: Commentary, New Translation, Special Studies* (1978; repr., Jewish Theological Seminary of America, 2011), 22.

voices and wept"). Fifth, they not only join in his sorrow (the wailing and weeping), but also attempt to join in his suffering via two signs of solidarity. They "[tear] their robes" (cf. 1:20) and grab a fistful of dirt from the ash heap and toss it "toward heaven" and on their own "heads." These actions are as symbolic as they are sympathetic. With them the friends also express solidarity, as if to say: "Your troubles are now our troubles. Your ash heap . . . well, move over. Let us sit with you, brother." Sixth, because "they saw that his suffering was very great," they show further sympathy ("the Hebrew word for 'sympathize' is *nud*, which denotes shaking the head or body back and forth as an indication of taking on the pain or grief of another")[12] and solidarity through sitting ("They sat with him on the ground")[13] and silence ("No one spoke a word to him") for the perfect amount of time (for "seven days and seven nights"; cf. the use of "seven" in 1:2; 42:8, 13).[14] "The extended silence . . . mirrors the traditional Jewish practice of the guests remaining silent until the primary mourner speaks. 'Comforters are not permitted to say a word until the mourner opens [the conversation].'"[15] As these brothers mourned their brother's losses—his wealth, his health, and his children—their patience is pictured as limitless.

While there *will be* much to criticize with the friends as the story continues, *here* there is so much to commend. They do what few people would do. They hear about Job's troubles, and they reply not by sending commiserations through messengers but by traveling themselves from three different regions. Word comes to them, they drop whatever they are doing, and they reorganize their schedules and come as a group so that they might travel together to show Job their sympathy and try to bring him some comfort. Remarkable!

In so doing, Job's counselors exemplify the qualities of loyal friendship and supportive sympathy. When they receive news of Job's troubles, they take immediate action. How often do we, in comparison, fail to act at all? When we hear of a death in our extended family, do we reach out with a call or card of condolence? When we discover that someone from church

12. Gerald H. Wilson, *Job*, Understanding the Bible Commentary 10 (Baker, 2007), 33.

13. It is as if they are mourning the dead (see Isa. 3:26; 47:1; Lam. 2:10).

14. Seven days is also the appropriate amount of time to mourn the dead (cf. Gen. 50:10; 1 Sam. 31:13; cf. *Sir.* 22:12). "Among Jews the period of mourning after the funeral is known as *Shiva*, from *sheva*, 'seven.'" Wilson, *Job*, 34.

15. Wilson, 34, quoting *Talmud Bavli, Mo'ed Qatan* 28b.

has been hospitalized, do we make the effort to visit and sit by the person's side? Do we pray for the person, or perhaps read him or her a comforting psalm and sing a soothing hymn? Moreover, akin to Eliphaz, Bildad, and Zophar, are we willing to suspend our own schedules in order to travel to a friend who is experiencing debilitating despair or facing imminent death? Job's friends sacrificed weeks of their own time to show their sympathy and try to bring comfort. Imagine life on the ash heap, enduring months of isolation, and then suddenly, in the distance, seeing three friends emerge. What a sight for sore eyes (and a body inflicted with sores)!

In 2 Corinthians 7:6, Paul writes that "God, who comforts the downcast, comforted us by the coming of Titus." The arrival of Eliphaz, Bildad, and Zophar surely comforts Job in similar ways. What also surely comforts Job, as it would comfort any grieving soul, is their empathy expressed in their incarnational ministry. By weeping alongside Job, tearing their garments as Job did, accepting the ash heap alongside Job, and refraining from speaking to Job, they exemplify gospel grieving. Rather than checking into the presidential suite at the Ritz-Carlton down the road, they sit on the zero-stars ash heap outside Uz. They do not recite Romans 8:28 ("all things work together for good"), but embody the spirit of Revelation 8:1 ("there was silence"). Sometimes when we enter the home of a fellow Christian who is nearing the end of his or her life or step through the door at the hospital and witness the inexplicable sufferings of someone we nurtured in the faith for many years, words are unnecessary. Our mere presence is felt. It is enough for us to be there, to hold the person's hand and to join him or her in weeping.

There is much to commend about Job's friends in Job 2:11–13. Yet it is difficult not to read what they later say to Job back into these verses. As we observe this moment, we can't help but wish we had some duct tape for their mouths! The sharing in his sorrows, the silence, the tears: it is all so beautiful. They should have called it a day—or a week, to be more accurate. If they had just ridden off into the sunset after the seven days of silence, they would have gone down in history as the picture of friendship. Artists would have immortalized them in portraits, composers would have written oratorios in their honor, and Christians would have named their children after them. But alas, such is not the case. As we will soon witness, a storm is on the horizon. A whirlwind of words is about to sweep through Job's ash heap. His so-called "friends" (Job 2:11), who were once regarded as "close" and "intimate" (19:14, 19), are about to unleash their full armory of rebukes, accusations, scorn, and mockery. Neither sticks nor stones will break Job's bones, but words will crush his inner spirit. He will soon cry out, "How long will you torment me and break me in pieces with words?" (19:2).

What is recorded in Job 2:11–13 is not all that will be said of Job's friends. In chapter 4 and following, Eliphaz, Bildad, and Zophar will turn against Job, misjudging his motives and attacking his assertions. This is the *last* test, but it is not the *least* of the tests. How will Job fare? Will we once again hear the author's affirmation, "In all this Job did not sin with his lips" (Job 2:10)? Will Job remain steadfast in his integrity, continue to fear God, and trust in God's sovereign, just, and merciful providence? We will find out soon.

Right Responses to Wrongs

Shortly after I began a sermon series on Job, I received an email from a good friend about a tragic boating accident. Her brother-in-law had been speeding along up a nearby river and came upon a neck-level cable wire that was left from a walking bridge that had been removed a few years before. He ducked in time, but his friend was clotheslined by the cable and thrown out of the boat. He drowned. She wrote that her "brother-in-law walked away fine physically but is not doing well emotionally," and that her sister was having "a hard time knowing how to comfort him." Then she asked: "First, can you please pray for them? Second, do you have any encouragement for him and my sister that I could pass along?"

How does one reply to that? How does one respond *wisely* to that tragedy? Here is part of my reply:

> My dear friend,
>
> Oh, my. What a horrific tragedy! Like Job's three friends at the end of Job 2, how else shall we respond? Unbelief (they couldn't believe it was Job when they finally saw him), deep sobbing ("they raised their voices and wept"), and silence ("no one spoke a word to him"). It is so hard to know what to say. The thought that comes to mind, especially for your brother-in-law, is to remember the gospel—that Jesus forgives *all* sin and that good news is

> his only hope. He will never get over this in any real sense and always feel responsible. So he will need to remind himself regularly that he is forgiven.

In Job 2:1–13, through both Job's and his friends' wise responses, God offers us his wisdom on how to respond to inexplicable tragedies. The wise trust our sovereign God, comfort others through the sacrifice of time and the gift of our presence, and walk closely with each other so that together we might continue our closer walk with the Lord, "a man of sorrows and acquainted with grief" (Isa. 53:3).

First Cycle of Speeches

5

Job: Why Is Light Given to Him Who Suffers?

Job 3:1–26

After this Job opened his mouth and cursed the day of his birth.
(Job 3:1)

Near the start of his book *Walking with God Through Pain and Suffering*, Tim Keller writes:

> No matter what precautions we take, no matter how well we have put together a good life, no matter how hard we have worked to be healthy, wealthy, comfortable with friends and family, and successful with our career—something will inevitably ruin it. No amount of money, power, and planning can prevent bereavement, dire illness, relationship betrayal, financial disaster, or a host of other troubles from entering your life. Human life is fatally fragile and subject to forces beyond our power to manage. Life is tragic.[1]

The Bible tells us that we live in a fallen world and that we are fallen creatures who are born dead in our sins and will die because of our sins.

1. Timothy Keller, *Walking with God Through Pain and Suffering* (Riverhead Books, 2013), 3.

The book of Job is a great illustration of the effects of original sin. Just "as predictably as flames shoot upwards from a fire" (Job 5:7 TLB), so all human beings are "born and bred" (v. 7 MSG) for problems, sorrows, and conflicts. Even incomparable and seemingly impeccable Job, for all his uprightness and integrity, is "born to trouble" (v. 7).[2] Job has lost his health and wealth, and many of his closest relationships have been severed by death (all his children and most of his servants are dead) or disagreements (his wife is accusatory and then silent). While a glimmer of light comes with the arrival of Job's three friends, the severity of God's bitter providence weighs Job down to the deepest darkness.

On the one hand, Job 3 introduces (or is the impetus for) the first of three cycles of speeches between Job and his friends (Job 3–27): Cycle One (3–14), Cycle Two (15–21), Cycle Three (22–27), followed by an interlude (28) and return to Job's final words—his "reminiscences, affliction, and oath of innocence," as John Walton labels chapters 29, 30, and 31.[3]

On the other hand, it serves as Job's third response to his tragedies in Job 1–2. After Job lost his wealth, including his offspring (Job 1:13–19), and lost his health (2:7–8), his responses model patience, resistance, faithfulness, and the fear of the Lord. Now, after his close and wise friends offer him companionship and show him sympathy, a somewhat unexpected response emerges. Job "breaks the protracted silence with an explosive speech,"[4] which is summarized in 3:1: "After this Job opened his mouth and cursed the day of his birth." This is unexpected because Job's responses thus far have been filled with faith and hope (1:21; 2:9–10), and his friends are demonstrating the deepest bond of friendship (2:11–13). Why not offer another remarkable confession of faith, or a pious prayer that holds out hope for the future? Such an outburst is expected, however, because such a sad soliloquy fits the sad situation. After suffering what Job has suffered, his question is reasonable: "Why is light [life] given to him who is in mis-

2. The word "trouble" (*'amal*), first employed in Job 3:10, will be repeatedly used by Job to summarize his sufferings (e.g., Job 4:8; 5:6, 7; 7:3; 11:16; 15:35; 16:2; 20:22).

3. John H. Walton, *Job*, NIVAC (Zondervan, 2012), 29. But since I take Job 28 not to be an interlude from the Joban poet but to be from Job himself, I view Job 27–31 as his final words. That said, I align with C. L. Seow that these chapters are not part of the dialogue, as signaled by the unique phrase "Job again took up his taunt" (Job 27:1) and not "the formulaic 'and So-and-So answered and said.'" *Job 1–21: Interpretation and Commentary*, Illuminations (Eerdmans, 2013), 67. I also take the monologues in Job 3 ("Job opened his mouth," 3:1) and 31 ("The words of Job are ended," 31:40) to form an inclusio.

4. Gerald H. Wilson, *Job*, Understanding the Bible Commentary 10 (Baker, 2007), 35.

ery?" (3:20), or "Why is light given to one burdened with grief" and whose "existence is bitter" (CSB)?

What Job says here will prompt an aggressive interchange of ideas. Stay tuned for the fight of words. Between Job's short opening lament over life (Job 3) and his long closing response on the mystery of God's ways and Job's personal integrity (chaps. 26–31), an aggressive interchange of ideas—two full cycles of dialogue—will emerge. He was "born to trouble" (5:7), and the moment he closes his curse of the day of his birth, he is about to hear from his friends more trouble than he could ever imagine. But for now, let us quiet our hearts, open our ears, and listen carefully to Job's hopeless cry so that we might feel something of his depths of despair and learn from his lament over life. And let us also so engage with the poetry itself—which is vividly real, fiery, impassioned, despairing, broken, and "at times quiet and shadowy as the grave itself"—that we might "taste something of Job's bitterness" as we "imagine this great man sitting next to [us], at times weeping, at times shouting, at times only able to whisper, at other times caught up in rapturous transport at the thought of somehow reconciling with God."[5]

Job's lament, using the man's own questions and exclamations, can be divided into three parts:

- Let That Day Be Darkness! (Job 3:1–10)
- Why Did I Not Die at Birth? (vv. 11–19)
- Why Is Light Given? (vv. 20–26)

Let That Day Be Darkness! (Job 3:1–10)

We start with Job 3:1–10, which contains Job's curse, not of God, but of his birth (which is more of "a parody of a curse" because "he curses a day in the past that cannot really be changed").[6] The opening verse offers a summary of his sad soliloquy. The narrator's comment that "Job . . . cursed the day of his birth" (Job 3:1) echoes Job's opening line: "Let the day perish

5. Eric Ortlund, *Suffering Wisely and Well: The Grief of Job and the Grace of God* (Crossway, 2022), 92. The five descriptors are Ortlund's. "Sometimes the best way to engage with poetry is not so much to analyze but to immerse oneself in the verbal music and images—to sit with the words and let them linger and percolate" (94).

6. Richard P. Belcher Jr., *Job: The Mystery of Suffering and God's Sovereignty*, Focus on the Bible (Christian Focus, 2017), 34–35.

on which I was born, and the night that said, 'A man is conceived'" (v. 3). Here, either he curses his birthday and the announcement that came later that day after his mother's labor ("It's a boy!") or he curses the moment his mother comprehended his conception and told his father ("I'm pregnant").

Job goes on, pounding his dark, deep theme into his hearers' heads. Using the same Hebrew verb form (the English word "let," used thirteen times in the ESV's translation of Job 3:3–9, and indicating a wish), and his main metaphor of darkness covering the light of his first moment of life,[7] Job wishes that darkness[8] and forces of darkness[9] would cover his conception announcement or birth (that or the "day," Job 3:4, 5, 6, 8) and any joyful shout surrounding it ("let no joyful cry enter it," v. 7).[10] "Let that day be darkness!" (v. 4). He thus prays the least likely Old Testament prayer: he asks for barrenness, for "the doors of [his] mother's womb" to be "shut" (v. 10). Sarah and Hannah roll over in their graves.

Job's metaphors reach deeper darkness than the wails of the once-barren. He asks "God above," who said "let there be light" on the first day (Gen. 1:3), not to shine any light on his birthday (Job 1:4). Soak in his sorrows as you read his mournful wail on his first day of life (here referred to seven times as "it"):

> Let gloom and deep darkness claim it.
> Let [dark] clouds dwell upon it;
> let the blackness of the day [night] terrify it.
> That night—let thick darkness seize it!
> Let it not rejoice among the days of the year;
> let it not come into the number of the months.
> Behold, let that night be barren;
> let no joyful cry enter it. (Job 3:5–7)

Job goes further. He dives deeper into the darkness. He descends to the bottom of the ocean and then ascends to the highest heavens; moving from the depths of the sea to the heights of the heavens, he laments life's intolerability:

7. Let not "light shine upon it" (Job 3:4); "let it hope for light, but have none" (v. 9).

8. "Darkness" (Job 3:4); "gloom and deep darkness" (v. 5); "the blackness of the day" (v. 5); "thick darkness" (v. 6; "let the stars . . . be dark," v. 9).

9. "Clouds" (Job 3:5); "Leviathan" (v. 8).

10. The "joyful cry" could reflect the moment of sexual consummation, namely, "sounds of pleasure from that night" (MSG).

Let those curse it who curse the day,
  who are ready to rouse up Leviathan.
Let the stars of its dawn be dark;
  let it hope for light, but have none,
  nor see the eyelids of the morning,
because it did not shut the doors of my mother's womb,
  nor hide trouble from my eyes. (Job 3:8–10)

Job prays that those who might join him in cursing the day of his birth (his friends who are listening?)[11] do something to bring the most powerful and awful creature from the deeps of the sea ("rouse up Leviathan," Job 3:8; cf. 41:1–34) and the mightiest powers from the highest heavens ("the stars of its dawn," 3:9) to reverse the course, so as to cancel the present pain ("hide trouble from my eyes," 3:10) by ripping his birthday off the calendar.

Why Did I Not Die at Birth? (Job 3:11–19)

As the first half of this poem (Job 3:3–10) is dominated by one theme (the day of Job's birth), one key word ("let"), and one main metaphor ("darkness"), the second half takes up that same theme with a new key word ("why," vv. 11, 12, 16, 20, 23), focusing on why Job did not die at birth (the first four occurrences of "why") if he was to live in such misery (the final two occurrences).

Job's first question is straightforward. In light of his past and present pain, he asks, "Why did I not die at birth?" followed by a parallel question, "Why did I not . . . come out from the womb and expire?" (Job 3:11). From there, his second question follows the birthing process. Job asks, "Why did" his mother rock him on her lap ("the knees receive me") and bring him to her breast to sustain him ("Or why the breasts, that I should nurse?," v. 12)? Job wishes he had died during or after the delivery. His third question, another parallelism—"Or why was I not as a hidden stillborn child"/"as infants who never see the light?" (v. 16)—wishes that he had died earlier—in the womb.

After the first two questions (in Job 3:11–12) and third question (in v. 16), Job offers reasons why his death, which he describes as sleep ("lain down," "slept," v. 13), would be best:

11. "Let them curse it that curse the day, who are ready to raise up their mourning" (Job 3:8 KJV).

> For then I would have lain down and been quiet;
>   I would have slept; then I would have been at rest,
> with kings and counselors of the earth
>   who rebuilt ruins for themselves,
> or with princes who had gold,
>   who filled their houses with silver.
> Or why was I not as a hidden stillborn child,
>   as infants who never see the light?
> There the wicked cease from troubling,
>   and there the weary are at rest.
> There the prisoners are at ease together;
>   they hear not the voice of the taskmaster.
> The small and the great are there,
>   and the slave is free from his master. (Job 3:13–19)

First, Job envisions that death would offer rest ("then I would have been at rest," Job 3:13; "the weary are at rest," v. 17; peace and "quiet," v. 13) and social equity, in that both the renowned upper class ("Kings and counselors of the earth who rebuilt ruins for themselves, or . . . princes who had gold, who filled their houses with silver," vv. 14–15) and the despised lower class ("the wicked," v. 17; "the prisoners," v. 18; "the small . . . and the slave," v. 19) "are at rest" and "are at ease together" (vv. 17, 18), even that the slave is "free from his master" (v. 19) and "the voice of the taskmaster" (v. 18). To him, death is better than life.

Have you ever felt this way—the desire to die? One family event was so emotionally traumatic for me that when I lay down to sleep that night, I felt that my heart was literally going to burst. I was so heartbroken that I begged God to take my life. I couldn't imagine anything more painful, and I couldn't see any hope of a future. Another time, my desire to die was related to physical pain. My family was on vacation in Northern Michigan when suddenly I needed a root canal. I knew that a root canal was the solution because I have felt that pain twice before in my life. A throbbing pain; a little tooth but a total body-consuming pain. It was Sunday. Every dentist office we called—the few within the region—was closed. Finally, a dentist returned the message I'd left on his emergency hotline, and we drove about two hours south to his office for the procedure. A few times during those hours of waiting, especially when I felt hopeless (that I'd have to wait till Monday), I envisioned death as better than life. So I have experienced both emotional pain and physical pain that have brought me to desire death. Job, however, had *at the same time* physical pain (the sores), emotional pain (the loss of his wealth, children, and to some extent his relationship with his wife), and spiritual pain (he must have been thinking: "What are you doing, God? Why are you doing what you are doing? And where are you, God?").

Why Is Light Given? (Job 3:20–26)

In the final seven verses, Job continues his personal and philosophical musings. His perspective, however, moves beyond his own sufferings to any and all who suffer. Starting with Job 3:20–23, he asks:

> Why is light given to him who is in misery,
> and life to the bitter in soul,
> who long for death, but it comes not,
> and dig for it more than for hidden treasures,
> who rejoice exceedingly
> and are glad when they find the grave?
> Why is light given to a man whose way is hidden,
> whom God has hedged in?

Job wonders why God allows people to be born if their lives are to be characterized by such severe suffering and misery ("Why is light given to him who is in misery?," Job 3:20). Using humor, along with hyperbole and irony, he highlights the sad situation, describing the miserable or "the bitter in soul" (v. 20) as looking "for death . . . more than" they would dig "for hidden treasures" (v. 21) and then "who rejoice exceedingly and are glad when they find the grave" (v. 22). Repeating the question above, *why* (as perhaps an inclusio), with a slight variance, "Why is light given to a man" (v. 23), Job wonders why someone is born if that person does not understand why he is suffering ("whose way is hidden, whom God has hedged in," v. 23). We sometimes talk about not putting God in a box. The image here is that God has put Job in a box. There are walls all around him. He cannot get out. He cannot see what God is doing.

While Job apparently connects reasons with his questions (notice the "for" at the start of verses 24 and 25 of Job 3), Job concludes his philosophical questions with personal reflections:

For *my* sighing comes instead of *my* bread,
  and *my* groanings are poured out like water.
For the thing that *I* fear comes upon *me*,
  and what *I* dread befalls *me*.[12]
I am not at ease, nor am *I* quiet;
  I have no rest, but trouble comes. (Job 3:24–26)

Notice the first-person personal pronouns highlighted above. Notice also Job's heartbreak. He has none of the "ease," "quiet," or "rest" that he thinks death would bring (Job 3:26). Instead of daily bread, he suffers insatiable emptiness ("sighing," and "groanings . . . poured out like water," v. 24). Notice, finally, his final prophetic phrase: "but trouble comes" (v. 26). Trouble is indeed coming. Job will receive only trouble and no rest from his friends' counsel. Only God's voice will soothe his soul, albeit without explicitly answering the question *why*.

Three Reflective Applications

Having explained Job 3, we can apply it with three reflections.

First, life is in God's hands. During one season of family meals, my family worked through Job. Each night, the final question I asked was "Do you have any questions?" There were always lots of questions! For this text, my youngest son, Simeon, asked, "Why didn't Job just kill himself?" Blunt question, but good question. I answered, "Job didn't contemplate, or at least communicate, any suicidal thoughts because he didn't view it as a legitimate option." Put differently, Job believes that life—even his own life (no matter how hard it gets)—is in God's hands. He survives "his darkest hour" by resisting both the temptation to curse God and the temptation to take "his fate into his own hands."[13] Admittedly, Christians commit suicide. Mental illness is a reality. Intense suffering is sometimes unbearable. But the godly response to physical and emotional and spiritual suffering is to do what Job does: to lament, but to leave life in God's hands, knowing and trusting that he alone has the authority to give life and take it.

12. What did Job fear? Perhaps what we all fear. The loss of wealth. The loss of his health. The loss of his children. The loss of his good relationship with his wife. The loss of his relationship with God.

13. John E. Hartley, *The Book of Job*, NICOT (Eerdmans, 1988), 101.

Second, learn how to process depression, grief, and trauma. Learn to lament! Commenting on Job 3, Pastor Chuck Swindoll writes:

> Early on (back in the early 1960s) when a Christian suffered from a depression that resulted in this kind of thinking and candid admission, you never said so publicly. You swallowed your sorrow. The first book I read on this subject, covering emotional turmoil and mental illness among Christians[,] was considered heresy by most of my evangelical friends. The pervasive opinion then was simple: Christians didn't have breakdowns. Furthermore, you certainly didn't stay depressed![14]

That fanciful perspective on emotional and spiritual struggles is, as Swindoll then points out, not biblical. Job 3 provides us with a realistic and God-approved/Spirit-inspired picture of and poem from a devastated man. I say "God-approved/Spirit-inspired" because Job's lament is part of the canon and because God will later declare that Job has "spoken of me what is right" (Job 42:7, 8). As Andreas Köstenberger and Gregory Goswell summarize, "The surprising divine evaluation of the tortured hero at the end of the book . . . requires the reader to approve of what Job says—though his bold speeches must have regularly shocked the reader—and to disapprove of what the friends say—though, on first hearing, what they say may sound thoroughly orthodox."[15]

At this point in the drama, God is not speaking to Job, and Job is not (not yet, at least) speaking *to* God, only *about* God. He is not cursing God (per his wife's suggestion), but he also is not praying to God (Job 3:4 and 23 are the only times that Job has mentioned God, and both verses are in some way negative). Such indirect discourse might be because Job is taming his tongue. He deeply desires to curse God. Certainly, he longs for death and agrees with his wife that to curse God would deliver an immediate death sentence. But he refuses to cross that line. He still fears God—not *for nothing* (for none of God's blessings). He wants—for better or worse—to stay in a relationship with his Creator, even if God is silent to his ash-heap supplications. On this point, Eric Ortlund's observation is excellent:

14. Charles R. Swindoll, *Job: A Man of Heroic Endurance* (Word, 2004), 68.

15. Andreas J. Köstenberger and Gregory Goswell, *Biblical Theology: A Canonical Thematic and Ethical Approach* (Crossway, 2023), 287.

> Without friendship of God, Job wants none of it. It is hard to hear Job utter a curse against the whole of his existence, but his motives are noble. Strange as it might sound, Job's curse on the day of his birth actually expresses the same high view of God as 1:21, only in a negative way. Furthermore, Job is right to value intimacy with God more than a blessed life. The only thing he is wrong about is how God really views him. . . . How terrible even the best and happiest of lives become without the friendship of God![16]

So God is silent. But so too are Job's friends. And his public lament is an honest invitation for a friend—divine or human—to help.[17] Of course, he knows that by opening up to them, he makes himself vulnerable—open to attack (which he, tragically, receives). But that doesn't mean that what he does here isn't indeed the right thing to do. It is the right thing, for he is trying to process his depression, grief, and trauma with his friends, three wise men who he hopes will share some wisdom, perhaps have a good answer to his question *why*.

In his article "The Coming Pastoral Crash," John Dobbs listed twelve reasons why pastors were in "particular danger" of crashing during the COVID-19 crisis.[18] For example, they were serving in ways for which they had had no training or experience, exhausted (fewer gatherings do not equal less work), not feeding their souls, and conforming to a seven-day schedule (no day off). Regarding the state of their mental well-being, Dobbs concluded that pastors spend significant time helping other people with their problems, but do not take care of their own problems. How true of pastors then and now. But also, how true of most other Christians!

As Job vents his anguish and anger,[19] he is honest and vulnerable. He shares his deepest sorrows with his friends. Might that venting of deepest emotions and expressions be the lesson that God is teaching through this dark passage,[20] one of the darkest in the Bible? If so, here is your homework:

16. Ortlund, *Suffering Wisely and Well*, 95.

17. Christopher Ash argues that Job is "not speaking to his friends" but "just speaking with himself." *Job: The Wisdom of the Cross*, Preaching the Word (Crossway, 2014), 65. I disagree for two reasons. First, Job 4:1 begins, "Then Eliphaz the Temanite answered." Eliphaz is listening to what Job says and responding to it. Second, it makes great sense that Job has decided to open up to his friends because, at this point in the story, they have proved to be true and dear friends. They have traveled a distance to see him. They have then showed empathy (they sat with him) and sympathy (they sat in silence with him for seven days and nights).

18. John Dobbs, "The Coming Pastoral Crash," *Baptist Bible Tribune*, May 21, 2020, https://www.tribune.org/the-coming-pastoral-crash/.

19. See August H. Konkel, *Job*, Cornerstone Biblical Commentary 6 (Tyndale House, 2006), 48.

20. Or, as David L. Allen labels the text, "the lowest of several low points in the book." *Exalting*

to think about someone you can talk to about your troubles (write down a name or make an appointment) and then take that next step. Share with someone the laments of life. Let someone else enter into your mess.

Third, remember that God entered into our mess and rejoice in that gospel. Job's six interrogatives—*why*, *why*, *why*, *why*, *why*, *why*—will be promptly answered by his friends: "Why? Let us tell you why. Because you have sinned!" But his questions will not be answered by God when he finally opens his mouth (Job 38–41). The *why* question just lingers on throughout the Old Testament (over three hundred times) until we find it on the lips of our Lord Jesus: "My God, my God, *why* have you forsaken me?" (Matt. 27:46). Our Redeemer—and Job's—has the question *why* on his lips when he dies. He does not ask God his Father, as Job does, why, if he was to suffer this much, he was born in the first place. Instead, his *why* question takes us back to the very reason he was born. He was born to die. He was born to suffer and die. He was born to be God-forsaken: "to be sin" so that we might be forgiven of our sins (see 2 Cor. 5:18–21).[21] Job thought he was forsaken by God. But he was not. God's silence did not mean Job's forsakenness. Jesus, however, *was* forsaken. He was forsaken so that we might not suffer eternal silence and separation from God.

God doesn't directly answer—in the book of Job or elsewhere in Scripture—the question "Why is there suffering?" but he does enter into it. It is called the incarnation and the atonement. Without Jesus' atoning sacrifice, our hands are stained with blood. We are guilty. Without the Word's becoming flesh and dying in his flesh as the God-man, we have no hope of eternal life, eternal joy, or eternal fellowship with the wise and just and loving God. So as we read this rather depressing poem in Job 3, let us thank God for Job's honesty. But let us also thank God for the gospel, for our great Redeemer, who, in his death, redeemed us, saving us from sin and Satan.

Jesus in Job, Christ-Centered Exposition (Holman Reference, 2022), 71.

21. "Job's passion, the cry of a righteous man afflicted beyond measure for the cause of God, can be heard in the cry of Jesus from the cross." Douglas D. Webster, *More Than a Sermon: The Purpose and Practice of Christian Preaching* (Lexham, 2024), 179.

6

Eliphaz: God Is Just; Are You, Job?

Job 4:1–5:27

Behold, blessed is the one whom God reproves; therefore despise not the discipline of the Almighty. For he wounds, but he binds up; he shatters, but his hands heal. He will deliver you from six troubles; in seven no evil shall touch you. (Job 5:17–19)

I was called into the principal's office. I didn't know why. I was young, maybe in third grade. Sister Mary Bernard, the principal, walked into the room. She sat behind her large wooden desk, wearing her blue-and-white nun's habit. She didn't smile. She didn't ask me how I was doing. Instead, she asked me whether I had been in the library yesterday. I nodded. She asked what I had done there. I said that I had helped the librarian put away books. "Anything else?" she inquired. She lowered her glasses. I was silent. I clutched my chair. She stood up, walked across the room, and grabbed a few books. "Look familiar?" she asked. "No," I said. She opened each book. There was something scribbled over each Table of Contents. In large letters of permanent fluorescent orange was scribbled a name. Mine! "Did you do this?" I wasn't the only O'Donnell in the school, but I was the only Douglas and the only Douglas Sean. Who else would do such a thing? Yes, I had done it! I lowered my head in shame. I was guilty. Caught. Punished.

Have you ever been caught? Or, conversely, have you ever been accused of something you haven't done? Sadly, I don't have any of those stories to share. But you might. Certainly, the world does. Our prisons are full of inmates with such stories, some of which are true. In Job 4–5, we are introduced to Eliphaz, who has called Job into the principal's office, in effect, to hear from God Almighty! Eliphaz speaks those words from God about God (Job 4:6, 9, 17; 5:8, 17) to Job. Without showing any tenderhearted emotional response to Job's heartfelt admission, he offers a forty-seven-verse poetic rebuke (4:2–5:27) in the form of a two-point sermon in response to Job's depressing monologue (3:3–26). He wants Job to *get that*, first, *he is guilty before God* and second, *that he needs to go to God* for restoration. This outline might make for a good evangelistic talk today, but is it the foolishness of God (the wisdom of the cross!) or the folly of man that is proclaimed to Job?

Guilty Before God (Job 4:1–5:7)

"Eliphaz the Temanite"[1] is the first to respond to Job's last speech ("answered," Job 4:1), likely because he is the eldest. He focuses on Job's guilt before God in two ways. First, Eliphaz claims that Job has been impatient. In Job 4:2, he asks, "If one ventures a word with you, will you be impatient?" Then in verse 5, he answers his own rhetorical question in the affirmative: "But now it [trouble] has come to you, and you are impatient." To the reader familiar with the prologue, this allegation seems out of line, for in those opening chapters, Job comes across as the exemplar of patient endurance (as James 5:11 well summarizes, "You have heard of the steadfastness of Job"). Moreover, in his response to Eliphaz, Job explicitly acknowledges that he is only human:

> This would be my comfort;
>   I would even exult in pain unsparing,
>   for I have not denied the words of the Holy One.

1. "The three friends . . . all have southern origins known in the OT. Eliphaz is from Teman, an important city in Edom (Gen. 36:11, 15; Ezek. 25:13; Amos 1:11–12), which was apparently known for its wisdom (Jer. 49:7)." Kenneth Laing Harris and August Konkel, "Job," in *ESV Study Bible* (Crossway, 2008), 876.

> What is my strength, that I should wait?
> And what is my end, that I should be patient?
> Is my strength the strength of stones, or is my flesh bronze? (Job 6:10–12)

Eliphaz personally observed Job's unwavering determination during their seven-day silence, in which Job displayed remarkable patience and refrained from complaining or cursing, even amid his afflictions. Thus, as Thomas Aquinas suggests, Eliphaz must be basing his accusation of impatience solely on Job's desire to die (his sad soliloquy in Job 3:3–26): "He took Job's expression of hatred for his life," his "despair," and his "bitterness" as expressions of "impatience," and he took "his profession of innocence for presumption."[2]

The second way in which Eliphaz seeks to implicate Job is by highlighting God's absolute holiness. After he has complimented Job's character—his own "integrity" (Job 4:6b), "fear of God" (v. 6a), and kindness to others ("you have instructed many, . . . strengthened the weak hands[,] . . . upheld him who was stumbling, . . . made firm the feeble knees," vv. 3–4)—he offers his first dose of the three friends' retribution theology (vv. 7–11), followed by his reminder of God's perfect purity (vv. 12–21). Eliphaz introduces both ideas with rhetorical questions. In Job 4:7, using a synonymous parallelism, he says:

> Remember:[3]
> who that was innocent ever perished?
> Or where were the upright cut off?

The answer is obvious: people get what is coming to them ("those who plow iniquity and sow trouble reap the same," Job 4:8).[4] What they reap is God's judgment ("by the breath of God they perish," v. 9). Such is the nature of the world; no creature is exempt. Just as the mighty lioness cannot protect her cubs if she cannot eat ("The roar of the lion, the voice of the fierce lion, the teeth of the young lions are broken. The strong lion perishes for lack of

2. Thomas Aquinas, "Explanation of the Letter of Job," quoted in *ESV Church History Study Bible: Voices from the Past, Wisdom for the Present* (Crossway, 2023), 708.

3. With the verb "remember," Eliphaz is assuming that both he and Job hold to the same truths and have experienced those truths lived out in the world.

4. "Eliphaz's observation is that evil (*awen*) and trouble (*amal*) come only to those who plow and sow them (see Prov. 11:18; 22:8)." Gerald H. Wilson, *Job*, Understanding the Bible Commentary 10 (Baker, 2007), 45.

prey, and the cubs of the lioness are scattered," vv. 10–11), so even great Job cannot alter God's moral law: the upright always prosper and the wicked always perish.

Eliphaz's second rhetorical question—"Can mortal man be in the right before God? Can a man be pure before his Maker?" (Job 4:17)—focuses on God's righteousness and, by implication, man's unrighteousness. While the point is obvious and stated elsewhere throughout Scripture (e.g., Ps. 143:2; Prov. 20:9; Eccl. 7:20), Eliphaz introduces it as a supernatural revelation ("A spirit glided past my face," Job 4:15), "a word . . . brought" to him (v. 12) in a nightmare that frightened him ("the hair of my flesh stood up," v. 15).[5] He states:

> Amid thoughts from visions of the night,
>   when deep sleep falls on men,
> dread came upon me, and trembling,
>   which made all my bones shake.
> A spirit glided past my face;
>   the hair of my flesh stood up.
> It stood still,
>   but I could not discern its appearance.
> A form was before my eyes;
>   there was silence, then I heard a voice. (Job 4:13–16)

Eliphaz wants such a prophetic vision to scare some sense into Job too. He seeks to remind Job that if God is so holy that even his angels are not perfectly holy in his sight, what then of mortal men ("those who dwell in houses of clay," Job 4:19), who "perish forever" (v. 20), "die . . . without wisdom" (v. 21), and are forgotten ("crushed like the moth," v. 19c)? Thus he continues:

> Even in his servants [angels] he puts no trust,
>   and his angels he charges with error;
>   how much more those who dwell in houses of clay,
>   whose foundation is in the dust,
>   who are crushed like the moth.

5. "Dreams are, of course, a valid mode of revelation in the Old Testament (e.g., Gen. 40–41; Joel 3:1)" and the New Testament (Matt. 1:20; 2:12, 13, 19, 22), and possibly one way that Job himself learned of God. See Eric Ortlund, *Suffering Wisely and Well: The Grief of Job and the Grace of God* (Crossway, 2022), 67.

Between morning and evening they are beaten to pieces;
  they perish forever without anyone regarding it.
Is not their tent-cord plucked up within them,
  do they not die, and that without wisdom? (Job 4:18–21)

Job has to bear the second half of this sermon (Job 5) before he can respond. But here, at the end of chapter 4, we can picture him muttering under his breath: "Duh. Thanks for the theology lesson, old friend." Job well recognizes that only God possesses perfect purity. He would likely concur with the analogy about the angels in Job 4:18: if God charges even the supernatural servants in heaven with error, then clay-made man on earth must be full of folly. We can ascertain this perspective based on Job's actions in 1:5 (his efforts to sanctify his children because he knew the potential depths and deception of sin) and from his plea to God in 7:21, "Why do you not pardon my transgression and take away my iniquity?"

Job will acknowledge his status as a sinner, but that is not the issue at hand. The real concern lies in Job's lack of awareness regarding the specific sin that may have caused such calamities. "If I sin, what do I do to you, you watcher of mankind? Why have you made me your mark?" (Job 7:20). Job would agree with Eliphaz regarding God's discipline: "Blessed is the one whom God reproves" (5:17). What he will not agree with is the assumption that he is under the discipline of God for a crime that he did not commit or does not know he committed. Job would say "Amen" to 1 John 1:8 ("If we say we have no sin, we deceive ourselves, and the truth is not in us"), as well as to verse 9 ("If we confess our sins, he is faithful and just to forgive us our sins and to cleanse us from all unrighteousness"). But he needs a sin to confess first! Thus, he cries out in effect, "God, Eliphaz, anybody—show me my specific calamity-causing sin!"

In Job 5:1–7, Eliphaz reiterates his perspective, recalling his earlier vision (Job 4:12–21) and advising Job that his recourse should be to God (cf. 5:8), rather than seeking assistance from any earthly being or even appealing to celestial beings ("Call now; is there anyone who will answer you? To which of the holy ones will you turn?," 5:1). Eliphaz anticipates that Job will eventually alter his request—from desiring death to escape suffering to asking for divine relief from his current anguish.[6] Furthermore, he emphasizes his belief in retribution theology:

6. See Wilson, *Job*, 50.

> Surely vexation kills the fool,
> and jealousy slays the simple.
> I have seen the fool taking root,
> but suddenly I cursed his dwelling.
> His children are far from safety;
> they are crushed in the gate,
> and there is no one to deliver them.
> The hungry eat his harvest,
> and he takes it even out of thorns,
> and the thirsty pant after his wealth.
> For affliction does not come from the dust,
> nor does trouble sprout from the ground,
> but man is born to trouble
> as the sparks fly upward. (Job 5:2–7)

Here Eliphaz reminds Job that suffering does not arise from nothing ("affliction does not come from the dust," Job 5:6) and cautions him of the consequences ("His children . . . are crushed in the gate," v. 4; "The hungry eat his harvest," v. 5) of sin (e.g., "vexation . . . and jealousy," v. 2).

In Job 4:2–5:27, Eliphaz is claiming that Job has been guilty of impatience during his sufferings and impurity before the perfectly pure God. Job must have felt like Josef K. in Franz Kafka's novel *The Trial* (1925). In that book, Josef K. is detained for a crime that is unclear. He does not know why and for what he was arrested. He is prosecuted by someone as detached and "objective" as Eliphaz. He cannot get an impartial hearing. He is even ridiculed by his uncle, who first supported him. All the time, as Josef K. goes from cell to courtroom and cell to courtroom, he racks his brain, trying to guess what crime he may have committed, and he despairs of ever finding out. Kafka may not have been reading the book of Job when he wrote his celebrated work, but both stories portray an innocent sufferer who is mocked and mistreated. Like Josef K., Job has had enough. He wants this trial to stop. But he will have to endure Eliphaz's pious closing remarks *patiently.*

Go to God (Job 5:8–27)

After Eliphaz has pressed home his first point, *get that you are guilty*, he moves on to the second point, *go to God* (best summarized in Job 5:8:

"As for me, I would seek God, and to God would I commit my cause"). He follows that bit of personal counsel with a beautiful poem addressing God's attributes and actions (Job 5:9–16), part of which (v. 13) Paul quotes in 1 Corinthians 3:19.[7] We might call this Eliphaz's "'Why Go to God' Poem," which includes notable literary features such as eight words that start with *aleph* (the first letter in the Hebrew alphabet) in Job 5:8, seven couplets, a plethora of parallelisms, and a series of reversals.[8] Moreover, the poem is replete with theological insights and language rooted in Scripture (see table 6.1).[9]

Table 6.1. Scriptural Quotes and Allusions in Eliphaz's "'Why Go to God' Poem"

Job 5:8–16	A Sample of Possible Echoes, Allusions, and Quotes
"As for me, I would seek God, and to God would I commit my cause" (v. 8)	2 Sam. 12:16; 1 Chron. 22:19
"who does great things and unsearchable, marvelous things without number" (v. 9)	Pss. 40:5; 71:19
"He gives rain on the earth and sends waters on the fields" (v. 10)	1 Sam. 12:17–18; Ps. 65:9–10
"He sets on high those who are lowly, and those who mourn are lifted to safety" (v. 11)	1 Sam. 2:5–8
"He frustrates the devices of the crafty, so that their hands achieve no success. He catches the wise in their own craftiness, and the schemes of the wily are brought to a quick end" (vv. 12–13)	1 Cor. 3:19

7. In *The Pious Sage in Job: Eliphaz in the Context of Wisdom Theodicy* (Wipf & Stock, 2016), Kyle C. Dunham claims that Paul uses Eliphaz's words "as part of a rhetorical strategy of irony in 1 Cor. 3:18–23," in that "the citation bolsters Paul's point that the one who professes to be wise [like Eliphaz, who is later rebuked by Yahweh] cannot escape the judgment of God by worldly cunning or ingenuity no matter how eloquent a sophist he or she claims to be." In this way, "Paul may quote from Eliphaz in a compelling way [and believing that he 'pronounces the truth'] without necessarily endorsing every aspect of what the sage declares to and about God in the book of Job" (41).

8. "In this section Eliphaz describes a series of reversals in which God's unfathomable power and purposes turn worldly perspectives on their ears. . . . The parallels with the Beatitudes in the Sermon on the Mount (Matt. 5:3–10), while far from exact, are certainly interesting. In both texts, God's will and purposes turn worldly expectations upside down." Wilson, *Job*, 53–54.

9. The same can be said of Job 5:17 (cf. Prov. 3:11–12; Heb. 12:4–11); Job 5:18 (cf. Deut. 32:39; Hos. 6:1–2); Job 5:19 (cf. Ps. 34:19); and Job 5:20 (cf. Hos. 13:14).

"They meet with darkness in the daytime and grope at noonday as in the night" (v. 14)	Deut. 28:29
"But he saves the needy from the sword of their mouth and from the hand of the mighty" (v. 15)	Ps. 35:10
"So the poor have hope, and injustice shuts her mouth" (v. 16)	Ps. 107:42

Eliphaz has misread the situation, and thus his wise words above are applied foolishly. Yet he does accurately proclaim certain universal truths. For example, he is right that in light of who God is and what he will do, humans should "seek God" (Job 5:8) through prayer. In chapters 1–2, Job has been faithful *to* God. In chapter 3, Job speaks *about* God. But it is not until chapter 7, toward the end of Job's second speech, that we get to hear him address God personally. And it is an interesting prayer, an honest one—one that is filled with questions:

> What is man, that you make so much of him,
> and that you set your heart on him,
> visit him every morning
> and test him every moment? (Job 7:17–18)

> Why do you not pardon my transgression [maybe Eliphaz is right]
> and take away my iniquity? (Job 7:21a)

Also, Eliphaz is right that God is just and that in his great and unsearchable control of his creation he eventually brings about vindication for those who fear him: "he sets on high those who are lowly, . . . frustrates the devices of the crafty, . . . [and] saves the needy" (Job 5:11, 12, 15). In fact, the sage-prophet Eliphaz as much as promises this for Job in the next section of his poem (vv. 17–27):

> Behold, blessed is the one whom God reproves;
> therefore despise not the discipline of the Almighty.
> For he wounds, but he binds up;
> he shatters, but his hands heal.
> He will deliver you from six troubles;
> in seven no evil shall touch you.

In famine he will redeem you from death,
and in war from the power of the sword.
You shall be hidden from the lash of the tongue,
and shall not fear destruction when it comes.
At destruction and famine you shall laugh,
and shall not fear the beasts of the earth.
For you shall be in league with the stones of the field,
and the beasts of the field shall be at peace with you.
You shall know that your tent is at peace,
and you shall inspect your fold and miss nothing.
You shall know also that your offspring shall be many,
and your descendants as the grass of the earth.
You shall come to your grave in ripe old age,
like a sheaf gathered up in its season.
Behold, this we have searched out; it is true.
Hear, and know it for your good.

The opening and closing phrases of this concluding poem feature a "behold" (Job 5:17, 27). The second "behold" concludes with a reminder to Job that all that has been said is simply a reiteration of what the traditional wisdom community ("we have searched out") decrees about this situation ("it is true") and about what Job should do ("Hear, and know it for your good," v. 27), namely, admit his guilt and go to God. The first "behold" (v. 17) is a beatitude ("blessed is the one whom God reproves") introducing a poem about the blessings of God's discipline ("therefore despise not the discipline of the Almighty"). What follows are future assurances for those who do not hold contempt for God's refining discipline.

These promises are a ploy to entice Job to repent; yet, ironically, they ultimately transform into fulfilled prophecies. When Eliphaz asserts that God "will deliver you" (Job 5:19), "he will redeem you from death" (v. 20), "you shall be hidden from the lash of the tongue" (v. 21), "you shall . . . miss nothing" from your "fold" (v. 24), "you shall know . . . that your offspring shall be many" (v. 25), and "you shall come to your grave in ripe old age" (v. 26), he foretells the blessings that Job will receive in Job 42:10–17 (see table 6.2).

Table 6.2. Echoes of Job 5:19–26 in Job 42:7–17

Job 5:19–26	Job 42:7–17
God "will deliver you" (v. 19); "he will redeem you from death" (v. 20)	Presumably, Job is restored to health. He is certainly made right with God (see v. 9b)
"You shall be hidden from the lash of the tongue" (v. 21)	Job is vindicated; his friends are rebuked for their false words (vv. 7–8)
"You shall . . . miss nothing" from your "fold" (v. 24)	His fortunes are doubled, including his livestock (v. 12)
"You shall know . . . that your offspring shall be many" (v. 25)	He has ten more children (v. 13) and many grandchildren and great-grandchildren (v. 16)
"You shall come to your grave in ripe old age" (v. 26)	He lives 140 more years (vv. 16–17)

Job's life is spared, and he experiences the joy of having ten more children. Additionally, he is bestowed with abundant wealth, including twenty-two thousand animals, vast financial resources, and a golden ring. Moreover, he is blessed to live a full and ideal lifespan of 140 more years. Despite the seemingly insensitive nature of Eliphaz's theological perspective toward Job, he does serve as a reminder to Job (and to us) that there is "hope" (see Job 4:6). He asserts that those who fear God and live lives of integrity have a bright future ahead. Suffering is temporary because healing and restoration are on the horizon. That said, as Eric Ortlund observes, "The thing we must not miss in chapter 4 is that Eliphaz, despite his good intentions, despite his pastoral tact, despite the fact that he has empirical evidence (v. 8) for thinking as he does, evidence that is complemented by a mystical experience (vv. 11–12), and even despite the fact that he has some scriptural backing, is not only completely misinterpreting Job's situation—he is acting as a mouthpiece for the devil as he does."[10]

Seeing What Eliphaz Should Have Seen

We all know that "the world is not a random place; actions have consequences, and the consequences correspond to the actions"[11]—that "whatever

10. Ortlund, *Suffering Wisely and Well*, 69.
11. Christopher Ash, *Job: The Wisdom of the Cross*, Preaching the Word (Crossway, 2014), 104.

one sows, that will he also reap" (Gal. 6:7), and that good things happen to good people and bad things happen to bad people. But not always—life is not that simple. Apparently, Eliphaz didn't get the memo. As we have examined the first response to Job's sufferings and speech, we are introduced to Eliphaz, Bildad, and Zophar's retribution theology. It is not fully developed or complete at this stage. In fact, chapters 4–5 of Job sound tame compared to the subsequent speeches, such as Eliphaz's harsh rebuke: "Is not your evil abundant? There is no end to your iniquities" (Job 22:5). But what we have here is the first sermon to suffering Job, one that is filled with a mixture of truth and error.

So that we might avoid falling into the same folly as Eliphaz, it is crucial for us to perceive what he should have *seen*. Sight is an important theme in the book of Job. Job repeatedly describes a "deep darkness" that engulfs him, not pertaining solely to physical suffering but more fundamentally to his inability to perceive the nature and intentions of God. When God eventually unveils himself to Job in chapters 38–41, Job responds to this revelation by declaring, "I had heard of you by the hearing of the ear, but now my eye sees you" (Job 42:5).

Eliphaz also employs the language of sight in his sermon to Job in chapters 4–5. He utilizes it to express commonsense observations derived from personal experience. In Job 4:8, he observes, "As I have seen, those who plow iniquity and sow trouble reap the same." Then in 5:3, he reiterates this idea: "I have seen the fool taking root, but suddenly I cursed his dwelling." Put simply, Eliphaz has seen that sin has consequences. He clarifies to Job that just as crops wither as a result of specific causes, such as a bad seed or inadequate cultivation, there are evident reasons behind Job's afflictions. His suggestions are Job's high anthropology (Job thinks his sin is not the cause of his calamities) and his low theology (Job should be praising God, not cursing his existence). Yet it is not Job but Eliphaz who is blind to himself and his God. While Eliphaz claims that he has received a vision at night and heard a voice (a so-called word from the Lord; cf. Job 4:12–16), his vision is still obscured. He is not seeing straight. Or, better, he is simply shortsighted.

How so? Here are three ways.[12] *First, Eliphaz does not see Satan.* That is, the possibility of otherworldly opposition does not register on his retribution-theology radar. He assumes that the only force fighting against Job is

12. For these three applications, see Ash, chaps. 5–6.

Job himself, and thus he attributes his suffering solely to the evil inherent in his fallen nature. Although Job's own flesh is undoubtedly waging war against him, as it does with all of us, there is more to the story, as we are aware. We have read Job chapters 1–2, and we understand that "Satan" is to blame. We know that Job is having a devil of a fight with the devil, or at least a supernatural being who is acting devilishly. So while Eliphaz asserts that he has had supernatural spiritual vision, what he truly needs is a futuristic visit from the apostle Paul—a trip to the seventh heaven and a dose of Ephesians 6:11–12: "Put on the whole armor of God, that you may be able to stand against the schemes of the devil. For we do not wrestle against flesh and blood, but against the rulers, against the authorities, against the cosmic powers over this present darkness, against the spiritual forces of evil in the heavenly places." Eliphaz needs to know not only that Satan can hinder us ("we wanted to come to you—I, Paul, again and again—but Satan hindered us," 1 Thess. 2:18), but that he is out to devour us ("Your adversary the devil prowls around like a roaring lion, seeking someone to devour," 1 Peter 5:8). There is a spiritual battle within us; there is a spiritual battle all around us.

Eliphaz doesn't see Satan, but we should. We should regularly pray the Lord's Prayer, which, of course, ends with the plea "deliver us from evil" (Matt. 6:13; or "the evil one," *tou ponerou*). We should echo Martin Luther's Morning Prayer:

> I thank Thee, my Heavenly Father, through Jesus Christ, Thy dear Son, that Thou hast kept me this night from all harm and danger; and I pray Thee to keep me this day also from sin and all evil, that all my doings and life may please Thee. For into Thy hands I commend myself, my body and soul, and all things. Let Thy holy angel be with me, that the Wicked Foe may have no power over me. Amen.[13]

We are to see what Eliphaz does not see, namely, that Satan is for real. Although he is not the cause of all suffering, Satan surely loves to tempt and test and try God's people, as he has Job. As he is responsible for Job's sores and losses, so he is responsible at times (and we often do not know when) for taking from us, tempting us, squeezing us with all the powers of hell. Just because God is sovereign over Satan, this does not mean that Satan—"the

13. Martin Luther, "Morning Prayer," in Small Catechism, *Evangelical Lutheran Hymnal* (Ohio Synodical Printing House, 1880), 332–33.

ruler of this world" (John 12:31; 14:30; 16:11)—is not at work in this world, busily travailing against Christ's kingdom.

Second, Eliphaz does not see the possibility of a heavenly mediator. In Job 5:1, he asks: "Call now; is there anyone who will answer you? To which of the holy ones will you turn?" Evidently, Eliphaz doesn't think that mere mortals, such as Job, can find access to God through any supernatural being. To him, there is not an angel or a messianic mediator to call upon. It is just sinful Job versus holy God. But that is not the full story, and Job knows it. As we will see later on, he knows that he has, or at least hopes that he has, a "witness . . . in heaven" (Job 16:19) and even a "Redeemer" who "lives" (19:25). Of course, we know so much more. We see that "there is one God, and there is one mediator between God and men, the man Christ Jesus" (1 Tim. 2:5). As Christians, we know that there is someone strong enough to save. We know that in the fullness of time, God sent Jesus to save us from our sins and to crush Satan's head—to vindicate the righteous and punish the wicked. In Jesus, we have salvation. In Jesus, we have a Mediator. In Jesus, we have deliverance from our suffering.

Third, and related to the second point, *Eliphaz does not see the cross.* He does not understand that an innocent Mediator might one day mediate between God and man through human suffering. If he had seen Jesus on the tree, he would have agreed with the mockers: "If you are the Son of God, come down from the cross" (Matt. 27:40). If he had been a disciple, he would have wanted Jesus to recover like Superman from this kryptonite moment—to push the nails out from his hands and feet, whisk away the wicked to the Phantom Zone, and rescue the weeping women. We can surmise that if Eliphaz had been at Calvary, the furthest thought from his mind would have been to grasp that Jesus played the role of the true Super Man by being the Suffering Man. Through his sacrificial death and then glorious resurrection and eternal enthronement, he has forgiven sins, destroyed the works of the devil, and brought meaning to all innocent suffering.

What a blessed vantage point we have! We can answer Eliphaz's question, "Who that was innocent ever perished?" (Job 4:7), with the simplest of Sunday-school answers: Jesus! "The word of the cross," as Paul writes, "is folly to those who are perishing, but to us who are being saved it is the power of God" (1 Cor. 1:18). What else is the word of the cross? It is wisdom, the very wisdom of God. "Jews demand signs and Greeks seek wisdom, but we preach Christ crucified, a stumbling block to Jews and folly to Gentiles, but to those who are called, both Jews and Greeks, Christ the power of God and the wisdom of God" (vv. 22–24). The wisdom of the cross is the word from the Lord that Eliphaz needed. It is the wisdom that we all need.

Eliphaz is a fool in that he doesn't see the cross, the possibility of a mediator, and the reality and activity of Satan. May we, by God's grace, perceive what he should have *seen*: that Satan is real and that he wages war against us; but also that Jesus is the "one mediator between God and men" (1 Tim. 2:5) who delivered us from the power of sin, death, and the devil through the sacrifice of his cross.

7

Job: Three Arrows

Job 6:1–7:21

For the arrows of the Almighty are in me; my spirit drinks their poison; the terrors of God are arrayed against me. (Job 6:4)

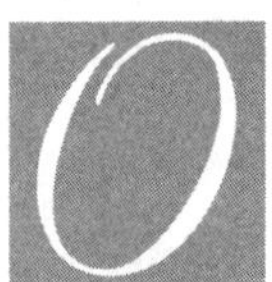

On July 7, 2015, the author and activist Anne Lamott posted this entry on her Facebook page:

> 29 years ago I woke up sick, shamed, hungover, and in deep animal confusion. . . . I was 32, with three published books. . . . I gave talks and readings that hundreds of people came to. I had won a Guggenheim Fellowship, although, like many fabulous writers, I was drunk . . . every day. I was penniless and bulimic. . . . My soul was rotted out from mental illness and physical abuse. My insides felt like Swiss cheese, until I had that first cool, refreshing drink.

Here Lamott is talking about drinking alcohol, as if that solved her daily problems or made them temporarily go away. But she knew that this was just one of her problems, as she goes on to describe showing up to an Alcoholics Anonymous meeting, or some counseling group: "There were all these other women who had what I had, who'd thought what I'd thought, who'd done what I'd done, who had betrayed their . . . deepest values, who sat with me that day, and said, 'Guess what? Me, too. I have that too. Let me get you a glass of water.'"

The book of Job offers the Bible's version of the "me, too"—not "me, too" as it relates to alcoholism, eating disorders, or sexual abuse, but "me, too" in the sense that we too can relate to Job's sufferings, especially what might cause the most pressing pain, the pain of friends turning against you, of allies acting like enemies. Additionally, Job's story addresses the experience of the pain of feeling as though *God* is against you, that "the arrows of the Almighty are in me" (as Job graphically puts it in 6:4), that the God whom we fear and who we know loves us is acting (or we think is acting) more like an adversary than an advocate.

Here in chapters 6–7, Job—after days and nights of racking his brain for answers (what he calls "months of emptiness," Job 7:3) and listening to Eliphaz's bad advice—cannot identify some secret sin that he needs to bring to light that might offer him a renewed life and relationship with God. He is not, for example, like David in Psalm 32:3–4, where the king laments how his unconfessed iniquity is devastating his body ("my bones wasted away . . . [and] my strength was dried up") until he confesses his transgressions. Since Job cannot calculate the cause of his physical, emotional, and spiritual anguish, he lays the blame of his pain on his sovereign God and God's inexplicable will (Job 6:1–13), a piercing pain that is only intensified by his friends' incorrect analyses (vv. 14–30). Job wonders (7:1–21) whether, if he has indeed sinned, God won't reveal the sin or graciously just erase the offense. Yes, he turns to God (finally, he is praying!) for answers. But heaven remains silent. Job's many questions remain unanswered.

Have you experienced the silence of heaven? Sure, you have. Me, too!

The title of this chapter, however, is not "Me, Too," but "Three Arrows," because that is the language that Job uses. In Job 6:1–13, Job speaks about *the arrows of the Almighty* in him. Then in 6:14–30, Job speaks about his own arrows—*the arrows of Job*, some piercing words that he aims at *his friends*. Finally, in 7:1–21, Job directs his aim upward, what might be called *the arrows of Job—up to Yahweh*. As David Allen explains: "He went straight to God and asked two questions, 'Why?' and 'Why me?' He refused to take God's silence for an answer or to let God off the hook."[1]

That's the overview and outline. After we dig deeper into the details next, we conclude (after we have survived all the arrows) with two safe places to

1. David L. Allen, *Exalting Jesus in Job*, Christ-Centered Exposition (Holman Reference, 2022), 3; cf. Eugene Peterson, *Job: Led by Suffering to the Heart of God* (NavPress, 1996), 5.

stand, places where we can look back on this battlefield and pick up some of the broken arrows and see what is valuable for us among the wreckage.

The Arrows of the Almighty

In Job 4–5, Eliphaz advised Job to *get* that he is guilty before God and then *go* to God for forgiveness and restoration. He specifically accused his friend of being impatient. Here in chapters 6–7, Job gives an answer to Eliphaz (and the other friends as well—the "you" throughout is plural). He claims that he has every reason to be upset and frustrated by his situation. For Job says that if someone took all his anger ("vexation") and agony ("calamity," Job 6:2) and weighed it on a scale, it would be "heavier than the sand of the sea" (v. 3a). Picture the impossible—every milligram of sand gathered from all the seas placed on a scale as large as the surface of Jupiter. That's pain—beyond measure! That is why Job's words have come across as "rash" (v. 3b). He cannot keep silent any more than a beast keeps silent when it is hungry (the donkey brays "when he has grass"; the ox lows "over his fodder," v. 5).

Job's friends fail to understand the situation correctly, and he is through with them. He will not stomach their insipid ("tasteless," Job 6:6; "loathsome," v. 7b) accusations, for he is not under the rod of God because of some iniquity ("I have not denied the words of the Holy One," v. 10). Instead, God has attacked him without cause ("the arrows of the Almighty are in me," v. 4; cf. Lam 3:12–13). As Daniel Estes notes: "The Old Testament often pictures Yahweh as a divine warrior who fights for his people (Zeph. 3:17), as he does notably in the exodus when he defeats Pharaoh and the army of Egypt (Ex. 15:1–18). Job, however, feels that instead of being his faithful protector, God has been his fierce enemy. Bending the familiar Old Testament image of God as the divine warrior fighting for his people. Job pictures him instead as an enemy attacking him with poisoned arrows that penetrate both his body and spirit."[2] Job has already conveyed his desire for death (Job 3). Now he wants the Divine Warrior to finish him off: "Oh that I might have my request, and that God would fulfill my hope" (Job 6:8), namely, to "crush me . . . and cut me off!" (v. 9). Job sees death as his only possibility of future "comfort" (v. 10). He has reached his limit, perhaps the human limit, of patience ("What is my strength, that I should wait?," v. 11). His body can take only so much

2. Daniel J. Estes, *Job*, Teach the Text (Baker, 2013), 39.

("Is my strength the strength of stones, or is my flesh bronze?," v. 12). His self-resolve has vanished ("Have I any help in me?," v. 13). For those who have endured constant and excruciating pain, the idea of death as a form of relief is familiar. This notion is even more prevalent for those who lived in eras before ours, when powerful painkillers such as morphine were not available for severe physical pain, and various drugs were not accessible for psychological and emotional distress.

The Arrows of Job—into His Friends

To summarize Job 6:1–13, Job defends his words to his friends because God's arrows are in him. He is suffering not for some sin (at least none that he recognizes) but simply because God, for some inexplicable reason, has deemed it so. Moving, then, to 6:14–30 and sticking (pun intended) with the arrow analogy, Job shifts to his own arrow aimed at *his friends* "for their failure of true friendship."[3] Instead of showing him steadfast love ("kindness," *hesed*), they have proved disloyal. As Gerald Wilson explains:

> When the pursuit of survival exhausts our energies, we have little left to sustain our faith. This is when we most need believing friends who resist the temptation to criticize our struggling faith, and instead come alongside us to give testimony of the continuing faithfulness of God that we have such difficulty seeing through our pain. This is precisely what Job's friends fail to do. They are so focused on what they consider to be Job's failure, that they trivialize his pain and confusion and condemn, rather than comfort him.[4]

Job's aphorism about his so-called friends is as sharp as any arrow: "He who withholds kindness from a friend forsakes the fear of the Almighty" (Job 6:14). Put differently, "The way you are treating me shows that you have forsaken the ways of God." Ouch!

Next, in verses 15–20 of Job 6, Job continues his attack by comparing his struggle with his friends to the disappointment of thirsty men coming to a dry source of water. Job is dying of thirst—of the living waters that come from true wisdom:

3. Gerald H. Wilson, *Job*, Understanding the Bible Commentary 10 (Baker, 2007), 61.
4. Wilson, 61.

My brothers are treacherous as a torrent-bed,
as torrential streams that pass away,
which are dark with ice,
and where the snow hides itself.
When they melt, they disappear;
when it is hot, they vanish from their place.
The caravans turn aside from their course;
they go up into the waste and perish.
The caravans of Tema look,
the travelers of Sheba hope.
They are ashamed because they were confident;
they come there and are disappointed. (Job 6:15–20)

Here Job compares his friends to a wadi in the "waste" (Job 6:18b; the Arabian Desert), a raging river that forms when the summer's heat melts the mountain ice and snow and creates temporary "torrential streams" (v. 15b) that quickly evaporate ("pass away," v. 15b; "vanish," v. 17b) before offering sustenance for desperate and exhausted travelers (those who have turned "aside from their course," v. 18; "caravans of Tema[,] . . . travelers of Sheba," v. 19). Like that dry riverbed, the supposed wisdom of Job's friends has proved to be an unreliable source in sustaining him through his suffering. Just as these weary travelers, who were "confident" that there would be water in the wadi when they arrived, are "ashamed" and "disappointed" (v. 20) once they see that the streambed is dry, so Job wants his friends to recognize that their counsel comes from overconfident and misguided perceptions of his situation.

Then Job takes the arrow from his friends out of his soul and sticks it into theirs. His friends are like that empty riverbed: "You have now become nothing" (Job 6:21a). As they look at Job ("you see my calamity," v. 21b), they are as "afraid" as those wanderers at the waterless wadi. They shrink back in fear instead of moving toward him in friendship. Job has not asked for much; he has not asked them for resources or rescue:

Have I said, "Make me a gift"?
Or, "From your wealth offer a bribe for me"?
Or, "Deliver me from the adversary's hand"?
Or, "Redeem me from the hand of the ruthless"? (Job 6:22–23)

Instead, he seeks wisdom. "Teach me, and I will be silent," Job says; "make me understand how I have gone astray" (Job 6:24). He is open to painfully honest rebukes ("How forceful are upright words!," v. 25a). But their wisdom and words have thus far proved worthless: "But what does reproof from you reprove?" (v. 25b). In other words, their criticisms amount to nothing! They think they have Job's problem solved ("Do you mean to correct what I say?," v. 26a NIV) and treat his disagreement with their diagnosis with disdain. To them, Job is full of hot air ("the speech of a despairing man is wind," v. 26b). But their charges are baseless and their accusations heartless. Job is a person, not an object. His erstwhile *friends* are treating him like a commodity, not a companion ("You . . . bargain over your friend"), acting as cruelly as poker sharks gambling over a desolate child's life ("You would even cast lots over the fatherless," v. 27).

But there is time for Job's friends to change. They think he needs to repent, and he thinks *they* need to repent—to "turn now" (Job 6:29). Verses 28–30 express his call to repentance:

> But now, be pleased to look at me,
>   for I will not lie to your face.
> Please turn; let no injustice be done.
>   Turn now; my vindication is at stake.
> Is there any injustice on my tongue?
>   Cannot my palate discern the cause of calamity?

In essence, Job concludes: "You look me in the eye, and I will look you in the eye. Let us treat each other like friends. I promise that I will not exaggerate the pain, hide any sins, or lie to you, and you promise to be fair-minded, for 'my vindication is at stake' [Job 6:29b]. Please believe me. You must believe me when I say that my words are not the 'cause of' my 'calamity' [v. 30b]."

This is a good place to hit the pause button and interject an application. For a personality test that I took for work, I know that I am someone who can get along with every type of personality except the dominant personality, if that person is in authority over me. Also, because I like to get along with everyone and usually do, I don't often have conflicts with people. But when I do, my natural inclination is avoidance. (I imagine a "me, too" from many readers.) Job doesn't avoid his conflict. He doesn't ask his friends to get out of town and leave him alone. He doesn't flee the situation. Instead, he admirably attacks the issues at hand. He speaks his mind. He's actually trying to bring some resolution and reconciliation with his "brothers," as he calls them (Job 6:15).

Resolution and reconciliation, of course, cannot take place without confession of sin. Yet Job's friends don't interrupt him here and say: "Sorry. We were wrong. We are zipping our lips and turning around. We repent." Nevertheless, what Job does is right. As blessed peacemakers, we should emulate his actions.

The Arrows of Job—Upward to God

As we return to Job's response, we see that Job shifts from confronting *his friends* ("Please turn," Job 6:29) to complaining ("I will complain in the bitterness of my soul," 7:11) to *his God*. His complaint is, we might say, east of Eden. The crunch of the thorns and thistles from Genesis 3:17–19 can be felt beneath Job's feet. "Man" has a "hard service on earth," he complains (Job 7:1a). His workdays are long ("his days [are] like the days of a hired hand," v. 1b) and his toil under the sun without respite ("like a slave who longs for the shadow," v. 2a). Although man works hard, he does so for meager pay, if he gets paid at all (he "looks for his wages," v. 2b). Life is hard for all humans. True for Job. True for me. True for you. Charles Spurgeon answers the question "Why does God allow for seasons of melancholy?" by saying, "Is it not first that *they are men*? Being men, they are compassed with infirmity, and heirs of sorrow."[5] Indeed!

Next, after Job 7:1–2, Job turns to himself. Notice the change from "man" to "me," "my," and "I," used sixteen times in verses 3–10. (In fact, in chapter 7, "I" is used twenty times, "my" seventeen times, and "me" thirteen times.) Job will return to man (humanity) in verse 17 ("What is man . . . ?"), but he will continually view the plight of all people in light of his own issues.

In Job 7:3, Job applies the analogy that he used of man in verse 2 to himself: worse than the man who toils all week and receives paltry compensation in exchange, Job suffers ("Nights of misery are apportioned to me," Job 7:3b) for nothing ("I am allotted months of emptiness," v. 3a). He inherits futility, along with insomnia. "The night is long" ("When I lie down I say, 'When shall I arise?'"); he tosses in his sleep ("I am full of tossing till the dawn," v. 4).

5. Charles Spurgeon, *Lectures to My Students* (Christian Focus, 2005), 177.

Job's days are even worse than his nights! They come and go, one sunrise after the next, quickly ending without a thread of hope ("My days are swifter than a weaver's shuttle and come to their end without hope," Job 7:6). Day after day, nothing has changed: he has not been healed; he has not died. But his body is like a walking corpse ("My flesh is clothed with worms and dirt") that regenerates sores ("My skin hardens, then breaks out afresh," v. 5).

Job's reflection on his days and nights (Job 7:3b–6) and weeks and months (vv. 1–3a) leaves him realistic ("my life is a breath") but not optimistic ("my eye will never again see good," v. 7). The reason that he is pessimistic is related to God's omnipresence, a theme to which he will return later (v. 20), and to humankind's transiency. As God looks on him ("Your eyes are on me," v. 8b), and perhaps people do as well ("The eye of him who sees me," v. 8a),[6] nothing is done to rescue Job. Just as he will die ("I shall be gone," v. 8b; "no more," v. 8a), man ("he," vv. 9, 10), who has worked so hard (vv. 1–2), labors in vain. (Apparently, Job has been reading Ecclesiastes, or else creating Qoheleth's first draft!) The grave (*Sheol* in Hebrew) will swallow him up: "As the cloud fades and vanishes, so he who goes down to Sheol does not come up; he returns no more to his house, nor does his place know him anymore" (vv. 9–10).

Job has had enough. He can shut his mouth no longer ("I will not restrain my mouth; I will speak," Job 7:11a–b) about the "anguish of" his "spirit" and the "bitterness of" his "soul" (v. 11b–c). He does not grasp what God is doing or why God has made him his focus, as if he is some special locus of malevolence: "Am I the sea, or a sea monster, that you set a guard over me?" (v. 12). Even at night, when Job finally falls asleep, God sends nightmares: "When I say, 'My bed will comfort me, my couch will ease my complaint,' then you scare me with dreams and terrify me with visions" (vv. 13–14). Job knows that he will "not live forever" (his "days are a breath," v. 16; *hebel*). But he wants to die now! Even death by strangulation ("I would choose strangling") would be a better option than what he is now enduring ("death rather than my bones," v. 15). "Leave me alone" (v. 16b), Job cries out to God, "or finish the job!"

The arrows go upward. We might interject, "Put down your bow, Job!" But no. Job is not done with his imprecatory prayer. He proceeds more directly to aim his arrows at the Almighty. Yet he dulls their edges. He does not

6. The parallel here ("the eye of him"/"your eyes," Job 7:8) could refer to God.

make accusations; rather, he asks six pointed questions. The first is "What is man, that you make so much of him, and that you set your heart on him, visit him every morning and test him every moment?" (Job 7:17–18). Unlike Psalm 8, which asks, "What is man that you are mindful of him, . . . that you care for him?" (Ps. 8:4) and begins and ends in praise, "O Lord, our Lord, how majestic is your name in all the earth!" (vv. 1, 9), in Job 7:17–18 God's mindfulness of man begins and ends only in despair. To Job, God's all-seeing eye is overbearing (Job cannot even swallow his spit without God's knowing; cf. Job 7:19). God's watchful eye ("you watcher of mankind," v. 20a) is not that of a protective father or merciful deliverer (as it was for Israel; see Pss. 12:7; 25:20; 40:11; 61:7) or even of a tester of mankind (cf. Ps. 11:4; Eccl. 3:18). Rather, the Almighty's eye lines up his arrows ("Why have you made me your mark?," Job 7:20; cf. 6:4). Job wants to be ignored, not oppressed by the Almighty's omnipresence. If he cannot be ignored, he simply wants to be forgiven for whatever infinitesimal iniquity is causing his colossal catastrophe: "Why do you not pardon my transgression and take away my iniquity" before I die ("I shall lie in the earth") and our relationship is over ("you will seek me, but I shall not be," 7:21)?

Job's final question (Job 7:21) is as important and as exaggerated as the first (vv. 17–18). He is looking for some sin as eagerly as his friends are. He is hoping to find something—even the smallest sin—that he could confess to release God's harsh hand, his brutal and illogical attack, "illogical" in that it does not represent a fair chastisement for a possible secret sin. But he is unable to discover anything, and the particular transgressions that his friends accuse him of do not align with his own sincere self-evaluation and sober perception. Therefore, he implores God to deliver him by not only identifying the sin but also granting forgiveness for it.

Applications to Job's Expressions of Anguish

Job is overwhelmed by the arrows of the Almighty. His physical strength falters (Job 6:11–12), his soul is engulfed in despair (v. 4)—"it is not his body that absorbs this poison but rather his spirit, an apt metaphor for Job's depression"[7]—and the weight of his afflictions becomes unbearable (v. 2).

7. Tremper Longman III, *Job*, Baker Commentary on the Old Testament Wisdom and Psalms (Baker Academic, 2012), 137.

Job wants to die. But "even in the midst of his death wish, Job refuses to break relationship with God."[8] Remarkably and admittedly, he never entertains thoughts of suicide, or at least never expresses such contemplation. He understands that taking his own life is not an option for one who follows God's commands ("the words of the Holy One," v. 10). While he yearns for death, he does not yearn for God's disfavor. He refuses to jeopardize his relationship with Yahweh (12:9; 28:28). The only way he sees out of the maze of his misery is for God himself to take his life or forgive him.

Friendship with God

Whatever we might think of Job's solution, we should appreciate and apply two aspects of his relationship with God. First, he fears God more than he fears death. Moreover, he loves God more than he loves himself. Second, he is honest with God, a point to press. We might desire Job to return to his more pious-sounding responses to pain ("The Lord gave, and the Lord has taken away; blessed be the name of the Lord," Job 1:21; cf. 2:9–10). We might wish that he were more hopeful. Job's friends certainly believed that hope should have been a distinguishing mark of his faith in God (cf. 4:6; 11:18), and in contrast to "the wicked [who] have no hope (8:13; 11:20)."[9] We might even assess his prayer (in chap. 7) as impudent (thinking, "How dare he talk that way to God!"). Alternatively, we might find the authenticity and integrity of his lamentations to be soothing to our souls. Like the pained psalmists, the weeping prophets, and the suffering saints, God's people can cry out, "How long, O Lord?" (e.g., Ps. 13:1; Hab. 1:2; Rev. 6:10) and "Why[, God?]" (Job 3:11, 12, 16, 20, 23; 7:20, 21).

Our depressing thoughts, even our longings for death and frustrations with God, can become appropriate prayers. When we are healthy and happy, we should turn to God in praise and thanksgiving. But when we are sick and sad, we should cast "all" our "anxieties on" God—our physical, emotional, social, financial, and *theological* concerns—even if we cannot sense that he "cares for" us (see 1 Peter 5:7). We should join in the chorus of the oppressed.

Stephen Nichols's excellent book *Getting the Blues: What Blues Music Teaches Us About Suffering and Salvation* explains both how blues music

8. Longman, 139.

9. "Although Job readily admits his feeling of hopelessness, he strongly argues against their deduction that he then necessarily must be wicked." Estes, *Job*, 45–46.

ultimately comes from "the music of slavery, the spirituals,"[10] and that the slave spirituals are some of the greatest songs in the Christian musical canon. Consider a few lines from "Nobody Knows the Trouble I've Seen":

> Sometimes I'm standing crying,
> Tears running down my face,
> I cry to the Lord, have mercy,
> Help me run this all race.
>
> Oh Lord, I have so many trials,
> So many pains and woes,
> I'm asking for faith and comfort,
> Lord, help me to carry this load.
>
> Nobody knows the trouble I've seen;
> Well, no [he corrects himself], nobody knows but Jesus.

Can we affirm these words and sing this song?

Job 6 and 7 are crucial chapters for contemporary Christians, a generation that is often rightly categorized as theologically shallow and superficially pious. We are "happy-clappy" Christians, as it used to be said, or, as said more recently, Christians who envision "Jesus singing a praise chorus at the grave of Lazarus."[11] Of course, that is not what our Lord did at the gravesite. "Jesus wept" (John 11:35). It is okay to weep over death, to lament during suffering, and to pray, as he did, "Remove this cup" (Luke 22:42) and "My God, my God, why have you forsaken me?" (Matt. 27:46). It's okay for us to cry out, "Come, Lord Jesus!" (Rev. 22:20), and to bellow out with heartfelt anticipation, "Swing low, sweet chariot, coming for to carry me home."

Friends with People

Another lesson from this passage relates to friendship, an important theme in Job (the Hebrew word *rea'* for "friend" is used fourteen times), just as it is an important experience in all our lives. How hard it is to find a faithful friend—a Jonathan for David or a Timothy for Paul. Job's friends started well (and they will end well), but their whirlwind of words pushes

10. Stephen J. Nichols, *Getting the Blues: What Blues Music Teaches Us About Suffering and Salvation* (Brazos, 2008), 29.

11. Christopher Ash, *Job: The Wisdom of the Cross*, Preaching the Word (Crossway, 2014), 68.

Job to the edge. To change the metaphor, Eliphaz has not soothed his friend's wounds but salted them. This is just the beginning of Job's third test—his final, torturous endurance test. He has been tested by the loss of his possessions, children, and servants. He has been tested by the loss of his health. And now—from Job chapter 4 to chapter 37, which give record of real days in his life—he has to endure his friends' false accusations and awful advice.

Relationships matter. The greatest commandment focuses on our relationship with God; the second greatest focuses on our relationship with people. Job feels as though he has joined Adam and Eve after being banished from the garden. He is not in relational harmony with his God, his wife, or his friends. In due course, however, God will speak, and the impact of his divine words will restore the relationships among all involved.

In no trite way, we can be thankful for "What a Friend We Have in Jesus." God has spoken to us in his Son, the final Word (Heb. 1:1–2), and that Word is soothing to our souls and renewing to all our relationships. We have a Mediator between God and man, someone acquainted with our sufferings (Isa. 53:3) and powerful enough to vindicate the righteous. Moreover, we have Christ's church—all those who are in relationship with God and one another through trust in Jesus. We have true "brothers" (Job 6:15) and sisters who hold us up when we feel the arrows of painful providence in our lives, friends who do not respond to our "blunt, even rageful, expressions of anguished questioning of God" with pious platitudes but who really hear us and feel alongside us "the pain that threatens to engulf" us.[12] Paul puts it beautifully: the "God of all comfort . . . comforts us in all our affliction, *so that* we may be able to comfort those who are in any affliction" (2 Cor. 1:3–4). Because we ourselves are "comforted by God," and because we ourselves "share abundantly in Christ's sufferings, so through Christ we share abundantly in comfort too" (vv. 4–5). Out of mutual suffering comes mutual comfort![13]

A Drenched Cardinal

A friend once sent an encouraging note to my wife that featured some extraordinary and apropos images. The note begins: "Hello Emily! I just

12. Wilson, *Job*, 62.
13. I am indebted to Longman (*Job*, 152) for connecting Job 6–7 to 2 Corinthians 1:3–7.

wanted to let you know that I have been praying for you and Pastor O and wanted to say thank you for all that you do." Emily's friend goes on to talk about what she has been praying for herself and everyone around her. Her word to describe prayer of late is "drenched." She wants us all to be *drenched* by God's Word. Here is the first image she gives: "As though standing under a waterfall and standing on a rock. The roar of the powerful and yet graceful water, pouring over my entire body, the noise of the water drowning out the lies that are so close to me."

Then she moves on to this image, one so fitting for what we have been exploring in Job:

> When I looked out my window on one of those rainy mornings recently, I saw a cardinal and he was wet. It made me smile. Drenched is what came to mind, he was drenched! And yet he was singing. The storm that passed in the night didn't stop him from singing. (Sing to the Lord a new song!) There are so many storms going on right now, so many unknowns (and it even reminds me of Job). The storms can be uncomfortable, but God can use them for good.

Are we drenched? That's fine. Are we singing that new song? Are we taking in all of God's Word like a mighty waterfall and standing beneath the weight only because we trust that God is working all things together for our good? And are we willing to stand next to others? To hold out our hand? To be a good friend? A true comfort? May it be so. May it be so as we Christians come together to let the pure words of God and the tumultuous waters of God's bitter providence drench us as we sing a new song even through the sorrows.

8

Bildad: New Singer, Same Old Tune

Job 8:1–22

If you are pure and upright, surely then he [God] will rouse himself for you and restore your rightful habitation.
(Job 8:6)

Leif Enger's novel *Peace like a River* features the Land family of Roofing, Minnesota—Jeremiah (the dad), Davy (a teenager), Reuben (an eleven-year-old), and Swede (their younger sister). Mr. Land is the janitor at the local high school. One night during a football game, he catches two teenage thugs—Israel Finch and Tommy Basca—in the girls' locker room, harassing and assaulting Davy's girlfriend. He takes care of the boys, whopping them with a broom handle. A few days later, they retaliate by coming by the house and abducting Swede for a few hours. They want to give her and the family a good scare, and they do. Sometime shortly thereafter, they return and break into the Lands' house at night. They are up to no good. When they appear at Davy's bedroom door, Reuben flips on the lights and Davy, without hesitation, shoots the two bullies dead. To Davy, who is arrested for manslaughter, he didn't kill those boys in self-defense but for what they did to his girlfriend and sister.

Bildad: New Singer, Same Old Tune

A few days later, as Reuben the narrator tells the story, "Lots of people we didn't know were calling and dropping by," such as newspaper reporters and TV correspondents and "bold and ambitious lawyers." But Reuben notes that "a lot of people we did know, and whose cheerful encouragement I'll bet Dad could've used, were staying away." He then lists some examples:

> I think of Oscar Larson, who liked to take Dad fishing because it seemed the walleyes always gathered round when Dad was in the boat. And of Gary Sweet, the butcher, whose walk-in freezer Dad had fixed during the July hot spell the previous summer, saving the integrity of uncounted beeves. I think of Ron Simonson, the odd-jobs man, who could count on Dad for occasional work—sharpening mower blades, shingling the garage, doing such tasks as Dad would've been delighted to do himself had Ron not needed employment. And I think, can't help it, of those friends of Job's in the Old Testament, the men who came to Job as he lay there in his bed of ashes, all twisted with boils and the loss of his children, and said to him, *Now what did you go and do?*[1]

"Now what did you go and do?" is the perfect Minnesotan paraphrase of the ancient Hebrew text before us. In Job 8, Bildad the Shuhite inserts his opinion to the argument over the cause of Job's calamities.[2] Echoing Eliphaz's retribution theology (chaps. 4–5), Bildad offers the clearest expression of their system of thought, which may be summarized as follows:

> God is in absolute control of his creation; he is completely just and fair; thus, he always punishes the wicked and blesses the righteous. If he were ever to do otherwise, he would necessarily be unjust, which is inconceivable. *Therefore*, if someone is suffering, he *must* have sinned and is being punished justly for his sin. And, presumably, if someone shows the signs of God's blessings (such as health and wealth), he must have been good.[3]

More concisely: "Retribution theology is based on the idea that sin leads to suffering and thus that suffering is a sign of sin."[4] "Now what did you go and do?"—'cuz you musta done somethin'—is another way to put it.

1. Leif Enger, *Peace like a River* (Grove, 2001), 58–59.

2. "Bildad is from Shuah, a name of one of the sons of Abraham from his marriage to Keturah, whose brother was Midian and whose nephews were Sheba and Dedan (Gen. 25:2; 1 Chron. 1:32), the latter being the name of a place in Edom or Arabia." Kenneth Laing Harris and August Konkel, "Job," in *ESV Study Bible* (Crossway, 2008), note on Job 2:11.

3. See Christopher Ash, *Job: The Wisdom of the Cross*, Preaching the Word (Crossway, 2014), 90 (author's paraphrase).

4. Tremper Longman III, *Job*, Baker Commentary on the Old Testament Wisdom and Psalms

Grounding his argument in tradition (Job 8:8–10), Bildad covers all his theological bases. Because "the Almighty" (vv. 3, 5) is absolutely sovereign and always just ("Does God pervert justice?," v. 3a), Job's sin—as is true for all the godless (whom he talks about in some detail, vv. 11–19; including Job's children, v. 4)—has been punished. The solution is simple: stop pretending to be innocent ("How long will you say these things?," v. 2) and ask God for forgiveness ("Seek God and plead . . . for mercy," v. 5). If Job does this, Bildad guarantees that the blessings will flow (vv. 7, 19–22). Even "laughter" (v. 21) will follow.

Bildad is a new singer singing—sadly for Job—the same old tune. His reply can be divided into four sections. First, he gives a concise summary of the retribution principle (Job 8:1–7). Second, he states that such theology is grounded in tradition (vv. 8–10). Third, he also states that such theology is supported by observation (vv. 11–19). Fourth, he concludes by speaking briefly about the benefits of submitting to the system (vv. 20–22).

A Concise Summary of the Retribution Principle (Job 8:1–7)

Starting with Job 8:1–7, Bildad shows none of the politeness, appreciation, and warmth that Eliphaz did in 4:3–4: "Behold, you [Job] have instructed many, and you have strengthened the weak hands. Your words have upheld him who was stumbling, and you have made firm the feeble knees." In fact, from here on out, opening insults will characterize the friends' speeches. Moreover, in the next three rebuttals, each will begin by calling Job a windbag: "Should a multitude of words go unanswered?" (Job 11:2a); "Should a wise man answer with windy knowledge, and fill his belly with the east wind? Should he argue in unprofitable talk, or in words with which he can do no good?" (15:2–3); "How long will it be until you put an end to words?" (18:2a MEV).

Bildad starts this bad trend by immediately blasting Job with a merciless assessment. He dismisses Job's ardent assertions and loud lamentations ("How long will you say these things?," Job 8:2a) as a lot of hot air (Job's "words" are like "a great wind," v. 2b; namely, they cannot be grasped and should not be held on to). He might also mean that Job's words are destructive. The phrase "a great wind" is used earlier in Job 1:19 for *the mighty wind* that "struck the

(Baker Academic, 2012), 159.

four corners" of Job's oldest son's house, causing the walls to collapse on and kill all of Job's children.[5] Bildad follows such unpastoral insensitivity with analytical and abstract theology. His tone is as cold and clinical as an operating suite as he dissects Job's defense. With the tightness of his theological system, he finds no room for innocent suffering. Like the men on Malta who saw the snake fastened on Paul's arm as a sign that justice will punish a murderer (Acts 28:4), Bildad sees the signs of suffering as sure evidences of Job's sin.

Job's sin, however, must not be as awful as his children's. Because God is just (Job 8:3), Bildad reasons, Job's children got their just deserts (God "has delivered them into the hand of their transgression," v. 4). But Job is still alive! So too are his options. He can continue to act impertinently, or he can go earnestly to the Almighty ("seek God," v. 5a). God is gracious, so Bildad tells Job to "plead . . . for mercy" (v. 5b), that is, to confess his sins. Or if Job is "pure and upright" (v. 6a), as the suffering man has maintained, there is no need for concern: God will come to Job's aid ("then he will rouse himself for you," v. 6b) and restore his good status ("[He will] restore your rightful habitation. And though your beginning was small, your latter days will be very great," vv. 6c–7).

It is also possible that Job 8:6 is part 2 of Bildad's suggested repentance ritual. First, Job should beg for God's forgiveness. Second, he should walk in holiness. The logic would then be as follows: "if" he seeks mercy (Job 8:5), and "if" he starts to amend his ways (v. 6a), then God will reward him (vv. 6b–7).[6] Bildad is being cynical here, but note that, ironically, he is right. In the final chapters of the book of Job, God will rise up (chaps. 38–41), exonerate Job (42:7–9), and restore and enlarge Job's fortunes (vv. 10–17). Job's "beginning" will seem "small," compared to the "very great" blessings of his "latter days" (8:7). In Job 42:12, we read, "And the Lord blessed the latter days of Job more than his beginning," and then it lists double the number of livestock.

Such Theology Is Grounded in Tradition (Job 8:8–10)

In Job 8:1–7, Bildad starts with his "A Concise Summary of the Retribution Principle." Next, in verses 8–10, he claims that "Such Theology Is Grounded in Tradition."

5. In Job 1:19, the Hebrew for the ESV translation "a great wind" is *ruach gedolah*, and in 8:2 it is *ruach kabbir* (lit. a *mighty* wind).

6. "A series of initial 'ifs' (Heb. *'im* [starting in v. 4]) binds his arrangement into a cohesive unit." Gerald H. Wilson, *Job*, Understanding the Bible Commentary 10 (Baker, 2007), 73.

Have you ever seen the musical *Fiddler on the Roof*, where Tevye, a poor Jewish milkman, sings the song "Tradition," which begins with a sixfold repetition of the word *tradition*, followed by a celebration of the traditional roles and rules of a Jewish household?

> The Papa, the Papa! Tradition!
> The Mama, the Mama! Tradition!
> The sons, the sons! Tradition!
> The daughters, the daughters! Tradition!

Tevye has five daughters, and his struggle throughout the story will be to maintain Jewish religious and cultural values as his daughters are influenced by the changing world around them. Bildad's values are the same as Tevye's—influenced by tradition!

Bildad is certain of his censure of and counsel to Job because his thought is substantiated by tradition. This might be the author's way of ironically taking his first jab at his own wisdom tradition, or the prevalent one within his culture. Bildad advises Job to see beyond his experience so that he might "inquire" into the past ("bygone ages") and to "consider" what tradition's sages have discovered ("what the fathers have searched out," Job 8:8). His reason makes sense: while there are exceptions (e.g., "I understand more than the aged, for I keep your precepts," says the psalmist in Psalm 119:100),[7] the older person is typically wiser than the younger,[8] and thus the Old Testament Wisdom Literature often commands the young to listen to their elders, teachers, and parents.

Elihu's attitude is the opposite of that of Generation Z—people born in the late 1990s and early 2000s. This demographic tends to value authenticity (e.g., the internet influencer who shares all her flaws and failures of everyday life) more than age, experience, and expertise. For example, if a group of top scientists for the National Institute of Allergy and Infectious Diseases recommends that everyone get the flu shot this winter to stop the spread of

7. "Wisdom is with the aged" (Job 12:12a). See also Elihu's claim in Job 32:6–9.

8. While Elihu acknowledges and shares this cultural value at the beginning of his speech ("I am young in years, and you are aged; therefore I was timid and afraid to declare my opinion to you. I said, 'Let days speak, and many years teach wisdom,'" Job 32:6–7), he also believes that God-inspired revelation—no matter the age—is more important ("But it is the spirit in man, the breath of the Almighty, that makes him understand. It is not the old who are wise, nor the aged who understand what is right," vv. 8–9).

influenza, people may or may not listen. But if a social media star their age says, "Got the shot!" and records herself walking into a drugstore, getting the shot, and placing a Band-Aid over the small wound, and posts the video online, they will follow her advice. They are indeed influenced by this influencer!

Bildad is Gen A, not Z, and as such he believes that the older person is almost always wiser than the younger. Moreover, he believes that the cumulative gathering of wisdom over time about God, people, and how the world works—that which is observed, studied, accepted as consensus, and handed down—is a reasonable foundation for one's thoughts and actions. So Bildad asks Job to consider time-tested tradition concerning the matter at hand. Surely, compared with the wisdom of the ages, what Job thinks he knows is inconsequential ("we are but of yesterday and know nothing, for our days on earth are a shadow," Job 8:9). Heed the wisdom of the ancients, for their voice is reliable: "Will they not teach you and tell you and utter words out of their understanding?" (v. 10).

Many confessional Christians, myself included, resonate with Bildad's theology here. This is not only because it is rooted in various teachings of the Bible, but also because it aligns perfectly with certain dispositions. Confessional Christians have a strong inclination to trust experts and hold tradition in high regard. This explains why I am a Presbyterian—seriously. Perhaps one of the greatest assemblies of theologians (certainly in the English-speaking world) gathered at Westminster Abbey in London from 1643 to 1653 and summarized the Bible's teaching in what many Christians find to be the most precise and accurate formulation to date (the Westminster Standards). This group of over 120 ministers also produced two documents—*Form of Church Government* and *Directory for Worship*. These documents, which have had a profound influence on the Presbyterian Church in America (PCA), provide detailed, helpful, and biblically grounded guidelines for corporate worship, church discipline, and the like.

By this standard, Bildad, who would have been a bad pastor but a well-organized PCA clerk and an excellent lawyer, presents an orderly argument. He gives an opening statement in "A Concise Summary of the Retribution Principle (Job 8:1–7)." Then he builds his case in "Such Theology Is Grounded in Tradition (Job 8:8–10)." Finally, he presents further evidence and submits the case file, which could be called "Such Theology Is Supported by Observation (Job 8:11–19)."

Such Theology Is Supported by Observation (Job 8:11–19)

Such wisdom as the ancients can impart is what Bildad offers Job next. In one of the most beautiful poems in the Bible, elements and analogies are employed to press home the point that traditional retribution theology is correct. The first synonymous parallelism contains two rhetorical questions that self-contain the obvious answer (Job 8:11):

Can papyrus	grow	where there is no marsh?
Can reeds	flourish	where there is no water?

Without water, plants do not grow. Papyrus and reeds, which can grow swiftly, plentifully, and to high heights, will "wither before any other plant," even "while yet in flower and not cut down" (Job 8:12). So too is the destiny of the godless. "All who forget God" (v. 13a, not for a moment but as a lifestyle), namely, those without God in their lives ("the godless"), whatever hope they might have, "shall perish" like the two plants (v. 13b). True enough. But is this true for Job? Bildad doesn't stop to ask. On he goes, loading beautiful but cruel line after beautiful but cruel line atop Job, like heaping "burning coals on his head" (Prov. 25:22).

Next, Bildad switches metaphors and adds another brilliant image and parallelism (Job 8:14):

His confidence	is severed, . . .
His trust	is a spider's web.

The future of the wicked is as tenuous as the few-days' masterpiece of an Australian garden orb weaver. Worse than that (and piling on the parallelisms!), even something seemingly stable cannot hold him up (Job 8:15):

He leans	against his house,	but it does not stand;
He lays	hold of it,	but it does not endure.

This is great poetry. But we must remember that this is more than a beautiful poem; it is a rebuke directed at Job. The "he" throughout is *him*. Job has lost his possessions, family, health, reputation—everything but his life, his now-miserable life! It has happened as quickly as a mischievous boy obliterates a spider's web with a twig. Thus we can view verses 16–19 of Job 8 as pointed—like a rod to the back, not a twig to the web—directly at our protagonist. Job was like a well-watered plant basking happily in the sun's rays ("before the sun," Job 8:16a). His branches ("his shoots") grew so vast that they "spread over" the "garden" (v. 16b). Not only that, his roots wrapped around a seemingly permanent foundation ("His roots entwine the stone heap," v. 17a). In fact, all that this plant experiences testifies, "I will be around forever!" ("he looks upon a house of stones," v. 17b). Yet like a weed, if he is pulled out of his seemingly solid underpinning ("If he is destroyed from his place," v. 18a), the gardener (God) will refute the relationship: "He will deny him, saying, 'I have never seen you'" (v. 18b, author's translation), or in Jesus' words, "I never knew you" (Matt. 7:23).

As Bildad ends his poem with "behold" (*hen*, which we might paraphrase as "See this!" or "Listen up!"), we are to behold the outcome of the unrighteous. "Behold, this is the joy of his way, and out of the soil others will spring" (Job 8:19). The irony is thick: there is no "joy" for the wicked. Why? They are soon to be gone.[9] The final phrase—"and out of the soil others will spring"—could refer to how the godly will grow in the place of the wicked, or to how one wicked generation produces another (i.e., there will be no end to evil offspring). Either way, Job is on the short end of the prosperous-plant analogy. Likely Bildad is saying that like the godless, if Job does not repent, another weed will take his place.

The Benefits of Submitting to the System (Job 8:20–22)

No doubt—this is, thus far, a solid argument. Let's see how Bildad rests his case. Here comes his closing argument, "The Benefits of Submitting to the System (Job 8:20–22)." This part of his speech too is impressive upon first reading, and quite convincing! Bildad offers a second "behold" (*hen*; cf. v. 19), hoping that Job will listen to his final consideration (v. 20):

Behold, God	will not reject	a blameless man, nor
	take the hand	of evildoers.

This antithetical parallelism ("will . . . reject" is the opposite of "take the hand"; "blameless" the opposite of "evildoers") restates and summarizes

9. "While Bildad's speech affirms retribution, he accepts the delay of its effective enactment to allow for suffering such as Job's." Wilson, *Job*, 82.

Bildad's theology and also initiates his final subtle appeal to Job to heed his earlier, not-so-subtle advice ("seek God and plead . . . for mercy," Job 8:5).

Again the aphorisms and imagery are amazing (e.g., God's taking someone by the hand as symbolizing a loving and protective relationship, or, in the case of the wicked, the lack thereof), but the theology is too unbending. Bildad has no room in his tight theological system for a "blameless" (*tam*) sufferer such as Job.[10] Yet to the reader, as well as Job (see what he says in response in Job chaps. 9–10!), Bildad's rigidity seems not only ruthless but unrealistic. Does he really think that every stillborn baby is a sign of God's rejection and every person born blind a token of Yahweh's retribution? What would he make of the widow's son who dies in 1 Kings 17 for no fault of his own? What would he make of psalmists who challenge the idea that bad things always come to bad people and good things to good people: "All this has come upon us, though we have not forgotten you, and we have not been false to your covenant" (Ps. 44:17; cf. Pss. 73; 88; 89)? What would he make of the blind man in the Gospel of John whose blindness from birth was caused neither by his sin nor by that of his parents, but so that Jesus—at that very moment—might display "the works of God . . . in him" (John 9:3)?

We wonder. We do not know. What we do know is that Job 8:21–22 ends on a hopeful note (hopelessly unrealistic as it pertains to Job). *If* Job heeds Bildad's advice to repent, positive benefits are certain to follow. His life will be filled with happiness (Job 8:21):

[God] will yet fill	your mouth	with laughter, and
	your lips	with shouting.

This passionate celebration (with joyful laughs and shouts) is based in part on Job's adversaries' receiving their just due: "Those who hate you will be clothed with shame, and the tent of the wicked will be no more" (Job 8:22).

There are ironies in this final line. First, Job's friends, who have become his enemies (Job 27:7, *'oyebi*), will indeed soon be "clothed with shame"—the shame of having God reprimand them (42:7–8) and of having to offer a massive and expensive sacrifice through the blameless man they repeatedly shamed (42:9). Second, God in his mercy will not judge these men (cf. "the wicked will be no more," 8:22) but instead forgive them through Job. Let us rejoice and

10. The Hebrew word *tam* is used of Job in 1:1, 8; 2:3; and by Job of himself in 9:20 ("though I am blameless").

be glad that God's system of world management is not as rigid as Bildad's! Indeed, let us thank the Lord that he works, whenever he wants, outside the predictable and automatic patterns of Bildad's retribution principle, that he is not pressed into some inflexible formula, and that he moves in mysterious ways.[11] Let us offer our gratitude especially for the mystery of the incarnation and atonement, in which God did not act as expected or anticipated.

Be Not like Bildad

Above is an attempt to explain Job 8. Below is an attempt to apply it. When close friends are heartbroken—depressed over the loss of a job, devastated by the loss of a loved one, distressed by the loss of health—it is difficult to know what to say and how to act around them. We might act awkwardly; we might say something stupid. Yet whatever we do and say, Job 8 teaches us not to act and talk like Bildad.

First, we are not to *act* arrogantly and abrasively. Bildad is completely certain of his theological assessment. He is confident of his claims and critiques. He even knows, through a logical deduction, that Job's children have sinned (Job 8:4)! Worse than that, he is callous, clinical, and condescending in his criticisms. His bedside manner is more than lacking; it is as sharp as a surgeon's scalpel without a visit from the anesthesiologist. He opens with a rebuke (v. 2) rather than a word of "sympathy and comfort" (his original intent; see 2:11), followed by "Oh, and your children—remember those whom you prayed for every day and then you buried in one day—died due to their wicked behavior" (cf. 8:4). Bildad makes no attempt to soothe Job's soul; he simply wants to solve a theological problem. While he asks the right question, "Does God pervert justice?" (v. 3; cf. 40:8), he leaves no room for God to be God. This moralist from Shuah thinks he knows the mind of God. But to assume and assert such knowledge is not safe. He is sure to be humbled soon (cf. 42:7–9).

We too must be humbled now. Bildad's folly should serve as a wake-up call. We must approach those who are hurting with kindness and humility. We must not think that we know all the answers; we must not spout out all the answers.[12] We must be careful not to act like "a doctor who confidently

11. Daniel J. Estes, *Job*, Teach the Text (Baker, 2013), 53.

12. For an excellent resource on this topic, see Nancy Guthrie, *What Grieving People Wish You Knew About What Really Helps (and What Really Hurts)* (Crossway, 2016).

prescribes . . . [a] cure without first taking care to diagnose correctly [the] disease." As Daniel Estes exhorts, "In trying to give the right answers to others, we must be careful to give answers that are truly relevant to their situations."[13] Moreover, we must remember that sometimes weeping alongside is the highest comfort (Job 2:12; cf. 30:25), silence most soothing (2:13), and closet prayer super supportive (Matt. 6:6). Bildad takes the general guidelines found in verses such as Proverbs 21:21 ("Whoever pursues righteousness and kindness will find life, righteousness, and honor") and its opposite (Deut. 28:15, "if you will not obey the voice of the Lord . . . , then all these curses shall come upon you and overtake you") as inflexible prophetic perimeters that box God in. The rules must determine how God must act. Bildad is wrong to limit God in any way; let us not ever be so wrong.

Second, we are not to *speak* falsely about God to God's people. Both the Old Testament and the New Testament repeatedly warn, with earnestness and severity, about false teachers and false teaching.[14] Bildad's version of the health-and-wealth or so-called prosperity gospel is damnable. Bildad is right that God is absolutely sovereign (Job 8:3, 5) and just (v. 3) and punishes the wicked (vv. 11–19), rewards the righteous (vv. 7, 20–22),[15] and forgives those who plead for mercy (v. 5). But to assert that the godly do not suffer is satanic, because it fails to grasp the possible benefits and purposes of suffering. Suffering can humble us; it can refine our faith. Most importantly, suffering can draw us closer to Jesus Christ, the Suffering Servant whose substitutionary suffering has atoned for all our sins, whose sorrowing sympathy aids us in every trial.

Closer to Christ

Let me conclude by explaining and illustrating the sanctifying effect of suffering. First, suffering can—often does—refine our faith. Job doesn't know the purpose of his sufferings. Like most of us when we are suffering, we can't see any purpose and so cry out, "Why?" and "Stop!" But all suffering

13. Estes, *Job*, 54.

14. E.g., Deut. 18:18–22; Jer. 14:14–16; 23:14; Matt. 7:15; 2 Cor. 11:13; 2 Peter 2:1–3.

15. While the book of Job was written to correct Bildad-type theology (suffering is not always connected to sin), other parts of the Old Testament clearly advocate the general principle that God judges the wicked and rewards the righteous in this life (e.g., Prov. 15:19; 21:21). The conditions of the law, for example, must not be forgotten: "if you faithfully obey, . . . all these blessings shall come upon you" (Deut. 28:1–2, 15). This is not only an Old Testament teaching (cf. 1 Cor. 11:30).

for all of God's people, according to the Bible, has purpose. All suffering, somehow and in some way, works for our good (see Rom. 8:28).

Anne Henegar's article "This Feels Familiar: Chronic Sufferers Can Help Equip the Church" shares lessons from her experience of suffering from chronic illness. Henegar writes: "I'm convinced that God wastes none of our pain. Nothing's on his editing floor. We will emerge from this wilderness. We will be refined and redefined." She gives an example from her mother's life. "My mother," she writes, "died three years ago after an 18-year battle with cancer. One of my 'grief tasks' from my beloved counselor is to work my way through the contents of Mom's iPad. I found a surprising treasure in her dictionary app. Her heavenly transformation was mapped across the words she searched for: Chemotherapy. Steadfast. Liberty. Fear. Iniquity. Mortify. Seraphim. Hilarity. Immanence. Holy. Maelstrom. Hosanna. Sanctify. Consummate. Glory. Though wasting away, she was being transformed day by day."[16]

In his first epistle to those Christians who were living as "elect exiles" in the world (1 Peter 1:1), Peter begins the body of his word of encouragement with the exclamation "Blessed be the God and Father of our Lord Jesus Christ!"—followed by what he has, in his grace, done for his church:

> According to his great mercy, he has caused us to be born again to a living hope through the resurrection of Jesus Christ from the dead, to an inheritance that is imperishable, undefiled, and unfading, kept in heaven for you, who by God's power are being guarded through faith for a salvation ready to be revealed in the last time. In this you rejoice, though now for a little while, if necessary, you have been grieved by various trials, so that the tested genuineness of your faith—more precious than gold that perishes though it is tested by fire—may be found to result in praise and glory and honor at the revelation of Jesus Christ. Though you have not seen him, you love him. Though you do not now see him, you believe in him and rejoice with joy that is inexpressible and filled with glory, obtaining the outcome of your faith, the salvation of your souls. (1 Peter 1:3–9)

Later, Peter concludes with a final statement on suffering: "And after you have suffered a little while, the God of all grace, who has called you to

16. Anne Henegar, "This Feels Familiar," *byFaith* 68, no. 2 (2020): 13–14, https://byfaithonline.com/this-feels-familiar-covid-quarantine/.

his eternal glory in Christ, will himself restore, confirm, strengthen, and establish you" (1 Peter 5:10). Suffering can—often does—refine our faith.

Second, and more importantly, suffering can draw us closer to Christ, the Suffering Servant whose substitutionary suffering has atoned for all our sins. In his blasphemous book *River Out of Eden: A Darwinian View of Life*, the brilliant-in-the-head but hard-in-the-heart Oxford don Richard Dawkins writes:

> The total amount of suffering per year in the natural world is beyond all decent contemplation. . . . In a universe of blind physical forces and genetic replication, some people are going to get hurt, other people are going to get lucky, and you won't find any rhyme or reason in it, nor any justice. The universe that we observe has precisely the properties we should expect if there is, at bottom, no design, no purpose, no evil, no good, nothing but pitiless indifference.[17]

Not true! Our God who rules the universe is not silent about suffering. He enters into it. The Son of God is born to suffer and die. The second person of the Trinity was spat on, brutally beaten, mocked, and nailed to a tree. That is not indifference. To Dawkins's repudiation of design, we might reply, "Know the wisdom of the cross." Or, as Peter preached at Pentecost, "This Jesus [was] delivered up according to the definite plan and foreknowledge of God" (Acts 2:23). There is a divine design, a predetermined plan. "No purpose," the don decrees. We answer: "Know the plan of God—the Lamb slaughtered for our sins," a Savior whose mission was "foreknown before the foundation of the world" (1 Peter 1:20; cf. Rev. 13:8). "No goodness," says he. "The sufferings of our Savior are rightly called the gospel—good news!" say we. Yes, there is, "at bottom" (at the deepest foundation of it all), design, purpose, meaning, and even goodness attached to all our suffering. So suffering can—often does—refine our faith. And as it refines our faith, suffering can draw us closer to Christ, the Suffering Servant whose substitutionary suffering has atoned for all our sins.

17. Richard Dawkins, *River Out of Eden: A Darwinian View of Life* (Basic Books, 1996), 132–33.

9

Job: Can I Get a Witness?

Job 9:1–35

There is no arbiter between us, who might lay his hand on us both. (Job 9:33)

We start with a satellite view of Job's response in Job chapters 9–10. The distant view features four obvious observations of both literary and theological import. First, every dialogue between Job and his friends begins with the same phrase: *wayya'an . . . wayyo'mar* ("then . . . answered and said")[1] and as C. L. Seow notes, "Job typically speaks of the friends collectively, not individually."[2] Second, Job's reply is twice as long as Bildad's rebuke. Third, while Job is replying to Bildad directly (Job 8) and Eliphaz indirectly (chaps. 4–5), God is both his subject and object. Right from the start, God is mentioned (9:2); and from that verse forward, God is mentioned seventy-five times.[3] To Job, God is the

1. Eliphaz, Job 4:1; 15:1; 22:1; Bildad, 8:1; 18:1; 25:1; Zophar, 11:1; 20:1; Elihu, 32:6; 34:1; 35:1; Job, 6:1; 9:1; 12:1; 19:1; 21:1; 23:1; 26:1.

2. C. L. Seow, *Job 1–21: Interpretation and Commentary*, Illuminations (Eerdmans, 2013), 542.

3. Three times as "God" (Job 9:2, 13; 10:2); once as the "accuser" (or "judge," 9:15; *meshophet*); the rest as pronouns: "he" (17×), "him" (17×), "his" (3×), "you" (21×), "your" (10×); including God and Job as "we" (1×) and "us" (2×). In Job 9:2–24, Job speaks about God (only "he," "him," and "his" are used), in 9:25–35 both to and about God ("he," "him," "you," "we," and "us" are used), and in 10:1–22 only to God (only "you" and "your" are used).

wise and mighty Creator, Ruler, and Judge. Fourth, other than his focus on God, Job centers on his innocence and pain. "I am not guilty," he states in 10:7, offering an excellent summary of his earlier assertions: "I am in the right" (9:15, 20) and "I am blameless" (vv. 20, 21). His pain is physical ("my wounds," v. 17); yet his emphasis here is on his spiritual and psychological anguish ("I loathe my life," v. 21; 10:1; cf. 7:16; "my suffering," 9:28; "the bitterness of my soul," 10:1).

Job's main "complaint" (Job 10:1), then, in light of the third and fourth observations above, is that he cannot comprehend how to bridge the gap between himself and God. He sees neither a savior to rescue him from God's afflictions ("There is none to deliver out of your hand," v. 7) nor an "arbiter" (9:33) who can successfully argue his case. Moreover, even if he could find a lawyer specializing in *God v. man* litigation and receive a court date with His Holiness himself (v. 32), he grasps that his claims of innocence could easily be proven ignorant up against God's cross-examinations ("How then can I answer him?," v. 14; "I cannot answer him," v. 15). He also understands that since he cannot possibly perceive who God is and how he works (v. 11), the odds of his winning the case against a perfectly wise and strong God ("He is wise in heart and mighty in strength," v. 4) are as slim as getting a two-thousand-pound camel through the eye of a sewing needle. Job is hopeless because, to him at this point, God's ways are incomprehensible.

So in his reply to Bildad, Job is honest with God. He thinks God is against him. Job makes this accusation first *about* God ("he crushes me," Job 9:17) and then *to* God ("*you* bring fresh troops against me," 10:17). But he cannot understand God's motives for such awful afflictions. Once again, he moves from the third-person pronoun to the second ("*he* . . . multiplies my wounds without cause," 9:17; "let me know why *you* contend against me," 10:2).[4] "This is unfair!" is his honest accusation (see 9:22–24; 10:3). Why does he, or others in similar situations, suffer so? Job desires to be in the know, but he will settle for salvation from God by God. (He wants the gospel, we might say!) Thus, he begs God to have mercy, and cries out, as we might put it, "Let me die in peace!"[5]

4. Other examples: "Let *him* take his rod away from me" (Job 9:34), compared with "[*You*, God!] do not condemn me" (10:2) and "[*you*] cease, and leave me alone" (10:20).

5. See Job 10:20–22; cf. 9:25–26.

Two Major Obstacles to a Trial with God (Job 9:1–10)

So much for the satellite view of Job's response to Bildad. In what follows, we take a more microscopic look at some vital particulars. In this chapter, we look at the first half of Job's response (Job 9:1–35), starting with Job 9:1–3:

> Then Job answered and said:
>
> "Truly I know that it is so:
> But how can a man be in the right before God?
> If one wished to contend with him,
> one could not answer him once in a thousand times."

Bildad advised Job to "seek God and plead with the Almighty for mercy" (Job 8:5). While Job agrees that an appearance before God is his desire ("Truly I know that it is so," 9:2), he cannot figure out how such a meeting is possible. If he could get a hearing, how would he "contend with" God (v. 3)? Two major obstacles, as he sees it, stand in his way.

Man's inability to achieve ethical faultlessness is the first obstacle. Agreeing with and echoing Eliphaz ("Can mortal man be in the right before God?," Job 4:17),[6] Job muses, "How can a man be in the right before God?" (9:2).[7] He knows that no specific sin has led to his catastrophes and sufferings (see vv. 15, 21; 10:7); yet he grasps that God's holiness is holier than anything that any holy human can attain, including and admittedly himself (see 13:23). That said, the focus here might also be on his hope of vindication. He cannot be right "*before* God" (*me'eloah*, 4:17), but he can be right *with* God (*'im-'ēl*, 9:2 KJV). That is, he can come into the presence of God and be vindicated by God, just as an innocent person is exonerated by a judge in a fair trial. He wants to be "proved right" (Isa. 43:26).

6. Eliphaz will later express a similar sentiment: "What is man, that he can be pure? Or he who is born of a woman, that he can be righteous?" (Job 15:14).

7. As Seow observes: "In the first movement of the speech (ch. 9), one finds a cluster of terms at home in the court of law: *tsadaq*, 'to be in the right' (9:2, 15, 20); *rasha'*, 'to be in the wrong' (9:20, 22, 29); *tam*, 'blameless' (9:20, 21, 22); *naqi*, 'innocent' (9:23); *niqqa*, 'to exonerate' (9:28); *'nh*, 'to answer' (9:3, 14, 15, 16, 32); *meshopheti*, 'my (legal) adversary' (9:15); *ya'id*, 'to testify' (v. 19b); *mishpat*, 'justice' (9:19, 32); *rib*, '(legal) dispute' (9:3); *shophetim*, 'judges' (9:24); and *mokiach*, 'one who effects right' (9:33). Furthermore, this chapter is framed by 'so' (*ken*) and 'not so' (*lo'-ken*), terms that also mean 'right' and 'not right' (9:2, 35)." He also notes that this "possibility of a legal dispute with God" is a theme that Job reverts to repeatedly until "his final words in ch. 31" and that "nowhere elsewhere in the Bible do we have a human being taking up a case *with* God." *Job 1–21*, 541–42.

The second obstacle that Job faces is his idea of subpoenaing God for questioning. He knows that this idea is ill advised, for if he could actually get God to take the stand, the Lord would not take the Fifth but pepper him with question after question![8] "If one wished to contend with him, one could not answer him once in a thousand times" (Job 9:3).[9] Job grasps that his wisdom is no match for God's. It would be impossible for him to fare well in a trial against his all-holy and all-wise God.

This is why, in Job 9:4–10, Job moves from legal language to an impressive ode on God's awesome authority:

> He is wise in heart and mighty in strength
> —who has hardened himself against him, and succeeded?—
> he who removes mountains, and they know it not,
> when he overturns them in his anger,
> who shakes the earth out of its place,
> and its pillars tremble;
> who commands the sun, and it does not rise;
> who seals up the stars;
> who alone stretched out the heavens
> and trampled the waves of the sea;
> who made the Bear and Orion,
> the Pleiades and the chambers of the south;
> who does great things beyond searching out,
> and marvelous things beyond number.

Here the attribute of God's obvious but incalculable strength is the theme, where his strength is demonstrated in doing the impossible and ruling the earth, heavens, and seas. The concluding verse—"who does great things beyond searching out, and marvelous things beyond number" (Job 9:10)—which is reflective of Eliphaz's doxology (cf. 5:9), simply highlights that Job is only scraping the surface of God's transcendent power, for the limits of such strength are beyond human comprehension.

First, God's strength is demonstrated in doing the impossible *on earth*. Here God is viewed not merely as touching the mountains so that they

8. True enough! In chapters 38–41, God asks Job over sixty questions, a barrage of interrogations that leaves Job stunned, temporarily silent, and quickly repentant.

9. The phrase "once in a thousand times" is "a Hebrew idiom for impossible odds (so v. 3b; see 32:23; Deut 32:30; Josh 23:10; Eccl 7:28)." Seow, *Job 1–21*, 544.

smoke (Ps. 144:5) but as picking up Mount Everest and Pikes Peak ("he who removes mountains") so quickly and forcefully that they have no idea how they ended up in Sodom ("and they know it not," Job 9:5a), or at the bottom of the sea (Mark 11:23; Rev. 8:8), as the case may be. In fact, his power is vaster than power over a few mountains: he can lift the earth ("who shakes the earth out of its place") from its foundations ("and its pillars tremble," Job 9:6). This image is bigger than God's sending an earthquake. Rather, God can move the entire earth, just as he moved many mountains.

Second, God's strength is demonstrated in doing the impossible *in the heavens and seas*. Between what God does in relation to the lights of the universe—in general ("commands the sun, . . . seals up the stars," Job 9:7) and with specific constellations ("made the Bear and Orion, the Pleiades and the chambers of the south," v. 9)—stands the emphatic antithetical parallelism (v. 8):

who alone	stretched out	the heavens and
	trampled	the waves of the sea.

This imagery is that of God's awesome strength stretching throughout the universe. His power is so great that he can effortlessly shift mountains and the earth itself (Job 9:5), and at his command, even the sun and stars can be extinguished (v. 7). Moreover, God possesses the ability to walk on water (v. 8b), symbolizing his mastery over any malevolent and chaotic forces that may resist him. Just as the "thick darkness" (Ps. 18:9//2 Sam. 22:10) lies beneath his feet, so too do the dark waters.

The theme of God's power connects to Job's earlier statements (Job 9:2–3) in addressing Job's second obstacle. The idea of subpoenaing God is misguided not only because the success rate is zero ("who has hardened himself against him, and succeeded?," v. 4b) but also because God is "wise in heart" and "mighty in strength" (v. 4a). God is smart and strong!

Job's hymn could represent, as Seow phrases it, "his anti-doxology" and a "parody" of Eliphaz's doxology (Job 5:9),[10] in that Job has fallen victim to God's *disastrous* wonderworks—his overturning of Job's foundations (literally the "pillars," v. 6, of his oldest son's house, 1:19) arising from God's "anger" (9:5). Yet it is more likely (since the hymn is overly positive in its

10. Seow, 545.

praise!) that Job offers a sincere doxology, which shows "a hunger for God."[11] Moreover: "Without really foreseeing the full implications of his own line of argument, Job is proceeding exactly as any preacher of the gospel must proceed. That is, he is establishing the fact that the chasm between man's sin and God's holiness is so impossibly wide that all human attempts to bridge it are exposed as utterly useless."[12]

With that gospel connection noted, and before we move to the second section of Job's words (Job 9:11–24), it is good for us to pause and ponder other possible connections to Jesus Christ. We do this not merely because it is the Christian preacher's duty—as modeled and taught by Christ himself (Luke 4, 24)—to preach Christ from all the Scriptures, but also because the New Testament offers two echoes of the poetry in Job 9:1–10. The most obvious echo comes in verse 8. The phrase "who alone . . . trampled the waves of the sea" ought to remind the Christian reader of Jesus' miracle of walking on water. The other echo arises in the language of Colossians 1, where Paul poetically writes of Jesus' being "the image of the invisible God," the one by whom "all things were created, in heaven and on earth" (Col. 1:15, 16), which would include the heaven (the sun and stars, Job 9:7–9) and earth (the mountains, v. 5) and sea (the waves, v. 8). Indeed, as Job "lauds the transcendent, untouchable power and holiness of the Almighty God," our minds should turn, as Paul's did, to the untouchable power and holiness of "the Almighty" (Rev. 1:8) incarnate Son of God; he performed miracles—"marvelous things beyond number" (Job 9:10; cf. John 21:25)—and tossed Mount Zion, the place where sins were atoned for in the Old Testament, into the sea. As Mike Mason writes:

> What wonderful irony there is in seeing Job set out to describe the immortal and invisible God, and in the process paint a stunningly accurate portrait of the earthly Jesus! Or was it the other way around? That is, did Jesus Christ, having been born into this world, set out deliberately to spend his life painting a visible and tangible portrait of his unseen Father as described in the Old Testament? For that is certainly just what Jesus came to do: to fulfill the Scriptures, making the transcendent God immanent. The staggering wonder of the Incarnation is that the same God who by definition stands absolutely

11. Robert S. Fyall, *How Does God Treat His Friends?* (Christian Focus, 1995), 65.

12. Mike Mason, *The Gospel According to Job: An Honest Look at Pain and Doubt from the Life of One Who Lost Everything* (Crossway, 1994), 112.

> above and outside the universe, perfect and uncreated and inscrutable, in the historical person of Jesus entered his own creation and so made himself visible, understandable, available.[13]

How Can I Answer Him? (Job 9:11–24)

After Job's magnificent hymn lauding "God's wisdom, strength, creative power, anger, commanding might, and great and marvelous deeds,"[14] Job pauses in his praise. He gives no concluding doxology. Rather, he bemoans the problem of such transcendent sovereignty. God's presence is unattainable. In Job 9:11, Job starts with "behold" to attract his hearers' attention and also to underline the irony—since he cannot behold God:

> he passes by me, and I see him not;
> he moves on, but I do not perceive him.

Unlike Moses, who perceived when "the Lord passed before him" (Ex. 34:6, with the Hebrew verb *'abar*), Job is unaware of God's mysterious movements; God "passes" (*'abar*) by him (Job 9:11), but Job is blind to his actions.

Beyond God's unattainable presence is God's incontestable nature, a theme that Job will develop further in Job 9:13–21. Following his second "behold," Job asks two rhetorical questions. First, when God takes something ("he snatches away"), "who can turn him back?" (Job 9:12). Just as Job was not strong enough to protect his possessions from sudden loss, no one is strong enough to hold back God's hand. Moreover, the second question, "Who will say to him, 'What are you doing?'" (v. 12), reinforces the idea that even individuals who may be inclined to question God's inexplicable and apparently unfair actions do not possess enough clout to compel him to cease or to condemn him for any wrongdoing.

Such sovereign strength, as Job sees it, is not working toward his deliverance. Here he cannot sing with the psalmist of God's answering his cry for help ("In my distress I called upon the Lord; . . . [and] he heard my voice") and coming to the rescue ("He bowed the heavens and came down. . . . He rescued me") because of his godly character ("The Lord dealt with me according to my righteousness," Ps. 18:6, 9, 17, 20). Instead, God has silently abandoned him.

13. Mason, 113–14.

14. David Atkinson, *The Message of Job*, The Bible Speaks Today (InterVarsity Press, 1991), 77.

In Job 9:13–21, Job continues to sigh over God's strength:

How then can I answer him,
   choosing my words with him?
Though I am in the right, I cannot answer him;
   I must appeal for mercy to my accuser.
If I summoned him and he answered me,
   I would not believe that he was listening to my voice.
For he crushes me with a tempest
   and multiplies my wounds without cause;
he will not let me get my breath,
   but fills me with bitterness. (Job 9:14–18)

If the allies of the strong and seemingly supernatural sea monster ("the helpers of Rahab") submit to God ("lie prostrate beneath Him," NKJV), how can a mere human like Job change God's mind if he chooses to target someone ("God will not turn back his anger," Job 9:13)?[15]

Beyond sighing over God's strength, Job also and again speaks of the ill-advised idea of a court date with the divine. In the poetic depiction above, Job takes center stage as he assumes the role of the defendant, while God, adopting the role of the prosecuting attorney, poses a series of questions to which Job gives no reply. His refusal to answer stems not from an attempt to conceal something, but rather from his genuine lack of knowledge. Even when words come to mind, he struggles to articulate them properly: "How then can I answer him, choosing my words with him?" (Job 9:14).

Nor is this Job's only legal problem. The only way forward is to obstruct the judicial process by requesting that the prosecuting attorney, who acts as his "accuser," also assume the role of his judge ("my accuser" is *meshopti* in Hebrew, often rendered "judge"): "Though I am in the right, I cannot answer him; I must appeal for mercy to my accuser" (Job 9:15). Job seeks "mercy" from this accuser-turned-judge. Even if his plea were to be granted, however, a new problem would arise. Job doubts that he would ever receive a hearing if God consented to act as the judge: "If I summoned him and he answered me, I would not believe that he was listening to my voice" (v. 16).

15. The word for "anger" is literally *nose* (*'ap*), which relates to the almost dragonlike picture of God's strength over any opposition: "By the breath of God they perish, and by the blast of his *anger* they are consumed" (Job 4:9; cf. 9:5).

In verses 17–18 of Job 9, Job reminds us why: "For he crushes me with a tempest and multiplies my wounds without cause; he will not let me get my breath, but fills me with bitterness." God's hand of suffering is too much. Job feels as if he is attempting to carry a cyclone above his head, while his sores breed like mosquitoes after a bite of blood (v. 17). Concurrently, with every breath he inhales, God seemingly fills his mouth with a bitter concoction akin to a wormwood smoothie (v. 18). So Job gives up:

> If it is a contest of strength, behold, he is mighty!
> If it is a matter of justice, who can summon him?
> Though I am in the right, my own mouth would condemn me;
> though I am blameless, he would prove me perverse.
> I am blameless; I regard not myself;
> I loathe my life. (Job 9:19–21)

Within these verses, Job provides a summary of the themes covered in verses 2–18 of Job 9, intertwining them with his hypothetical courtroom scenario. God wins the man-versus-God weightlifting competition. He also wins the legal dispute in two ways. First, God cannot be subpoenaed ("who can summon him?," Job 9:19b). Second, if he were to appear in the courtroom, he would assume the role of the prosecuting attorney, not the accused, posing questions to Job that would serve only to make him look guilty (vv. 19b–20). Faced with this reality, what options does Job have? The stark realization that he cannot sue God and emerge victorious leads him to despise his own life. He reacknowledges his innocence ("I am blameless"), yet he no longer concerns himself with the consequences or outcome of his situation ("I regard not myself," v. 21a). He sounds suicidal: "I loathe my life" (v. 21b).

Job perceives God as unjust because God fails to rescue him from his afflictions and vindicate him as righteous (see Job 10:2–7). Furthermore, Job asserts here that God's injustice stems from a recurring pattern wherein he treats the righteous ("the blameless," 9:22; "the innocent," v. 23) and the unrighteous ("the wicked," v. 22) in a similar manner: "It is all one; therefore I say, 'He destroys both the blameless and the wicked'" (v. 22).

In Job 9:23–24, Job develops this theme further but takes it to a darker place:

> When disaster brings sudden death,
> he mocks at the calamity of the innocent.

The earth is given into the hand of the wicked;
  he covers the faces of its judges—
if it is not he, who then is it?

Here Job revisits his own harrowing experiences (as depicted in Job 1:13–19): "When disaster [or, in Job's case, lightning and a great wind] brings sudden death" (as to his children and servants), God "mocks at the calamity [or "despair," *massat*] of the innocent" (9:23). That God *mocks* Job's despair is a strong accusation. Putting forth the image of God not only as folding his arms (he does not care) but as hurling insults is a statement that Job will live to regret (cf. 42:1–6)—so too the exaggerated claim that the ungodly govern the world without any intervention from God. The phrase "the earth is given into the hand of the wicked" implies that God has granted this power; the clause "he covers the faces of its judges" (9:24) restates the same idea at a deeper and more diabolical level—the corruption has reached even the judicial system; and the concluding question, "If it is not [God], who then is it?" takes the theme to ground zero. If injustice exists, Job believes, then God must be to blame.

Job's assessment of God is certainly off and perhaps sinful,[16] and God will confront him on this matter (see Job 38:2–40:2, which ends, "Shall a faultfinder contend with the Almighty?," 40:2a). We perhaps empathize with Job, however, for why is he undergoing such severe sufferings, and when will God rescue him? Why would anyone in Job's situation not answer Bildad's question, "Does God pervert justice?" (8:3), with a resounding "yes," or at least a hesitant "It certainly seems that way"?

Unsatisfying Alternatives (Job 9:25–35)

From his honest accusations against God, Job next uses three images of speed—an Olympian-caliber sprinter, fast boat, and swooping eagle—to illustrate his transient life:

16. Eric Ortlund labels Job in 9:22–24 as blameworthy and sinful, which is certainly possible, but in my estimation (because of 42:7, 9) uncertain. "Doubtless many of his harsh criticisms of God, however understandable they might have been, were simply sinful to utter. How can it be anything but morally blameworthy to claim that God laughs when innocent lives are ruined?" *Piercing Leviathan: God's Defeat of Evil in the Book of Job*, New Studies in Biblical Theology (IVP Academic, 2021), 59.

> My days are swifter than a runner;
> they flee away; they see no good.
> They go by like skiffs of reed,
> like an eagle swooping on the prey. (Job 9:25–26)

Then in Job 9:27–35, he returns to courtroom imagery (cf. Job 9:2–3, 14–16, 19):

> If I say, "I will forget my complaint,
> I will put off my sad face, and be of good cheer,"
> I become afraid of all my suffering,
> for I know you will not hold me innocent.
> I shall be condemned;
> why then do I labor in vain?
> If I wash myself with snow
> and cleanse my hands with lye,
> yet you will plunge me into a pit,
> and my own clothes will abhor me.
> For he is not a man, as I am, that I might answer him,
> that we should come to trial together.
> There is no arbiter between us,
> who might lay his hand on us both.
> Let him take his rod away from me,
> and let not dread of him terrify me.
> Then I would speak without fear of him,
> for I am not so in myself.

In this speech, as Daniel Estes explains: "Job turns over in his mind whether he should enter a legal complaint as a plaintiff against God . . . , because God appears to be almost arbitrary in his treatment of humans. As he thinks it through, Job finds himself left with three unsatisfying alternatives."[17]

These alternatives are as follows. First, Job could drop his complaint against God ("If I say, 'I will forget my complaint,'" Job 9:27a). In fact, he could change his disposition and demeanor completely (saying, "I will put off my sad face, and be of good cheer," v. 27b). The problem with this option is that he dreads further punishment, either for no reason at all or for pretending that he is not in pain: "I become afraid of all my suffering, for I know you

17. Daniel J. Estes, *Job*, Teach the Text (Baker, 2013), 56.

will not hold me innocent" (v. 28). If he is to be "condemned" (v. 29a) for staying on the ash heap and looking as he does or for getting up, taking a shower, and returning to work, why make any changes ("why then do I labor in vain?," v. 29b)? It is better to stay put and do nothing.

Second, Job could try to purify himself. He could "wash" his body with a pure natural substance ("snow") and "cleanse" his "hands" with a powerful man-made compound ("lye," Job 9:30). He could do it twice, which might be part of the reason for the poetic redundancy: I wash/cleanse; myself/my hands; with snow/with lye. "Yet" (v. 31a, and an ominous word in this context) how effective would any purification ritual prove? God's righteous requirements will not be met. Job would soon be dirty—as soon as God decided to act against him again ("you will plunge me into a pit," v. 31a). Then all his scrubbing with pure frozen rain and super-soap will be in vain. For, as he speaks humorously and with hyperbole and personification, even his garments getting a whiff of him after soaking in the sewer again will be repulsed by his skunky scent: "my own clothes will abhor me" (v. 31b).

Third, Job contemplates finding an impartial umpire to arbitrate. He reasons that if he cannot bring a lawsuit against God ("he is not a man, as I am"), or provide adequate answers to God's cross-examination ("that we should come to trial together," Job 9:32), perhaps some supernatural arbiter can bridge the divide between the two parties. Again, another problem arises: this might be a good idea, but where would he find such a mediator? "There is no arbiter between us, who might lay his hand on us both" (v. 33). The image here is gentle and sweet. Oh, that someone among the heavenly beings or on the earth would take one hand and place it on God and place another on Job, and then say to each party, "Can we both get along?"[18] Job will not give up on this idea (cf. 16:19–21; 19:23–27; 33:23–28). He is surely on to something, but he does not quite know what.

Having considered and dismissed these three potential solutions, Job ultimately returns to the only practical option he can conceive. He asks God to remove his wrath: "Let him take his rod away from me, and let not dread of him terrify me" (Job 9:34). Job wants to move beyond an unhealthy terror of God and return to a holy fear of him. He also wants to speak to God and

18. Job longs for, as Derek Thomas puts it, "one as powerful as God and as compassionate and understanding as a true friend." *The Storm Breaks: Job Simply Explained*, Welwyn Commentary Series (repr., Evangelical Press, 2005), 110.

of God without fear of further repercussions: “Then I would speak without fear of him, for I am not so in myself” (v. 35).

The Low Point That Reveals a High Point

Eric Ortlund is right that this chapter records “Job’s absolute low point in the debate,” where Job “utters his darkest suspicions about God” and gives his clearest and sharpest “protest against divine injustice.” As Ortlund also says, “Dreadful as this chapter is, Job is not arrogantly and casually railing against a God before whom he has never trembled.”[19] Job loves, believes in, and wants to hear from God. In fact, it is striking that—in the lightning flashes of hope and momentary glints of praise that are all soaked in his deepest doubts and depressing lamentations—what grieves “Job most deeply out of all his losses is the loss of intimacy with God.”[20] He does not cry out, “Why take my children?” or “Why ruin my illustrious financial enterprises and wipe out my labor force so that I cannot easily rebuild?” or “Why destroy my body deep down to my bones?” He cries out for vindication from God, while under his breath or in the same breath, he cries out for a restored relationship with God. He wants God most of all!

Moreover, because the intimate relationship with God that he experienced before his extreme sufferings has been lost, Job longs for a solution. One idea that comes to mind and out of his mouth is that of a mediator between himself and God, but to his knowledge there is none (Job 9:33; cf. 10:7). This is the first time, but not the last, that Job speaks of a personal witness. “His perception that a mediator does exist grows stronger as the book progresses,”[21] for later he will speak of his “witness . . . in heaven” who will be his attorney before God (“he who testifies for me,” 16:19; and “he would argue the case of a man with God,” v. 21). This “mediator,” he hopes, will “declare to man what is right for him” (33:23); he will, through a merciful ransom (“he is merciful to him . . . ; ‘I have found a ransom,’” v. 24a, c), deliver him from hell (“Deliver him from going down into the pit,” v. 24b) and judgment (“his rod,” 9:34), and thus Job will not only be “accept[ed]”

19. Job will do this elsewhere (see Job 12:13–25; 19:5–12; 21:7–33; 24:1), “but,” as Eric Ortlund notes, “states it most sharply here.” *Suffering Wisely and Well: The Grief of Job and the Grace of God* (Crossway, 2022), 98–100.

20. Ortlund, 98.

21. C. J. Williams, *The Shadow of Christ in the Book of Job* (Wipf & Stock, 2017), 65.

by God but also find joy and satisfaction in life ("he sees [God's] face with a shout of joy," 33:25–26).

As Christians, we find it difficult to read Job 9 without pitying Job. We pity his sufferings. But we also pity his lack of knowledge. We wish he had the revelation of Job 1:6–12 and 2:1–6 to help him understand why he was suffering, and by whose hand. We also wish he could read about the advocate we have in Jesus and the hope we have of life after death through his mediation for us:

> We have an advocate with the Father, Jesus Christ the righteous. He is the propitiation for our sins, and not for ours only but also for the sins of the whole world. (1 John 2:1b–2)
>
> He is the mediator of a new covenant, so that those who are called may receive the promised eternal inheritance. (Heb. 9:15; cf. 12:24)
>
> There is one God, and there is one mediator between God and men, the man Christ Jesus. (1 Tim. 2:5)

Let us be thankful that Job's statement "There is no arbiter between us" (Job 9:33) is not true for us, and no longer true for Job. Now, in Christ, all of God's people know of and rejoice in "that one who stands both on the side of God and on our side, the one who is able to mediate, to reconcile, to arbitrate between us."[22] More than that, we know that Jesus' meditation is not merely that of what Job hoped for (someone who can both sympathize with his pain and vindicate him), but that of fully appeasing God's wrath against our sin. In his propitiatory death, Jesus has finally removed God's "rod" and the "dread" of his terrible judgment (v. 34). As Bill and Will Kynes express it: "Job, in his deep pain, sees the problem, and Job, in his deep longing, points us to the only solution—the solution found in the gospel of the triune God."[23]

22. Bill Kynes and Will Kynes, *Wrestling with God: Defiant Faith in the Face of Suffering* (IVP Academic, 2022), 99.

23. Kynes and Kynes, 99.

10

Job: Pleading to God

Job 10:1–22

I loathe my life; I will give free utterance to my complaint;
I will speak in the bitterness of my soul. (Job 10:1)

In Forest Park, Queens, Natan (Nathan) Rapoport's *Statue of Job* (1968) is displayed. The sculptor depicts Job as standing with his right hand covering his left hand and his arms pressing against his chest in the form of an inverted V. Over his head is a torn prayer shawl and on his left arm there is a serial number, which indicates Rapoport's depiction of Job as an inmate in a Nazi concentration camp. Job's head is tilted back, as if he is looking up to heaven and asking the questions "Why have you made me your mark?" (Job 7:20), "What are you doing?" (9:12b), and as we come now to the second movement of Job's second response, "Why did you bring me out from the womb?" (10:18).

In Job chapter 10, the scene and speech patterns have not shifted much from chapter 9. Job is still talking about abhorring his existence ("I loathe my life," Job 10:1; "Would that I had died before any eye had seen me and were as though I had not been, carried from the womb to the grave," vv. 18b–19; cf. 9:21). Although Job now turns to prayer, addressing God directly ("I will say to God," 10:2; "Why did *you* . . . ," v. 18a), we wonder whether he has fallen into an abysmal despair. Is he really praying to God, or is he actually accusing him in "prayer"?

Five Questions (Job 10:1–17)

The start of Job's direct address to God is less than promising. He follows his "I loathe my life" with

> I will give free utterance   to my complaint;
> I will speak   in the bitterness of my soul. (Job 10:1)

The pain is too deep for Job to pray respectfully; he has abandoned himself to bitterness. So while he lingers briefly on familiar themes such as his hope for deliverance ("I will say to God, Do not condemn me") and desire for understanding ("let me know why you contend against me," Job 10:2), the thrust of the petition is antagonistic and accusatory:

> Does it seem good to you to oppress,
> to despise the work of your hands
> and favor the designs of the wicked?
> Have you eyes of flesh?
> Do you see as man sees?
> Are your days as the days of man,
> or your years as a man's years,
> that you seek out my iniquity
> and search for my sin,
> although you know that I am not guilty,
> and there is none to deliver out of your hand?
> Your hands fashioned and made me,
> and now you have destroyed me altogether.
> Remember that you have made me like clay;
> and will you return me to the dust?
> Did you not pour me out like milk
> and curdle me like cheese? (Job 10:3–10)

With these five questions Job indicts God's workings in the world and personal care (or lack thereof) of Job. The first question is "Does it seem good to you to oppress?" (Job 10:3). More pointedly, why does God seem "to despise" someone whom he has seemingly crafted to follow his ways ("the work of your hands") but to reward someone who disregards his laws ("and favor the designs of the wicked," v. 3)? It is one thing to say that God "makes his sun rise on the evil and on the good, and sends rain on the just and on the unjust" (Matt. 5:45), but why, in Job's case, is the sovereign Lord sending him only thunderstorms and the wicked only rainbows after the storm? "Job's questions," Kelly Kapic comments, "express the fear experienced by many who suffer, who often interpret their experiences as God's judgment and disapproval of them."[1]

In this way, Job expresses a common concern expressed by God's people. Think of the first half of Psalm 73, where Asaph bemoans "the prosperity of the wicked" (v. 3b) with exaggerated analogies:

> For they have no pangs until death;
> their bodies are fat and sleek.
> They are not in trouble as others are;
> they are not stricken like the rest of mankind.
> Therefore pride is their necklace;
> violence covers them as a garment.
> Their eyes swell out through fatness;
> their hearts overflow with follies.
> They scoff and speak with malice;
> loftily they threaten oppression.
> They set their mouths against the heavens,
> and their tongue struts through the earth.
> Therefore his people turn back to them,
> and find no fault in them.
> And they say, "How can God know?
> Is there knowledge in the Most High?"
> Behold, these are the wicked;
> always at ease, they increase in riches. (Ps. 73:4–12)

In contrast to the wicked wealthy, Asaph suffers ("all the day long I have been stricken," Ps. 73:14a) even though he has kept his intentions pure ("heart

1. Kelly M. Kapic, *Embodied Hope: A Theological Meditation on Pain and Suffering* (IVP Academic, 2017), 64.

clean") and his actions unadulterated ("washed my hands in innocence," v. 13). All his costly obedience seems to be "in vain" (v. 13a)!

Another example of this common experience is expressed in Harriet Beecher Stowe's *Uncle Tom's Cabin*, a book that dramatically depicts the widespread brutalities of slavery in the antebellum South. In perhaps the most theologically charged scene in her celebrated novel, the runaway slaves George and his wife, Eliza—along with Simeon, an old white Quaker who is assisting in their escape—learn that a party of slave traders and officers of the law are close at hand. In his anger, fear, and frustration, George thunders:

> Is God on their side? Does he see all they do? Why does he let such things happen? . . . They are rich, and healthy, and happy . . . , expecting to go to heaven; and they get along so easy in the world, and have it all their own way; [while] poor, honest, faithful Christians—Christians . . . better than they—are lying in the very dust under their feet. They buy 'em and sell 'em, and make trade of their heart's blood, and groans and tears—and God *lets* them.[2]

Asaph's perception of God's just and providential care will change only after he goes into the temple and has a renewed vision of God's wrath coming upon all wrongdoers and his compassion showering his saints. "For me it is good," the psalmist says, "to be near God; I have made the Lord God my refuge" (Ps. 73:28a). Similarly, it is only when Simeon reads and explains Psalm 73 to George that the words "breathed by the friendly old man stole like sacred music over the harassed and chafed spirit of George." George then sees the truths that "it is often those who have least of all in this life whom he chooseth for the kingdom" and that there is a coming kingdom ("If this world were all, . . . you might, indeed, ask, 'where is the Lord?'") wherein God will finally and forever establish perfect justice ("He will make all right hereafter"). He understands that he can continue to trust God through his suffering as a fugitive slave ("Put thy trust in him . . . , no matter what befalls you here").[3]

Job needs a similar renewed vision of God, which he will soon receive. But for now, he feels far from God and far from understanding the ways

2. Harriet Beecher Stowe, *Uncle Tom's Cabin*, Everyman's Library (repr., Knopf, 1994), 216. Some of the wording around the quote comes from Douglas Sean O'Donnell, *God's Lyrics: Rediscovering Worship Through Old Testament Songs* (P&R Publishing, 2010), 87, 105–6.

3. Stowe, *Uncle Tom's Cabin*, 216–17.

of God in his life. Thus, he continues with his second question: "Have you eyes of flesh?" (Job 10:4a). Put differently, "Do you see as man sees?" (v. 4b). Put less poetically and more pointedly, "God, is your perception of reality as shortsighted as that of human beings?"

This question arises because Job perceives God's actions as resembling those of a mere mortal, a human judge lacking complete knowledge of the situation. Job knows that this cannot be the case, so he supports his second question by asking his third: "Are your days as the days of man, or your years as a man's years, that you seek out my iniquity and search for my sin, although you know that I am not guilty, and there is none to deliver out of your hand?" (Job 10:5–7). Here Job is essentially accusing God of putting him in an impossible predicament. If God knows that Job is innocent (which, as the infinite God, he does), why is he actively searching for some moral flaw? What is Job to do? He cannot call on anyone but God to rescue him from God. He knows, as Eric Ortlund states, that "he cannot autonomously make a claim to righteousness on his own; he needs God to vindicate him and show him to be in the right."[4]

The fourth question follows right on the thematic tail of the third. We might paraphrase it this way: "Why, why, why? God, please tell me why!" The fuller sense of it is this: "If you meticulously created me ('Your hands fashioned and made me,' Job 10:8a), why would you hastily abolish me ('and now you have destroyed me altogether,' v. 8b)?" In Job 10:9, Job presents this point differently. He implores God to "remember" (*zakar*)! This phrasing can carry negative connotations, namely, suggesting that Job is reproaching God for being forgetful, a charge often leveled against Israel (e.g., Judg. 3:7; 1 Sam. 12:9). Or the plea for remembrance can be positive, invoking God's recollection of his promises to someone or to his people (see Gen. 8:1; 9:15; 19:29; 30:22; Ex. 2:24; 6:5). With Job's statement and question—"Remember that you have made me like clay; and will you return me to the dust?" (Job 10:9)—the connotation might be both positive and negative. Job is not holding out much hope at this time. Yet an ounce of optimism might remain. Despite being a fragile human ("you have made me like clay") destined for death ("return . . . to the dust," v. 9; cf. Eccl. 12:7), Job is hopeful that God will remember why he created this unique

4. Eric Ortlund, *Suffering Wisely and Well: The Grief of Job and the Grace of God* (Crossway, 2022), 102.

individual—someone who has honored, loved, and served him so well—and then restore him.

If the fourth question has an ounce of optimism, the fifth and final question of this section quickly drains all positivity from Job's outlook. The sense is a pause in questions, followed by an accusation:

Did you not	pour me out	like milk
and	curdle me	like cheese? (Job 10:10)

Here Job remembers that his relationship with God as of late has been sour; God has treated him like milk well past its expiration date. Some commentators take the reference to milk and curdled cheese in Job 10:10 as a veiled reference to semen and the embryo produced through sexual reproduction, which could fit thematically with the reality that Job bemoans the loss of his own offspring.[5] Whether this is the case or not, what follows takes us not to the moment of conception but to the gestation period:

> You clothed me with skin and flesh,
>   and knit me together with bones and sinews.[6]
> You have granted me life and steadfast love,
>   and your care has preserved my spirit. (Job 10:11–12)

What a picture of divine intimacy and of personal rapport! Job is no deist. His God took the time to fashion him—and everyone else—knitting each muscle and ligament and clothing human beings with billions of freckles and millions of beauty marks, something echoed later by the psalmist:

> For you formed my inward parts;
>   you knitted me together in my mother's womb.
> I praise you, for I am fearfully and wonderfully made.
> Wonderful are your works;
>   my soul knows it very well.
> My frame was not hidden from you,
> when I was being made in secret,
>   intricately woven in the depths of the earth.
> Your eyes saw my unformed substance;
> in your book were written, every one of them,

5. E.g., John E. Hartley, *The Book of Job*, NICOT (Eerdmans, 1988), 187.

6. The verb translated "knit me together" (*tesokekeni*) is used only twice in Scripture: Job 10:11 and Psalm 139:13.

the days that were formed for me,
when as yet there was none of them. (Ps. 139:13–16)

In Job 10:12, Job continues in this theologically sentimental mood: "You have granted me life and steadfast love, and your care has preserved my spirit." He pauses to praise. Like the psalmist, he acknowledges that God (not just Job's parents) has given him life and, more than that, has carefully and caringly guarded every step and breath that Job has taken. The clause "your care has preserved my spirit" is an oasis in the desert of despair for Job.

The "yet" (as the ESV renders it) that starts Job 10:13, however, sours any sentimentality. Job questions the rationale behind God's creation of him if the true intention, shrouded in secrecy and malevolence, is to inflict punishment on him: "Yet these things you hid in your heart; I know that this was your purpose." He continues:

If I sin, you watch me
and do not acquit me of my iniquity.
If I am guilty, woe to me!
If I am in the right, I cannot lift up my head,
for I am filled with disgrace
and look on my affliction.
And were my head lifted up, you would hunt me like a lion
and again work wonders against me. (Job 10:14–16)

The particle "if" (*'im*) begins both verses 14 and 15 of Job 10. The ESV also includes an implied "if" in verse 15b. This one word, used three times, introduces Job's three thoughts here. First, in verse 14, he questions why God doesn't simply forgive him if his suffering is a result of some sin. Job sees no sin. But he is not God. God can and should use his omniscience to assist Job: "If I sin, you watch me and do not acquit me of my iniquity." Second, in verse 15a, Job admits that if he has sinned ("If I am guilty"), he deserves what has been handed out ("woe to me!"). But third, if he has not sinned ("If I am in the right"), then nothing has changed—he remains disgraced; namely, as he contemplates his current condition ("look on my affliction"), he is drowning in dishonor ("I am filled with disgrace") to the point at which he is too embarrassed to hold up his head and look his friends in the eye ("I cannot lift up my head," Job 10:15). Even if he could do so ("And were my head lifted up," v. 16a), it would only make him a bigger target. He thinks God "would hunt" him "like a lion" and once "again work" his awesome power ("wonders," *pala'*) "against" him (v. 16). Both images are frightful, and both echo other scriptural language of judgment. In Hosea (5:14; 13:7–8) and Amos (3:4, 8; 5:19), God is pictured as "executing his judgment against his people as a lion rends its prey,"[7] and in Exodus 3:20, God speaks of stretching out his hand to "strike Egypt with . . . wonders" (*pala'*) in order to compel Pharaoh to release God's people.

In Job 10:17a–b, Job returns to the courtroom, where God recommences his accusations:

You	renew	your witnesses	against me
and	increase	your vexation	toward me.

Even worse, there is no order in this court. Instead of the bailiff handcuffing Job and bringing him back to his cell, God commands his army to take Job away (and perhaps do violence to him): "you bring fresh troops against me" (Job 10:17c).

At this point, some commentators believe that Job here "crosses the line by calling into question God's justice."[8] Other commentators disagree. Francis Andersen argues that if we are to read all of Job's words through the lens of God's repeated commendation of Job (Job 42:7–8), then we should not concede "that later on [after Job 2] Job weakened, and fell into sinful speech." As Andersen rightly explains: "However impious and shocking some of the statements he makes during the dialogue may seem to us, his transgression of the conventional bounds of decorous religious talk might incur the disapprobation of cautiously reverent men, but the only censure they receive from God is that Job obscured the divine purpose by talking in ignorance."[9]

Leave Me Alone (Job 10:18–22)

Like the previous section (Job 10:11–17), this final section (vv. 18–22) begins with Job's recollection of his gestation: "Why did you bring me out

7. Tremper Longman III, *Job*, Baker Commentary on the Old Testament Wisdom and Psalms (Baker Academic, 2012), 180.

8. Richard P. Belcher Jr., *Job: The Mystery of Suffering and God's Sovereignty*, Focus on the Bible (Christian Focus, 2017), 71.

9. Francis I. Andersen, *Job*, Tyndale Old Testament Commentaries 13 (InterVarsity Press, 1976), 94.

from the womb?" (v. 18). Moreover, as in Job 10:3–10, Job asks God questions. The first question is about his birth: Job again (cf. 3:11–16) wonders why God brought him into the world and wishes he had been stillborn: "Would that I had died before any eye had seen me and were as though I had not been, carried from the womb to the grave" (10:18b–19).

The second question is about his impending death: "Are not my days few?" (Job 10:20). Job's logic (the "then" in the second line below) in this section is simple: he reasons with God, saying in effect, "If I am soon to die and go to a dark place, then stop the suffering so that I can enjoy a few last moments of sunshine."

> Are not my days few?
> Then cease, and leave me alone, that I may find a little cheer
> before I go—and I shall not return—
> to the land of *darkness* and *deep shadow*,
> the land of *gloom* like thick *darkness*,
> like *deep shadow* without any order,
> where light is as thick *darkness*. (Job 10:20–22)

Job's imagery ends by shedding great light on his dark night of the soul (note the use of the language of darkness, italicized above). He has no hope in death; he has no hope in life. But he would prefer the "land of darkness" to his apartment of ash in Uz.

Lower than Low

Near the end of the previous chapter, I quoted Eric Ortlund's observation that Job 9 records "Job's absolute low point in the debate." I suggest, however, that Job 10 takes us even lower, into the deep darkness of Job's plight! If we are honest (as Job is), we all know what it is like to feel that our souls are "cast down" and that we are experiencing "turmoil within," to "[thirst] for God" as "a deer pants for flowing streams" but find him distant ("When shall I come and appear before God?"), to cry uncontrollably ("My tears have been my food day and night") and cry to God, "Why have you forgotten me?" (Ps. 42:1, 2, 5, 9). It might be crippling depression, chronic illness, or the loss of a loved one that weighs heavy on our souls; when we cry out to God for help, there is silence. We wonder: "Does God care? Has he left us to suffer alone?" The book of Job reminds us that such feelings are realities for God's people. And building on the Andersen quote above, if we take God's commendation of Job's words (that he has "spoken of me what is right," Job 42:7, 8) that God approves Job's words of confusion, despair, desolation, and even anger here in Job 9–10, then this book also reminds us that there is nothing we can say to God that God cannot handle.

Job Knows That God Can Handle His Laments

That there is nothing we can say to God that he cannot handle is the first flicker of light we are to see from Job's dark thoughts. Pastor Chuck Swindoll tells the story about his time as a student at Dallas Theological Seminary, when he and his wife became best friends with Dennis and Lucy. While there, Lucy had a little boy, "whom Dennis absolutely adored." After Dennis graduated, they moved to Los Angeles, where he earned his PhD in psychology. One day, "their little boy stumbled into a swimming pool in a neighbor's backyard and drowned." Dennis was devastated. Years later, he shared with Swindoll how he had responded afterward: "I got in my car, . . . and I grabbed that steering wheel and I drove about every freeway in Los Angeles. And during those hours I *screamed* out to God expressing all the grief and the anger and the sadness and the confusion from deep within my soul. I said things to him in that car that I'd never said before to *anybody*. I screamed it out, and it wasn't very nice. I just vomited everything out to God." Near dawn, Dennis arrived home. In the driveway, with his shirt dripping with sweat and his face soaked wet from giant heaves, he rested his head on the wheel and was comforted with the thought: "God can handle it! He can handle everything I said."[10]

Do we believe that God can handle our words of distress? Do we believe (to plant this truth in biblical and Christological soil) that, like our Lord Jesus, our souls can be "very sorrowful" (Matt. 26:38)—so sorrowful that we can offer "loud cries and tears" (Heb. 5:7; "Jesus cried out with a loud voice," Matt. 27:46a) as we ask God to withdraw suffering ("My Father, if it be possible, let this cup pass from me; nevertheless, not as I will, but as you will," 26:39) and beg for his presence and comfort ("My God, my God, why have you forsaken me?," 27:46)? As C. J. Williams rightly asserts: in Jesus,

10. Charles R. Swindoll, *Job: A Man of Heroic Endurance* (Word, 2004), 71.

as with his followers, "there is no conflict between faithful submission and the honest expression of human anguish."[11]

Williams also says: "The Bible always shows us the human side of the heroes of faith. Job is not a superhuman example of perfect patience frozen in time. He is flesh and blood, susceptible to passion and confusion."[12] When we pray, therefore, we should pray with passion, expressing our emotions sincerely. Even when we feel perplexed or uncertain, we should remember that God can handle both the prayer that praises his providential rule ("The LORD gave, and the LORD has taken away; blessed be the name of the LORD," Job 1:21) and the prayer that questions it ("Why is light given to him who is in misery, and life to the bitter in soul?," 3:20). God can handle it! He can receive accusations such as "the arrows of the Almighty are in me; my spirit drinks their poison; the terrors of God are arrayed against me" (6:4) and "Why do you hide your face and count me as your enemy?" (13:24). He can take complaints such as "Oh that I might have my request, and that God would fulfill my hope [to die], that it would please God to crush me, that he would let loose his hand and cut me off!" (6:8–9) and "Though he slay me, I will hope in him; yet I will argue my ways to his face" (13:15).[13] God can handle it!

Job Still Holds Fast His Integrity

The second flicker of light we see glimmering from Job's dark thoughts is that he maintains his personal integrity. After the first wave of trials, the Lord said of Job to Satan, "He still holds fast his integrity, although you incited me against him to destroy him without reason" (Job 2:3). In context, Job's integrity would include resisting the temptation to curse God, as earlier recommended by his wife: "Do you still hold fast your integrity? Curse God and die" (v. 9). But it would also include resisting "the desires of the flesh" (1 John 2:16), as the apostle John phrases it. It is not uncommon for Christians, especially men, who experience painful suffering or great loss to turn to drunkenness or sexual immorality for some "relief," "to forget the pain," or as a subtle protest against God's bitter providence. They might not curse God to his face, but they do not fear God by turning away from evil. Job refuses to do this. God is silent, and seems so distant that he cannot see.

11. C. J. Williams, *The Shadow of Christ in the Book of Job* (Wipf & Stock, 2017), 40.

12. Williams, 40.

13. "Job does not hold back in any of his speeches (see 16:6), and the Joban poet does not censor or mute or 'pretty up' any of Job's criticisms of God." Ortlund, *Suffering Wisely and Well*, 100.

Yet Job remains blameless and upright. As he will later say, "Till I die I will not put away my integrity from me" (Job 27:5)—a consistent faithfulness that he hopes God both sees and will soon acknowledge ("let God know my integrity!," 31:6). Let us be known for such integrity as well. When we experience severe sufferings, let us guard our thoughts, words, and actions.

Job Sticks with God

The third flicker of light to see from Job's dark thoughts is that he sticks with God, not only here but till the end. "In the midst of his darkness," Roland de Pury points out, Job refuses to "flee to some better kind of God," but stays close to "the very God who is crushing him."[14] Even though he feels that the Lord has abandoned him, Job refuses to abandon the Lord. As Bill Kynes says of him:

> He never gives up his desire to hear from God, to meet with God, and to be vindicated by God. Though Job is arguing with his friends, his real audience throughout this dispute is God. In speech after speech, after dispensing with the friends' arguments, he turns his attention back to God. He continues to seek him, to confront him, to pray to him. It is very clear throughout the book that Job's deepest longing is not the restoration of his prosperity but the restoration of his relationship with God.[15]

Amen! As much as Job is suffering physically, his deepest pain—expressed over and over in his responses—is that he is "suffering under a broken relationship with God and bereft of his friendship."[16] Christopher Ash labels this desire as "a passionate longing," and speaks of how Job "longs above all the longings of the human heart to be in the presence of God" and "to speak to God face-to-face." Because of his love for God, Job declares repeatedly: "I want to meet God. I want to be right with God. I want to be reconciled to God. I want to be justified, vindicated, seen to be right with God."[17]

Job's desires and his faithful resilience are models for us in times of deep sorrow and inexplicable pain. Ash recounts the story of the famous Bible

14. Roland de Pury, *Hiob—der Mensch im Aufruher* (Neukirchener, 1957), 23, quoted in Bill Kynes and Will Kynes, *Wrestling with God: Defiant Faith in the Face of Suffering* (IVP Academic, 2022), 102.

15. Kynes and Kynes, *Wrestling with God*, 84.

16. Ortlund, *Suffering Wisely and Well*, 101.

17. Christopher Ash, *Trusting God in the Darkness: A Guide to Understanding the Book of Job* (Crossway, 2021), 66–67.

translator J. B. Phillips. When he was five, Phillips's mother was diagnosed with cancer, and for ten years "she suffered terribly" until she died. Because his childhood was consumed with watching her waste away month by month and year by year, "he said of that time, 'I gave up my religious faith utterly, for what use was prayer and talk of the love of God when I returned daily to this horrible caricature of the sprightly, witty mother I had known and loved?'"[18] Of course, later in life Phillips would return to God and dedicate his life to service for Christ. But some professing Christians never recover. One churchgoing couple I know lost their two-year-old child and shortly thereafter walked away from faith in God. That is not uncommon. Excruciating traumas can easily lead to easy exits. But in the trials, and through such harrowing events, we must not retreat from wrestling with God in prayer, finding his comfort through his people, and worshiping the one who gives and takes away.

God Sticks with Job

The first flicker of light to see from Job's dark thoughts encourages us to pray honest laments to God, knowing that God can handle it! The second is that Job maintains his personal integrity. The third is that he sticks with God, not only here but till the end. The fourth is that God sticks with Job.

While we pity Job's lack of knowledge, we should not overlook aspects of his theological and experiential shortsightedness. Not everything he does and says is a model for us to emulate. When we undergo adversity, like Job we should admit and even admire God's total sovereignty. We should also, as noted above, pray honestly and forthrightly about our needs. We can even question God (Job 10:3–10; cf. esp. Ps. 77:7–9).

That said, we must be careful not to place God in the dock, expecting him to answer our every question. We certainly should not accuse God of injustice, for he embodies and defines perfect justice and defines it (see God's rebuke, Job 40:8). Like Job, we are prone to oversimplify our situation in light of God's power. Like Job, we find it easy to question God's justice when our agonies make his will for us seem so unfair. We must strive, however, as Job previously taught us (2:10), to "be content to receive bad as well as good from God,"[19] even if it appears through our agonies that all that we

18. Ash, 67, quoting Gaius Davies, *Genius, Grief, and Grace: A Doctor Looks at Suffering and Success* (Christian Focus, 2001), 313–14.

19. John Goldingay, *Job for Everyone*, Old Testament for Everyone (Westminster John Knox, 2013), 55.

are experiencing is bad. (As fallen humans living in a fallen world, we know that fallen things happen!)

We should also keep in mind that God still loves us in the silence and is consistently molding us into the image of his Son, "a son" who "learned obedience through what he suffered" (Heb. 5:8). Put differently, God sticks with Job throughout Job's sufferings and throughout his laments, accusations, confessions, and questions. Job asks God to "look on [his] affliction" (Job 10:15)—something that God has been doing and will do, in providing a remedy for his sufferings. Let us be thankful that because God has looked upon Christ's afflictions for us, we know that he loves us through every test, trial, and tragedy and will, by the Spirit's power, help us endure till the end.

11

Zophar: God Exacts of You What Your Guilt Deserves

Job 11:1–20

Should a multitude of words go unanswered, and
a man full of talk be judged right? (Job 11:2)

Type "Christian bumper stickers" into Amazon.com and see what you get. Here are a few top-selling stickers from the list in 2024:

- Save Gas: Walk with Jesus
- I Stand at the Anthem and Kneel for the Cross
- Real Men Love Jesus
- She Who Kneels Before God Can Stand Before Anyone
- Do You Follow Jesus This Closely?
- It's Not a Religion, It's a Relationship

Of course, Zophar the Naamathite (Job 11:1)[1] would not understand the allusions to gas prices, American nationalism as it relates to professional

1. "Zophar is from Naamah, which is the name of a woman listed in the genealogy of Cain (Gen. 4:22), from whom the Kenites were descendants (Gen. 4:22). The Kenites are also mentioned in connection with the Midianites in the Sinai and Arabian deserts (Num. 10:29; Judg. 4:11)." Kenneth Laing Harris and August Konkel, "Job," in *ESV Study Bible* (Crossway, 2008), note on Job 2:11.

sports, Christ's death on the cross, or, for that matter, bumper stickers on automobiles. Given his poem on God's transcendent otherness, he would see all such slogans as trite, especially the last one. Yet he does, ironically enough, have a slogan of his own that he slaps all over poor Job: God Exacts of You What Your Guilt Deserves.

Before we get to that slap, notice Zophar's role in the drama of the book of Job. "Zophar the Naamathite" has not only an interesting name, but a unique role. He is the last of the three friends to speak and speaks only twice. He remains silent, for some reason,[2] after Job's ninth speech, thus breaking the pattern of Job 3–31:

- Job/Eliphaz
- Job/Bildad
- Job/Zophar
- Job/Eliphaz
- Job/Bildad
- Job/Zophar
- Job/Eliphaz
- Job/Bildad
- Job/[_____]

Zophar's speech in Job 11 is short, sharp, and straightforward. It is *short*, only 110 words, but is not as short as one might imagine, given his rebuke to Job ("Should a multitude of words go unanswered?," Job 11:2a). It is also *sharp*. Zophar certainly shows more intense indignation than his two friends, and thus wastes no time cutting into Job's character,[3] calling him a "man full of talk" (v. 2b) and in a backhanded way a "stupid man" (v. 12) who belongs to "worthless men" (v. 11). He also claims that Job has deserved what has come to him, and what will be coming to him (righteous judgment: "Should . . . a man full of talk be judged right?," v. 2b) if he does not repent (vv. 14, 20). Finally, his speech is *straightforward*: like Eliphaz and Bildad, he holds strictly to the retribution principle. This formula is logical to him:

2. "Ironically [see Job 11:2], in the third cycle of speeches, it is Zophar who is reduced to silence and who does not participate in the final round in chapter 27." Daniel J. Estes, *Job*, Teach the Text (Baker, 2013), 69.

3. "Zophar has heard Job talk about God in ways that are horrifying to him. . . . It is no wonder that Zophar is ready to burst with righteous indignation at this foul blasphemer." John C. Holbert, *Preaching Job*, Preaching Classic Texts (Chalice, 1999), 50.

Sin = [it will always cause] Suffering
Job + He Is Suffering = Job Must Have Sinned

In his three-point sermon, Zophar works out the logic. First, in verses 1–6 of Job 11, he assumes that the "equation" above is true: "God exacts of you [what] your guilt deserves" (Job 11:6c) is his bumper-sticker theology. Second, in verses 7–12, he holds out the wisdom of God, hoping that in light of such wisdom, Job will recognize his folly. Third, if Job will do so, Zophar claims in verses 13–20 that all will be restored (e.g., "your life will be brighter than the noonday," v. 17a). If Job will not repent, however, the fate awaiting him will be worse than going to the "land of darkness" (10:21): death or Zophar's version of hell.

An Exacting God (Job 11:1–6)

Zophar first states that God is an exacting God. After Job's long response to Bildad (Job 9 *and* 10), Zophar pounces on this "man full of talk," who uses "a multitude of words" (11:2). Coming from Israel's wisdom tradition, which was based on both direct divine revelation and careful analysis of life (including the wisdom traditions of other nations around Israel), this is an excellent angle of attack. For if Proverbs 10:19, or some similar ancient and accepted proverbs,[4] is true ("When words are many, transgression is not lacking") always and in general,[5] then Job has already transgressed. With two accusing questions that center on Job's words, Zophar seeks to silence (and answer—"answered," Job 11:1; "unanswered," v. 2; *'anah*) sinful Job: "Should a multitude of words go unanswered, and a man *full of talk* be judged right? Should *your babble* silence men, and when *you mock*, shall no one shame you?" (vv. 2–3).

Notice that three word-related sins are mentioned. First, Job is long-winded ("a multitude of words," paralleled with "full of talk," Job 11:2). Second, he has tried to "silence" good "men" (i.e., Eliphaz and Bildad) with proud claims ("babble," *bad*, v. 3a; elsewhere translated "boasting," Isa. 16:6; cf. Jer. 48:30).

4. See Prov. 12:18; 17:27; Eccl. 5:2, 3, 7; 6:11; 10:14.

5. "In classic wisdom teaching, the sage is the one who speaks *few* words, choosing them carefully and using them to good effect. The hot-headed fool speaks voluminously without thinking, and he often gets into trouble as a result." Gerald H. Wilson, *Job*, Understanding the Bible Commentary 10 (Baker, 2007), 112.

Third, he has ridiculed them with his empty rhetoric: "Should your babble silence men, and when you mock, shall no one shame you?" (Job 11:3).

Zophar is intervening now to tame such a tongue, answer Job's accusations, and make sure he is aware of his sins and shamed for them. In verses 4–6 of Job 11, Zophar presents himself as a prophet, who introduces God and God's point of view on Job's dilemma:[6]

> For you say, "My doctrine is pure,
> and I am clean in God's eyes."
> But oh, that God would speak
> and open his lips to you,
> and that he would tell you the secrets of wisdom!
> For he is manifold in understanding.
> Know then that God exacts of you less than your guilt deserves.

If Job would only be quiet and let God speak ("But oh, that God would speak and open his lips," Job 11:5), God would reveal "the secrets of wisdom," something of his "manifold . . . understanding," a word that would render the punishment that Job has endured a light sentence in view of his heavy sins ("Know then that God exacts of you less than your guilt deserves," v. 6). Or, as the NLT phrases this terribly unfair decree: "God is doubtless punishing you far less than you deserve!" Ouch! Zophar offers no such solace here. Instead, his unsympathetic systematics prevail. He gives Job the rough draft of his short theological tract (soon to be a bumper sticker), "God Exacts of You What Your Guilt Deserves." Zophar uses his unwise words on God's wisdom to expose Job's obvious folly—that guilt is oozing out of his mouth. Not only are Zophar's words unwise, but they are arrogant and hypocritical. For who "deputized him to relay the mysteries [of God] to the world"?[7] Moreover, how does he know what God will say, and by the logic of his own argument, how can he claim to know anything about God?

There are two problems with Zophar's then (and now!) popular and made-to-stick slogan. First, Zophar's zinger zigs and zags far off course. His retribution theology, along with the "strict deductive logic he uses to evaluate Job's situation,"[8] misses the mark. Job does *not* deserve what has

6. God is the central figure underlying all of Zophar's points in every verse of Job 11:4–20.

7. Holbert, *Preaching Job*, 53.

8. Estes, *Job*, 68. "By taking the retribution principle to its logical conclusion, Zophar insists that

happened to him. And for Zophar to suggest to his old friend that God has been lenient is not only incorrect but cruel. Moreover (and ironically!), "in some sense Zophar is proven right: There is a hidden wisdom, to which Job is not (yet) privy (cf. 1 Cor. 2:7). The irony, of course, lies in the fact that when Yahweh finally does speak according to Zophar's desire ([Job] 11:5), nothing is said of Job's guilt (11:6c)."[9]

Second, Zophar is mistaken in his accusation. Job never claimed to be "clean" (*bar*) in the sense of morally pure or sinless; he only claimed to be "blameless" (*tam*),[10] something that God himself has boasted of his servant (see Job 1:8; 2:3; cf. 1:1). At this point, we are not told what Job thinks or how he feels, but we know from his immediate reaction that he is upset ("No doubt you are the people, and wisdom will die with you," 12:2) and also that he feels misunderstood and mocked. Even though Job is "a blameless and upright" man (1:1, 8; 2:3), he is viewed as "a laughingstock" by his "friends" (12:4). Imagine the psychological pain.

In studying this section of Job, I turned to chapter 11 in Christopher Ash's commentary, which I thought covered Job 11. I was surprised by Ash's introduction, because I thought it didn't relate to the text (I was looking in the wrong chapter!). But when he answered the question "Why are we, as readers, told what is going on behind the scenes?" stating, "First, we gain from the sufferings of Job a deep insight into the sufferings of Christ,"[11] I thought, "Yes, what an excellent insight!" As Ash went on to talk about the "experience of God-forsakenness," my mind wandered to Christ's mockeries in the passion narrative, specifically what the Roman battalion did to him in the governor's headquarters before the crucifixion. After pointing out that they undressed and brutally beat Jesus (he was "scourged," Matt. 27:26), Matthew uses a chiastic structure to paint the paradox, namely, that their acknowledgment of Jesus as King and their adoration of him as a suffering Sovereign is precisely how disciples should react to the passion and death of Jesus.[12] The text reads:

---

suffering necessarily proceeds from sin" (68).

9. J. Gerald Janzen, *Job*, Interpretation: A Bible Commentary for Teaching and Preaching (John Knox, 1985), 100.

10. By substituting *bar* for *tam*, Zophar exaggerates Job's claim and "renders a portrayal of him that is inaccurate, careless, and even cruel." Estes, *Job*, 69. Even Job's later claim "my prayer is pure" (Job 16:17) "is hardly the same thing as claiming that he is pure." Holbert, *Preaching Job*, 52.

11. Christopher Ash, *Job: The Wisdom of the Cross*, Preaching the Word (Crossway, 2014), 159.

12. Part of this paragraph is from Douglas Sean O'Donnell, "Matthew," available at https://www

27 Then *the soldiers* of the governor *took Jesus into* the governor's headquarters, and they gathered the whole battalion before him.
28 And *they stripped him* and *put a scarlet robe on him*,
29a and twisting together a crown of thorns, they put it on his *head* and put a *reed* in his right hand.
29b And **kneeling before him**, they mocked him, saying, **"Hail, King of the Jews!"**
30 And they spit on him and took the *reed* and struck him on the *head*.
31a And when they had mocked him, *they stripped him* of the robe and *put his own clothes on him*
31b and [*the soldiers*] *led him away to* crucify him.

Like this moment in the passion of the Christ, the passion of Job in Job 11 features the mockery of an innocent man by misunderstanding men. But unlike Christ—who here and later at his trial and on the cross—could have used his divine power to judge his enemies (see Matt. 26:53; John 19:11), Job is absolutely powerless. This is why he will later say to his friends, "Bear with me, and I will speak, and after I have spoken, mock on" (Job 21:3). Here, in Job 11, with only fourteen verses left in Zophar's short sermon, Job will have to endure the accusation that he is not only foolish ("a stupid man," 11:12) but a "wicked" man, whose only "way of escape" is "lost" and whose only "hope" is death ("to breathe" his "last" breath, v. 20).

A Wise God (Job 11:7–12)

In Job 11:7–12, Zophar mocks on and moves on. He moves from distorting Job's words (Job 11:1–6) to employing a beautiful poem on the wisdom of God in an ugly way. Instead of using the theme of God's wisdom like a *window* that Job can open and see through to better understand God, he uses it like a *mirror* so that Job might see his smallness and insignificance as well as his gross deformities. Adding a few answers to Zophar's rhetorical questions in verses 7–9 demonstrates the point:

.thegospelcoalition.org/commentary/matthew/#section-76. "If the soldiers' appalling attitudes are removed from their actual actions—'the parody of the wreath of thorns as golden garland, a soldier's cloak as royal robe, a reed as scepter, and the adulation due Caesar conferred upon Christ'—they model the proper reaction to King Jesus." See Douglas Sean O'Donnell, *Matthew: All Authority in Heaven and on Earth*, Preaching the Word (Crossway, 2013), 852.

> Can you find out the deep things of God? [No!]
> Can you find out the limit of the Almighty? [Of course not!]
> It is higher than heaven—what can you do? [Nothing!]
> Deeper than Sheol—what can you know? [Nothing!]
> Its measure is longer than the earth
> and broader than the sea. (Job 11:7–9)

The repetition of the first-person personal pronoun "you" and the verb "can" in English ("can you," 4×) showcases that Zophar is giving Job a personal talking-to—a theological talking-*down*-to! Using a series of four questions, Zophar zings Job with the "profundity and sublimity of God," describing "God as someone who is too high, too deep, too long, and too wide to grasp," as "higher than the highest place imaginable (heaven), deeper than the deepest place (Sheol), longer than the longest place (the earth), and wider than the widest place (the sea)."[13] Of course, Job already knows what he can and cannot do. He cannot contend with God (Job 9:3) or understand all his ways (vv. 11–12). He also knows that God alone is the all-wise and almighty Creator (v. 4), "who alone stretched out the heavens" (v. 8) and can remove mountains and command the sun to rise (vv. 5–7). He knows that God "does great things beyond searching out, and marvelous things beyond number" (v. 10). He would readily embrace the Pauline doxology of Romans 11:33–36. What he will not embrace, however, is reported "wisdom" on the wisdom of God from fools: "No doubt you are the people, and wisdom will die with you" (Job 12:2).

Zophar concludes his belittling poem to Job on the greatness of God with two final rhetorical questions:

> If he passes through and imprisons
> and summons the court, who can turn him back?
> For he knows worthless men;
> when he sees iniquity, will he not consider it? (Job 11:10–11)

His description of God moves from metaphors depicting God as Creator to metaphors about him as Judge. Perhaps playing off Job's legal language in chapter 9, where he begged for a hearing before God, his "judge" (Job 9:15), so as to vindicate himself (vv. 14–20), Zophar envisions in Job 11:10–11 God's

13. Tremper Longman III, *Job*, Baker Commentary on the Old Testament Wisdom and Psalms (Baker Academic, 2012), 187–88. "The transcendent infinity of God contrasts with the finite character of the world in its fourfold dimensionality: height, depth, length, breadth." Janzen, *Job*, 98.

coming to earth ("he passes through"), tossing Job in jail ("and imprisons"), and holding a trial ("summons the court," 11:10). Job has no option; he must attend, as must everyone else who is summoned ("who can turn him back?," v. 10b). Once court is in session, Zophar reminds Job that God is not dumb. He knows the difference between a good man and a wicked one ("he knows worthless men"), between an evil action ("he sees iniquity," v. 11) and a righteous one. Job's appearance in court will be his downfall! He will be declared guilty.

Zophar follows this scene with a shrouded insult, in which it is clear even to us (and Job!) that Job is the target of his taunt: "But a stupid man will get understanding when a wild donkey's colt is born a man!" (Job 11:12). The point of this clever but cruel proverb is that it is more probable that a wild donkey would give birth to a full-grown man than that the "incorrigible idiot"[14] Job would apply the wisdom of Zophar's brilliant sermon.

A Rewarding God (Job 11:13–20)

With Job 11:12, Zophar is trying to shame (and even bully!) Job into turning away from his sin. With verses 13–20, he is trying to woo (Job 11:15–19) and warn (v. 20) him to the winning side. With a few conditional particles ("if," vv. 13–14) and temporal particles ("then," v. 15), and now turning from the third person to the second person, Zophar implores Job directly to repent. The call is seemingly loving and the imagery certainly inspiring: "If you prepare your heart, you will stretch out your hands toward him. If iniquity is in your hand, put it far away, and let not injustice dwell in your tents" (vv. 13–14). According to Derek Thomas, Zophar suggests that the possible "iniquity," and thus cause for Job's demise, is that "Job's wealth had been acquired by extortion."[15]

Here repentance involves four actions. Inwardly, Job is to set his mind on God ("prepare your heart," Job 11:13a). Outwardly, he is to acknowledge God as God and reach out to him for mercy ("stretch out your hands toward him," v. 13b; cf. 1 Kings 8:38//2 Chron. 6:29).[16] Personally, he is to stop sinning ("If

14. Estes, *Job*, 69.

15. Derek Thomas, *The Storm Breaks: Job Simply Explained*, Welwyn Commentary Series (repr., Evangelical Press, 2005), 117.

16. "To stretch out his hands to God" is "a gesture of submission and supplication—like persons drowning at sea who stretch out their hands eagerly to those who would draw them into the safety of the lifeboat." Wilson, *Job*, 119.

iniquity is in your hand, put it far away," Job 11:14a). Publicly, he is to deal justly and lovingly with his household, friends, and neighbors ("let not injustice dwell in your tents," v. 14b).

Zophar's counsel is clear and his promises sure. If Job repents, restoration will follow:

> Surely then you will lift up your face without blemish;
>   you will be secure and will not fear.
> You will forget your misery;
>   you will remember it as waters that have passed away.
> And your life will be brighter than the noonday;
>   its darkness will be like the morning. (Job 11:15–17)

Such restoration is described in terms that would be to Job's liking. He has been asking God not for renewed wealth or health but to pull him out of the darkness of despair. As he proved in Job 1:20–21 and 2:10, Job can live without his wealth and health. What he cannot live without is being in a right relationship with God. That relationship seems severed because God has been silent about Job's sufferings. So Zophar's words here are "tempting," if we can put it that way, because Job longs for what Zophar offers. Job wants to be unashamed ("Surely . . . you will lift up your face without blemish"),[17] safe, and without fear (Job 11:15). He wants to "forget" his "misery," as one forgets a wave that has crashed to shore ("you will remember it as waters that have passed away," v. 16). He wants light, not darkness: "And your life will be brighter than the noonday; its darkness will be like the morning" (v. 17; cf. 10:21–22). He wants the security and safety that comes from hope, as well as the prestige that comes from being recognized as wise: "And you will feel secure, because there is hope; you will look around and take your rest in security. You will lie down, and none will make you afraid; many will court your favor" (11:18–19). If Job repents, the rest he longs for (see 3:26; 7:4) will be granted and hope, which eludes him (see 6:11–13; 7:6), restored.

Having attempted to woo Job with the promises of restoration that come with repentance, Zophar concludes by warning him of the condemnation

17. The phrase "without blemish" (Job 11:15) might refer to the scars and scabs on Job's face, or it might be a metaphor for being unashamed or having a clear conscience. Job's suffering had brought him so low that he was unrecognizable even to his friends. In their sympathy, his friends raised (*nś'*) their voices and mourned to heaven on Job's behalf, but here Zophar refers to a day when Job may yet lift (*nś'*) his own face again.

to come following a lack of repentance. Moving from the second person directly addressing Job ("you," used twenty times above), the final verse uses the third person. This general principle is true not just for Job but for everyone else: "But the eyes of the wicked will fail; all way of escape will be lost to them, and their hope is to breathe their last" (Job 11:20). Unlike Eliphaz (5:25–27) and Bildad (8:20–22), but like Job (10:20–22), Zophar ends on a sour note. He is holding out hope for Job, but wants to make clear that there is no hope for the wicked. If Job refuses to heed his word, he will "die without hope, in black despair."[18]

Two Ways to Avoid Zophar's Bad Behavior

What are we to do with Zophar's short sermon? What Zophar has said about God is good and right, but what he says about God *to Job* is wrong and evil. Job was his punching bag, and solid theology his gloves. Truths about God should be used to teach, not taunt. The Bible should be used to build up, not bully or belittle. That said, if we remove the situation and take in the theology, Zophar has something to teach the church today. Before I highlight a few truths that we can glean from him, however, I start with two ways in which we should avoid his bad behavior.

Have a Better Bedside Manner

First, we should have a better bedside manner. As David Allen observes: "Zophar's bedside manner leaves something to be desired. It is a wonder Job did not throw him out of the hospital room!"[19] Changing metaphors, Allen states that Zophar approached Job "like a telemarketer," in that he was "insensitive, brusque, and [wouldn't] take no for an answer" and that he left the "same message the previous two friends" did.[20] Daniel Estes compares Zophar to Inspector Javert in Victor Hugo's *Les Misérables*, who unremittingly pursues the protagonist, Jean Valjean, a former criminal who is now a good man. "In Javert's obsession with duty at the expense of compassion, he becomes a maniacal, avenging force. Like Zophar, he does not take into

18. John Gill, "An Exposition of the Old Testament," in *ESV Church History Study Bible: Voices from the Past, Wisdom for the Present* (Crossway, 2023), 718.

19. David L. Allen, *Exalting Jesus in Job*, Christ-Centered Exposition (Holman Reference, 2022), 85.

20. Allen, 83.

account the circumstances of the person he hunts."[21] Francis Andersen, in my favorite summary and statement about Zophar, compares him to flat beer:

> There is not a breath of compassion in his speech. It is true that in Job's *multitude of words* so far there have been elements of impatience and exaggeration. Job will later regret this (42:6). But that is an apology to God, not men. Job has no obligation to keep to the prim conventions of pious talk just to satisfy people like Zophar. Zophar's cold disapproval shows how little he has heard Job's heart. His censorious chiding shows how little he has sensed Job's hurt. Job's bewilderment and his outbursts are natural; in them we find his humanity, and our own. Zophar detached the words from the man, and hears them only as *babble* and mockery (verse 2). This is quite unfair. Zophar's wisdom is a bloodless retreat into theory. It is very proper, theologically familiar and unobjectionable. But it is flat beer compared with Job's seismic sincerity.[22]

Whether we compare Zophar to flat beer, a neurotic policeman, an annoying telemarketer, or a heartless doctor, we should take his impersonal and unempathetic behavior as the opposite of the example of how to serve friends in great need. People in such a position do not need theological jargon mixed with preconceived dogmatics, abstract reasoning, and snide sarcasm, along with the offer of an "erroneous prescription" for a misconstrued ailment.[23] They need someone who sympathizes, listens, takes seriously their expressions of their sufferings, offers comfort, and prays for them.

Have a Place for Grace

Second, we should emphasize the gospel, the message of God's grace. In the *Knowing the Bible* study booklets—which cover all the books of the Bible—the authors are tasked with connecting the sections of Scripture that they are covering with the gospel (called "Gospel Glimpses"). Eric Ortlund's gospel-glimpse lesson on Job 4:1–14:22 is labeled "Gospel Failure." Ortlund writes:

> Job's friends display a theology of strict merit: God dispenses suffering to sinners, but repentance qualifies you for God's mercy (contrast Rom. 5:6–8).

21. Estes, *Job*, 73.

22. Francis I. Andersen, *Job*, Tyndale Old Testament Commentaries 13 (InterVarsity Press, 1976), 156.

23. See Estes, *Job*, 68.

> This prevents them from considering the possibility that God might treat a sinner better than he deserves. And just as they do not have a category for grace in their relationship with God, so are they utterly ungracious with Job, telling him that all of his suffering is justly deserved (Job 8:2–3)—or maybe is even *less* than he deserves (11:6).[24]

Let us avoid making the same mistake. Let us have as a major category in our relationship with God a place for grace, and let us extend that grace to others. What is more, let us rejoice in the truth that God treats sinners like us better than we deserve.

Applying Good Theology Used Badly for Our Good

In the first paragraph on his first of three sermons on Job 11, John Calvin begins:

> The points which are made here are true in themselves despite the fact that they are poorly applied to the person of Job. Consequently, we have instruction that is valid and useful, provided we have the wisdom and discretion to determine how to use it right. In brief, we are shown here that if we consider how man is able to stand before God, we must not demonstrate how clever we are with language, thinking that we will win our cause with empty rhetoric, but we must acknowledge God's majesty and be humble and astonished by it. To do this, we must realise it is impossible for us to inquire into that wisdom which we cannot understand but which everybody must bow and yield to.[25]

So how do we use Zophar's counsel rightly? We start where Calvin does.

Have a High View of God

It is usually a recipe for disaster to take what is said within a specific historical context in the Bible out of context and apply it to our situation or the situation of our hearers. Yet some of what Job's friends said about God—if taken out of the context of their falsely accusing Job—is theologically brilliant. Like that of the other friends, Zophar's theology is God-saturated and God-centered, and some of what he says is like a nugget of gold found

24. Eric Ortlund, *Job: A 12-Week Study*, Knowing the Bible (Crossway, 2017), 32.

25. John Calvin, *Sermons on Job*, vol. 1, *Chapters 1–14*, trans. Rob Roy McGregor (Banner of Truth, 2022), 511.

in a pile of rubble, and can be used (out of context!) to turn our eyes heavenward—to the infinite God and his mysterious workings.

God is, as Zophar preaches, "manifold in understanding" (Job 11:6), and we cannot (nor can righteous Job) "find out the deep things of God" or "find out the limit of the Almighty" (v. 7). Job will learn as much when God speaks to him later; we should learn it even now. When reading Job 11:7–9, we must understand that we cannot fully grasp the incomprehensible wisdom of God, and we should quietly say, "Amen, preach it!" Moreover, we should pray with hands raised in awe of God and then pause in prayer and shout out, as Paul did:

> Oh, the depth of the riches and wisdom and knowledge of God! How unsearchable are his judgments and how inscrutable his ways!
>
> "For who has known the mind of the Lord,
>   or who has been his counselor?"
> "Or who has given a gift to him
>   that he might be repaid?"
>
> For from him and through him and to him are all things. To him be glory forever. Amen. (Rom. 11:33–36)

Repent and Seek God's Mercy

In counseling Job to "prepare [his] heart" and "stretch out [his] hands toward" God (Job 11:13) by removing "iniquity" from his "hand" and "injustice" from his "tents" (v. 14), Zophar offers the right counsel on repentance and restoration to the wrong person. Job is innocent; he doesn't need to purify his heart ("[make] thine heart pure," LXX) and clean his hands ("Scrub your hands of sin") and household ("and refuse to entertain evil in your home," MSG). But whenever we do need to purify ourselves (we are not so innocent so often!), what excellent advice! When we sin, we should be so "cut to the heart" (Acts 2:37) that we turn from sin and turn to God.

Yes, admittedly (and it is hard to admit), we can learn from Zophar's theology of repentance. We are not Job, and certainly not Jesus. Thus, we should follow the *first* of Martin Luther's Ninety-Five Theses, "When our Lord and Master, Jesus Christ, said, 'Repent,' he called for the entire life of believers to be one of repentance." Even more importantly, we should pray daily, "Forgive us our debts" (Matt. 6:12), as Jesus taught us to pray, and we should seek to do so with our hearts in the right place, our hands stretched out to heaven, and our lives walking in step with the Spirit and in accord with Christ's commands, believing that repentance brings restoration and that holiness usually leads to happiness, and sometimes renewed health.

Extol the Immanence of Our Transcendent God

In his groundbreaking book *Preaching Christ from the Old Testament*,[26] Sidney Greidanus has taught a generation of pastors seven ways in which one can legitimately move from every genre found in the Old Testament to Christ in the New Testament: redemptive-historical progression, promise-fulfillment, typology, analogy, longitudinal themes, New Testament reference, and contrast. In some of the applications above, we have used what Greidanus calls "contrast" to show the dissimilarity between Zophar's counsel and the teaching of Jesus. A final application of Zophar's words would fall into the categories of both contrast and redemptive-historical progression.

The most foundational and important truth of the New Testament is that the transcendent God, whom Zophar rightly extols, became a man and dwelt on earth among us. Thus, the last application is that we should extol the immanence of our transcendent God. Put differently and more specifically, we should rejoice that the divine *Logos*, through whom everything in creation was made (John 1:1–3; Col. 1:16), "became flesh and dwelt among us" (John 1:14); we should celebrate that "Immanuel (which means, God with us)" lived and died for us (he saved "his people from their sins," Matt. 1:21, 23; cf. Col. 1:20). We should long for the time when Christ returns and God forever dwells in the midst of his people.

26. Sidney Greidanus, *Preaching Christ from the Old Testament: A Contemporary Hermeneutical Method* (Eerdmans, 1999).

12

Job: Hope for God's Vindication?

Job 12:1–14:22

All the days of my service I would wait, till my renewal should come. (Job 14:14)

There is a movie genre—somewhere under the "action" category, and featuring stars such as Jackie Chan, Sylvester Stallone, Arnold Schwarzenegger, and Clint Eastwood—in which the hero remarkably defeats wave after wave of fearsome enemies. Job faces only three men, supposed "friends," not enemies, and yet as readers, we feel that same intensity and suspense as we read his responses to their attacks. Will the hero survive? How will he continue to defend himself? Who will win?

Job 12–14 records the conclusion of the first cycle (Job 4:1–14:22). This is Job's third reply to his friends ("Then Job answered and said," 12:1) but not the end of the war of words between friends. Another barrage of word-bullets is coming! After Job catches his breath from Zophar's attack (chap. 11), he fires back! He unleashes a lengthy rebuttal, responding to aspects of his opponents' speeches—notably, the theme of the wisdom of God. He commences with a choice insult ("No doubt you are the people, and wisdom will die with you," 12:2),[1] followed by a lengthy defense of his knowledge (12:3–13:2), which

1. Eugene Peterson's paraphrase captures the biting sarcasm well: "I'm sure you speak for all the experts, and when you die there'll be no one left to tell us how to live" (Job 12:2 MSG).

starts and ends with synonymous claims: "I have understanding as well as you" (12:3)[2]//"What you know, I also know" (13:2); "I am not inferior to you" (12:3; 13:2). In Job's estimation, his wisdom is neither inferior to nor equal with theirs, but superior. He knows something of God's wisdom and strength (12:13–25), as they do. But he knows what they do not know (or will not acknowledge!), namely, that it is not his sin but God's hand that is the ultimate cause of his sufferings ("Who . . . does not know that the hand of the Lord has done this?," v. 9). That claim is the start of the first of four major movements in his response to Zophar.

The First Movement: The Hand of the Lord Has Done This (Job 12:3–13:2)

After Job states that he knows as much as, and even more than, his friends do, he shares how upset he is that they not only are not taking him seriously but are seriously mocking him. Twice in Job 12:4, he labels himself a "laughingstock." Yet that inclusio of their incorrect estimation is set (as in a parenthetical thought) between God's estimation of and relationship with him:

> I am a laughingstock to my friends;
> I, who called to God and he answered me,
> a just and blameless man, am a laughingstock.

Here, in self-defense, Job is reminding his friends—as they laugh at him—that this is no laughing matter. He is guiltless and is still in relationship with the God who labeled him "a blameless and upright man" (Job 1:8), despite God's silence and the sufferings that Job is experiencing.

Next, in Job 12:5–9, Job recapitulates his friends' lack of wisdom. He starts, "In the thought of one who is at ease there is contempt for misfortune; it is ready for those whose feet slip" (Job 12:5). Job's friends are approaching his situation as *ivory-tower* theologians. That is, while once they had their heads and hearts on the ashes with Job and offered sympathy for Job's sufferings, now they are far removed—not physically, but emotionally and intellectually.

2. Job 13:2 (quoted above) parallels the previous verse: "Behold, my eye has seen all this, my ear has heard and understood it" (Job 13:1), summarizing in an ideological way the physical expressions of seeing and hearing.

They are "at ease" as they theologize, while Job is still in pain. They are like rich and inexperienced politicians meeting in a fancy boardroom of a New York skyscraper, creating legislation for the immigration of Syrian refugees. They are far too removed from the reality on the ground. As a result, whereas they once showed sympathy for his sufferings, now Job's friends express "contempt for [his] misfortune" (v. 5).

These men hold such disdain because they have concluded that Job's wrongdoing is the reason for his sufferings. Adversity ("it") is akin to a snare, one that will entrap sinners as soon as they succumb to sin ("it is ready for those whose feet slip," Job 12:5b). The friends are mistaken, however. They lack proper context to comprehend Job's predicament. Job illustrates this point by using the opposite of his situation: "The tents of robbers are at peace, and those who provoke God are secure, who bring their god in their hand" (v. 6). Sometimes wicked men (such as thieves) reap the rewards of the "blessed" life: prosperity ("are at peace")[3] and security ("are secure," v. 6). Even though they "provoke God" with their actions and idolatry (perhaps "their god in their hand" [v. 6] also means that they trust in their ill-gotten gains; cf. 31:24–28), he does not punish them immediately. If this is true (evil men are not always punished close in time to their crimes), then why would Job's story not also be true (a good man is sometimes punished)?

Job explores this idea further in Job 12:7–13, calling on creation—the beasts, the birds, the fish (cf. Gen. 1:20, 25), and even the bushes![4]—to testify to the truth of his claim that Yahweh is the cause of his calamities:

> But ask the beasts, and they will teach you;
> the birds of the heavens, and they will tell you;
> or the bushes of the earth, and they will teach you;
> and the fish of the sea will declare to you.
> Who among all these does not know
> that the hand of the LORD has done this?

3. The Hebrew word *yishlayu* can also be rendered "prosper." Thus, Peterson's paraphrase is as perfect as a paraphrase can be: "Crooks reside safely in high-security houses, insolent blasphemers live in luxury; they've bought and paid for a god [an idol—their money in hand?] who'll protect them" (Job 12:6 MSG).

4. The ESV translates the three Hebrew words *'o siach la'arets* as "or the bushes of the earth" (Job 12:8). Yet I favor the alternative translation, listed in the footnote, "or speak to the earth," followed by "and it will teach you." The idea, then, is that "the beasts and birds (every creation on earth) and the fish (and all the creatures that swim the seas) will teach you."

In his hand is the life of every living thing
and the breath of all mankind.
Does not the ear test words
as the palate tastes food?
Wisdom is with the aged,
and understanding in length of days.

With God are wisdom and might;
he has counsel and understanding. (Job 12:7–13)

God is completely sovereign. He can do whatever he deems right: "In his hand is the life of every living thing and the breath of all mankind" (Job 12:10). Just as the ear is designed for hearing ("Does not the ear test words . . .") and mouths water over a freshly stirred and served dish of Louisiana jambalaya (". . . as the palate tastes food?," v. 11), God's exercising an absolute, free sovereignty is basic to how the world works. While it is true that the older you get, the more you know from experience and observation ("Wisdom is with the aged," or, put a slightly different way, "understanding in length of days," v. 12), God's wisdom surely surpasses even that of the oldest and wisest of humans. For "with God are wisdom and might; he has counsel and understanding" (v. 13; cf. v. 16; 9:4).

Job expands our vision of God's supremacy with a poem centered on God's "wisdom and might" (Job 12:13) or "strength and sound wisdom" (v. 16):

If he tears down, none can rebuild;
if he shuts a man in, none can open.
If he withholds the waters, they dry up;
if he sends them out, they overwhelm the land.
With him are strength and sound wisdom;
the deceived and the deceiver are his.
He leads counselors away stripped,
and judges he makes fools.
He looses the bonds of kings
and binds a waistcloth on their hips.
He leads priests away stripped
and overthrows the mighty.
He deprives of speech those who are trusted
and takes away the discernment of the elders.

> He pours contempt on princes
> and loosens the belt of the strong.
> He uncovers the deeps out of darkness
> and brings deep darkness to light.
> He makes nations great, and he destroys them;
> he enlarges nations, and leads them away.
> He takes away understanding from the chiefs of the people of the earth
> and makes them wander in a trackless waste.
> They grope in the dark without light,
> and he makes them stagger like a drunken man. (Job 12:14–25)

Each line begins with the phrase "if he" or "with him," or simply "he" (only Job 12:25 is the exception), followed by various actions, which are a mix of synonymous, antithetic, and synthetic parallels: God tears down, shuts in, withholds, sends out, leads away, makes, looses, overthrows, deprives, takes away, pours (out), loosens, uncovers, brings, destroys, and enlarges. All these actions involve something that God does in his "strength and sound wisdom" (v. 16) that cannot be thwarted. He cannot be thwarted by anything on earth ("the waters" or "the land," v. 15) or under the earth ("the deeps," v. 22a). He cannot be thwarted by "nations" (cf. v. 23) or by men, no matter how wise, holy, respected, or powerful those men might be—"counselors" (v. 17a), "judges" (v. 17b), "kings" (v. 18), "priests" (v. 19a), "the mighty" (v. 19b), "the elders" (v. 20b), "princes" (v. 21a), and "the strong" (v. 21b). Even "the chiefs of the people of the earth" (v. 24a) cannot resist God's will.

Job 12:24–25 offers the longest comparison, with verse 25 breaking the pattern. Its purpose is to underscore the idea that if God can make even the greatest people on earth "wander in a trackless waste" (Job 12:24) or "grope in the dark" or "stagger like a drunken man" (v. 25)—think of Nebuchadnezzar (Dan. 4:33)—then his power is irresistible. Job's point is plain. In Job 12:16, which deviates from the pattern by commencing with the phrase "with him" instead of "if he" or "he," the main point of the poem is emphasized: "With him are strength and sound wisdom; the deceived and the deceiver are his." Like Paul's poem on love to the loveless church in Corinth (1 Cor. 13), Job's poem in Job 12:14–25 is a rebuke. Its purpose is not only to showcase God's amazing power and wisdom but also to teach or remind Eliphaz, Bildad, and Zophar that God, in his wisdom, can use his sovereign power as he sees fit. They have somehow been deceived and are imploring Job to join in such deception (12:16; cf. 13:9b). Job will have none of it!

THE SECOND MOVEMENT: AS FOR YOU (JOB 13:3–12)

The second movement centers on Job's friends. In Job 13:4–12, the poor man switches his focus from his knowledge of God to what he knows about his friends ("As for you," Job 13:4; with "you" and "your" repeated seventeen times). He knows that they are wrong (e.g., "you speak falsely for God," v. 7a). He also knows that they will someday be judged for how they have treated him (e.g., "He will surely rebuke you," v. 10a). (And he is right; read Job 42.)

The second movement starts with Job's reintroducing the idea of talking directly to God about his situation: "But I would speak to the Almighty, and I desire to argue my case with God" (Job 13:3). He wants to "speak to the Almighty" and "argue" his "case with God" himself. He will do so later in the book, in a kind of solo mock trial. First, however, he returns to confronting his friends. His accusatory "As for you," which starts Job 13:4, is followed by a list of what they have done wrong and the divine judgment that is on its way because of their behavior:

> As for you, you whitewash with lies;
>   worthless physicians are you all.
> Oh that you would keep silent,
>   and it would be your wisdom!
> Hear now my argument
>   and listen to the pleadings of my lips.
> Will you speak falsely for God
>   and speak deceitfully for him?
> Will you show partiality toward him?
>   Will you plead the case for God?
> Will it be well with you when he searches you out?
>   Or can you deceive him, as one deceives a man?
> He will surely rebuke you
>   if in secret you show partiality.
> Will not his majesty terrify you,
>   and the dread of him fall upon you?
> Your maxims are proverbs of ashes;
>   your defenses are defenses of clay. (Job 13:4–12)

Their list of offenses is outlined as follows (see table 12.1).

Table 12.1. Offenses of Job's Friends

Crime	Specific Accusation
They have been atrocious surgeons of the soul	"worthless physicians are you all" (Job 13:4b)
They have been false teachers	"you whitewash with lies" (v. 4a); "you speak falsely for God and speak deceitfully for him" (v. 7)
Their testimony has been slanted	"you show partiality toward [God]" (v. 8) (or "you slant your testimony in his favor," NLT)
Their wisdom is worthless	"Your maxims are proverbs of ashes; your defenses are defenses of clay" (v. 12)

Job's solution is for his friends to keep their "wisdom" to themselves ("Oh that you would keep silent, and it would be your wisdom!," Job 13:5) and listen afresh to his version of the story ("Hear now my argument and listen to the pleadings of my lips," v. 6). Job not only wants to point out their sins; he also wants them to grasp the fact that judgment for such sins is looming. In Job 13:7–9 and 11, using a series of questions, Job informs them that their court date with God is not looking so promising. The first two questions remind them of what they have done wrong in relation to God (note the terms "for" and "toward"):

Will you	speak falsely	for God
and	speak deceitfully	for him? (Job 13:7)
Will you	show partiality	toward him?
Will you	plead the case	for God? (v. 8)

The second two questions speak of God's coming judgment. The friends' day in court will end with a guilty verdict:

> Will it be well with you when he searches you out?
> Or can you deceive him, as one deceives a man? (Job 13:9)

Will not	his majesty	terrify you,
and	the dread of him	fall upon you? (v. 11)

In Job 13:10, Job asks no rhetorical questions. He instead makes a prophetic assertion: "He will surely rebuke you if in secret you show partiality."

The Third Movement: Job's Hope and Prayer for Salvation (Job 13:13–27)

In the third movement, Job returns to his initial goal from verse 3 of Job 13: he will speak both about God (Job 13:13–19) and to God (vv. 20–27), seeking to argue his case. Both at the start of verses 13–19 and in the middle, he reiterates what he said in verses 5 and 6, namely, that his friends should listen to him as he speaks: "Let me have silence, and I will speak" (v. 13a); "Keep listening to my words, and let my declaration be in your ears" (v. 17). Job will live with the repercussions of his words ("and let come on me what may," v. 13b). He is not afraid, however, to present his case to God ("argue my ways to his face," v. 15b). While this might seem like a perilous proposal, he does not believe that he is putting his life in jeopardy: "Why should I take my flesh in my teeth and put my life in my hand?" (v. 14).

Put simply, Job sees no risk here. He is in no mortal danger, for his case is irrefutable—he knows that he is innocent: "Behold, I have prepared my case; I know that I shall be in the right" (Job 13:18) when he is able to "argue my [his] ways to his face" (v. 15b). He knows that God will not even grant him a hearing if this is not the case: "the godless shall not come before him" (v. 16b). He knows that his friends cannot substantiate their claims: "Who is there who will contend with me? For then I would be silent and die" (v. 19). Thus, if God indeed hears his case, Job is optimistic that the Judge's verdict will be just. "Though he slay me, I will hope in him" (v. 15a). God might destroy him, but Job trusts that in the end, the Lord will vindicate the righteous: "This will be my salvation" (v. 16a).

With this groundwork laid (he has almost talked himself into actually filing the claim), Job addresses God (Job 13:20–27). Yet the scene is not what is expected. There is no courtroom. Instead, we find a prayerful conversation in preparation for the case. Perhaps at this point Job realizes that direct complaint to God will get him nowhere. So he humbly asks God for help. He petitions, "Only grant me two things, then I will not hide myself from your face" (v. 20).

First, Job expresses his genuine hope for deliverance *from* God *by* God: "withdraw your hand far from me, and let not dread of you terrify me" (Job 13:21). Once Job's health is restored, he will be ready to present his case. Second, "call, and I will answer; or let me speak, and you reply to me" (v. 22). Job knows that some present sin, or sin of the past few months, is not the cause of his sufferings. But he also knows that he is a sinner (cf. 7:21; 9:29–31) and that he has a sinful teenage past (cf. 13:23, 26b). So he asks God to reveal whatever sin might be hindering the two of them from meeting face to face to discuss and resolve the matter: "How many are my iniquities and my sins? Make me know my transgression and my sin" (v. 23). What a great prayer to pray every day!

At this point, one gets the impression that Job is genuinely hopeful that all that he has laid out makes sense. God might actually agree to Job's plan. But with the word "why" that begins Job 13:24 and "your enemy" that ends it, a shadow covers these glimmers of light. In verses 24–27, Job seems to return to his personal land of darkness (Job 10:21). He starts:

> Why do you hide your face
> and count me as your enemy?
> Will you frighten a driven leaf
> and pursue dry chaff? (Job 13:24–25)

Despair has consumed him. Job struggles to comprehend why, after enduring countless days of excruciating suffering, God remains silent. Why not send a dream, a vision, or an angel? Why not write something on a stone or a scroll? Why not speak truth through the three worthless physicians? Instead of treating him like a friend, God is treating him as an enemy (like the wicked of Psalm 1:4). God's unwarranted opposition toward Job appears utterly senseless. Why would the mighty God of the universe pursue him like a "leaf" or "dry chaff" blown by the wind, only to catch the useless and decaying object and use it to "frighten" and torment him (Job 13:25)? To Job, his sufferings seem like "long-delayed punishment for his sins as a young man, which God has recorded and remembered."[5]

> For you write bitter things against me
> and make me inherit the iniquities of my youth. (Job 13:26)

5. Daniel J. Estes, *Job*, Teach the Text (Baker, 2013), 83.

To Job, "his present predicament" is that of a "prisoner closely confined and constantly watched."[6] He is incarcerated by the Almighty:

> You put my feet in the stocks
> and watch all my paths;
> you set a limit for the soles of my feet. (Job 13:27)

As Job has been "struck" physically "with loathsome sores" on "the sole of his foot" (Job 2:7), so has he been assailed psychologically by his *good* God. He cannot even move without God's watchful eye. He has not a moment of remission from his pain. Oh, that God would speak to him!

THE FOURTH MOVEMENT: YOU DESTROY THE HOPE OF MAN (JOB 13:28–14:22)

Job was strong and confident as he rebuked his friends at the start of his third reply. As he has begun to address God, at times there have been glimmers of hope. He hopes God will hear his case and vindicate him. In the fourth and final movement of his speech, however, despair overtakes him. This should not surprise us, since it has been Job's pattern thus far—every speech ends in a dark place.[7] But it perhaps makes us really empathetic to his sufferings. When will his trials end? When will Job receive answers? The cause of his despondency stems from his contemplation of humanity as a whole. Job sets aside his personal afflictions (mentioning himself only in Job 14:3, 13–17) as he delves into the unfortunate fate of the human condition, which becomes the focal point of these verses. The ESV begins Job 13:28 with the word "man," though in Hebrew, the text simply uses the pronoun "he" (*hu'*). Nevertheless, "man" serves as an appropriate way to start this final section because Adam-kind is the subject of Job's musings, with the term "man" appearing six times, twice as *'adam*. Indeed, the state of Adam's offspring takes center stage.[8]

First, Job focuses on the fragile and fleeting nature of Adam's offspring's existence. The statement that "man who is born of a woman is few of days and full of trouble" (Job 14:1) is surrounded by illustrations from creation:

6. John E. Hartley, *The Book of Job*, NICOT (Eerdmans, 1988), 228.

7. See Job 3:20–26; 7:19–21; 10:18–22.

8. The Hebrew word for "man" in Job 14:1 is *'adam*.

"Man wastes away like a rotten thing, like a garment that is moth-eaten" (13:28); "He comes out like a flower and withers; he flees like a shadow and continues not" (14:2). The question then arises: if man is like a decomposing pumpkin, an old moth-eaten wool sweater, a shriveling daisy, and a passing cloud, then why does God focus his attention on us ("do you open your eyes on such a one and bring me into judgment with you?," v. 3)? Job wonders why God would drag him into court ("bring me into judgment," v. 3b). Job is as sinful as any other human being, who can hardly look presentable before a perfectly pure Judge: "Who can bring a clean thing out of an unclean? There is not one" (v. 4). Job is as transient as any human being. He cannot live longer than God has ordained: "his days are determined, and the number of his months is with you, and you have appointed his limits that he cannot pass" (v. 5). In response, Job offers a solution—one that he has suggested before (7:16, 19; 10:20). He wants God to leave man alone ("look away from him and leave him alone," 14:6a) so that he can find some delight in the few days he might have left ("that he may enjoy, like a hired hand, his day," v. 6b)!

For his next petition, Job asks God to bury him in the grave ("Oh that you would hide me in Sheol," Job 14:13a). He gives two reasons for this apparently grim prayer. First, he hopes that Sheol will remove him from his present sufferings ("Conceal me until your wrath be past," v. 13b). Second, he hopes that Sheol is not the end of the story, that God will someday retrieve Job from this pit ("that you would appoint me a set time, and remember me!," v. 13c). What comes before Job 14:13 is his observation on the bleak reality of human death (vv. 7–12), but what follows is his hope that God might make an exception in his case (vv. 14–17).

In Job 14:7–12, Job contrasts man's death with the death of a tree that withers, dies, and is chopped down. But what happens next is amazing: just a few drops of water cause new life to sprout! A sapling buds out of the dead trunk. Poetically, Job says it this way:

> For there is hope for a tree,
>   if it be cut down, that it will sprout again,
>   and that its shoots will not cease.
> Though its root grow old in the earth,
>   and its stump die in the soil,
> yet at the scent of water it will bud
>   and put out branches like a young plant. (Job 14:7–9)

In contrast to a tree, a man dies and that is the end of him: "But a man dies and is laid low; man breathes his last, and where is he?" (Job 14:10). Man's death is like dried-up waters—"a river" or "lake" that "fail[s]" (or "disappears"), "wastes away and dries up" (v. 11). Once he is dead ("so a man lies down"), there is no hope of life again ("and rises not again," v. 12a); he is dead forevermore ("till the heavens are no more he will not awake or be roused out of his sleep," v. 12b–c).

In the midst of this grim reality, Job asks God to act. As mentioned earlier, he implores God to "hide" him "in Sheol" (Job 14:13a). Although the imagery of being cast into a pit or thrown into an open grave is unpleasant, Job seems to adopt a somewhat positive perspective. In verses 7–12 of Job 14, Job laments man's fate after death. In verses 14–17, however, he expresses hope that God might perform an even greater miracle than sprouting a new tree from a dead one. He desires God to resurrect him! His plan consists of two parts. First, to free him from his present pain, he asks God to send him to Sheol (v. 13a–b). Second, when the time is right, Job envisions that God will (1) remember what he did with Job and (2) retrieve him from the grave (v. 13c).

This plan makes good sense to Job. As it stands, there is currently no hope for such a resurrection ("If a man dies, shall he live again?," Job 14:14a). But if God is willing to offer life after death, Job is willing to wait in Sheol for it ("All the days of my service I would wait, till my renewal [or "change"] should come," v. 14b–c). It is difficult to know precisely what is being said in the second half of Job 14:14. What change is Job envisioning? If he is dead in Sheol, it must be a bodily resurrection. What he pictures next is his version of "Lazarus, come out" (John 11:43). God would beckon Job ("You would call"); Job would hear him ("and I would answer you," Job 14:15a); and then he would receive new life. This is one of the several places where we see people from the Old Testament grasping for the hope of eternal life.

Why would God raise Job from the dead? Two reasons are given. First, as the end of Job 14:15 states, "you would long for the work of your hands." Put differently, the reason for this resurrection is God's glory. "Wouldn't you, God, for your own glory, love to see a resurrection just as much as I'd like to experience one? My old life gone, buried in Sheol; my life now with you forever, as friends again." The second reason for Job's plea involves the forgiveness of man's iniquities. Job wants to be saved not only from Sheol, but also from his sin. He envisions God as dismissing incriminating evidence in the case of *God v. Job.* Although God would still oversee every aspect of Job's life ("you would number my steps," Job 14:16a), his omniscience would not be confining but freeing, for God would not keep track of every transgression ("you would not keep watch over my sin," v. 16b). Instead, "my transgression would be sealed up in a bag, and you would cover over my iniquity" (v. 17). What a remarkable picture of Job's desired salvation and our actual salvation: "Blessed are those whose lawless deeds are forgiven, and whose sins are covered; blessed is the man against whom the Lord will not count his sin" (Rom. 4:7–8, quoting Ps. 85:2). Yes, we know what Job could only dream of knowing: that Jesus has conquered the grave. We know that in his resurrection, we are made right with God (justified) and given the unshakable hope of release from sin, suffering, and death. What good news!

Our good news, and Job's too, does sound good. But Job doesn't dwell long on the positives. He wakes from his delightful daydream, and in his next lines provides a reality check:

> But the mountain falls and crumbles away,
>   and the rock is removed from its place;
> the waters wear away the stones;
>   the torrents wash away the soil of the earth;
>   so you destroy the hope of man.
> You prevail forever against him, and he passes;
>   you change his countenance, and send him away.
> His sons come to honor, and he does not know it;
>   they are brought low, and he perceives it not.
> He feels only the pain of his own body,
>   and he mourns only for himself. (Job 14:18–22)

These lines are Job's pessimistic admission that none of this will happen. The word "but" (Job 14:18) introduces the contrast. Just as a "mountain" erodes ("crumbles away," v. 18a) completely ("the rock is removed from its place," v. 18b), with stormwaters eating away "the stones" (v. 19a) and "the soil" (v. 19b), so God levels all anticipation of life after death ("you destroy the hope of man," v. 19c). Now, to Job, God is a destroyer, not a savior. When God overpowers a man at death, it is permanent ("You prevail forever against him, and he passes," v. 20). When man is sent to Sheol ("you . . .

send him away"), he is changed ("you change his countenance," v. 20b), but not for the better. In the grave, he is unaware of anything that happens on the earth above. If his children prosper, thrive, and enjoy life ("sons come to honor"), "he does not know it" (v. 21a); if they lose it all, get sick, and die ("are brought low"), "he perceives it not" (v. 21b). He sees none of their successes or failures. His eternal hell is a lonely place: "He feels only the pain of his own body, and he mourns only for himself" (v. 22). These are sober reminders of the reality of divine judgment—a judgment that should compel us to seek God's grace.

A Work of Art; Work on Us!

Job 12–14 offers many key Bible themes to explore—wisdom, sin, salvation, prayer, hope, judgment, forgiveness, death, and resurrection. In regard to wisdom, Job's poem on the wisdom of God is not merely beautiful ancient poetry (Job 12:14–25), something that we turn into a plaque to hang on the wall, but a work of art intended to work on us. In a fallen world, suffering and death, along with inexplicable injustices, are part of the curse (cf. Rom. 5:12–21). We must have the wisdom to recognize this. We must also let God rule his world with his wisdom, leaning on him instead of our own understanding (Prov. 3:5). If despair sets in because of our inability to figure things out, we should still remember that God is in complete control. Perhaps most importantly, when we find ourselves in circumstances beyond our wisdom or control, we must go to God. He might not give us answers. He might not even bring us immediate comfort. But we go to God in prayer because worship of our sovereign King is our highest calling, for "with him are strength and sound wisdom" (Job 12:16).

We can also learn something about our salvation from Job 12–14. Job's only possible solution to his sufferings—and sins—involves some sort of resurrection. While there are hints of such a resurrection in the Old Testament (e.g., Pss. 49:15; 73:24; Dan. 12:2), it is unclear what Job believes about the life to come. At times he appears confident that there is no life after death (e.g., Job 10:21; 16:22). Other times, however, he seems to imagine and hope that there might be something more (e.g., 14:13–17; 19:25–27). Of course, how blessed we are! We *know* that Jesus has conquered the grave. We *know* that in his resurrection, we are made right with God and given the unshakable hope of release from sin, suffering, and death.

It may be a coincidence, or else something very deliberate, that Paul in Philippians 1:19 uses the phrase "this will turn out for my deliverance" (*touto moi apobesetai eis soterian*), which is precisely the phrase used in the Greek version of Job 13:16, where it is translated "This will be my salvation." Both Paul and Job are simply asking to be delivered from their trying circumstances. Yet what Paul says next in Philippians is precisely what Job, and every other believer, needs to hear and heed: "it is my eager expectation and hope that I will not be at all ashamed, but that with full courage now as always Christ will be honored in my body, whether by life or by death. For to me to live is Christ, and to die is gain" (Phil. 1:20–21). Job was uncertain what awaited him after the grave. For our part, we are not afraid of death, for we know that death leads us into the very presence not of our destroyer but of our Savior ("to depart and be with Christ"), which is "far better" (v. 23) not only than our sufferings but also than anything that this world has to offer.

Second Cycle of Speeches

13

Eliphaz: Do You Limit Wisdom to Yourself?

Job 15:1–35

Have you listened in the council of God? And do you limit wisdom to yourself? (Job 15:8)

Mark Twain's "Story of the Bad Little Boy," first published in *California* magazine in 1865, is a parody of popular Sunday-school books of the time. It begins with a formulaic introduction: "Once there was a bad little boy whose name is Jim." The twist is that Jim, who does one terrible thing after another, has no pang of conscience for stealing ("all at once a terrible feeling didn't come over him"), has no thought of repentance ("he didn't kneel down all alone and promise never to be wicked any more, and rise up with a light, happy heart, and go and tell his mother all about it and beg her forgiveness"), and suffers no consequences for his crimes (he doesn't "languish in a sick bed for weeks"). He also suffers no penalty for boating and fishing on Sundays (he "didn't get drowned" and "struck by lightning"). Instead, "Jim bore a charmed life." He grew up, got married, raised a large family, and then one night, he "brained them all with an axe," and not only got away with murder but "got wealthy by all manner of cheating and rascality." As the story ends, Twain states that while Jim "is the infernalest wickedest scoundrel in his native village," he is a member of the House of Representatives ("belongs to the Legislature") and is "universally respected."[1]

If we were to continue Twain's parody, we could focus on how Jim used words for evil purposes while serving in government. He cursed, boasted, lied, flattered, made false promises, gossiped about his colleagues, ridiculed his adversaries, slandered the opposing political party, and rashly shouted in anger during debates. Jim did all that, and yet in the end, he became the President of the United States. Can you imagine a man with such a mouth obtaining that high office? We can, but Eliphaz cannot. His response to Job (Job 15:1–35), which opens the second and shorter cycle of speeches (15:1–21:34), focuses on Job's seemingly sinful words. He is certain that Job's words are the cause of his calamities and have broken apart his relationship with God.

Eating Away the Fear of God (Job 15:1–6)

Eliphaz starts the second cycle by reiterating what he said earlier, but now, as Gerald Janzen summarizes, "less sympathetically,"[2] or as I'll put it, with *no sympathy whatsoever.*[3] Gone are his gentle and courteous commendations ("you have instructed many, and you have strengthened the weak hands") and the encouraging acknowledgments (that the "fear of God" is Job's "confidence" and "the integrity of your [his] ways" his "hope," Job 4:3, 6). Here the fangs come out! Moreover, instead of actually hearing what Job has to say, Eliphaz only sides with his two friends. He draws on Bildad's bashing over the head and Zophar's zings to attack Job's claims and character.

As stated above, Eliphaz's response centers on Job's words (as italicized below). He starts with two rhetorical questions and colorful but cruel metaphors:

> Should a wise man *answer* with windy knowledge,
> and fill his belly with the east wind?

1. Mark Twain, "Story of the Bad Little Boy," https://twain.lib.virginia.edu/tomsawye/mtbadboy.html, accessed June 22, 2025.

2. J. Gerald Janzen, *Job*, Interpretation: A Bible Commentary for Teaching and Preaching (John Knox, 1985), 115.

3. Eliphaz begins each of the three cycles of dialogues (Job 4:1; 15:1; 22:1). The dialogue in the second cycle, as Daniel J. Estes summarizes, "becomes more strained, abusive, and insulting as the friends focus almost completely on the divine punishment due wicked people like Job." *Job*, Teach the Text (Baker, 2013), 92.

> Should he *argue* in unprofitable *talk*,
> or in *words* with which he can do no good? (Job 15:2–3)

Here Eliphaz echoes Bildad's "the words of your mouth be a great wind" (Job 8:2) with his metaphor of Job's "windy knowledge," words that are "unprofitable," or, better rendered—in keeping with the wind metaphor—"useless" or "empty." "A wise man," as the NLT expresses the sense, "wouldn't answer with such empty talk!" (15:2). Here Bildad envisions Job as inhaling the hot air that blows across the Arabian Desert ("the east wind," 15:2),[4] and then spewing out something more dangerous than hot air. His words are not only useless, but destructive: "But you are doing away with the fear of God," or, said in a slightly different way, you are "hindering meditation before God" (v. 4). Job's windy words are so strong that they have broken Job's covenant with God ("you are doing away [*tāpēr*, "break"][5] with the fear of God," v. 4a). Eliphaz claims that this severing of God's favor and diminishing of their relationship (the word "hindering" in v. 4b can also be translated "diminishing"; cf. Ezek. 16:27) is a sure consequence of Job's "crafty" tongue (Job 15:5):

> For your iniquity teaches your *mouth*,
> and you choose the *tongue* of the crafty.
> Your own *mouth* condemns you, and not I;
> your own *lips* testify against you. (Job 15:5–6)[6]

Earlier, Eliphaz was optimistic about Job's spiritual condition and possible turnaround. Now, after hearing from Job, he is convinced that Job is in a bad, almost irreversible, place. Reusing the second phrase of Job's own vulnerable admission ("Though I am in the right, my own mouth would condemn me," Job 9:20), he twists Job's words and uses them against him. Sin has been Job's schoolmaster ("your iniquity teaches your mouth," 15:5),

4. Throughout the Old Testament, "the east wind" destroys crops: "seven ears [of corn], withered, thin, and blighted by the east wind" (Gen. 41:23; "the east wind dried up its [the vineyard's] fruit," Ezek. 19:12); "the east wind, . . . rising from the wilderness," will "dry up" the "fountain" (Hos. 13:15; cf. "the wind from the desert," Jer. 13:24).

5. Tremper Longman III, *Job*, Baker Commentary on the Old Testament Wisdom and Psalms (Baker Academic, 2012), 224, citing T. F. Williams, *NIDOTTE* 3:696, records that this verb is used twenty-three times for Israel's breaking of the covenant.

6. Francis I. Andersen notes that the "speech organs—*mouth, tongue* and *lips*—are all subjects of four clauses in parallel." *Job*, Tyndale Old Testament Commentaries 13 (InterVarsity Press, 1976), 175.

his vocabulary that of the snake (cf. Gen. 3:1). The case is open and shut. Job's "own mouth condemns" him; his "own lips testify against" him (Job 15:6).

Eliphaz claims that Job's words are as oppressive and destructive as the east wind, but imagine how oppressive and destructive Eliphaz's words are to Job! He must feel like a marathon runner being met near the finish line with a cup of scorpion-pepper Tabasco sauce. Eliphaz could benefit from Jesus' warning on words: "on the day of judgment people will give account for every careless word they speak, for by your words you will be justified, and by your words you will be condemned" (Matt. 12:36–37). Eliphaz is cruel and careless here. His words are condemnable! *He*, not Job, has sinned with his mouth.

Drinking in Sin (Job 15:7–16)

In verses 7–14 of Job 15, "taking the tone of a belligerent prosecutor determined to prove his case, Eliphaz assaults Job with a barrage of humiliating questions intended to prove Job guilty."[7] The first eight rhetorical questions are rebukes for not listening to his friends' counsel:

> Are you the first man who was born?
> Or were you brought forth before the hills?
> Have you listened in the council of God?
> And do you limit wisdom to yourself?
> What do you know that we do not know?
> What do you understand that is not clear to us?
> Both the gray-haired and the aged are among us,
> older than your father.
> Are the comforts of God too small for you,
> or the word that deals gently with you?
> Why does your heart carry you away,
> and why do your eyes flash,
> that you turn your spirit against God
> and bring such words out of your mouth? (Job 15:7–13)

Eliphaz attacks Job's self-autonomy and the fact that his perception is grounded in the present, not the past. Job is not older than Adam ("Are

7. Estes, *Job*, 92.

you the first man who was born?") or the third day of creation ("Or were you brought forth before the hills?," Job 15:7). He certainly was not there at the moment when God, in his wisdom, created the earth (Prov. 8:23, 25a). This might be the sense of the question "Have you listened in the council of God?" (Job 15:8a). Or the meaning might be that "the council of God" represents others who are wise, which would then correspond with the second line, "And do you limit wisdom to yourself?" (v. 8b). Certainly, in Job 15:9 Eliphaz speaks of the wisdom of others, notably that of the three friends. Job is acting as though he knows more than they do. Eliphaz disagrees: "What do you know that we do not know? What do you understand that is not clear to us?" (v. 9). "The word group 'know,'" as Christopher Ash points out, "appears more than seventy times in Job. It is a vital question: how do we know what we claim to know? For Eliphaz and his friends, tradition is the best we can do."[8] Furthermore, Eliphaz claims that their wisdom, unlike Job's, has been "garnered through experience and observation and passed on from one generation to the next."[9] Those "older than" Job's "father" side with them ("are among us," v. 10). The "gray-haired and the aged" are Eliphaz, Bildad, and Zophar or perhaps represent the tradition—ancients from the past—that the three friends continue to stand on and are counseling Job with. Job is not listening to wisdom. He is not listening to God. He is not listening to God's voice through the tradition. "Are the comforts of God too small for you, or the word that deals gently with you?" (v. 11).

If the phrase "the word that deals gently with you" refers to the words of the friends, then we join Job in rolling his eyes. What? God has not spoken with Job; there is no comfort there. The friends have spoken of what is wrong about Job, and with great venom at times. There is certainly no comfort there, either. Job is rightly upset about such a lack of comfort. Yet Eliphaz considers Job's "righteous" (or at least "understandable") anger, and instead accuses him of iniquity. Job's passions ("your heart [carries] you away, . . . your eyes flash," Job 15:12) have gotten the better of him. Job's soliloquy and speeches ("words out of your mouth") confirm that every part of him rages against his Creator ("you turn your spirit against God," v. 13).

The last two of Eliphaz's ten rhetorical questions are intended to move Job to consider his case before a holy God:

8. Christopher Ash, *Job: The Wisdom of the Cross*, Preaching the Word (Crossway, 2014), 180.
9. C. L. Seow, *Job 1–21: Interpretation and Commentary*, Illuminations (Eerdmans, 2013), 143.

> What is man, that he can be pure?
> Or he who is born of a woman, that he can be righteous?
> Behold, God puts no trust in his holy ones,
> and the heavens are not pure in his sight;
> how much less one who is abominable and corrupt,
> a man who drinks injustice like water! (Job 15:14–16)

Here Eliphaz returns to the theme of human sinfulness in light of God's holiness (see Job 4:17–18). The logic is tight, the poetic parallelisms precise, and the theology almost right. But the application is absolutely off. It is true that man is totally depraved,[10] but not completely wicked.[11] God has "crowned" man with "glory and honor," and "given him dominion over" all of God's creation (Ps. 8:5, 6). Blaise Pascal summarized the paradox of humanity thus: "What a chimera then is man! What a novelty! What a monster, what a chaos, what a contradiction, what a prodigy! Judge of all things, imbecile worm of the earth; depositary of truth, a sink of uncertainty and error; the pride and refuse of the universe!"[12] It is true that the angels are not holy in the sense of God's absolute and eternal holiness. It is therefore also true that the man Job is not perfectly pure in God's sight. But Job has not claimed as much. Neither is it accurate that Job is "abominable and corrupt" (Job 15:16). Such a label should not be used for "blameless and upright" Job (1:1, 8; 2:3). It is certainly not true that he is so unrighteous that he "drinks injustice like water" (15:16). How ridiculous!

The Consequences of Such a Diet (Job 15:17–35)

In the last section (Job 15:17–35), which is a calculated jab at Job,[13] Eliphaz waxes eloquent on the fate of the "wicked man" (v. 20a), also called the

10. As John Calvin describes it, "We are so entirely controlled by the power of sin, that the whole mind, the whole heart, and all our actions are under its influence." *Commentaries on the Epistle of Paul the Apostle to the Romans*, trans. John Owen, vol. 19 of *Calvin's Commentaries* (Calvin Translation Society, 1849), 261.

11. "While agreeing that men are fragile and dirty (14:1–4), Job nevertheless thinks that people are precious to God (10:12f). Eliphaz goes to the extreme, dismissing man as *abominable and corrupt*." Andersen, *Job*, 177.

12. Blaise Pascal, *Thoughts, Letters, and Minor Works*, ed. Charles W. Eliot, trans. W. F. Trotter, Harvard Classics (P. F. Collier & Son, 1910), 147.

13. As Norman C. Habel points out, Eliphaz uses fourteen "allusions" from Job's own speeches that "reflect verbal irony and barbed innuendo designed to expose how Job testifies to characteristics in

"ruthless" (v. 20b) and the "godless" man (v. 34a). After a robust introduction ("I will show you," v. 17), Eliphaz shows Job what happens to the man who "stretche[s] out his hand against God" (v. 25a). Every line is about this man (note the plethora of pronouns: "he," "his," "him," thirty-two times), and every imaginable evil overcomes him, from present agonies (he "writhes in pain all his days," v. 20a) to future losses ("he will not be rich," v. 29a).

At this point, we have heard enough of Eliphaz's patronizing preaching; we can be sure (from Job's forthcoming response: "Shall windy words have an end?," Job 16:3a)[14] that, for his part, Job is done with Eliphaz's oratorical unkindness, and that such piercing words are causing severe psychological pain (see v. 5b). And at this point, Job would presumably prefer a stick to the shin or a stone thrown at his chest than his friends' seemingly unending false accusations. Alas, there is half a sermon left—a long-winded and harsh conclusion (15:17–35). Starting in Job 15:17–20, and shifting from "rhetorical questions to didactic language in the first person,"[15] Eliphaz states:

> I will show you; hear me,
>   and what I have seen I will declare
> (what wise men have told,
>   without hiding it from their fathers,
> to whom alone the land was given,
>   and no stranger passed among them).
> The wicked man writhes in pain all his days,
>   through all the years that are laid up for the ruthless.

If we think of Eliphaz's speech as a three-point sermon to Job, we might divide the material as follows. Point one: With your words, you are eating away the fear of God (Job 15:1–6). Point two: Because you have not listened to God through tradition, you are like a man who drinks in sin like water (vv. 7–16). Point three: Such a diet will not bode well for you (vv. 17–35). Eliphaz's sermon is reminiscent of the opening lines in Richard Watson's *The Philosopher's Diet*, where a professor emeritus of philosophy from the

himself that are typical of the wicked man." *The Book of Job: A Commentary*, Old Testament Library (Westminster, 1985), 251–52.

14. Andersen, *Job*, 179, observes the irony: "It is subtlety of our author that Eliphaz, who began by calling Job a wind-bag (verse 2), ends his own speech with a pile of verbiage. With tedious repetition, assertion not argument, he presents the doctrine 'you reap what you sow' in several forms."

15. Seow, *Job 1–21*, 703.

prestigious Washington University in St. Louis begins a diet book by saying: "Fat. I presume you want to get rid of it. Then quit eating so much."[16] Watson is being brutally honest, but he is also winsomely inviting his readers to a way "to take off weight and keep it off" by embracing "a philosophy of life."[17]

Eliphaz is lacking in both charming wit and a philosophy, or theology, that will actually help Job. In fact, here in Job 15, Eliphaz has not moved from his earlier stated vision: "Remember: who that was innocent ever perished? Or where were the upright cut off? As I have seen, those who plow iniquity and sow trouble reap the same" (Job 4:7–8). Here Eliphaz just expands on what he meant in 4:9: "By the breath of God they perish, and by the blast of his anger they are consumed." That is, both the wisdom tradition ("what wise men have told, without hiding it from their fathers," 15:18) and wise observation of life ("what I have seen I will declare," v. 17) teach the retribution principle: the good prosper, while the bad perish. The focus here is only on the downside of that principle, with the key verse being Eliphaz's opening line: "The wicked man writhes in pain all his days" (v. 20). All the lines that follow focus on this main point. The purpose of this poem on the wicked man is for Job to hear the wisdom of Eliphaz ("hear me," v. 17a) and see that he, like David caught in his sin, is *that* man ("You are the man!," 2 Sam. 12:7).

Job 15:21–24 illustrates various aspects of divine punishment that the wicked man suffers:

> Dreadful sounds are in his ears;
>   in prosperity the destroyer will come upon him.
> He does not believe that he will return out of darkness,
>   and he is marked for the sword.
> He wanders abroad for bread, saying, "Where is it?"
>   He knows that a day of darkness is ready at his hand;
> distress and anguish terrify him;
>   they prevail against him, like a king ready for battle.

Even in times of peace, suddenly the wicked man hears the sounds of marauders marching against his home. All his *shalom* quickly vanishes:

16. Richard Watson, *The Philosopher's Diet: How to Lose Weight and Change the World* (Godine, 1998), 3.

17. Watson, xiii.

"Dreadful sounds are in his ears; in prosperity the destroyer will come upon him" (Job 15:21). He fears going out at night ("He does not believe that he will return out of darkness") because his once-safe neighborhood is now filled with violence ("he is marked for the sword," v. 22). Verses 21–22 of Job 15 likely are flashbacks to Job's loss of property at the hands of the Sabeans and Chaldeans (1:13–19), and 15:23–24 describes the aftermath. He is hungry: "He wanders abroad for bread, saying, 'Where is it?'" (15:23a). He thinks that death is imminent ("He knows that a day of darkness is ready at his hand," v. 23b), and like a warrior king defeating his foes, "distress and anguish terrify him" and "prevail against him" (v. 24). He is a mess both physically and psychologically.

Next, Eliphaz tells his small congregation the cause of all these calamities: sin! The only specifically named sin, which makes the wicked man "wicked," is found in Job 15:25: all of this has come upon Job "because [through his complaints] he has stretched out his hand against God," and in doing so, he wrongly contests, disobeys, or "defies the Almighty." The phrase "he has stretched out his hand" is an image of confronting and challenging God. It is a clenched hand, a fist in the air—the ultimate posture of rebellion. This image is reinforced with another related image—that of the wicked man charging at God ("running stubbornly [or "defiantly"] against him") with a massive, "thickly bossed shield" in hand (Job 15:26). While the image is that of a battle scene, with Job rushing at Yahweh, the fact that a shield and not a sword is mentioned may symbolize his defensiveness. He is so stubborn in his position against God.

The ESV begins Job 15:27 with the word "because" (so also Job 15:25). This Hebrew particle (*ki*) can be translated as "because," "that," "when," or "though." Since a new thought seems to be in place (the *ki* does not relate directly to verses 25–26 but connects to what follows in verses 27–28), "though" also fits well, the sense being: "Though his face is covered with fat and his waist bulges with flesh, he will inhabit ruined towns and houses where no one lives, houses crumbling to rubble" (vv. 27–28 NIV). The irony is this: while this man is overweight ("he has covered his face with his fat and gathered fat upon his waist," as the ESV translates verse 27), he is not living high on the hog! His housing situation is pathetic. His cities are "desolate," his homes condemned ("houses that none should inhabit") and soon to be demolished ("ready to become heaps of ruins," v. 28; perhaps an allusion to 1:19: "a great wind . . . struck the four corners of the house, and it fell").

Like Job 15:21–24 and 27–28, verses 29–35 further illustrate various aspects of divine punishment. Job "will not be rich," and any "wealth" he has "will not endure" (Job 15:29a). He will leave no inheritance ("nor will his possessions spread over the earth," v. 29b). He himself will disappear with his money: he will not endure but will die ("not depart from darkness," v. 30a). By "the breath of [God's] mouth" he will be incinerated ("the flame will dry up his shoots," v. 30b–c). With these analogies of a consuming fire (also v. 34b below) and the drastic loss of possessions, Job's own sad story is likely echoed here ("The fire of God fell from heaven and burned up the sheep and the servants and consumed them," 1:16).

With a mix of metaphors from botany, business, and birth, Eliphaz concludes:

> Let him not trust in emptiness, deceiving himself,
> for emptiness will be his payment.
> It will be paid in full before his time,
> and his branch will not be green.
> He will shake off his unripe grape like the vine,
> and cast off his blossom like the olive tree.
> For the company of the godless is barren,
> and fire consumes the tents of bribery.
> They conceive trouble and give birth to evil,
> and their womb prepares deceit. (Job 15:31–35)

All the images above are of emptiness and ineffectiveness. The wicked man, who is self-deceived because he trusts not in Yahweh (but in "emptiness" instead, Job 15:31; or what is worthless, his riches or own wisdom), is a loser in life. He is paid "emptiness" (v. 31b), or "vanity is his recompence" (YLT). He does not flourish. He is like the branch that does not bud, the dead, raisinlike grape on the withered grapevine, the flower that falls dead from the olive tree.

The subtle (or not-so-subtle!) accusations are outrageous and ironic: outrageous because Eliphaz claims that Job's wealth was due to his wickedness, and ironic because if Judge Job has been having secret meetings with his high-profile clients in "the tents of bribery" (Job 15:34) to make some big-time cash on the side, then why didn't God judge him—as he does the wicked—before he made all his money? Moreover, Eliphaz's final two lines—

where he shifts from the singular (the wicked man) to the plural (the man with his shady company)—while poetically masterful,[18] are reprehensible. From-the-pit-of-hell reprehensible!

Applying Two Angles on Eliphaz's Otherwise Worthless Words

Eliphaz's sermonic poem exhibits a complete detachment from reality, not only disregarding Job's specific situation but also overlooking basic observations of life. Related to Job, has Job really gone from being a blameless, God-fearing man to a wicked infidel who "shakes his fist at God and vaunts himself against the Almighty" (Job 15:25 NIV)—or, as Ash shockingly puts it, gives "God the finger"?[19] Then, related to the world, does the wicked man really writhe "in pain *all* his days" (v. 20a)? Is the merciless man always poor (vv. 21b, 29)—so poor that he begs for bread (v. 23a) and shacks up in a shanty (v. 28b)? Do ill-gotten riches always evaporate (v. 29)? The ancient songwriter Asaph wholeheartedly disagrees. He begins his Spirit-inspired poem (Ps. 73) by bemoaning "the prosperity of the wicked" (v. 3b), who are "always at ease" as "they increase in riches" (v. 12), while "the rest of mankind" is "stricken" and "in trouble" (v. 5) and the righteous "rebuked every morning" (v. 14b).

Beyond Psalm 73, the Scriptures are filled with expressions and examples of the truth that *suffering is not always due to sin*. Remember the life and ministry of Jeremiah, the weeping prophet. Review the sufferings of the early church in Acts. Read the epistles and the Apocalypse. "Suffering," as Derek Thomas puts it, "is one of the 'marks' of the church."[20] Some of the Bible's heroes of faith were "destitute, afflicted, mistreated," while others endured "mocking and flogging, and even chains and imprisonment," and still others "were stoned, . . . sawn in two, . . . killed with the sword" or "were tortured" to death ("refusing to accept release," Heb. 11:35–37). Similarly,

18. Eliphaz begins his rebuke with the gross image of the desert air that comes from Job's belly (Job 15:2b), and he closes with a picture of the company of the wicked having sex ("They conceive"), gestating ("their womb prepares deceit," or as Robert Alter nicely phrases this awful idea, "pregnant with wretchedness"), and giving birth to their godless schemes ("give birth to evil," Job 15:35). See *The Wisdom Books: Job, Proverbs, and Ecclesiastes* (W. W. Norton & Company, 2010), 70.

19. Ash, *Job*, 184.

20. Derek Thomas, *The Storm Breaks: Job Simply Explained*, Welwyn Commentary Series (repr., Evangelical Press, 2005), 123.

all Christians, if we seek to live a godly life and faithfully share our faith, will run into some form of persecution, at the very least rejection or scorn (see 2 Tim. 3:12). Christ's holy church is a wholly suffering church; and as we suffer, so Christ suffers with us and through us (see Acts 9:4; Col. 1:24).

In *The Biggest Story Curriculum* for children, the lesson I wrote on Acts 4 is one that all of God's children—no matter the age—should learn:

> Here's a simple equation (like 1 + 1 + 1 = 3) for how the church grows: power + preaching + persecution = growth. It makes sense that God's *power* is necessary, and *preaching* makes sense too (people need to hear the good news). But how does *persecution* (God's people suffering for the gospel) grow the church? It is a bit of a mystery, but the answer to the mystery is connected to Christ. He suffered, so we must suffer; he is raised to glory; we too one day will be raised to glory. So, all that to say, as you read Acts 4 *keep an eye out* for another sermon, *see* how many people our powerful God saves, and *watch* what happens when the apostles run into some persecution.[21]

It is easy to make our response to Eliphaz's sermon a simple word to the wise: Do not preach like him! Do not tell someone who has suffered unimaginable losses that his intense emotions and passionate laments are uncalled for and that he should process his feelings in "cool, analytical, and objective" ways.[22] Avoid playing God by presumptuously judging between the godly and the ungodly. Refrain from scaring good people into false repentance. Resist the temptation to accuse every suffering saint of sin. Fight the urge to misconstrue the facts. Do not be so demeaning. Do not be so *mean*! But we should also take two other angles on Eliphaz's otherwise worthless words, one positive and the other corrective.

The positive takeaway is that we must not shy away from teaching the topics that Eliphaz teaches on. Do we boldly teach the utter sinfulness of man before a holy God? Do we warn sinners about the certain wrath of this wholly righteous God? Do we caution the wealthy about the dangers of riches and the fleetingness of possessions? These are all important biblical themes, when lovingly proclaimed and properly applied.

The corrective application emerges as we place Eliphaz's words in the context of all that God has made known in his Word. More specifically, our

21. *The Biggest Story Curriculum*, 6 vols. (Crossway, 2023), 5:19–20.
22. Estes, *Job*, 93.

theological "framework of assumptions"[23] must be shaped, developed, and refined from a close reading of Scripture, and read in light of the Light of the World—our Lord Jesus Christ. We fully see what God wants us to see in these verses only when we read them through the lens of Christ's death and resurrection. As stated in Luke 24:26, "Was it not necessary that the Christ should suffer?" and in verses 45–46: Jesus "opened their minds to understand the Scriptures, and said to them, 'Thus it is written ['in the Law of Moses and the Prophets and the Psalms,' v. 44], that the Christ should suffer and on the third day rise from the dead." Through Jesus, the perfectly innocent sacrifice and Savior, we gain a better understanding of God's greater intentions. In light of these things, it is clear that Eliphaz fails to foresee that at least one righteous man would "[writhe] in pain" and suffer the fate of having "the destroyer . . . come upon him" (Job 15:20–21). Therefore, Eliphaz's bold pronouncements—though true in places—also remind us of our persistent need to confront the wisdom of the world (i.e., "bad people suffer") with the wisdom of Christ crucified (1 Cor. 1:18–24).

23. Vern S. Poythress, "Kinds of Biblical Theology," *Westminster Theological Journal* 70, no. 1 (Spring 2008): 134. On this concept, see especially "IV. The Reverse Influence of Systematic Theology on Biblical Theology," 133–34.

14

Job: Where Then Is My Hope?

Job 16:1–17:16

Where then is my hope? Who will see my hope? (Job 17:15)

Peter Cartwright is known for losing a U.S. Congress seat to Abraham Lincoln. But he is better known for being a Methodist circuit rider who rode from town to town throughout the Wild West—then Tennessee and Kentucky—preaching the gospel and baptizing converts. Cartwright reportedly baptized twelve thousand people! There is a lot to admire about him. Like all great men, however, especially those of a rough and rugged temperament, he had his flaws. As the story is told:

> One day after he preached, a man came up to him and, to test the sincerity of Cartwright's Christianity, struck him on the right cheek and then again on the left. Through both blows Cartwright stood his ground. He did not retaliate. Yet when the man struck him a third time, this strong evangelist landed a nice upper cut on that chap's face. And as he did so he said, "My Lord said nothing about a third slap."[1]

1. Recounted in Douglas Sean O'Donnell, *Matthew: All Authority in Heaven and on Earth*, Preaching the Word (Crossway, 2013), 137. Professor Lyle Dorsett told this story in a class on evangelism at Wheaton College.

As well deserving as the blow might have been, Cartwright not only misapplied the spirit of Jesus' teaching, but arguably also disobeyed Christ's clear command to love our enemies. As we turn to Job 16:1, we find again the familiar and repeated Hebraism, "Then Job answered and said," which honestly shakes my sensibilities. Why such reserved narration? Should it not be "And then Job punched Eliphaz in the face!"? Job does not do so. But he comes close. He begins his fourth reply with some verbal attacks of his own, asserting that his three friends are "miserable comforters" and that if he were in their shoes, he would say and do the opposite, namely, he would bring strength and solace to the suffering (Job 16:1–5).

The rest of Job's speech centers again on how hopeless he is.[2] The questions "Where then is my hope?" and "Who will see my hope?" (Job 17:15) state the theme of these chapters perfectly. He is without hope because God, as Job sees the situation, is against him (16:6–17), and there is nothing he can do about it (16:18–17:16). He must somehow endure his broken relationships, the disdain of his friends ("my friends scorn me," 16:20), the mockery of men ("Men . . . have struck me insolently on the cheek," 16:10; cf. 17:2), and the silence ("my eye pours out tears to God," 16:20) and anger of God ("He has torn me in his wrath and hated me," v. 9a).

Job's Friends Are Against Him (Job 16:1–6)

Job has had enough; and he has heard enough! Job's friends are not doing their job. They came to "comfort him" (Job 2:11; *nakham*). Instead, they are "miserable comforters" (16:2; *menakhame ʿamal*): "I have heard many such things; miserable comforters are you all" (v. 2). Job is not the one filled with "windy knowledge" (15:2; cf. 8:2); *they* are: "Shall windy words have an end? Or what provokes you that you answer?" (16:3). Their useless and oppressive counsel (their "windy words," v. 3a) seems endless. He is sick of their hot air in his face. Job wonders what their problem is. What continues to incite them that they keep answering his laments with their lies ("Or what provokes you that you answer?," v. 3b)? He wants to be left alone.

In Job 16:4–6, Job imagines trading places with his interlocutors: "I also could speak as you do, if you were in my place" (Job 16:4a–b). He could act

2. Even Job's temporary glimmers of hope (Job 16:19; 17:9) are, in the context of the whole speech, quickly snuffed out.

as they are acting. He could prod them with dispassionate poetry ("I could join words together against you," v. 4c) and wag his head in disbelief and dismay ("and shake my head at you," v. 4d). Or he could take the high road, the path that they should be on: "I could strengthen you with my mouth, and the solace of my lips would assuage your pain" (v. 5). He could use his words to build them up, not tear them down, bringing strength and "solace," helping "assuage" their "pain." Job has tried everything. He has tried to comfort himself with such words of strength and solace, but even his own method does not work: "If I speak, my pain is not assuaged" (v. 6a). He has also tried refraining from offering himself words of comfort, and yet that too offers little relief ("and if I forbear, how much of it leaves me?," v. 6b).

Job will go on to speak more in the verses to come about the social pain he is experiencing. He is "desolate" of true "company" (Job 16:7), viewed by everyone as the embodiment of misfortune ("made . . . a byword," 17:6a), and some people even "spit" on him (v. 6a). He will also speak of the physical pain. People strike him "insolently on the cheek" (16:10), his skin is as rough and brittle as "sackcloth" (v. 15a), and his "strength" has completely left him ("laid . . . in the dust," v. 15b). But we should not lose sight that it is the emotional and spiritual pain (mixed with the physical, of course) that he likewise expresses. He feels as though his "kidneys" (a Hebrew idiom for what we'd call the heart) have been slashed open (v. 13),[3] his "face is red with weeping" (v. 16a), he has bags under his swollen eyes from night after night of his loss of sleep (his "eyelids" resemble "deep darkness," v. 16b; "eye . . . grown dim from vexation," 17:7a), and his whole body ("my members") has wasted away "like a shadow" (v. 7b). "My days are over," he laments. "My hopes have disappeared. My heart's desires are broken" (v. 11 NLT).

One wonders whether Job has come to the point—socially, physically, emotionally, and spiritually—at which the tears have stopped or are about to stop. He has nothing left to give. He has reached the place that Jerry Sittser describes after the loss of his wife, children, and mother in a car accident:

> I remember counting the consecutive days in which I cried. Tears came for forty days, and then they stopped, at least for a few days. I marveled at the genius of the ancient Hebrews, who set aside forty days for mourning, as if

3. After the loss of two children in infancy, Nancy Guthrie describes the pain as being like a "boulder on [her] chest." *What Grieving People Wish You Knew About What Really Helps (and What Really Hurts)* (Crossway, 2016), 12.

> forty days was enough. I learned later how foolish I was. It was only after those forty days that my mourning became too deep for tears. So my tears turned to brine, to a bitter and burning sensation of loss that tears could no longer express. In the months that followed I actually longed for the time when the sorrow had been fresh and tears came easily. That emotional release would have lifted the burden, if only for a while.[4]

For Job, as day after day has slipped by ("My days are past," Job 17:11a)—what he calls his "days of affliction" (30:16, 27) and "months of emptiness" (7:3)—perhaps now his mourning has become too deep for tears. From this point on, there is no further indication of Job's tears. These chapters record the last time that the words "weep" (see 16:16a) and "tears" (v. 20) are used.

God Is Against Him (Job 16:7–17)

Job cannot find comfort from his friends (Job 16:2–4). He cannot even comfort himself (v. 6). Is God, then, the solution? The suffering man answers with an emphatic "No!" In fact, in Job 16:7–11 (below), as well as verses 12–14, "the root reason why Job is suffering so intensely is not," as Christopher Ash summarizes, "contrary to what we might expect, because of his bankruptcy, his bereavements, or his bodily emaciation; it is because he is experiencing the felt hostility of God. God is the actor, the agent, and the attacker" in these verses.[5] Notice in italics below all that Job believes "God has" done to him:

> Surely now *God has worn me out*;
> *he has made desolate all my company.*
> And *he has shriveled me up*,
> which is a witness against me,
> and my leanness has risen up against me;
> it testifies to my face.
> *He has torn me in his wrath and hated me*;
> *he has gnashed his teeth at me*;
> my adversary [God!] *sharpens his eyes against me.*
> Men have gaped at me with their mouth;
> they have struck me insolently on the cheek;
> they mass themselves together against me.

4. Jerry Sittser, *A Grace Disguised: How the Soul Grows Through Loss* (Zondervan, 2021), 6.
5. Christopher Ash, *Job: The Wisdom of the Cross*, Preaching the Word (Crossway, 2014), 189.

> [Because] *God gives me up to the ungodly*
> and [God] *casts me into the hands of the wicked.*

Job believes that he is under God's "wrath" (Job 16:9a), an indignation that shows itself in both God's apparent attitude (the gnashing of teeth, the hateful glares) and his actions: God has "worn [him] out" (Job 16:7a), "shriveled [him] up" (v. 8a), "torn [him] in his wrath" (v. 9a), made "desolate" all his company ("casts me into the hands of the wicked," v. 11b), and provides every onlooker with evidence of Job's guilt before God (the state of his body is "a witness against me," v. 8a). Job also believes that another attack comes in the form of "men"—three men who could not believe their eyes when they first spotted Job (they "gaped at me," v. 10a; cf. 2:12) but who quickly united to turn against him ("they have struck me insolently on the cheek; they mass themselves together against me," 16:10b–c). Those who persecute him are not his friends only, but others from the surrounding lands who have come to see the spectacle and offer their abuse for Job's obvious iniquities: "Some great man! What a great sinner! Look at him!" Whether it is the friends, others, or both, Job admits defeat. He assumes that the warrior God is their commander-in-chief. "God gives me up to the ungodly," he complains, "and casts me into the hands of the wicked" (v. 11). *God* throws Job to the *ungodly*!? This is certainly how Job feels as he experiences the full arsenal of his friends' attack, as well as that of the mockers who stroll by to see the skinny statue of "The Wise Man of the East" deconstructed.

Job next recounts God's stealthy and severe strikes:

> I was at ease, and *he* [God] *broke me apart*;
> *he seized me by the neck and dashed me to pieces*;
> *he set me up as his target*;
> his archers surround me.
> *He slashes open my kidneys* and does not spare;
> *he pours out my gall* on the ground.
> *He breaks me* with breach upon breach;
> *he runs* upon me like a warrior. (Job 16:12–14)

Job has lost wealth, health, and children, along with his wife's and his friends' respect. The imagery—God's choking him, throwing him to the ground, and then having his archers use him as target practice and afterward slashing open his innards and watching his blood flow into the soil—is not as exaggerated as we might imagine. Job once enjoyed a life of prosperity and peace, but it did not end with a fairy-tale "happily ever after." Instead, for possibly months or even years, he has been relentlessly besieged by what appear to be cosmic forces set against him. He does not know what to do. He has done everything that he thinks he should do. He has repented of anything that he can possibly repent of: "I have sewed sackcloth upon my skin and have laid my strength in the dust" (Job 16:15).[6] He has turned to God for help. He is physically exhausted and spiritually drained ("my face is red with weeping, and on my eyelids is deep darkness," v. 16). But the sky seems made of stone. He does not understand why God will not hear his prayer and show mercy on him. He is, after all, innocent, and his cries for help sincere ("although there is no violence in my hands, and my prayer is pure," v. 17).

Job's honest evaluation of his situation finds an echo in Malcolm Guite's brilliant poem "Engine Against Th'Almightie," the seventh sonnet in his collection of reflections on George Herbert's exquisite sonnet "Prayer." On Herbert's seventh metaphor for prayer, Guite writes:

> Here in this shadowed valley, dark and bleak,
> We lay a bitter siege against the one
> Who was our heart's desire, but now withdraws
> Behind his battlements. Our prayers just break
> Against what seem like walls of silent stone.
> We make an engine of our injuries,
> And vault at God a volley of our sorrows:
> All the despair and anger that we feel.
> The catapult of our catastrophes
> Hurls up its heavy load, and flights of arrows
> Clatter against his walls, fall back and fail.
> How can we make him feel our miseries?
> We fling back famine at him, torture, cancer,
> Is he almighty then? Has he no answer?[7]

6. The ESV, with its alliteration, perfectly captures one of the greatest metaphors in the Bible. That Job has "sewed sackcloth" over his "skin" is a powerful image: he is in a constant state of humiliation before God.

7. Malcolm Guite, "Engine Against Th'Almightie," in *After Prayer: New Sonnets and Other Poems* (Canterbury Press, 2019), 10. Used by permission.

Like Job, Guite describes the seeming ineffectiveness of our prayers. The day in the "valley" is "shadowed" and "dark," and God ("our heart's desire") is inaccessible (he "withdraws behind his battlements"). We stand before the battlements and "catapult of our catastrophes" and sling "our sorrows" ("all the despair and anger that we feel"), but "our prayers just break against what seem like walls of silent stone," our many petitions, like "flights of arrows," crash and "clatter against his walls." The poem, which offers profound insights into our spiritual experience, ends with three questions about God: "How can we make him feel our miseries? . . . Is he almighty then? Has he no answer?"

Of course God is almighty. He has answers. He is intimately acquainted with our grief. As Christians, we know that the incarnation is the answer! In the coming of the Son of God, our deepest miseries were felt and sovereign love set on display. Jesus wept at Lazarus's tomb, prayed that his own sufferings would cease at Gethsemane, and cried out when he felt the deepest pain of forsakenness on the cross. So when we experience the silence of God in the deep and dark valleys of despair, we need to remember—in the words of Daniel 2:22—that God "knows what is in the darkness, and the light dwells with him."

Even Hope Will Not Lie in the Grave with Him (Job 16:18–17:16)

Job 16:18 is another beautifully crafted supplication, one that ties in to what Job has said in verses 7–17. He is not sure whether God can or will hear him, so he calls on the earth to vindicate him: "O earth, cover not my blood, and let my cry find no resting place" (Job 16:18; cf. v. 13). He also calls on someone in heaven to be his advocate: "Even now, behold, my witness is in heaven, and he who testifies for me is on high" (v. 19). He does not know whether heaven and earth will come to the rescue, but he has no other hope. Both his closest companions and his faithful God have forsaken him: "My friends scorn me; my eye pours out tears to God" (v. 20). But Job seems conflicted, as he speaks perhaps prophetically: "that he would argue the case of a man with God, as a son of man does with his neighbor" (v. 21). Who is the "he"? Is this "son of man" the Son of Man, the one who has come "to seek and to save" (Luke 19:10)? Is this intercessor the God-man? We know, but Job does not. Job is neither messianic nor optimistic. He knows that he will soon die: "For when a few years have come I shall go the way from which I shall not return" (Job 16:22).

Chapter 17 continues this theme of impending death: "My spirit is broken; my days are extinct; the graveyard is ready for me" (Job 17:1). Sheol awaits Job, where death will mock his existence: "So this is the greatest man of the east? Ha!" But for now, his friends do the job of mocking him. He is surrounded by deriders ("Surely there are mockers about me," v. 2a); he is forced to face their taunts ("my eye dwells on their provocation," v. 2b). Job needs God to put a down payment on his innocence ("Lay down a pledge for me," v. 3a) because no one else is wise enough and willing enough to do it, considering the circumstances ("who is there who will put up security for me?," v. 3b). Since he believes that God has barred his friends' minds from grasping the truth ("Since you have closed their hearts to understanding," v. 4a), Job hopes that they will not get the last word in the debate ("therefore you will not let them triumph," v. 4b). After all, their sin is obvious, and thus their retribution principle needs to be practiced on them! If they are going to mock and denounce Job, their children should suffer the consequences of their crimes: "He who informs against his friends to get a share of their property—the eyes of his children will fail" (v. 5).

Job's words are not careless; they are crafted against those who think he is crafty (cf. Job 15:5). Yet they are sad words. He is lost, confused. He turns again to contemplate God and his responsibility for Job's sorrows:

> He has made me a byword of the peoples,
>   and I am one before whom men spit.
> My eye has grown dim from vexation,
>   and all my members are like a shadow.
> The upright are appalled at this,
>   and the innocent stirs himself up against the godless.
> Yet the righteous holds to his way,
>   and he who has clean hands grows stronger and stronger.
> But you, come on again, all of you,
>   and I shall not find a wise man among you. (Job 17:6–10)

God, he says, "has made" him a "byword of the peoples" (the laughingstock of Uz) and the object of degrading physical scorn ("men spit" on him, Job

17:6). As a result of Job's sufferings, he can no longer see ("My eye has grown dim from vexation," v. 7a) or stand up straight. All his body parts ("members") are like sticks standing in the morning sun ("like a shadow," v. 7b). Yet under the shadow of the Almighty, Job still stands. He believes that his vindication is soon to come, for he knows that anyone who is truly blameless ("the upright" man) is appalled by what is happening to him, and such a man freely joins Job in his raging against the machine ("The upright are appalled at this, and the innocent stirs himself up against the godless," v. 8). Job trusts that his "godless" friends are not wise ("I shall not find a wise man among you," v. 10b). Sarcastically, he encourages them to give their attack another try ("But you, come on again," v. 10a). Meanwhile, he ("the righteous[,] . . . he who has clean hands") stands firm ("holds to his way"), and in doing so only "grows stronger and stronger" (v. 9).

Job's strength, however, has its limits. He can hold only so much weight over his head. In verses 11–16 of Job 17, he again descends (as he has done thus far in all his speeches) into the depths of despair. He is unlike the psalmists whose laments end in hopeful affirmations and praise.[8] He is more like Peter, who moves from a moment of great faith—walking on the water toward Christ—to suddenly seeing the storm afresh and quickly sinking into the sea. We see Job's feet sink below the waves:

> My days are past; my plans are broken off,
>   the desires of my heart.
> They make night into day:
>   "The light," they say, "is near to the darkness." (Job 17:11–12)

Job's good "days" are a thing of the "past," along with his heart's "desires" and "plans" for the future (Job 17:11). All that he might have hoped for is surely not going to happen ("broken off," v. 11). His friends have brought him to this place. They call good "evil" and evil "good" (cf. Isa. 5:20): "They make night into day: 'The light,' they say, 'is near to the darkness'" (Job 17:12). Job again embraces this darkness, piling morbid metaphor upon morbid metaphor:

8. The pattern of most biblical laments can be characterized by protest ("My eyes grow dim with waiting for my God," Ps. 69:3c–d), petition ("Deliver me from sinking in the mire; let me be delivered from my enemies and from the deep waters," v. 14), and praise ("I will praise the name of God with a song; I will magnify him with thanksgiving," v. 30).

> If I hope for Sheol as my house,
>   if I make my bed in darkness,
> if I say to the pit, "You are my father,"
>   and to the worm, "My mother," or "My sister,"
> where then is my hope?
>   Who will see my hope? (Job 17:13–15)

Even if Job embraces death as his abode ("Sheol" as his "house," the "darkness" of the grave as his "bed," Job 17:13) and as the only family he now has (calling his earthen tomb "father" and the decomposition of his body "mother" and "sister," v. 14), he will find no comfort. Will hope join him in the grave: "Will it go down to the bars of Sheol? Shall we descend together into the dust?" (v. 16)? Surely not. Hope is not going to rest in peace with him.

Under the Shadow of the Almighty, Job Still Stands

We might wonder why this debate between Job and his friends goes on so long. But it is part of the test. It is also part of the realism of Job's story. Real suffering rarely ends after a few hours, or in one day. We must keep this in mind when we go through extended periods of pain. We must also keep this in mind when attempting to comfort others.

Job begins this fourth reply to his friends by calling them "miserable comforters" (Job 16:2)—an apt summary of their role in his life. When he needed some soul therapy, they terrorized him with their theological talk. In his commentary on Job, John Goldingay uses Boaz as the type of comforter that Job needed instead and that we should be:

> In the story of Ruth, Boaz provides a neat example of the way "comfort" in the Old Testament can involve both words and actions. Boaz speaks appreciatively to Ruth about the way she has cared for Naomi and prays for Yahweh to bless her as she has come to seek refuge under his wings. Boaz has also taken action to ensure that Ruth can glean successfully and safely in his fields. One might see both the actions and words as expressions of the "comfort" she thanks him for.[9]

Be like Boaz, however, is not the only application of Job 16 and 17. *Marvel at Jesus* is another, one that goes to the depth of our faith. Job longed for a

9. John Goldingay, *Job for Everyone*, Old Testament for Everyone (Westminster John Knox, 2013), 84.

"witness . . . in heaven" who would testify on his behalf (Job 16:19). We have that witness in Jesus! Commenting on Job 16:18–21, David Jackson offers this insight into Job's thought process:

> If God is sovereign and all of this is God's doing; if God is just and he has declared Job to be righteous; if God cares for this image-of-God man that he has made out of the earth; if this is all real and not a dream—then there must be someone who can stand before God and speak on Job's behalf and present his case. God's courtroom must be a place where a righteous man can be defended and justified. So if God will not bring that courtroom to earth and if Job cannot ascend to heaven and enter it, there must be one who can represent him in heaven. The logic is inescapable and forces the realization that this mediator and advocate must be there.

From there, Jackson offers a beautiful connection to Christ and counsel for Christians, which I summarize as follows. When God in heaven seems silent, we must remember that our Mediator stands before the throne above on our behalf, and thus we can trust that justice, truth, and mercy always triumph.[10] Moreover, let us thank God—as a Puritan poet once phrased it—that "Thou hast given us a present, Jesus thy Son as Mediator between thyself and our souls, as middle-man who in a pit holds both him below and him above, for only he can span the chasm breached by sin, and satisfy divine justice."[11] That said, while we have in Jesus the Witness and Mediator that Job longed for, let us not forget that our "advocate with the Father," who turned away his wrath toward us ("He is the propitiation for our sins," 1 John 2:1, 2), did not arrive on the scene in a Rolls-Royce, step into the courtroom dressed in a $20,000 suit, and present our case with flawless oratorical skills. Instead, he endured the mockeries of men, the rejection of friends, and the wrath of God—everything that Job suffered, and infinitely more.[12]

The Mockeries of Men

First, we have a Mediator who has undergone the worst mockeries of men. Other than Psalm 22 and Isaiah 53, no other place in the Old Testament better

10. David R. Jackson, *Crying Out for Vindication: The Gospel According to Job*, Gospel According to the Old Testament (P&R Publishing, 2007), 96–97.

11. Adapted from Arthur Bennett, ed., *The Valley of Vision: A Collection of Puritan Prayers and Devotions* (Banner of Truth, 2006), 31.

12. A few lines from this final section come from Douglas Sean O'Donnell, *Mark: Arise and Follow the Son*, Expository Reflections on the Gospels 3 (Crossway, 2024), 462, 494–95.

depicts so vividly the reality of the mockery of an innocent sufferer. On the mount of his sufferings—the ash heap outside the city—Job was reviled by his friends ("My friends scorn me," Job 16:20) and had people who gawked at him with mouths wide open ("gaped at me with their mouth," v. 10a). He also had people who turned their stunned silence into violence. Job was spat on (17:6) and "struck . . . insolently on the cheek" (16:10b). Job sat there, enduring their disdain ("my eye dwells on their provocation," 17:2b).

Likewise, and furthermore (the furthest of the more!), Jesus endured men's mockery. Like Job's passion, Jesus' passion features the persecuted protagonist being struck in the face and spat on. After Jesus appeared before Pilate, the Roman soldiers struck Jesus' "head with a reed" as they spat "on him" (Mark 15:19), and then before the Sanhedrin "they spit in his face and struck him" and "slapped him" (Matt. 26:67). Moreover, throughout his passion, our Lord was mocked. Pilate mocked Jesus by labeling him "the King of the Jews," both when he was seeking to release him (Mark 15:9, 12) and as his sentence of condemnation (v. 26). The Roman soldiers "mocked" (v. 20) him repeatedly. Before the crucifixion, they clothed him in purple, placed a crown of thorns on his head, saluted him, struck him with a reed-made scepter, and bowed before him. During the crucifixion, they offered him mixed wine. Both Matthew and Mark tell us that the wine was mixed with something ("gall," Matt. 27:34a; "myrrh," Mark 15:23), which indicates that this was a cruel joke, like offering a thirsty man lemon juice and calling it lemonade or allowing this "king" to sip some rancorous wine.[13] After the crucifixion, the soldiers mocked Jesus by dividing his clothing. We read that "they . . . divided his garments among them, casting lots for them, to decide what each should take" (Mark 15:24). What this temporary casino at the foot of the cross shows—they gambled for his garments—is how insensitive they were to a dying man and how oblivious they were to the identity of Jesus and what he was doing right above them. It also once again shows that there are no limits to their mockery. They had nailed Jesus to a tree without his clothes on, or very little (perhaps a loincloth). How embarrassing! How shameful.

Finally, Jesus was "derided" by the Jews, "those who passed by" (Mark 15:29)[14] the cross (vv. 29–30), was "mocked" (v. 31) by "the chief priests with the scribes" (vv. 31–32a), and was even tormented by "those who were crucified

13. See Craig A. Evans, *Mark 8:27–16:20*, Word Biblical Commentary 34B (Thomas Nelson, 1988), 501.

14. Matthew adds that "those who passed by derided him, *wagging their heads*" (Matt. 27:39), a

with him" (v. 32b; "the robbers . . . also reviled him," Matt. 27:44; cf. Ps. 22:7, 13). Surely sticks and stones—or thorns and nails, in this case—hurt Jesus' body and bones, but a major part of Jesus' ex*cruc*iating pain was the consistent and persistent ridicule that he received in his last hours.

The Rejection of Friends

Second, we have a Mediator who endured the full rejection of his closest companions. As much as Job feels that he suffers alone (indeed, at this point, he has found no sympathy from friends or family), Jesus' isolation was far more intense.

After Jesus was arrested, Mark records one of the saddest verses of the Bible: "And they all [his eleven disciples] left him and fled" (Mark 14:50). The word "all" springs off the sheet. The word "left" is also striking, for in the first chapter of Mark's Gospel, some of Jesus' disciples had left (*aphienai*) their livelihoods to follow Jesus (1:18, 20); now, as he approached his moment of great suffering, they left (*aphienai*, 14:50) Jesus to save their own lives. At this point, not one of the Twelve would heed Mark 8:34 and "deny himself and take up his cross and follow." If Jesus felt abandoned by his friends when he prayed at Gethsemane, imagine how he felt here. Moreover, notice that as the Lamb of God was led away to slaughter (see Isa. 53:6–7), the darkest sheep—Judas—betrayed Jesus, while the others from the apostolic flock not only strayed, but "fled"! Even a would-be disciple joined them in their sprint to safety ("And a young man followed him, with nothing but a linen cloth about his body," but when the mob "seized him," or tried to, "he left the linen cloth and ran away naked," Mark 14:51–52). All have gone astray; all have run away. Literally. "As we are saved by Christ *alone*, our Savior has to suffer *alone*,"[15] writes one commentator. Of course, the good news of Jesus' betrayal by his closest friends is the path to our salvation. It is the lesson well summarized in Isaiah 53:6 and played out on the cross of Calvary:

> All we like sheep have gone astray;
>   we have turned—every one—to his own way;
> and [meanwhile] the Lord has laid on him
>   the iniquity of us all.

possible echo to Job's experience. That Job wished he could "shake [his] head" (Job 16:4) at his friends implies that they had been doing just that to him.

15. C. J. Williams, *The Shadow of Christ in the Book of Job* (Wipf & Stock, 2017), 43.

The Weight of God's Wrath

Third, we have a Mediator who, as the perfectly righteous and absolutely beloved Son of God, felt the full weight of God's wrath. Job felt something of the loss of God's presence and protection ("God gives me up to the ungodly and casts me into the hands of the wicked," Job 16:11); but Jesus experienced becoming sin for us and in doing so experienced the wrath of God on our behalf ("Jesus [was] delivered up according to the definite plan and foreknowledge of God" to be "crucified and killed by the hands of lawless men," Acts 2:23, and thus to be "the propitiation for our sins," 1 John 2:2).

In Matthew's Gospel, following the verbal ridicule (Matt. 27:41–44), we hear Jesus' cry of dereliction, "My God, my God, why have you forsaken me?" as darkness covered the land (vv. 45–46). This moment atop Golgotha takes us back to Jesus' prayers in Gethsemane. What Jesus dreaded more than anything else was the silence of and the separation from his Father—drinking the cup of God's holy judgment on sin. How could there be silence? How could there be separation? The answer is hinted at in Matthew 8:17, where the Evangelist quotes Isaiah 53:4, "He took our illnesses and bore our diseases," more directly stated by Jesus in Matthew 20:28: "the Son of Man came . . . to give his life as a ransom for many"—in other words, to "pour out" his blood "for many for the forgiveness of sins" (Matt. 26:28). How are sins forgiven? Jesus became sin for us, and in Jesus' becoming sin (cf. 2 Cor. 5:18–21), there was some inexplicable yet unavoidable silence and separation from the Father. His temporary damnation; our eternal salvation!

Here, Then, Is Our Hope

At this point in his story, Job is hopeless. He cries out, "Where then is my hope?" (Job 17:15). We, at this point (and every point) in our lives as Christians, have all the hope in the world. Or, more accurately, in heaven! Because Jesus—"our Savior and . . . our hope" (1 Tim. 1:1)—suffered the mockery, the physical pain, the social rejection, and the separation, we have the "hope of eternal life" (Titus 1:2; 3:7), "the hope laid up for [us] in heaven" (Col. 1:5), "the hope" that is described as "the hope of glory" (v. 27; cf. Rom. 5:2). Thus, we "rejoice in hope" (Rom. 12:12). We "share" now in "Christ's sufferings" so that we will "rejoice and be glad when his glory is revealed" (1 Peter 4:13). Yes, we know that we suffer nothing on earth that is not for our spiritual good. We know that the grave cannot hold us any longer than it held Jesus. We have the hope of eternal life and blessed joy. We have the hope of heaven.

15

Bildad: Bad Things Happen to Bad People

Job 18:1–21

Indeed, the light of the wicked is put out, and the flame of his fire does not shine. (Job 18:5)

Popular dystopian novels and the films that usually follow their success offer a real appeal to many millions. And to me. Aldous Huxley's *Brave New World* and George Orwell's *1984* are interesting and insightful works written in 1931 and 1949. A decade before Huxley's classic, Russian author Yevgeny Zamyatin wrote the novel *We*.[1] Orwell asserted that Huxley built on some of Zamyatin's themes—a claim that Huxley denied. Whatever the truth of Orwell's claim, the novel *We* captured well the premise of all future novels in this genre, namely, a world of conformity under a totalitarian regime.

In Job 18, Bildad, the traditionalist or the strict conformist to the traditional retribution regime, offers Job his second rebuttal. He wants eccentric and individualistic Job's "I" (the "you/r" italicized below) to conform to the conventional "we."

1. Zamyatin wrote Мы (*We*) in 1920–21, and it was translated and published in English in 1924.

How long will *you* hunt[2] for words?
  Consider, and then *we* will speak.
Why are *we* counted as cattle?
  Why are *we* stupid in *your* sight?
You who tear yourself in *your* anger,
  shall the earth be forsaken for *you*,
  or the rock be removed out of its place? (Job 18:2–4)[3]

Bildad knows nothing of computer software, but he believes that the world perfectly reflects the retribution algorithm. He holds that there are precise and predictable patterns to the moral order of the world. Job's responses from his experiences, which are radical to Bildad the theoretical ethicist, repudiate this reality. Job claims that Bildad's retribution algorithm does not accurately reflect how the world, under God's sovereign but mysterious rule, has been programmed to work for him. Bildad is befuddled, the Shuhite stunned. How can this be? It's blasphemy! Or near-blasphemy. It is certainly disrespectful to the time-tested totalitarian theological tenets. What about the *we*?

Job's folly is obvious to Bildad. He is an angry sinner ("You who tear yourself in your anger," or "tear yourself apart inside as you tore your clothing in two"), who arrogantly thinks the earth should be abandoned and a mountain moved to clear space for him ("shall the earth be forsaken for you, or the rock be removed out of its place?," Job 18:4). Job's "point of view is too self-centered and grandiose," and his "theology," according to Bildad, "is entirely too anthropocentric, indeed, egocentric."[4] He assumes that "the universe" should be "redesigned just for him."[5] Job still searches for something to say ("you hunt for words," v. 2),[6] or for word-traps to

2. Before Bildad moves to the singular "you" in Job 18:4, he starts with the plural in verses 2 and 3. He does this either to include Job with the wicked, the subject of much of this chapter, or as a "sarcastic allusion to Job's associating himself with the company of the righteous (cf. 17:8, 9)." Meredith Kline, "Job," in *Wycliffe Bible Commentary*, ed. Charles F. Pfeiffer and Everett F. Harrison (Moody, 1963), 475.

3. "Job ended his previous speech, in chapter 17, with a list of rhetorical questions, and Bildad opens his second speech in the same fashion. Once again, too, the speaker starts with a verbal barrage of insults (cf. Eliphaz in 15:2–3 and Job in 16:2–3)." Daniel J. Estes, *Job*, Teach the Text (Baker, 2013), 110. "The dialogue decreases and angry attacks directed at each other increase." Richard P. Belcher Jr., *Job: The Mystery of Suffering and God's Sovereignty*, Focus on the Bible (Christian Focus, 2017), 111. The friends' "later replies degenerate into irrelevant harangues on the woes of the wicked." Kline, "Job," 475.

4. C. L. Seow, *Job 1–21: Interpretation and Commentary*, Illuminations (Eerdmans, 2013), 778.

5. Kline, "Job," 475.

6. "How long will you say these things, and the words of your mouth be a great wind?" (Job 8:2).

lay,[7] after dismissing the caring counsel and wise words of the *we*: "we [are] counted as cattle" and "we" are seen as "stupid in your sight" (v. 3). Job thinks the friends are acting like "stupid, abominable, and even savage" beasts, but "it is Job himself who has acted so bestially ['*you* (singular) who tear *yourself* in *your* anger' (v. 4)]. Job as the predator preys on none other than himself. This is an image not just of a wild animal, a stupid creature, but a demented, self-destructive beast!"[8]

The *we* are not happy; and the *me*-on-behalf-of-them (Bildad) steps in to disabuse Job of his crazy claims. He offers a short sermon (Job 18:5–21). Job is surely glad for its brevity, if not for its content. Following his demeaning and accusatory introduction, Bildad blasts Job with his sermon's big idea: bad things happen to bad people. Or, as summarized elsewhere: "There are no exceptions to the rule that the wicked suffer God's punishment. Sin leads to suffering; and suffering is a sure sign that will lead the observant observer of the obvious to a sinner—like *you*, Job!"[9] Bildad's big idea is an awful idea, an evil idea—an awful and evil idea that is as new as the sun rising and setting on Job's well-worn ash heap.[10]

Bildad's Short Satanic Sermon (Job 18:5–21)

After the Shuhite seeks to silence his opponent with his introduction (which can be titled "You Shut Up and Cool Down and Let Cooler Heads Speak"), the pious preacher descends deeper into darkness. He titles his diatribe, "The Wick of the Wicked Is Snuffed Out," offering a word-painting of the wicked that closely resembles Job's own portrait.[11] Job knows this course in sub-biblical theology as Retribution Principle 101. Yet he is forcibly reenrolled for yet another semester in the School of Shame!

"In sharp contrast to his initial speech, where he outlines distinct outcomes for both the wicked ([Job] 8:11–15) and the righteous (8:16–19), Bildad now focuses solely on the destiny of the wicked, mirroring Eliphaz's approach

7. "How long will you set word snares?" (Job 18:2a). Marvin H. Pope, trans., *Job: Introduction, Translation and Notes*, Anchor Bible 15 (Doubleday, 1973), 132.

8. Seow, *Job 1–21*, 773.

9. Adapted from Douglas Sean O'Donnell, "Job," in *Ezra–Job*, vol. 4 of *ESV Expository Commentary*, ed. Iain M. Duguid, James M. Hamilton Jr., and Jay Sklar (Crossway, 2020), 402.

10. Job has heard this sermon, in various forms, before; see Job 4:7–11; 5:2–7; 8:3–4, 11–19; 11:11; 15:20–35.

11. Kline, "Job," 475. See also note 20 below.

in his second speech (15:2–35)."[12] He starts with his seemingly unshakable thesis that those who deny and disobey God will die: "Indeed, the light of the wicked is put out, and the flame of his fire does not shine" (v. 5).[13] Next, he offers a string of illustrations to support this irrefutable fact. Continuing with the light/darkness metaphor, Bildad speaks of the fate of the wicked before death: "The light is dark in his tent, and his lamp above him is put out" (v. 6). The first metaphors are about extinguished light. Job has talked much about darkness, the "deep darkness" (3:5; 12:22; 16:16) of his sufferings. Bildad says in effect: "You have not seen *deep* darkness yet. What you have experienced has all been surface stuff." The life ("the light," 18:5a, 6a; "the flame of his fire," v. 5b; "his lamp," v. 6b) of the ungodly is eventually "put out" completely (vv. 5a, 6b).[14] No light whatsoever! His lamp might flicker for a moment, but soon enough darkness encompasses his whole household ("dark in his tent," v. 6a). Perhaps his children die, his possessions are destroyed, and his health deteriorates. Then death comes to town. "If light is symbolic of life (3:20), wealth (22:28), and happiness," as Richard Belcher points out, "then darkness represents loss (15:30), sadness, and death (3:5)." Indeed, Job's "whole life is enveloped in darkness."[15]

Bildad's theology here is *biblical* (or at least resembling teaching found elsewhere in the Bible: e.g., "for the evil man has no future; the lamp of the wicked will be put out," Prov. 24:20), but in Job's case, its application is *diabolical*. Job, we can safely assume, is begging for a break from the babble ("How long will you torment me and break me in pieces with words?," Job 19:2). But no such relief is given; Bildad plows through his prepared speech. Though he has had nine chapters to prepare, the message has not changed, only the metaphors:

> His strong steps are shortened,
>   and his own schemes throw him down.
> For he is cast into a net by his own feet,
>   and he walks on its mesh.
> A trap seizes him by the heel;
>   a snare lays hold of him.

12. Seow, *Job 1–21*, 770.

13. Seow, 770.

14. While the image of "light" might include health and prosperity, it is clearly an allusion to life: "the light of life" (Job 33:30); and "Why is light given to him who is in misery, and life [given] to the bitter in soul?" (3:20). "Darkness" is also an allusion to death (3:5; 10:21; 17:13).

15. Belcher, *Job*, 112. See also John E. Hartley, *The Book of Job*, NICOT (Eerdmans, 1988), 275.

A rope is hidden for him in the ground,
    a trap for him in the path.
Terrors frighten him on every side,
    and chase him at his heels.
His strength is famished,
    and calamity is ready for his stumbling.
It consumes the parts of his skin;
    the firstborn of death consumes his limbs. (Job 18:7–13)

Job 18:7–13 describes a fugitive who is caught in his own devices and eventually meets the judgment that he has been running from (cf. Prov 1:10–19). He runs, but soon he is out of breath ("His strong steps are shortened," Job 18:7a). He falls to the ground; his own sin has leveled him ("his own schemes throw him down," v. 7b). When he regains some strength, he runs again. But his foot is soon caught ("he is cast into a net by his own feet, and he walks on its mesh," v. 8). We might imagine the man (of course, Bildad has Job in mind) as dragging himself along, step by slow step in this fishnet trap set for birds, and then suddenly, when it could seemingly get no worse, a metal bear trap "seizes him by the heel" (v. 9a). Imagine the pain! This "snare lays hold of him" (v. 9b). He is tired now. Bleeding. Screaming. Yet he moves on. But the way of the wicked is not safe ("the way of the wicked will perish," Ps. 1:6). Another trap is there to meet him: "A rope is hidden for him in the ground, a trap for him in the path" (Job 18:10). He falls into a third trap. Tired. Bleeding. Screaming. Now there is no way for him to move forward.

What comes next is worse than the three traps.[16] Terrors! "Terrors frighten him on every side" (Job 18:11a). He moves the mesh, snare, and rope an inch or so, but with every inch, terrors are chasing "him at his heels" (v. 11b). He has lost all might ("His strength is famished," v. 12a; or "strength . . . consumed by hunger," NRSV).[17] Death or "calamity" is hungry as well—waiting for the white flag to be raised ("calamity is ready for his stumbling," v. 12b).

16. In Job 18:8–10, Bildad uses six different words ("net," "mesh," "trap" [*pāḥ*], "snare," "rope," "trap" [*ûmalkuḏtô*]) for the traps that the wicked man gets caught in. "The series of six traps leads one to expect a climactic seventh, but the climax is not another latent or covert danger. Instead, one finds instead a plurality of malevolent forces—'terrors,' forces associated with death and the underworld (Tromp, 1969, 74–75)—surrounding the trapped prey." Seow, *Job 1–21*, 775.

17. David J. A. Clines translates Job 18:12a as "Disaster is hungry for them." *Job 1–20*, Word Biblical Commentary 17 (Word, 1989), 405. The verse might be a synonymous parallelism, as the NIV translates it: "*Calamity* is hungry for him; *disaster* is ready for him when he falls."

Death does not wait long to feast on the flesh. To quote from Edgar Allan Poe, "No more dallying with the King of Terrors."[18] Slowly, death begins to nibble, eating away the flesh of the entrapped man ("It consumes the parts of his skin," v. 13a). Even death's offspring ("the firstborn of death"—perhaps the oddest image in the Bible—v. 13b, likely symbolizing deadly diseases), like a brood of vultures, join in the grotesque gorging ("consumes his limbs," v. 13b). The wicked man is being eaten alive by death and its offspring!

If Bildad weren't so serious, the picture here would be almost comical in its exaggeration. It is reminiscent of the funny scene in the Steve Martin movie *The Jerk*, where Navin R. Johnson (played by Martin) has just learned that he's lost his fortune. As he walks out on his loving wife and his trusted dog, he is depicted as slowly sauntering down the road in his bathrobe, with his pants around his ankles and his hair disheveled. He is carrying a chair, an ashtray, matches, a wooden paddleball, a remote control, a lamp, and a magazine, and with each item he took from the house he says, "That's all I need." He is now bankrupt, homeless, and depressed. Bildad's description of the unrighteous is nearly as comical! Does he really believe that every man who disregards God's ways has an awful life before he experiences a more unremittingly awful death?

Consider the plight of a good friend—a dedicated pastor, husband, and father—losing his dear wife to ALS. As he transitions her to hospice care—a sweet Christian woman in her forties who has served her Savior for decades and walked faithfully in his ways—what would Bildad say to her? To her husband? To their three children? What hope would he offer? Does Bildad really believe that bad things happen only to bad people? Moreover, has Bildad forgotten the state of his friend who stands (or lies) right in front of him? He obviously knows what has happened, since he clearly makes connections to Job's situation.[19] Simply imagine what Job looks like at this point. In William Blake's famous paintings of Job, the characters in the drama—including Job—are depicted like bodybuilders. If Job was well built before his tragedies, it is doubtful whether he has kept his fine physique. More likely, Job is naked, skinny, and clutching

18. From Edgar Allan Poe's short story "The Pit and the Pendulum," in *The Gift: A Christmas and New Year's Present* (Carey & Hart, 1842), 150.

19. "Bildad gives a transparent allegory which is singularly cruel in its obvious reference to Job's bereavement. The last state, having *no offspring, descendant* or *survivor*, is the worst." Francis I. Andersen, *Job*, Tyndale Old Testament Commentaries 13 (InterVarsity Press, 1976), 190.

a loaf of bread in his hands, as the fifteenth-century Italian artist Sefer Emet depicts him.[20]

We don't know whether Job was hungry or cold, although he may have been. But we do know that Job was weak and emaciated ("My body is clothed with worms and scabs, my skin is broken and festering," Job 7:5 NIV; "my bones stick to my skin and to my flesh," 19:20a), and surely mourning the loss of his children, wealth, and status ("My face is red with weeping, dark shadows ring my eyes," 16:16 NIV; "my eyes have grown dim with grief," 17:7a NIV). Of Job's condition, Bill and Will Kynes ask: "Can you picture that? What a pathetic sight he is! Job is trapped in the depths of a deep, deep pit of despair."[21] We can picture that! But somehow Bildad is looking past Job, not at Job, for he offers no concern for his friend's needs. As Kynes and Kynes continue:

> Pity is just what these friends lack. Where is their compassion, their commiseration, their condolence? They fail to enter into the depth of Job's despair; they rationalize rather than sympathize; they speak to Job's mind, but totally bypass his heart. These are the cries of a broken and despairing man, a man who had once lived in the joyous blessing of Almighty God, but who now knows nothing but pain, loss, and grief. But they treat Job as if he were a student in a theology seminar.[22]

Job will soon beg Eliphaz, Bildad, and Zophar for mercy ("Have mercy on me, have mercy on me, O you my friends," Job 19:21), but here no mercy is offered. "When pain is to be borne," C. S. Lewis writes, "a little courage helps more than much knowledge, a little human sympathy more than much courage, and the least tincture of the love of God more than all."[23] Job needs their sympathy and love!

Bildad offers none of that. Instead, he believes, as with the sin of Achan (see Josh. 7:15), that "evil such as Job's so contaminates and destabilizes the created order that . . . it must be purged from the cosmos."[24] For in Job 18:14–20, Bildad continues his ridiculous rhetorical tirade, proposing that

20. For a visual, see Seow, *Job 1–21*, 772.

21. Bill Kynes and Will Kynes, *Wrestling with God: Defiant Faith in the Face of Suffering* (IVP Academic, 2022), 83.

22. Kynes and Kynes, 83–84.

23. C. S. Lewis, *The Problem of Pain* (Macmillan, 1948), vii.

24. J. Gerald Janzen, *Job*, Interpretation: A Bible Commentary for Teaching and Preaching (John Knox, 1985), 128.

the ruin of the wicked man's house ("tent," Job 18:6a, 14a, 15a; "habitation," v. 15b; "dwellings," "place," v. 21) and household ("memory," "name," v. 17; "posterity," "progeny," "survivor," v. 19) will surely follow the demise of the man himself (vv. 7–14):

> He is torn from the tent in which he trusted
>   and is brought to the king of terrors.
> In his tent dwells that which is none of his;
>   sulfur is scattered over his habitation.
> His roots dry up beneath,
>   and his branches wither above.
> His memory perishes from the earth,
>   and he has no name in the street.
> He is thrust from light into darkness,
>   and driven out of the world.
> He has no posterity or progeny among his people,
>   and no survivor where he used to live.
> They of the west are appalled at his day,
>   and horror seizes them of the east. (Job 18:14–20)

Not only has the wicked man been torn from his seemingly secure home and given death to devour, his secure reputation has been thrown out the window as well—or, to change the metaphor, is being eaten with the winds of time. Instead of being filled with children—his legacy—his house is hellish. Within ("in his tent dwells") and above ("over his habitation") are not children who bear his name but scattered "sulfur" that burns all into oblivion (Job 18:15). His fate is like that of Sodom and Gomorrah, with his ashes spread "in the land of forgetfulness" (Ps. 88:12).

Bildad is awful here. He is directly telling Job, with the loss of his children, that his legacy has vanished. Job knows this, bemoans this. But Bildad does not care. He has another harsh poetic pronouncement:

> His roots dry up beneath,
>   and his branches wither above.
> His memory perishes from the earth,
>   and he has no name in the street. (Job 18:16–17)

Not only is Job, according to Bildad, "thrust from light into darkness" or, put another way, "driven out of the world" (Job 18:18) and his offspring annihilated ("He has no posterity"/"among his people, . . . no survivor," v. 19), but everyone—all the people "of the west" and "of the east"—is disgusted by his life as well ("are appalled at his day"/"horror seizes them," v. 20).

Bildad completes his response with a final parallelism, a couplet conclusion on "the consequences of being caught"[25] (Job 18:21): "Surely

such are	the dwellings	of the unrighteous,
such is	the place	of him who knows not God."

Finally, "God" (*'el*) is mentioned, but not as Job's helper or refuge, or merciful Maker—but as fearsome Judge. Like the tail of a scorpion, the end of this sermon stings! Earlier Bildad claimed that Job, and the wicked like him, had forgotten God (Job 8:13); now he states that Job "knows not God" (18:21). Ouch! Unlike Jonathan Edwards's famous sermon "Sinners in the Hands of an Angry God," in which Edwards offers the hope of salvation,[26] Bildad's infamous sermon holds out absolutely no hope for Job. Bildad will be shocked, needless to say, when, in the final chapter, God holds out more than hope—he gives Job both vindication and reward. We can only imagine what Bildad would have made of the gospel, the good news that angels longed to see (see 1 Peter 1:12). Bildad wouldn't have believed his eyes if he saw the fulfillment of God's plan of salvation through Jesus, who "was numbered with the transgressors" so as to make "intercession for the transgressors" (Isa. 53:12). He would be utterly amazed that a member of the Holy Trinity would descend to earth, become a man, live a perfectly righteous life, and then suffer and die for sinners ("he bore the sin of many," v. 12), and (the gospel of amazing grace is even more amazing!) that through this atoning sacrifice God would hold out hope to even the vilest of sinners, to those who cling in faith to the cross of Christ.

Warning to the Wise

How should we reflect on and respond to what Bildad says in Job 18? There are some commendations mixed with condemnations, as well as a warning.

25. Seow, *Job 1–21*, 770.

26. For example, near the end of the sermon, Edwards preached, "And now you have an extraordinary opportunity, a day wherein Christ has thrown the door of mercy wide open, and stands calling and crying with a loud voice to poor sinners; a day wherein many are flocking to him, and pressing into the kingdom of God." Jonathan Edwards, "Sinners in the Hands of an Angry God," in *The Works of Jonathan Edwards*, ed. Edward Hickman, 2 vols. (Banner of Truth, 1992), 2:11.

We start with a warning, especially to Christian teachers. The folly of Bildad's counsel is reminiscent of the warning in James 3:1 that "not many of you should become teachers, . . . for you know that we who teach will be judged with greater strictness," along with the provocative taming-of-the-tongue sermon that follows shortly after that warning. That exposition contains lines that both Bildad and every believer need to hear. Bildad has set ablaze a great forest with his tongue. He has committed some serious sins—speech sins, sins of the untamed tongue.

We cannot underestimate the high calling of Christian leadership. We must, by God's gracious and powerful Holy Spirit, tame our tongues. For wisdom, as James goes on to say, is shown in "meekness," not false truths (James 3:13–14). We all need the "wisdom that comes down from above," a wisdom that is "pure, then peaceable, gentle, open to reason" (vv. 15–17). Such wisdom will produce "a harvest of righteousness" (v. 18). This is one answer or application to the question "How should we reflect on and respond to what Bildad says?"

Another application, also related to church leadership and teaching (but expansive enough to reach everyone in the pew today), relates to the scriptural qualifications for elders. One qualification for being an elder in Christ's church is ability to teach (2 Tim. 2:24). The rest of the qualifications, however, revolve around character, not skill or gifting. In fact, surrounding the important teaching proviso in Timothy are all the qualities that Bildad fails to demonstrate. Can we say that he is "not . . . quarrelsome but kind to everyone" (v. 24)? Can we say that he corrects his opponent "with gentleness," hoping that "God may perhaps grant [him] repentance leading to a knowledge of the truth" (v. 25; cf. Gal. 6:1)? Even though we know that the friends—not Job—need to "come to their senses" and "escape from the snare of the devil" (Satan), since they are, seemingly, "captured by him to do his will" (2 Tim. 2:26), can we even say that they, at any point, turn to God in prayer (calling on "the Lord from a pure heart," v. 22), asking for his view on the matter? Sadly, the answer to all these questions is no. Instead, Job's counselors breed this quarrel (contra Paul's admonition: "Have nothing to do with foolish, ignorant controversies; you know that they breed quarrels," v. 23)! Bildad is quarrelsome, is unkind, and offers corrections (wrong corrections) with a total lack of gentleness. Christian leader, Christian husband and wife, Christian mom or dad—don't be like Bildad!

A final answer to the question "How should we reflect on and respond to what Bildad says?" relates to the gospel. Speaking of the Bible's literary excellence, Jerome writes: "What is more polished than [the book of] Job?"[27] Bildad's words are indeed polished—as polished and sharp as Ehud's dagger (Judg. 3:21). His poetry is beautiful, some of the best in the whole literary masterpiece. Whether in his simple analogies ("Can reeds flourish where there is no water?," Job 8:11; "he lays hold of [his house], but it does not endure," v. 15) or clever word pictures ("His roots entwine the stone heap," v. 17; "he is cast into a net by his own feet," 18:8), the poet-philosopher impresses with his poetry but not his philosophy. Or his theology! Bildad's system of thought handcuffs God, puts him in a box, and closes the lid. It makes Yahweh not "I am who I am" (Ex. 3:14), but a robotic ruler who is as predictable as the atomic clock by which we set our watches.

The God of the Bible does not think or act predictably and mechanically. God does not bow the knee to some fixed formula. The unchangeable law of tradition is not his master. The prologue and epilogue of Job tell us as much. God's speeches in Job 38–41 shout from the housetops that his sovereign providence cannot be chained or reduced to simplistic explanations. The whole Bible, notably the gospel (God's becoming man and dying for our sins!), makes sure that we do not follow Bildad's philosophical and theological thought. We must leave room for God to be God, for his gospel of grace to be given and received, and for "the providential care of the Lord" to be "the ground for confident hope even when all seems hopeless."[28]

Earlier, I mentioned a friend whose dear wife was transitioning to hospice care. He sent out an email update that started in this way:

> I wanted to give you a quick update on my wife, and her battle with ALS. She is almost entirely wheelchair bound, cannot do even the smallest amount of self-care, now has a feeding tube in place, and her speech is almost entirely unintelligible. God has provided both the people and the funds for two remarkable caregivers when I am at work, since she needs constant care. She is in good spirits, trusting with courage and hope as she travails this path. Our children and I are dealing with true lament, yet we are thankful

27. Jerome, in his Latin translation of Eusebius of Caesarea's *Chronicon*, quoted in and translated by Michael Graves, *The Inspiration and Interpretation of Scripture: What the Early Church Can Teach Us* (Eerdmans, 2014), 78.

28. Estes, *Job*, 114.

> for the gift that she has been to each of us (we celebrate 25 years of marriage this July!) and for the true and mighty hope that is ours.

Bildad holds out no hope to Job. But we as Christians have all the hope in the world. And we as Christians should hold out hope (like a torch, a lantern, a lighthouse) to our brothers and sisters who are living through deep darkness, because we believe (unlike the *we* of the totalitarian regime of the retribution principle—bad things happen to bad people) that God is working through everything (even all the bad) for our good; yes, we believe that the providential care of the Lord is the very ground for our confident hope even when all seems hopeless.

The same hour I received that email from my friend, I was working on (how's this for the providence of God!) a sermon on the Sermon on the Plain, specifically on the verse where Jesus says, "Blessed are you who are hungry now, for you shall be satisfied" and "Blessed are you who weep now, for you shall laugh" (Luke 6:21), when I came across this sentence in Nick Perrin's commentary: "The repetition of [the word] *now* (*nyn*) in both of the beatitudes only sharpens the contrast: if this age is *now* fraught with sin, *now* mired in death, disease, deprivation and loss, the coming age will be no less extreme in its reversal of such things."[29] I sent the line to my friend, and he replied, within seconds, "Love it!"

Yes, we as followers of Jesus, love (!) and long for (!!) the great reversal that is soon to occur. We hold out hope because we have hope.

29. Nicholas Perrin, *Luke*, Tyndale New Testament Commentaries 3 (IVP Academic, 2022), 118.

16

Job: Have Mercy on Me, Have Mercy on Me, O You My Friends

Job 19:1–29

Have mercy on me, have mercy on me, O you my friends,
for the hand of God has touched me! (Job 19:21)

My fourth-grade teacher viewed personal note writing—handwritten notes passed from one student to another while she taught—as a near-capital offense. The punishment was to stay in during recess and write the definitions of five thousand words from the dictionary. Catholic schools back in the day!

One day, the most beautiful girl in class (Dana) passed me a note. It said "Doug + Amy," a simple and factually accurate statement. I did like Amy. I quickly replied with "Dana + Tom." A second after I turned around and stuffed the note under Dana's textbook, she lifted it, read it, grabbed the note she'd written off my desk, walked to the front, tossed her note into the trash, and handed mine to the teacher. She whispered in the teacher's ear, and the teacher then promptly pointed at me. "Douglas," she commanded, "come here!" I arose, defended myself, and showed evidence. We were *both* promptly sentenced. Sure enough, we spent the rest of recesses together that year, learning a whole lot of A-words. It was awful, atrocious, audacious—"audacious" in the sense of the second listed definition: "showing an imprudent lack of respect" (for me). I wished that we would get to the B-words so that I could write "betrayal," draw a picture of Dana, and slip the note on her desk.

Have you ever been betrayed by a friend? Most people have, and some (such as our Lord Jesus) have been betrayed unto death by those who knew them best and walked closely with them for years. Job was not betrayed unto death (although, at this point, he might have preferred that), but he was betrayed by his "close" and "intimate friends" (Job 19:14; 19). This chapter contains one of the most famous lines from the book of Job: "I know that my Redeemer lives" (v. 25). As we will see, in that section (vv. 23–27) Job does express hope for future vindication. But surrounding this fifth response to his friends are not rays of hope but more clouds of darkness.

Addressing his three "friends" (Job 19:14, 19, 21), Job denounces their friendship (vv. 1–6) because they have not accepted that God has brought these sufferings on Job for no reason ("know then that God has put me in the wrong," v. 6; "he has kindled his wrath against me," v. 11; "the hand of God has touched me!," v. 21). God has "stripped" Job of his "glory" (v. 9; cf. vv. 7–12) so much that those closest to him—his wife, brothers, and "intimate friends"—distance themselves from him (vv. 13–22). Job wants Eliphaz, Bildad, and Zophar to accept these facts and to be merciful to him ("Have mercy on me, have mercy on me, O you my friends," v. 21). He wants them to stop their pursuit of him ("Why do you, like God, pursue me?," v. 22a), and warns them what will happen if they do not: "be afraid of the sword" (vv. 28–29). Indeed, the final word—"judgment" (v. 29)—is a word of warning.

Tormented by Friends (Job 19:1–6)

We begin where Job begins Job 19, with his denouncement of his friends' friendship. Bildad has used opening questions about Job's words to begin his speeches ("How long will you say these things, and the words of your mouth be a great wind?," Job 8:2; "How long will you hunt for words?," 18:2a). In 19:1–2, Job questions Bildad's words, along with those of Eliphaz and

Zophar: "Then Job answered and said: 'How long will you [plural] torment me and break me in pieces with words?'" Job is not simply asking them to stop their useless talk; he is asking them to cease torturing him with their words. Their verbal reproaches seem endless ("these ten times," 19:3; cf. Gen. 31:7, 41; Num. 14:22), and his "friends" have no remorse for what they are doing to him: "These ten times you have cast reproach upon me; are you not ashamed to wrong me?" (Job 19:3). Job does not understand, for they have no case against him. He has committed no public, scandalous sin, and even if he is guilty of some small sin or inadvertent error, such a transgression and what God does with it are none of their business ("And even if it be true that I have erred, my error remains with myself," v. 4). Although they have no legal leg to stand on, they exalt themselves above Job ("you magnify yourselves against me") and use his humiliation as the only proof of his sin ("and make my disgrace an argument against me," v. 5).

Job wants his companions to know that this is not wise. He wants them to accept his innocence and understand that his sufferings are the result of God's sovereign will ("know then that God has put me in the wrong and closed his net about me," Job 19:6).

Stripped of His Glory (Job 19:7–12)

Like Habakkuk (see Hab. 1:2–4), Job cries out, "Violence!" (Job 19:7). The difference is that Job is speaking of God's attack against him. The other difference is that God answers Habakkuk immediately, while Job still waits to hear from God: "Behold, I cry out, 'Violence!' but I am not answered; I call for help, but there is no justice" (v. 7). Job feels that God has been unjust ("God has put me in the wrong," v. 6; "there is no justice," v. 7). Instead of treating Job like a righteous man, rewarding him with honor and lighting his way, God is treating him like the wicked:

> He has walled up my way, so that I cannot pass,
> and he has set darkness upon my paths.
> He has stripped from me my glory
> and taken the crown from my head.
> He breaks me down on every side, and I am gone,
> and my hope has he pulled up like a tree. (Job 19:8–10)

Moreover, instead of treating Job like a friend, providing for him and protecting him (cf. Job 1:10), God is treating him like an enemy:

> He has kindled his wrath against me
> and counts me as his adversary.
> His troops come on together;
> they have cast up their siege ramp against me
> and encamp around my tent. (Job 19:11–12)

With vivid imagery, Job describes his hopeless situation ("my hope has he pulled up like a tree," Job 19:10). One moment he feels completely trapped (God "has walled up my way, so that I cannot pass," v. 8a). Then, when he can move forward, he cannot see where he is going (God "has set darkness upon my paths," v. 8b). Job has lost all the high dignity that he once had (he is "stripped" of his "glory," v. 9). He is even the target of God's wrath ("He breaks me down on every side," v. 10a; "He has kindled his wrath against me. . . . His troops come . . . and encamp around my tent," vv. 11–12). On this image of God's mighty military laying siege to "little old Job in [his] one-man tent," Christopher Ash comments: "It is as if I go for a night's camping on my own. I wake, peep out of the tent, and all around me are tanks and gun emplacements, and overhead is the entire United States Air Force. All are bent on attacking me. We may surely feel with Job that there is a degree of overkill."[1]

There is an overkill of exaggeration, but there is also a sincere expression of despair by Job about God *to God*. Such an expression reminds me of the point in Carolyn S. Briggs's memoir *The Dark World: A Memoir of Salvation Found and Lost*, when she gives the account of her loss of faith. She portrays, by Joseph Minich's account, "a woman desperate to experience God, desperate to know that all things are in his [God's] control, desperate just to know that he is there." And she tells of the silence she met when she suffered spiritual abuse, when her friends battled cancer (and lost), and when her marriage failed.[2] Job too is met with divine silence through his sufferings, but he keeps his faith. He laments to God and complains against

1. Christopher Ash, *Trusting God in the Darkness: A Guide to Understanding the Book of Job* (Crossway, 2021), 74.

2. Joseph Minich, *Enduring Divine Absence: The Challenge of Modern Atheism* (Davenant Institute, 2018), 12.

God, but through both the doleful dirges and poignant protests (and even honest accusations!), he expresses extraordinary faith.

Ash speaks of the "unique pain" experienced only by believers—the pain that Job feels and expresses:

> There is a pain for the believer that gives suffering a unique sharpness. Suffering is the common experience of the human race. All sorts of people get ill; all kinds of people are touched by war, famine, and earthquake. And yet suffering touches the believer with a sharper and uniquely piercing pain.

He describes the problem of the believer's pain as follows:

> The worshiper truly believes that God is sovereign. He or she really believes that the living God is in control of his world. And so, when suffering comes, it must be God who ultimately sends it—after all, he is in control, is he not? It is not just that it hurts—although Job's suffering hurts abominably. It is more than this: it is the conviction that it is God who is in some sense doing the hurting.

Unbelievers might say that they are bothered by the injustice of suffering ("Why is a baby born with trisomy 18?"), but if they don't believe in a living and active God who is both completely sovereign and absolutely good, they don't face the same problem we do ("Why would you expect there to be sense and fairness in this world?"). If the innocent suffer, God must determine it. This is what Job believes as a believer ("if it is not he, who then is it?," Job 9:24), and he expresses such faith by laying the blame and the need for a solution at God's door (19:7–12). "The true believer," Ash continues, "will follow Job and rail passionately against the injustice of it all, calling on the sovereign God to do something. The believer takes seriously the 'godness' of God."[3]

Unloved by Loved Ones (Job 19:13–22)

From Job 19:6, Job has spoken about what God has done to him. His problem with pain is his problem with God, which he expresses in detail (see table 16.1).

3. Ash, *Trusting God in the Darkness*, 63, 64, 65.

Table 16.1. Job's Expressions of Pain at the Hand of God in Job 19

God has	put . . . in the wrong	v. 6a
[God has]	closed his net about [or around] me	v. 6b
He has	walled up my way, so that I cannot pass	v. 8a
He has	set darkness upon my paths	v. 8b
He has	stripped from me my glory	v. 9a
[He has]	taken the crown from my head	v. 9b
He	breaks me down on every side	v. 10a
He	has pulled up [my hope] like a tree [from the ground]	v. 10b
He	has kindled his wrath against me	v. 11a
[He]	counts me as his adversary	v. 11b
His troops	come on together [to conquer]	v. 12a

In Job 19:13, Job adds a final "He has": "He has put my brothers far from me, and those who knew me are wholly estranged from me." This complaint about being abandoned is followed by further embellishment and contemplation on the abandonment of his closest companions:

> My relatives have failed me,
>   my close friends have forgotten me.
> The guests in my house and my maidservants count me as a stranger;
>   I have become a foreigner in their eyes.
> I call to my servant, but he gives me no answer;
>   I must plead with him with my mouth for mercy.
> My breath is strange to my wife,
>   and I am a stench to the children of my own mother.
> Even young children despise me;
>   when I rise they talk against me.
> All my intimate friends abhor me,
>   and those whom I loved have turned against me. (Job 19:14–19)

Here Job bemoans the estrangement that his sufferings have caused between him and those closest to him: his "relatives" (Job 19:14a), "close friends" (v. 14b), "wife" (v. 17a), brothers ("the children of my own mother," v. 17b), and "intimate friends" (v. 19; likely the "brothers" of v. 13a and "close friends" of v. 14b, namely, Eliphaz, Bildad, and Zophar). He is even estranged from his household servants (vv. 15, 16), former houseguests (v. 15), and children from the community, or perhaps his nieces and nephews (v. 18). Collectively, they have all "failed" him (v. 14a), have "forgotten" him (v. 14b), are repulsed by him (v. 17), will not help him (v. 16), "despise" (v. 18a) and "abhor" him (v. 19a), and gossip against him (v. 18b). All those he has "loved have turned against" him (v. 19b). His own wife and brothers will not go near him: "My breath is strange to my wife, and I am a stench to the children of my own mother" (v. 17).[4] What "a pathetic picture of the isolation of the sufferer. Job is alienated, estranged, and forgotten."[5]

We can imagine the pain of such social estrangement and assaults, as well as the physical pain. Job is literally skin and bones ("My bones stick to my skin and to my flesh," Job 19:20a). He is barely alive. He has eluded death narrowly ("I have escaped by the skin of my teeth," v. 20b). Job needs mercy; he begs for it ("Have mercy on me, have mercy on me, O you my friends") and gives the reason for it ("for the hand of God has touched me!," v. 21). He needs Eliphaz, Bildad, and Zophar to be real friends and stop their verbal attacks ("Why do you, like God, pursue me?," v. 22a; cf. v. 2). He hopes his desperate physical condition is enough for them to show some compassion ("Why are you not satisfied with my flesh?," v. 22b).

A Glimmer of Hope (Job 19:23–27)

Following his plea for his friends to show mercy and stop attacking him (Job 19:21–22), Job returns to a theme touched on in Job 19:7. There he said, "Behold, I cry out, 'Violence!' but I am not answered; I call for help, but there is no justice." In verses 23–27, Job's heart faints within him (note the threefold repetition of "oh that") over the possibility of God's hearing and vindicating him. Job hopes that there might be a permanent written record of his vindication:

> *Oh that* my words were written!
>   *Oh that* they were inscribed in a book!
> *Oh that* with an iron pen and lead
>   they were engraved in the rock forever! (Job 19:23–24)

4. "My friends and companions stand aloof from my plague, and my nearest kin stand far off" (Ps. 38:11).

5. Ash, *Trusting God in the Darkness*, 74.

He hopes that there will be two witnesses to attest to the verdict "not guilty," one "inscribed in a book" (Job 19:23b) and another "engraved in the rock forever" (v. 24b).[6] Verses 25–27 of Job 19, three of the most famous verses of the book, stand out not only for their piercing clarity but also for their unusual tone. Job has been awfully hopeless since chapter 3. Even in Job 19:10, he described God's taking whatever deep root of hope Job still has and pulling it "up like a tree." But now a new seed of hope emerges. Light flashes across the stage of this depressing drama. We can almost hear Job singing his solo from the score of Handel's *Messiah*:[7]

> For I know that my Redeemer lives,
>   and at the last he will stand upon the earth.
> And after my skin has been thus destroyed,
>   yet in my flesh I shall see God,
> whom I shall see for myself,
>   and my eyes shall behold, and not another.
>   My heart faints within me! (Job 19:25–27)

Job uses the verb "I know" (*yadati*) to express his innocence and certainty (the sense being "I know that I shall be in the right"), and he ties that certainty to a certain "Redeemer" (*go'el*):

> In Israel, a *goel* was a family member with the official duty of preserving and defending the rights of his relatives. He might, for instance, buy back family property as a "kinsman-redeemer" (Lev 25:25), or avenge a murdered relative as "the avenger of blood" (Num 35:19). . . . The role of *goel* was intended to give human portrayal of God's redemption of his own household, the house of Israel. The Psalmist called him "my strength and my *goel*" (Ps. 19:14). God is the *goel* of his people as he delivers them from slavery in Egypt.[8]

By capitalizing the word "Redeemer" (Job 19:25), the ESV is either linking the word with "God" in Job 19:26 or making a Christological connection (the "Redeemer" is Jesus).[9] For example, C. J. Williams writes of the latter

6. "Of course, ironically, Job's words, here and elsewhere, are part of our unchangeable and enduring canonical Scriptures ('the word of the Lord remains forever,' 1 Peter 1:25; cf. Isa. 40:8)." C. J. Williams, *The Shadow of Christ in the Book of Job* (Wipf & Stock, 2017), 71.

7. George Frideric Handel, "I Know That My Redeemer Liveth," *Messiah* (1741).

8. Williams, *Shadow of Christ in the Book of Job*, 70–71.

9. "It is purely a divine reference, and perhaps the original depiction of God as *goel* in redemptive

interpretation: "His advocate, and ours, is the Lord Jesus Christ. In the covenant of grace, Christ is appointed as our representative. He makes our case for salvation, he covers us in his righteousness through the gift of faith, and he bears witness that we belong to him. The wrath of God, which all men so richly deserve for their sins, is satisfied for God's people by the righteous life and sacrificial death of our great advocate, Jesus Christ."[10]

Some commentators, however, think that the redeemer here is simply the advocate and witness that Job has described in Job 9:32–35 and 16:18–22. If this is true, then Job is once again asking for an intermediary or arbitrator who can represent him before Yahweh. The hope of this representation is restoration. But based on the immediate context, the context of the book, and the other Old Testament references, the most likely reading is that God himself is the "Redeemer" that Job hopes for. In the immediate context, "Job's description of his 'Redeemer' as one who 'lives' (Job 19:25) and his following reference to 'God' (v. 26) indicate he believes that God is the one who ultimately will vindicate him."[11] In the context of the book, we learn from chapter 42 that God himself, not some human or angel, redeems (in the sense of vindicates and restores) Job. Finally, "Redeemer" is a familiar title for God elsewhere in the Old Testament (see Ps. 19:14, Isa. 43:14; 44:6), and the same word describes God's activity with respect to both Israel as a nation (Ex. 6:6) and individuals (Gen. 48:16).

The phrase "at the last he will stand upon the earth" (Job 19:25b) likely refers to God as Job's Redeemer, taking the stand on his behalf at the end of the ages (judgment day).[12] Job perhaps envisions God as standing as a man next to him on the ash heap ("the earth" could be translated "the dust"). Here we might say, as John Hartley has, that "Job is beseeching the God in whom he has faith to help him against the God who is punishing him."[13] On that day ("at the last," v. 25) and in that place (upon the "ashes," 2:8; "earth," 19:25), another paradox occurs. Not only is the court case *God v. God*, but Job, who has talked about death as extinction (7:9; 10:21; 14:10, 12), here

history." Williams, 71. Taking the Christological position, Williams continues: "Job understood that God would become visible, and stand on the earth incarnate, as his Redeemer. The *goel* would make the invisible God visible" (71).

10. Williams, 68.

11. Kenneth Laing Harris and August Konkel, "Job," in *ESV Study Bible* (Crossway, 2008), 899.

12. "The last" could also, and simply, refer to "finally" or "at the end of Job's ordeal."

13. John E. Hartley, *The Book of Job*, NICOT (Eerdmans, 1988), 295.

speaks of dying ("after my skin has been thus destroyed," 19:26a) and yet somehow seeing God vindicate him ("yet in my flesh I shall see God," v. 26b), apparently in some resurrected state. "The references to skin, *flesh* and *eyes*," as Francis Andersen points out, "make it clear that Job expects to have this experience as a man, not just as a disembodied shade, or in his mind's eye."[14] Job envisions a resurrected body; and the thought of this beatific vision ("God, whom I shall see . . . and my eyes shall behold," vv. 26–27a–b)[15] and beautiful vindication is too much for him to take in ("My heart faints within me!," v. 27c). This future theophany is the ground of his hope.

Whatever Job's view at the time on the issue of a bodily resurrection,[16] we know from our Lord Jesus how to view the matter. It is clear from Jesus' interpretation of Exodus 3:6 ("I am the God of your father, the God of Abraham, the God of Isaac, and the God of Jacob") that Israel did believe, or should have believed, in life after death. Jesus rebukes the Sadducees' false view that there is no life after death, stating that Exodus 3:6 proves that God "is not God of the dead, but of the living" (Matt. 22:32)—in this instance, the patriarchs. Here Jesus points out that God's covenant with people presumes a continued relationship after death: when Abraham, Isaac, and Jacob died and were buried, not only were they "gathered to [their] people" (Gen. 25:8; 35:29; 49:33), but they were also gathered to their covenant-keeping God.

So while Job may not have been specifically thinking about Jesus' death and resurrection and the hope that Christians gain from those redemptive events when he uttered the words of Job 19:25–27, the earliest Christian commentators (from the time of Origen, c. 185–c. 253 on) were right to read this ancient text and Job's "extraordinary insight of faith"[17] in view of our

14. Francis I. Andersen, *Job*, Tyndale Old Testament Commentaries 13 (InterVarsity Press, 1976), 193. In *How Scripture Interprets Scripture: What Biblical Writers Can Teach Us About Reading the Bible* (Baker Academic, 2021), 154, Michael Graves renders Job 19:26–27 thus: "And after my skin has been destroyed, then from my flesh I will see God, whom I will see for myself; and my eyes will behold, and not a stranger. My feelings (kidneys) are consumed inside of me." And Graves thus concludes: "Job clearly believes that he will see God after his flesh has been destroyed. . . . He expects to see God after he dies."

15. On the phrases "will see, and my eyes," Albert the Great correctly notes that Job is speaking "not only of the heart [inwardly], but also of the body." St. Albert the Great, *On Job*, vol. 1, trans. Franklin T. Harkins, Fathers of the Church, Mediaeval Continuation 19 (Catholic University Press, 2019), 318.

16. Whatever Job's view, it was likely not, as Graves summarizes in his study of the Old Testament on the matter, "a fully formed theology of the afterlife but a vague assumption that people continue to exist in some way after they die." *How Scripture Interprets Scripture*, 149.

17. Ash, *Trusting God in the Darkness*, 80. Ash also labels these lines "perhaps the pinnacle of Job's faith in the darkness" (77).

Redeemer. Moreover, we can and should rejoice that we have a Redeemer, a Mediator who is both fully God and fully man (1 Tim. 2:5) and who has also turned away the full wrath of God on sinners (Rom. 5:9).

> The point at which Job arrives—anticipating a divine Redeemer to rescue him from divine wrath—takes us to the very heart of the gospel, and only makes sense from a Trinitarian understanding of salvation. The redemption of God rescues us from the wrath of God. The Father's justice is satisfied by the Son's sacrifice. God is *simul Iudex et Redemptor*—at the same time Judge and Redeemer.[18]

We should celebrate that we have been redeemed by his blood (Eph. 1:7; Col. 1:20; Rev. 5:9), and that we have a "living hope" (1 Peter 1:3) of physical resurrection, final vindication, and future glorification and beatific vision ("we know that when he appears we shall be like him, because we shall see him as he is," 1 John 3:2), all because Jesus has conquered the grave. We should joyfully sing Handel's great aria in the *Messiah*, where Job 19:25–26 is juxtaposed with 1 Corinthians 15:20, "But now is Christ risen from the dead, and become the firstfruits of them that slept" (KJV). As Hartley well summarizes:

> Job is working with the same logic of redemption that stands as the premise of the NT doctrine of the resurrection. Both hold to the dogma that God is just even though he permits unrequited injustices and the suffering of the innocent. God, himself, identified with Job's sufferings in the suffering of his Son, Jesus Christ, who suffered unto death even though he was innocent. Jesus overcame his ignominious death by rising from the grave. In his victory he, as God's Son and mankind's kinsman-redeemer, secured redemption for all who believe on him. While his followers may suffer in this life, he is their Redeemer, their Advocate before the Father. In this way Job's confidence in God as his Redeemer amidst excruciating suffering stands as a model for all Christians.[19]

A Warning to the "Wise" (Job 19:28–29)

After Job has spoken about how his friends have tormented him (Job

18. Williams, *Shadow of Christ in the Book of Job*, 72.
19. Hartley, *Job*, 297.

19:1–6) and his loved ones despised him (vv. 13–22), and how he has lost his former glory (vv. 7–12) but hopes for future redemption (vv. 23–27), he finally concludes with a warning to his three friends (vv. 28–29). Job has asked them, in the politest manner thus far, to stop pursuing him (cf. v. 22). In these final two verses, he warns them of what will happen if they do not stop:

> If you say, "How we will pursue him!"
> and, "The root of the matter is found in him,"
> be afraid of the sword,
> for wrath brings the punishment of the sword,
> that you may know there is a judgment. (Job 19:28–29)

Job cautions his companions that if they continue to harass him (Job 19:28a) with their false accusation that his sin is the root of his troubles (v. 28b), the wrath of God that he has been experiencing (vv. 11, 29) will come upon them. Hanging above them like the sword of Damocles, Yahweh's "sword" (twice in v. 29; cf. Isa. 66:16) is soon to drop.

In Johnny Cash's "God's Gonna Cut You Down,"[20] the legendary country singer/songwriter sings of God's certain, even if slow, judgment. The sinner—whether he is a liar, rambler, gambler, or back biter—can "run on for a long time," but "sooner or later" God will cut him down. Job too believes in that delayed but definite justice. Yet God will not cut down Job's friends because they behaved like an immoral motorcycle gang ("midnight riders," as Cash styles them), but as sophisticated but satanic subterfuges who have twisted theological truths. Because of their sins, God will cut them down—mercifully, not by condemning them, but by disciplining them. Stay tuned to see what will happen to them before this story is over!

Also stay attuned to the truth that underlies both Job's warning and confession. Like Job, we should believe that vindication for the righteous will come, even if it does not come in our lifetime. Jesus' parable of the rich man and Lazarus makes this very point (Luke 16:19–31). We can trust God to do what is right in his right timing. We can "take courage" as we wait upon the Lord (Ps. 27:14), who is the God of justice.

20. Johnny Cash, "God's Gonna Cut You Down," on *America V: A Hundred Highways* (Universal Music Group, 2006).

17

Zophar: Heaven Reveals the Iniquity of the Wicked; the Earth Rises Up Against Him

Job 20:1–29

Do you not know this from of old, since man was placed on earth, that the exulting of the wicked is short, and the joy of the godless but for a moment? (Job 20:4–5)

John Updike's short story "Pigeon Feathers" features David Kern, the story's protagonist, and walks the reader through David's theological wrestling with the idea of a bodily resurrection. After the thirteen-year-old and his family move to a country farmhouse, David reads the atheist H. G. Wells's *The Outline of History*, a book that claims that the Christian movement was based on myths and that Jesus was no more than a mere human. Such claims shake David's spiritual foundations. One day in catechism class at his local Lutheran church, after he has experienced a terrifying "vision of death" during a nighttime visit to the outhouse, he asks Rev. Dobson about the resurrection of the body. The theologically liberal minister compared what happens to us after death to the way that Abraham Lincoln's goodness lives after him. Such an answer is less than satisfying. It only further confuses and frustrates the boy.

It takes an unusual event and observation to restore and renew David's faith. His grandmother asks him to take his Remington .22 to the barn and get rid of the pesky pigeons. David quickly gets to work. One after another he picks off all the pigeons. As he starts to bury the birds, David notices the complex and beautiful design of their feathers: "across the surface of the infinitely adjusted yet somehow effortless mechanics of the feathers played idle designs of color, no two alike, designs executed, it seemed, in a controlled rapture, with a joy that hung level in the air above and behind him." With this observation, David comes to the realization of eternal beauty. He is now "robed in this certainty: that the God who had lavished such craft upon these worthless birds would not destroy His whole Creation by refusing to let David live forever."[1]

Job may not, at this point in the drama, be "robed in . . . certainty" about the resurrection. But he certainly has more than a glimmer of hope about the future—if not the near future, the distant future (an afterlife!). How, then, in Job chapter 20, do Job's friends respond to his Hallelujah Chorus? Effectively, they rip his sheet music in two!

"Zophar the Naamathite" (Job 20:1), in his final words in the book, offers an immediate response ("my thoughts answer me, because of my haste within me") to what he correctly views as Job's criticism and reprimand (see esp. 19:2, 28–29): "I hear censure that insults me" (20:2–3a). And it is from his so-called spirit-inspired "understanding" ("out of my understanding a spirit answers me," v. 3)[2] that he strikes up the band and beats the same old retribution-principle drum: Sin. Leads. To. Suffering. And. Judgment. Sin. Leads. To. Suffering. And. Judgment.[3] Verse 27 of Job 20 is a more poetic summary: "The heavens will reveal his iniquity, and the earth will rise up against him." The powers of heaven and earth will expose the evildoer eventually. Even after Job's insulting censure, Zophar is sure that the E-B-Z brain trust is reliable in its assessment of Job's spiritual status (20:1–3). From the first moment that man stepped on earth, a system of punishment and

1. John Updike, *Pigeon Feathers and Other Stories* (Alfred A. Knopf, 1962).

2. The word "inspired" is used here because perhaps Zophar, with the use of the word "spirit" (*ruach*), is claiming divine inspiration for his speech. This is more clearly the case with Eliphaz (Job 4:15) and Elihu (32:8).

3. "Zophar intends this rehearsal of traditional sentiments regarding the fate of the wicked more as a pronouncement of judgment than as an encouragement to repent." Gerald H. Wilson, *Job*, Understanding the Bible Commentary 10 (Baker, 2007), 214.

reward was put in place: do good things, get good things; do bad things, get bad things. Even if the wicked experience some joy and prosperity, the hammer of divine justice will soon fall.

In view of his set system of theology, Zophar preaches a three-point sermon. First, God will not let the wicked experience pleasure (Job 20:4–11) or, second, prosperity (vv. 20–29) for too long. Why? Because God is holy, and thus, third, he will not let the wickedness of the wicked triumph (vv. 12–19).

The Short-Lived Joys of the Wicked (Job 20:4–11)

After his introductory remarks, Zophar replies to Job's bold attestations to the three friends—"know [*yada*'] then that God has put me in the wrong" (Job 19:6) and "I know [*yada*'] that my Redeemer lives" (v. 25), saying, or implying, that Job is not in the know after all:

> Do you not know [*yada*'] this from of old,
> since man was placed on earth,
> that the exulting of the wicked is short,
> and the joy of the godless but for a moment? (Job 20:4–5)

Zophar's thesis here is clear: any honor and happiness that the ungodly man might experience is like a candle burning in the wind (cf. Job's analogy in Job 21:18). Zophar elaborates on this thesis with further illustrations of the short-lived joys of the wicked. Zophar's poetic lines soar higher than Bildad's:

> Though his height mount up to the heavens,
> and his head reach to the clouds,
> he will perish forever like his own dung;
> those who have seen him will say, "Where is he?" (Job 20:6–7)

These verses describe the brevity of the wicked man's honor and reputation. Even if a reprobate somehow obtains success in this life ("his height mount up to the heavens"/"his head reach to the clouds," Job 20:6), he is eventually like "dung" sitting on a sulfur sidewalk: he will dissolve into the dirt (cf. v. 7). "The contrast could not be greater—from the heights of human glory to the ignobility of human waste!"[4]

4. Wilson, 214.

Verses 8–11 of Job 20 further embellish this theme of transience—that the name of the wicked will perish like human waste. Job has responded to Bildad's claim about the wicked man (namely, Job!)[5]—"His memory perishes from the earth, and he has no name in the street" (18:17)—with his hope that an eternal book and an everlasting monument would be created to memorialize his words, a way of perpetuating his good name forever:[6]

> Oh that my words were written!
> Oh that they were inscribed in a book!
> Oh that with an iron pen and lead
> they were engraved in the rock forever! (Job 19:23–24)

Zophar has already added his voice to the debate with his retort that the exultation and joy of the wicked is short-lived (Job 20:5) and that they perish (v. 7); now he goes on to show how the name of the wicked is forgotten, his children suffer want, and his body dies and turns to dust:

> He will fly away like a dream and not be found;
> he will be chased away like a vision of the night.
> The eye that saw him will see him no more,
> nor will his place any more behold him.
> His children will seek the favor of the poor,
> and his hands will give back his wealth.
> His bones are full of his youthful vigor,
> but it will lie down with him in the dust. (Job 20:8–11)

The question "Where is he?" (Job 20:7b) lingers. The wicked man is nowhere to be found. He is like "a dream"/"a vision of the night," and his achievements are surreal: they "fly away"/"[are] chased away" (v. 8; cf. Prov. 23:5). All that he had and was is gone. The dream is over; reality sets in. "Where is he?" (Job 20:7b). Nowhere. Gone. He goes unnoticed even by his own household: "The eye that saw him will see him no more, nor will his place any more behold him" (v. 9).

5. "Though nowhere in this second response does Zophar directly accuse Job of being wicked (cf. 11:4–6, 13–14), the way in which he reverses Job's language and applies it to the wicked leaves little doubt as to what he implies." J. Gerald Janzen, *Job*, Interpretation: A Bible Commentary for Teaching and Preaching (John Knox, 1985), 152.

6. Adapted from Janzen, 151–52.

Ah, but that is not all. The judgment is not over. Next, the bad man's iniquity is visited on his offspring. His children become so poor that they must beg from the destitute for sustenance ("His children will seek the favor of the poor") because their father had to return all his exploited earnings ("his hands will give back his wealth," Job 20:10). Though he might seem healthy at the moment (his "bones are full of . . . youthful vigor"), such strength will vanish at his sudden death ("but it will lie down with him in the dust," v. 11). Zophar's comments in Job 20:4–11 are cruel cuts into Job as they echo his awful day of loss. In one day, Job went from the penthouse to the poorhouse and his children from a lively party to nailed coffins. These verses are also specific replies to Job's first edition of Handel's *Messiah*, as Gerald Janzen elucidates:

> The reference in verse 8 to the transience of dream and vision cruelly if indirectly dashes cold water on Job's vision of 19:25–27. For Job has hoped, beyond death and dust, in a renewal of the sight of God. Zophar adopts the language of seeing to assert that the wicked will be seen no more. Job has entertained the prospect that his bones, though denuded by wasting and death (19:20), will be restored to flesh (19:26). Zophar counters this theme as well: the bones of the wicked, though for a time full of youthful vigor, that is, full of healthy flesh (cf. 33:19–25, esp. v. 25), will come to nothing. This destiny is signaled by a vivid reversal of Job's words in 19:25b. There Job has said "the last one shall arise on behalf of (*'al*) dust." Here Zophar counters, "[his vigor] shall lie down with him in (*'al*) dust."[7]

But is Zophar right? It is true that "pride" does go "before destruction, and a haughty spirit before a fall" (Prov. 16:18), but is it also true that "the greatest of all the people of the east" (Job 1:3) has fallen into such disgrace because of his arrogance or some other sin? We know the answer. Job does too. But Zophar is still blind, and in his blindness he continues his barrage of true statements falsely applied.

Before we continue on, let us pause here to acknowledge our own blindness and ask for God's forgiveness. Here is a prayer that my wife, Emily, wrote in response to this text: "Father, we confess today that, like Job's friends, we have failed to truly listen to those hurting around us. We have shut down conversations by believing we know what someone thinks and believes before

7. Janzen, 151–52.

we have done the loving task of listening well." This prayer was written for liturgical use. The congregation responds by saying, "Forgive us." Yes, may God forgive us for our clogged ears, false diagnoses, and misguided offers of wrong and unhelpful remedies.

The Wickedness of the Wicked (Job 20:12–19)

In Job 18:4–21, Bildad explored the theme of *place* and crafted an elaborate depiction of the wicked being cast out from their dwelling—an image we interpreted as symbolizing the obliteration of their physical existence (death and losses after death, including knowledge of their name). Zophar now takes up a similar theme, focusing on the concept of *portion* (encompassing sustenance and possessions), and proceeds to extensively elaborate on the portion of the wicked.

While the "evil" of the wicked man is mentioned in Job 20:12, the only specific sin named comes in verse 19: "he has crushed and abandoned the poor; he has seized a house that he did not build." The picture that we might envision, which is close to what Zophar sees, is that of a real estate mogul who has pushed out the poor for profit. He offers reasonable rent, but then drives up the price, leaving his neighbor high and dry. Ah, but as Proverbs says, so too does Zophar: "Whoever oppresses the poor to increase his own wealth . . . will only come to poverty" (Prov. 22:16; cf. Job 20:21, 28). Moreover, this "whoever" (Job!) will eat his losses first:

> Though evil is sweet in his mouth,
>   though he hides it under his tongue,
> though he is loath to let it go
>   and holds it in his mouth,
> yet his food is turned in his stomach;
>   it is the venom of cobras within him.
> He swallows down riches and vomits them up again;
>   God casts them out of his belly.
> He will suck the poison of cobras;
>   the tongue of a viper will kill him.
> He will not look upon the rivers,
>   the streams flowing with honey and curds.
> He will give back the fruit of his toil
>   and will not swallow it down;

from the profit of his trading
he will get no enjoyment.
For he has crushed and abandoned the poor;
he has seized a house that he did not build. (Job 20:12–19)

Eating is the main metaphor in these verses, with terms such as "sweet in his mouth" (Job 20:12a), "under his tongue" (v. 12b), "in his mouth" (v. 13b), "food . . . in his stomach" (v. 14a), "swallows" (v. 15a), "vomits" (v. 15a), "belly" (v. 15b), "suck" (v. 16a), "tongue" (v. 16b), "honey and curds" (v. 17b), "fruit" (v. 18a), and "swallow" (v. 18b). The overall image is disgusting: the wicked man is destroyed by his own appetite for evil. Put differently, his evil eats him alive.

The picture that comes to my mind is that of Jabba Desilijic Tiure (commonly labeled "Jabba the Hutt"), a grotesque character in *Star Wars*. Jabba is the size of a hippo, but his body looks like a mix of a crocodile (greenish brown scaly skin with a long tail), a slimy slug, and an NFL offensive lineman on steroids (his neck is as big as his head). He is "a crime lord from Tatooine, a sparsely inhabited circumbinary desert planet located in the galaxy's Outer Rim Territories," according to the *Star Wars* fandom webpage. He is depicted as a brutal and vengeful gangster who renders violent verdicts as he sits in one place and stuffs food into his mouth. It is hard to picture Job like this, but Zophar sees things differently.

Transitioning back to his pulpit outside Uz, Zophar continues to describe how this Jabba-like creature (whom he sees as Job) is destroyed by his own appetite for evil. First, the man sits down to enjoy a delicacy. While it is "sweet in his mouth"—so sweet that he savors it "under his tongue" and "holds it in his mouth"—he is actually eating "evil" (Job 20:12–13). Then what he is "loath to let . . . go" will not let go of him (v. 13a). The "food" in "his stomach" turns to wormwood (v. 14a); it is like "the venom of cobras within him" (v. 14b). What he has swallowed down are ill-gained "riches" (v. 15a; cf. vv. 18d–19; see also 1 Tim. 6:10). Then he "vomits them up again" (Job 20:15a). This is one perspective on the scene; the other is God's, who also "casts them out of his belly" (v. 15b).

The image is not that of a spew of the stew on the table; rather, it is of the wicked man's wealth being taken from him (cf. Job 20:10). Verses 16–18 of Job 20 continue with both the food metaphors and the theme of the consequences for the wicked man's wickedness. Instead of the "delicious but deadly food" of verses 12–15,[8] the cuisine of verse 16 is repulsive: "He will suck the poison of cobras; the tongue of a viper will kill him." This venomous meal is his last meal. No more picnics along the riverbank ("He will not look upon the rivers"), with delicious delights to feast on ("honey and curds," v. 17). No more fine wines to sip. It's payback time! "He will give back the fruit of his toil and will not swallow it down; from the profit of his trading he will get no enjoyment" (v. 18). The joys of this wealthy wicked man have been short-lived.

The Prosperity of the Wicked Will Not Endure (Job 20:20–29)

In the final section of the sermon, Zophar continues with more of his digestion metaphors ("no contentment in his belly," Job 20:20a; "nothing left after he had eaten," v. 21a; "fill his belly to the full," v. 23a) and adds military ones ("an iron weapon," v. 24a; "a bronze arrow," v. 24b). Three main points are made here. The first two have already been made: first, the joys of the wicked are temporary; second, the prosperity of the wicked will not endure.

The first point appears to be made in Job 20:20: "Because he knew no contentment in his belly, he will not let anything in which he delights escape him." The sense of this verse is difficult. Perhaps it means that his "greed will lead to cravings that cannot be satisfied,"[9] or, in the words of Isaiah 48:22, "There is no peace . . . for the wicked."

The second point is made in Job 20:21, 28. After the wicked man indulged in his ill-gotten gains, "there was nothing left after he had eaten" (Job 20:21a). Put less metaphorically, "his prosperity will not endure" (v. 21b). Or as phrased in verse 28, "The possessions of his house will be carried away, dragged off in the day of God's wrath."

The words "God's wrath" introduce us to the third point found in these final verses, namely, that God will strike the wicked man's body and soul before he dies. While people will attack him ("the hand of everyone in misery will come against him," Job 20:22b) and all creation testify against him ("The heavens will reveal his iniquity, and the earth will rise up against him," v. 27), the enemy to fear most is God. When the wicked man is resting

8. Robert L. Alden, *Job*, New American Commentary 11 (Broadman & Holman, 1993), 215.
9. Daniel J. Estes, *Job*, Teach the Text (Baker, 2013), 124.

at ease with a full stomach ("in the fullness of his sufficiency," v. 22a; "fill his belly to the full," v. 23a), God's judgment will strike him. He will suffer in soul ("he will be in distress," v. 22a; "terrors come upon him," v. 25c). He will suffer in body: "To fill his belly to the full, God will send his burning anger against him and rain it upon him into his body" (v. 23). The scene of divine judgment will play out like this (and notice the shift from food to battle to black hellfire imagery):

> He will flee from an iron weapon;
> a bronze arrow will strike him through.
> It is drawn forth and comes out of his body;
> the glittering point comes out of his gallbladder;
> terrors come upon him.
> Utter darkness is laid up for his treasures;
> a fire not fanned will devour him;
> what is left in his tent will be consumed. (Job 20:24–26)

Wicked men such as Job, Zophar is saying, experience a living hell: utter darkness; an unquenchable fire; an impaled body. Zophar's version of the inferno of Elohim's anger is as fierce as Dante's![10] Moreover, finally, and to be absolutely clear, Zophar concludes his speech, saying that such burning anger has been divinely decreed: "This is the wicked man's portion from God, the heritage decreed for him by God" (Job 20:29).

Get God's Grace

Zophar is right that God has ordained such punishment for the wicked. Indeed, Jesus himself, in the parable of the rich fool (Luke 12:13–21), teaches many of the same lessons as we learn here in Job 20, such as (1) watch out for wealth and (2) God often judges evildoers unexpectedly. We need to be warned about the dangers of wealth. Jesus said, "Take care, and be on your guard against all covetousness, for one's life does not consist in the abundance of his possessions" (Luke 12:15). We need to be reminded of the righteous, and potentially sudden, judgment of God. For as Jesus taught in his parable: "God said to him, 'Fool! This night your soul is required of you, and the

10. For example, Dante depicts Judas as being headfirst inside Lucifer's mouth with his back skinned by the cruelest creature's claws. *Inferno*, circle 9, canto 34:58–63.

things you have prepared, whose will they be?' So is the one who lays up treasure for himself and is not rich toward God" (vv. 20–21; cf. Jer. 17:11).

But we also need to learn about God's grace. In his commentary on Job, Christopher Ash asks an excellent question: "Why do we have to go on and on listening to these dreadful speeches?" His answer is important: "These speeches stand as a warning to us to guard grace jealously."[11] What Job needs from Zophar is not a reminder of the deceitfulness of riches, the fleetingness of earthly pleasures, or the burning heat of God's anger. He needs soothing words—God's grace for sinners; God's grace for sufferers. He needs to hear a sermon not on Romans 6:23a ("For the wages of sin is death"), but on Romans 6:23b ("but the free gift of God is eternal life in Christ Jesus our Lord"). He needs to hear a sermon not on Deuteronomy 32:35 ("In due time their foot will slip" [NIV]—the text for Jonathan Edwards's famous "Sinners in the Hands of an Angry God"), but on 2 Corinthians 12:7–10:

> To keep me from becoming conceited . . . , a thorn was given me in the flesh, a messenger of Satan to harass me. . . . Three times I pleaded with the Lord about this, that it should leave me. But he said to me, "My grace is sufficient for you, for my power is made perfect in weakness." Therefore I will boast all the more gladly of my weaknesses, so that the power of Christ may rest upon me. For the sake of Christ, then, I am content with weaknesses, insults, hardships, persecutions, and calamities. For when I am weak, then I am strong.

Eschew Arrogance

Get grace is one lesson to learn from Zophar's wrong response to Job. *Eschew arrogance* is a second lesson. In their rebukes of Job, Eliphaz appealed to private revelations and Bildad to long-established traditions. But Zophar, both here and earlier, appeals "to nothing except his arrogant confidence in his own importance and wisdom."[12] Even though he is the youngest of the three friends, he is "compelled to speak from the storehouse of *his* great 'understanding'! (Job 20:3)."[13] God, so he believes, has "deputized him to relay the mysteries to the world."[14] How arrogant! And how illogical. For

11. Christopher Ash, *Job: The Wisdom of the Cross*, Preaching the Word (Crossway, 2014), 219.

12. Derek Thomas, *The Storm Breaks: Job Simply Explained*, Welwyn Commentary Series (repr., Evangelical Press, 2005), 112.

13. Thomas, 168, emphasis mine.

14. John C. Holbert, *Preaching Job*, Preaching Classic Texts (Chalice, 1999), 53.

how does he know what God will say, and by the logic of his own argument, how can he claim to know anything about God?

Of course, that is not to say that there is no divine wisdom in Zophar's zings. His message here "taken in the abstract . . . is an almost perfect sermon, one of remarkable consistency and pointed application,"[15] and his earlier ode to God's incomprehensible wisdom (Job 12:7–12) is awesome: God's wisdom and knowledge are limitless, are beyond human comprehension, and ensure that justice will be seen to be done. That will preach and should be preached! As Derek Thomas points out, however, "we must not miss the entire sarcasm and cutting edge of its intention,"[16] and we should agree that Zophar "would have made better use of his excellent doctrine . . . if he had humbly recognized the limitations of his own knowledge of divine providence and had not presumed to understand Job's sufferings to perfection."[17]

It is easy to fall into this same trap, especially for well-trained, highly educated pastors. We may not say, as Zophar did in his *first speech*, that "God exacts of you less than your guilt deserves" (Job 11:6), that someone is "stupid" (v. 12), that the person is to blame for the death of children, and that there is no hope of restoration with God, or now here in his *final speech* that the person we are counseling "will perish forever like his own dung" (20:7), that the person's children will beg for bread from the poor (v. 10), that the poison of a viper will kill him (v. 16), and that God himself will send "burning anger" like rain from heaven that somehow falls deep "into his body" (v. 23)! And we may not imply that besides all the obvious sins, such a person must, like Job, "be hiding some whopper of iniquity and worthlessness (11:11), which God's court of law will consider soon enough."[18] As Paul Zahl counsels:

> When we treat sufferers this way—and we have all probably done so at one time or another, if only in our thoughts—we are acting as divine Sherlock Holmeses and divine "hanging judges." When people set themselves up to make judgments for God, they can become malicious, like Zophar; and un-*healing*, like all three of Job's friends. In response to such pride, Jesus says, "Judge not, that you be not judged" (Matt. 7:1).[19]

15. Thomas, *The Storm Breaks*, 168.

16. Thomas, 115–16.

17. Meredith Kline, "Job," in *Wycliffe Bible Commentary*, ed. Charles F. Pfeiffer and Everett F. Harrison (Moody, 1963), 468, quoted in Thomas, *The Storm Breaks*, 116.

18. Paul F. M. Zahl, "Job," in *ESV Gospel Transformation Study Bible* (Crossway, 2018), 681.

19. Zahl, 681.

Preach Not the Prosperity Gospel

Get grace is one lesson to learn from Zophar's wrong response to Job. *Eschew arrogance* is a second lesson. *Preach not the prosperity gospel* is a third.

One of the most interesting, and sad, insights that Alexis de Tocqueville offers from his lengthy visit to America centers on America's obsession with the love of money. In his *Letters from America* (1832), he writes, "The one passion that runs deep, the only one that stirs the human heart day in and day out, is the acquisition of wealth."[20] Later in his classic book *Democracy in America* (1835), Tocqueville dedicates a whole chapter ("On the Taste for Material Well-Being in America") on the theme, namely, that "love of well-being has become the national and dominant taste" and that "the desire to acquire the goods of this world is the dominant passion of Americans."[21] Saddest of all is his observation that "American preachers refer to this world constantly."[22] They freely feed the hand that feeds them.

The popular prosperity gospel of our day—in America and around the world—is not new. In fact, it is as old as one of the oldest books, if not the oldest book, in the Bible. In Job 11, Zophar promised Job "instant health and wealth (pleasure, profit, and position)" and a "life . . . of unmixed joy" if he simply followed his program. Zophar also preached the converse (especially here in Job 20), namely, that it is "not just that God rewards those who follow him with material, this-worldly blessings" but that he "likewise punishes those who do not by withdrawing these things" and that he "does so *immediately*."[23]

Of course, the Bible does teach that there can be material blessings for those who turn from sin and live God's way. We know this from Scripture and experience. Countless times, men who are living in sin (wasting money on gambling, alcohol, and sexual immorality), and who are unmotivated at work, after their conversions turn from those behaviors and become clean, diligent, loyal, and honest men, with happy households and successful careers. The opposite is true too. Think of the businessman who lost his fortune because he cheated one too many people or was caught by the authorities,

20. Alexis de Tocqueville, *Letters from America*, ed. Frederick Brown (Yale University Press, 2010), 44.

21. Alexis de Tocqueville, *Democracy in America*, ed. Olivier Zunz (Literary Classics of the United States, 2002), 617, 619, 623.

22. Tocqueville, *Democracy in America*, 616.

23. Thomas, *The Storm Breaks*, 118.

the adulterer who destroyed his marriage and is now plagued with an incurable sexually transmitted disease, or the pastor who is defrocked due solely to his own sinful failings. God does judge sin, sometimes immediately, or almost immediately. Remember Nadab and Abihu, who were consumed by fire because they offered "unauthorized fire before the Lord" (Lev. 10:1); Naaman's servant Gehazi, whom God judged with leprosy for his greed (2 Kings 5); and Ananias and Sapphira, who lied and died (Acts 5). But not always! What Zophar gets right is that evildoers do not prosper. What he gets wrong is the timing. As Lydia Brownback observes:

> While evil doesn't prosper in the long run, it sometimes seems to pay off for a season. [Zophar] is right when he says that bad things happen to bad people—evil and evildoers will indeed be judged and destroyed. But he's wrong when he claims that tragedies and difficulties are the direct and immediate consequence of particular sins. The truth is, evil sometimes does seem to prosper—for a season. Sin *does* seem to pay off sometimes.[24]

Job has already pointed this out. In his observation of life on earth, he has witnessed that "robbers" live "at peace," that "those who provoke God" through their idolatry "are secure" (Job 12:6), and that judges are made fools, kings are shamed, priests are humiliated, the mighty are overthrown, preachers are silenced, and the wisdom of the wise elders is snatched away (vv. 17–20). He will make the same point again, in his next rebuttal: "the wicked . . . reach old age, and grow mighty in power" (21:7); they are blessed with children and grandchildren (v. 8; their children also dance, sing, and "rejoice to the sound of the pipe," vv. 11–12); they enjoy safety (v. 9), healthy animals (v. 10), and prosperity (vv. 13, 16); and even in their old age they die at the top of their game (with "full vigor" [or "bone" (*ḇeʿeṣem*)], v. 23), and then are respected even in their graves ("When he is carried to the grave, watch is kept over his tomb," v. 32). The godly are not always healthy and wealthy and the godless sick and poor. As we read Zophar's prosperity gospel, therefore, let us reject it and replace it (to return to our first application) with the gospel of grace—in which a persecutor of the church can become an apostle, a greedy tax collector a hungering-for-righteousness soul-winner, and a prostitute perfectly pure in heart.

24. Lydia Brownback, *Job: Trusting God When Suffering Comes*, Flourish Bible Study (Crossway, 2023), 32. Brownback says this of Eliphaz, but the same is true of Zophar.

18

Job: The Inexplicable Blessedness of the Wicked

Job 21:1–34

Why do the wicked live, reach old age, and grow mighty in power? (Job 21:7)

In his book *When Trouble Comes*, Phil Ryken begins by retelling the story of a spring semester as president of Wheaton College during which, "over the course of several long and difficult weeks," he plummeted "deeper and deeper into discouragement until eventually there were days when [he] wondered if [he] had the will to live." He credits prayer as a sustaining force. He knew that neighbors and former college roommates were regularly lifting him up to the Lord. He pressed on in prayer as well:

> Meanwhile I was praying, too. In my prayers, I told God exactly what I was thinking, just like Job did when he was afflicted. Sometimes I didn't know what to ask or couldn't find the words to form an intelligible petition. I could only say, "Help me, Jesus" or "Son of David, have mercy on me!" Or I could only groan, literally.

Ryken also mentions how he got a little (or a lot of!) help from an old friend, as well as a good wife. He writes of a providential call from Jon Dennis, the pastor of Chicago's Holy Trinity Church, who checked up on him. That care elicited Phil's admission that he "was losing the will to live," but also Jon's sincere verbalization of love ("it made a big difference . . . right at that moment" to hear "that he loved me"). A similar but even deeper relational love was expressed by his wife, Lisa, "when she would read psalms over [him] until [he] fell asleep, quieting [his] anxious spirit with the true words of God."[1]

Needless to say, that is not how Job has been treated—either by his wife or by his friends. We don't know whether Job wandered off the ash heap to scrape up or beg for some food and gather clothing or blankets to survive the cold nights and the unexpected cold fronts, but we do know that those closest to him were likely lacking in good works (James 2:15–16; 1 John 3:17) and certainly lacking in good words. They may have helped warm his body and fill his belly (someone had to help a person who was so sick), but they neglected the deeper need of empathy and affection, the "I love you" and the "Let me read until you fall asleep in my arms." The nakedness of his soul and the hunger of his heart were laid bare and starving.[2]

Now for another round of the verbal boxing match; and once again, Job has had it! He wants to land the knockout punch by laying to the mat—for the ten count—his friends' bad theology. Thus, instead of offering a personal reflection on his sufferings or a prayer to God, "he confines his remarks to his friends"[3] and in doing so "counteracts Zophar's every assertion"[4] (see table 18.1 on the next page).

Zophar is blind to the way that the world works and how God has chosen to rule. The wicked do not always die sudden deaths as they drink the venom of asps and watch their children bleed to death with God-induced iron spears sticking out of their necks. No, "the wicked live" (Job 21:7)! They "live," as Job explains in the body of his rebuttal, in the sense that they prosper (vv. 7–16) and that God lets them do so (vv. 17–21). "How often is it that the lamp of the wicked is put out?" (v. 17), Job asks. "Not often," answers the shuddering, dismayed, and utterly impatient sufferer (cf. vv. 1–6).

1. Phil Ryken, *When Trouble Comes* (Crossway, 2016), 11, 19, 20–21.

2. See J. Gerald Janzen, *Job*, Interpretation: A Bible Commentary for Teaching and Preaching (John Knox, 1985), 154.

3. Francis I. Andersen, *Job*, Tyndale Old Testament Commentaries 13 (InterVarsity Press, 1976), 197–98.

4. Roy Zuck, *Job*, Everyman's Bible Commentary (Moody, 1978), 98.

Table 18.1. Job's Counterattacks[5]

Zophar's Claims About the Wicked (Chap. 20)	Job's Counterclaims About the Wicked (Chap. 21)
"will perish forever like his own dung" (v. 7)	"reach old age" (v. 7)
"the exulting of the wicked is short" (v. 5)	"grow mighty in power" (v. 7)
"his height" no longer "mount[s] up to the heavens, and his head reach to the clouds" (v. 6); lose their "youthful vigor" (v. 11)	offspring and descendants "are established . . . before their eyes" (v. 8)
"what is left in [their tent] will be consumed" (v. 26); "his prosperity will not endure" (vv. 21, 23); "the possessions of his house will be carried away" (v. 28)	"houses are safe from fear" (v. 9a), their bulls breed and cows calve without miscarriage (v. 10)
will receive God's "burning anger" (v. 23) and be "dragged off in the day of God's wrath" (v. 28)	the rod of God is not upon them (v. 9b)
have "children [who] will seek the favor of the poor" (v. 10)	their children dance and sing to the tambourine and lyre, and "rejoice to the sound of the pipe" (vv. 11–12)
"swallows down riches and vomits them up again" (v. 15) and cannot enjoy "the profit of his trading" (vv. 17–18)	"spend their days in prosperity" (v. 13)
iniquity is revealed by the heavens (v. 27)	resist serving almighty God, seeing no profit in praying to him (vv. 14–15)
"his hands will give back his wealth" (v. 10); puts his iniquity on his children (21:19)	see their own destruction (vv. 19–21)

5. Zuck, 88, switched to the ESV.

Zophar's Claims About the Wicked (Chap. 20) continued	Job's Counterclaims About the Wicked (Chap. 21) continued
will be forgotten at death (20:7–9), will "perish forever like his own dung" (v. 7), will "fly away like a dream and not be found" (v. 8), "his place [will no longer] behold him" (v. 9)	receive an honorable burial, where "watch is kept over his tomb" (vv. 32–33)

Job does not conclude with a prayer to God, but he does offer a reflection on God. With a second almost theophany-like moment (Job 21:22–26; cf. 19:25–27), Job grasps that God can do whatever he wants ("Will any teach God knowledge, seeing that he judges those who are on high?," 21:22). Job understands that humans cannot understand God completely. For, using his ash-heap observation of how the world works, Job reckons that the righteous and the wicked look the same after the dust smothers them and the worms devour their flesh ("They lie down alike in the dust, and the worms cover them," v. 26).

Job ends his refutation autobiographically, as he began ("I" [6×], "me" [5×], "my" [3×] in Job 21:1–6, 27–34). He also ends with that great word "behold" (v. 27; used at key points throughout Job—e.g., 1:12; 2:6; 28:28). Job wants his friends to *see* something special. What is it? That they are wrong. Their attempts to "comfort"—their false and futile doctrines on retribution—are "empty nothings" (21:34). In truth, the wicked fare far better than pure and pious Job.

Mocking the Mockers, with a Tear in His Eye (Job 21:1–6)

With an autobiographical opening (note the use of "I," "me," and "my" in each of the six opening verses), Job mocks his mockers, yet with a tear in his eye. The mocking sarcasm is obvious:

Then Job answered and said:

"Keep listening to my words,
and let this be your comfort.
Bear with me, and I will speak,
and after I have spoken, mock on." (Job 21:1–3)

Here Job is asking his friends to offer him some real *consolation* by being quiet and finally paying attention to what he actually says, as the CSB suggests: "Pay close attention to my words; let this be the consolation you offer" (Job 21:2). Yet he is not overly optimistic, for he knows that every word he speaks can and will be used against him ("after I have spoken, mock on," v. 3b). Even so, he risks giving his verbal sparring partners more ammunition for their next insensitive attack because he holds out some hope that they might actually be enlightened, repent, and finally show sympathy for the *spiritual sufferings* he faces.

Beginning with a double rhetorical question, Job directs his complaint not against his human companions ("is my complaint against man [*'adam*]?," Job 21:4a) but against God ("Why should I not be impatient?," v. 4b).[6] It is true that Job is "impatient" (vv. 2, 5), but it is a justifiable impatience, since God refuses to speak to him and settle the situation. Job also wants his friends' sympathy for his *physical sufferings*. He wants them to make a fresh examination of his sore and skinny body and be so "appalled" that they are left speechless: "Look at me and be appalled, and lay your hand over your mouth" (v. 5). He further wants their sympathy for his *psychological sufferings*. When Job recalls what happened to his children and wealth on that one day and his loss of status and reputation ever since ("when I remember"), he is "dismayed" (or "terrified," v. 6a). He is so terrified that it affects his body ("shuddering seizes my flesh," v. 6b).

As a contemporary comparison, Jerry Sittser describes the sudden and traumatic loss of his mother, wife, and daughter in a car accident as being like "an atomic blast [that] went off, leaving the landscape of [his] life a wasteland," stating that his suffering was so "immediate and intense" that it felt as though his body had fallen off a cliff and smacked the ground.[7] He also speaks of his "catastrophic loss" as wreaking "destruction like a massive flood":

> It is unrelenting, unforgiving, and uncontrollable, brutally erosive to body, mind, and spirit. Sometimes loss does its damage instantly, as if it were a flood resulting from a broken dam that releases a great torrent of water, sweeping away everything in its path. Sometimes loss does its damage gradually, as if

6. When Job has used the language of "complaint" (see Job 7:13; 9:27; 10:1), it is clear that his complaint is toward God.

7. Jerry Sittser, *A Grace Disguised: How the Soul Grows Through Loss* (Zondervan, 2021), 12–13.

> it were a flood resulting from unceasing rain that causes rivers and lakes to swell until they spill over their banks, engulfing, saturating, and destroying whatever the water touches. In either case, catastrophic loss leaves the landscape of one's life forever changed.[8]

Similarly, Job's spiritual, physical, and psychological landscape has been hit by a tsunami.

The Wicked Prosper, You Idiots! (Job 21:7–16)

In Job 21:7–16, Job moves from a request for commiseration to a corrective of his friends' theology. When Zophar asserts that the wicked inevitably suffer, despite some temporary enjoyment of wealth and the pleasures that money can buy, Job argues to the contrary: the wicked often prosper in life, and God appears to permit it. These two arguments are the two points of Job's discourse, which ironically echoes Eliphaz's earlier portrayal of the virtuous man.[9]

First, in Job 21:7–16, Job observes that the wicked flourish:

> Why do the wicked live,
> reach old age, and grow mighty in power?
> Their offspring are established in their presence,
> and their descendants before their eyes.
> Their houses are safe from fear,
> and no rod of God is upon them.
> Their bull breeds without fail;
> their cow calves and does not miscarry.
> They send out their little boys like a flock,
> and their children dance.
> They sing to the tambourine and the lyre
> and rejoice to the sound of the pipe.
> They spend their days in prosperity,
> and in peace they go down to Sheol.
> They say to God, "Depart from us!
> We do not desire the knowledge of your ways.
> What is the Almighty, that we should serve him?
> And what profit do we get if we pray to him?"

8. Sittser, 2.
9. See Andersen, *Job*, 19.

> Behold, is not their prosperity in their hand?
> The counsel of the wicked is far from me.

Using exaggerated generalizations, Job lists how "the wicked" (mentioned three times in Job 21:7–17, and bookending his poem, v. 7 and v. 17) reside in safety ("Their houses are safe from fear," v. 9a), "grow mighty in power" (v. 7b), increase in wealth ("They spend their days in prosperity," v. 13a; "prosperity [is] in their hand," v. 16a), live long lives ("live, reach old age," v. 7), see their children and grandchildren ("Their offspring are established in their presence, and their descendants before their eyes," v. 8), and die peaceful deaths ("in peace they go down to Sheol," v. 13b). More than that, their livestock are fruitful and multiply: "Their bull breeds without fail; their cow calves and does not miscarry" (v. 10). Furthermore, perhaps most ironic of all, the children of the wicked are happy: "They send out their little boys like a flock, and their children dance. They sing to the tambourine and the lyre and rejoice to the sound of the pipe" (vv. 11–12)—or, as Ken Taylor in TLB paraphrases, "They have many happy children, they spend their time singing and dancing."

Second, God lets the wicked and their children sing and skip and dance through life. Job says it this way: "no rod of God is upon them" (Job 21:9b). God does not discipline them through disasters. He lets them live their happy lives, even though they do not acknowledge his gifts; the phrase "Behold, is not their prosperity in their hand?" (v. 16a) can also be rendered "But their prosperity is not their own doing" (NET). Moreover, God lets them live their happy lives, even though they deride him and his ways. They say to God, as Robert Alter translates: "Turn away from us, we have no desire to know Your ways. Who is Shaddai that we should serve Him, and what use for us to entreat Him?" (vv. 14–15).[10] To them, praise and prayer are of no profit, revelation of God's law—such as "Beware lest you say in your heart, 'My power and the might of my hand have gotten me this wealth'" (Deut. 8:17)—is not needed, and allegiance to the Almighty is wholly impractical. Job does not understand why God allows the wicked to go on their merry way. "It's beyond me how they can carry on like this!" (Job 21:16 MSG)[11] is

10. Robert Alter, *The Wisdom Books: Job, Proverbs, and Ecclesiastes* (W. W. Norton & Company, 2010), 90.

11. "And all these good and bad things are going to be doled out without any apparent pattern to them, without any discernible method in the madness. People who think they see a pattern (as Job's

Eugene Peterson's rendering of "The counsel of the wicked is far from me." Job also takes "far" not to mean "far from understanding the mysterious ways of God" (although he is far from that too!), but to mean "far from listening to and walking with the wicked" despite the temporary perks. Yes, even though Job acknowledges that crime does sometimes pay, that honesty is not always the best policy for financial success, and that ungodly actions may not poorly affect the bank account or show on the bad medical test results, nevertheless he wants nothing to do with the wicked. This is what is so remarkable about Job. He will not walk "in the counsel of the wicked," stand "in the way of sinners," or sit "in the seat of scoffers," even if he does not see the fruit of his righteousness, even if it cannot be said of him at this moment: "In all that he does, he prospers" (Ps. 1:1, 3). Job will maintain his moral integrity, refusing to compromise it, regardless of the wealth and security that the wicked might possess.

Let this be a lesson for us. We can acknowledge "how much easier it would be to live a godly life if there were immediate rewards for good conduct and immediate punishment for wrongdoing," and alongside Job, we can complain that life isn't fair. "But that is precisely the point," as Mike Mason states; "life is *not* fair. It is grossly unfair. Why? Not because God is unfair, or nonexistent, but rather because in large measure he holds back his fairness, his justice, for a future dispensation."[12] He does so for at least three reasons: first, because he is loving ("he makes his sun rise on the evil and on the good, and sends rain on the just and on the unjust," Matt. 5:45); second, because he is slow to anger, often waiting for someone's sin, or a group of people's sin, to reach "its full measure" (Gen. 15:16 NIV; "the iniquity of the Amorites is not yet complete"); and third, because he is rich in kindness ("Or do you presume on the riches of his kindness and forbearance and patience, not knowing that God's kindness is meant to lead you to repentance?," Rom. 2:4; cf. 2 Peter 3:9).

The faithful follower remains righteous in thought, word, and deed while he or she waits for God to show his final mercy or wrath: "Having faith in God means living daily with the hard reality of delay—the delay of the full expression of his kingdom."[13] Having faith also means remembering our

---

friends do) are simply fooling themselves." Mike Mason, *The Gospel According to Job: An Honest Look at Pain and Doubt from the Life of One Who Lost Everything* (Crossway, 1994), 231.

12. Mason, 235–36.

13. Mason, 235.

friendship with God, as Joseph did, when up against a strong temptation ("How then can I do this great wickedness and sin against God?," Gen. 39:9); as Daniel did, when exiled in a kingdom opposed to God's commands ("Daniel resolved that he would not defile himself with the king's food," Dan. 1:8); and as Job did, resisting the lure of the wicked who prosper in this world.[14]

How Often Is the Lamp of the Wicked Put Out? (Job 21:17–21)

As the previous section opened with a question ("Why do the wicked live, reach old age, and grow mighty in power?," Job 21:7), so too does this next section (v. 17). Job moves from *why* (why do the wicked, who brashly reject God and refuse to serve him or seek his help, live long lives, become powerful and prosperous, have safe homes and happy homesteads, and see their children and grandchildren flourish?)[15] to *how often*:

> How often is it that the lamp of the wicked is put out?
> That their calamity comes upon them?
> That God distributes pains in his anger?
> That they are like straw before the wind,
> and like chaff that the storm carries away?
> You say, "God stores up their iniquity for their children."
> Let him pay it out to them, that they may know it.
> Let their own eyes see their destruction,
> and let them drink of the wrath of the Almighty.
> For what do they care for their houses after them,
> when the number of their months is cut off? (Job 21:17–21)

This second question closely resembles the first, representing an alternative formulation of the identical challenge that Job faces. It also aligns with the second point of Job's speech in Job 21:7–16, where he contends that God permits the prosperity of the wicked. Eliphaz has asserted that the children of the wicked "are far from safety" and "are crushed at the gate" (Job 5:4); Zophar has claimed that the wicked and their offspring are destroyed, often quite suddenly ("You say, 'God stores up their iniquity for their children,'"

14. See Barry G. Webb, *Job*, Evangelical Biblical Theology Commentary (Lexham Academic, 2023), 264–65.

15. See Webb, 258.

21:19; cf. 20:4–29); and Bildad believes that "the light of the wicked is put out" (18:5)—the sense being that the wicked die young. Job disagrees. It is rare ("how often," 21:17a) that God punishes the wicked during their lifetimes—that "calamity comes upon them" (v. 17b), that they experience agony ("That God distributes pains in his anger," v. 17c), or, metaphorically, that they are "like straw before the wind, and like chaff that the storm carries away" (v. 18). "Come on, friends," is the sense of Job's thought here. "How often [in the real world] is it that the lamp of the wicked is put out?" (v. 17a). The friends claim that God knows and counts each sin that the wicked commit, a debt that their children will pay ("God stores up their iniquity for their children," v. 19a). Job says: "Well, when is that collection coming? It's been due for a while, God!" ("Let him pay it out to them, that they may know it," v. 19b). Job thinks that the wicked should experience now what he is experiencing: "Let their own eyes see their destruction, and let them drink of the wrath of the Almighty" (v. 20). But he knows that this is usually not the case. He also knows that once they die and have been buried for a few months ("when the number of their months is cut off," v. 21b), the wicked no longer worry about what will happen to their children and grandchildren ("For what do they care for their houses after them . . . ?," v. 21a). They will also not care less what "happens to their family after they are dead" (NLT).

Will You Teach God Knowledge? (Job 21:22–26)

In Job 21:22–26, Job pauses his direct rebuttal to ponder the incomprehensible way in which God governs the world, and how "God's exercise of justice transcends what humans can comprehend."[16] Starting with another rhetorical question, Job clarifies his confusion:

Will any teach God knowledge,
  seeing that he judges those who are on high?
One dies in his full vigor,
  being wholly at ease and secure,
his pails full of milk
  and the marrow of his bones moist.
Another dies in bitterness of soul,
  never having tasted of prosperity.

16. Daniel J. Estes, *Job*, Teach the Text (Baker, 2013), 130.

> They lie down alike in the dust,
> and the worms cover them. (Job 21:22–26)

As Job observes the world, he knows that "life is more complicated" than his friends' philosophy that "the righteous always prosper and the evil always fail."[17] It is not apparent—certainly not as black-and-white as Eliphaz, Bildad, and Zophar claim—that the retribution principle holds true in every case. Job illustrates the grayness of actual life with an illustration of two deaths ("one dies," Job 21:23a; "another dies," v. 25a). The first man dies "in his full vigor, being wholly at ease and secure" (v. 23), his body having been well nourished and his bones healthy ("his pails full of milk and the marrow of his bones moist," v. 24) his whole life. The second man dies an awful death ("dies in bitterness of soul") after living a miserable life ("never having tasted of prosperity," v. 25). We might picture the first man as the wicked man described above in Job 21:7–16 and righteous Job as the second man. Job, however, does not tell us who is who. What he does say is that what the two men now have in common is their decaying dead bodies: "They lie down alike in the dust, and the worms cover them" (v. 26). Death makes their lives—whether lived for the glory of God or for the glory of self—indistinguishable. The point Job is making is the one he has been making since verse 7, namely, that the bad live the good life or the wicked are not always judged in their lifetime. The slightly new nuance is that even the death of the wicked does not necessarily correspond with how he lived. He might have a painful death or a peaceful one. God alone determines.

This principle is illustrated elsewhere in the Bible. For example, Acts 12:22–23 records the swift demise of the wicked Herod the Great: the moment after he readily received the praise for his speech ("The voice of a god, and not of a man!"), "an angel of the Lord struck him down, because he did not give God the glory, and he was eaten by worms and breathed his last." But Scripture also records, in Jesus' parable of Lazarus and the rich man, the death of a rich man who seemingly lived a long, and certainly enjoyable (he "was clothed in purple and fine linen" and he "feasted sumptuously every day," Luke 16:19), life ("remember that you in your lifetime received your good things," v. 25). These examples highlight that God's judgment is not bound to the timing or circumstances of one's life or death; his justice

17. Andersen, *Job*, 19.

transcends human understanding and operates on a divine timeline that often eludes our immediate perception.

There Is Nothing Left of Your Answers but Falsehood (Job 21:27–34)

In Job 21:27–34, Job returns to his direct and personal confrontation of his friends, bookending this section with accusations. The first is an accusation of their evil intentions ("Behold, I know your thoughts and your schemes to wrong me," Job 21:27) and the second of their useless and untrue counsel ("How can your empty clichés comfort me? All your explanations are lies!," v. 34 NLT).[18] In between those two accusations, Job revisits his argument. He first returns to the good life of bad people (cf. vv. 7–21) and how it is obvious to anyone who has observed the world that the wicked are not always judged. Using questions, Job features his friends' perspective that both the name and the place of the wicked perish with them. "For you say, 'Where is the house of the prince? Where is the tent in which the wicked lived?'" (v. 28). He follows their viewpoint with his:

> Have you not asked those who travel the roads,
> and do you not accept their testimony
> that the evil man is spared in the day of calamity,
> that he is rescued in the day of wrath?
> Who declares his way to his face,
> and who repays him for what he has done? (Job 21:29–31)

Job counsels his friends, saying that simple observation, or simply asking someone who has seen the world (receiving the "testimony" of "those who travel the roads," Job 21:29), will tell them that God's anger does not always show itself against the "evil man" ("he is rescued in the day of wrath," v. 30). God neither rebukes the wicked ("Who declares his way to his face . . . ?," v. 31a) nor recompenses them for their crimes ("who repays him for what he has done?," v. 31b). Moreover, the funeral of the ungodly is glorious. After a massive procession to the gravesite ("When he is carried to the grave, . . . all mankind follows after him, and those who go before him are innumer-

18. "What Job is offered for comfort is *hebel* ["empty"], the Preacher's favourite word [in Ecclesiastes] for the 'vanity' (*empty nothings*) or futility of everything human." Andersen, 19.

able," vv. 32a–33b–c), he is lowered into the ground ("Sweet to him are the [dirt] clods of the valley,"[19] v. 33a), where he rests in peace, and his burial site is maintained and protected ("watch is kept over his tomb," v. 32b). Job concludes with another sarcastic jab at his friends' "comfort":

> How then will you comfort me with empty nothings?
> There is nothing left of your answers but falsehood. (Job 21:34)

Job opened "ironically by urging his friends to give him the 'consolation' of being quiet and listening to him" (Job 21:2); now "he ends by referring sarcastically to their previous exhortations as 'futile comfort.'"[20] To hold to his friends' false doctrine is "vanity [*hāb-el*] and a striving after wind" (Eccl. 1:14); it is like trying to catch the winds of a hurricane with a butterfly net. Vain! Foolish! In Job's *hāb-el*-filled sufferings ("In my vain life"), he has seen what the Preacher saw: "There is a righteous man who perishes in his righteousness, and there is a wicked man who prolongs his life in his evildoing" (Eccl. 7:15), and thus he knows that his friends' clichés are only so much hot air!

Four Shortcomings of Job; Four Lessons for Us

Job might have called his friends' counsel futile and compared it to hot air, but he has endured burning breath after burning breath from word after word that has had its effect on him; as a result, in Job 21 he clearly and directly expresses his impatience with Eliphaz, Bildad, and Zophar. Job's shortness of spirit, however, is not (in my estimation) his shortcoming here. He had every right to express himself the way he did. Rather, there are four other shortcomings.

Job Exaggerates the Opposite

First, Job exaggerates the opposite of the retribution principle, presenting the picture that the wicked rarely, if ever, suffer and are punished. This is simply not true! When we are impatient (and angry!), it is easy to exaggerate or overcompensate, turning what is true (sometimes the wicked prosper) into an unchangeable truth (the wicked always prosper).

19. Marvin H. Pope, *Job: Introduction, Translation and Notes*, Anchor Bible 15 (Doubleday, 1973), 157.

20. Webb, *Job*, 256.

Job Forgets Judgment Day

Second, Job forgets judgment day. It could be argued that he doesn't believe that there will be a judgment day, since his perspective on the afterlife isn't always clear or consistent. But from his best moments, when he longs for his Redeemer and dreams of a bodily resurrection from the dead (Job 19:25–27), we are led to suspect that he believes in both the vindication of the righteous and the condemnation of the wicked. He certainly believes Ecclesiastes 12:13 ("Fear God and keep his commandments, for this is the whole duty of man"), so why not assume that he believes Ecclesiastes 12:14 as well ("For God will bring every deed into judgment, with every secret thing, whether good or evil")?

Whatever Job might believe about God's final judgment, our revelation is clear. We should remind ourselves that the wicked might escape retribution in this world, but that they are certain to face it on judgment day and in the world to come. As David Allen states: "What good would it do for you to have a fortune yet not be able to access it? That is the ultimate condition of all who die without Christ. Regardless of their earthly wealth, position, or power, without Christ they face an eternal destiny separated from God."[21] Life might be unfair now, but it will not always be. God's just judgment is coming soon. So too is his salvation.

Job Has Lost Sight of God's Sovereignty

The third way in which Job is shortsighted is that he has lost sight of the hope of God's sovereignty. Job's vision is impaired by his injuries. The wicked do not always prosper in the way he describes. Moreover, and most importantly, God will judge the wicked and vindicate the righteous. Put simply, Job needs Job 38–42! All believers need that revelation—to see God and to hear from God that he is in control and working in accordance with his wise plan.

Job Has Stopped Praying

A final way that Job is shortsighted is that he doesn't pray. He has turned on his friends, when what he needs to do most is to turn to God in prayer. In Luke 18:1–8, Jesus taught his disciples the parable of the persistent widow "to the effect that they ought always to pray and not lose heart":

21. David L. Allen, *Exalting Jesus in Job*, Christ-Centered Exposition (Holman Reference, 2022), 112.

> "In a certain city there was a judge who neither feared God nor respected man. And there was a widow in that city who kept coming to him and saying, 'Give me justice against my adversary.' For a while he refused, but afterward he said to himself, 'Though I neither fear God nor respect man, yet because this widow keeps bothering me, I will give her justice, so that she will not beat me down by her continual coming.'" And the Lord said, "Hear what the unrighteous judge says. And will not God give justice to his elect, who cry to him day and night? Will he delay long over them? I tell you, he will give justice to them speedily."

In Job 21, it appears that Job has lost heart, for he has stopped praying! Let us not, in our pain, make the same mistake. If we struggle with how to say our prayers, we can sing a classic hymn such as "Dear Refuge of My Weary Soul," which begins:

> Dear Refuge of my weary soul,
> on Thee, when sorrows rise,
> on Thee, when waves of trouble roll,
> my fainting hope relies.[22]

Or try the hymn "Be Still, My Soul," which starts:

> Be still, my soul; the Lord is on thy side;
> bear patiently the cross of grief or pain.
> Leave to thy God to order and provide;
> in ev'ry change He faithful will remain.
> Be still, my soul; thy best, thy heav'nly Friend
> through thorny ways leads to a joyful end.[23]

Other resources abound! As a final example, pray this stirring prayer from "A Liturgy for Those Enduring Lasting Pain":

> O Christ who endured
> the anguish of the garden,
> and the agony of the cross,
> willingly taking upon yourself the sum of all our suffering,

22. Anne Steele, "Dear Refuge of My Weary Soul" (1760).
23. Katharina von Schlegel, "Be Still, My Soul" (1752), trans. Jane Borthwick (1855).

heal me or hold me now,
for I am unable to bear
this pain alone.

Either give me respite
from this agony,
or give me grace to
endure what I cannot
on my own.

Meet me in the secret
place of my torment, O Jesus,
which no other person, save you,
can know or touch,
for you alone
have already carried the full weight of it,
sharing in this moment
—and in all moments—
of my suffering and death,
that I might also share
in the fullness of your resurrection.

Do not abandon me here, O Christ!
Do not leave me to face this hurt alone.

However intense my affliction grows,
let your presence and power be manifest
ever more profoundly.

Even if this pain expands to fill all of
my awareness, so that I can hardly move,
or speak, or form a coherent thought—even
then fling wide your doors and draw me into
your place of refuge, O Lord, or, better yet,
seek me and find me where I have collapsed.
There gather me into your arms, carry me to
your hiding place, and tend to my distress.

Where can I go, but to you, Jesus?
And who but you can come to me?

Either take this pain away, O Christ,
or enfold me in the embrace of your Spirit
and cradle me through it.

For I cannot bear it alone. I
cannot bear it alone.[24]

24. Douglas Kaine McKelvey, *Every Moment Holy: Death, Grief, and Hope* (Rabbit Room Press, 2021), 83–84.

Third Cycle of Speeches

19

Eliphaz: Accusation and Exhortation

Job 22:1–30

Is not your evil abundant? There is no end to your iniquities.
(Job 22:5)

My wife received a family heirloom—a 1933 record player—which is housed in a beautifully designed wooden case that is about four feet tall. To generate power, springs are used. The problem, however, is that there is something wrong with the springs. So the record player is cranked, but the slowly spinning record never gets past the first song.

Like a broken record player, Eliphaz never seems to get past his only argument. As he began the first cycle of dialogues (Job 4:1), so he begins the third and final cycle. The three friends have little left to say. Bildad speaks only a few sentences (25:1–6) and Zophar none at all. In this chapter, Eliphaz offers what amounts to thirty recorded verses from the same album. "Job's counselors have only one song to sing and they have sung it to death!"[1] says

1. Derek Thomas, *The Storm Breaks: Job Simply Explained*, Welwyn Commentary Series (repr., Evangelical Press, 2005), 133.

Derek Thomas. That song sounds like this: once again hoping that Job will see his sins (22:2–11)—notably, how he has spoken with theological naiveté (vv. 12–20)—Eliphaz promises that repentance of such sins will lead to restoration (vv. 21–30).

Does the Almighty Concern Himself with Your Cause? (Job 22:2–3)

"Eliphaz the Temanite" (Job 22:1), a once-"caring" friend (cf. 2:11), essentially tells Job that, now, he couldn't care less about his troubles. The two questions in Job 22:2–3 center on God's transcendence and self-sufficiency. God does not need man's help in running the universe ("Can a man be profitable to God?," Job 22:2a). Not even a smart, sensible, and skilled man could lend God a hand ("Surely he who is wise is profitable to himself," v. 2b). In contrast with the depiction of God in the prologue, where he takes great notice of Job's piety, Eliphaz claims that God receives no pleasure or profit from Job's so-called blameless and upright life. "Is it any pleasure to the Almighty if you are in the right, or is it gain to him if you make your ways blameless?" (v. 3). As if a perfectly holy God gains something from a human's holiness. Surely not!

In this chapter, Eliphaz frequently (5×) refers to God as "the Almighty" (*shadday*), which is more frequent than in any other chapter. This could be because Job has recently used this name (Job 21:15, 20), or it might be chosen to emphasize the sense of distance and detachment that Eliphaz wants to convey. Either way, the Almighty has not been impressed by Job's actions; he has not even noticed them.

Job's Ethical Iniquities; God's Holy Judgments (Job 22:4–11)

In Job 22:4–11, Eliphaz begins with another question, a sarcastic one: "Is it for your fear of him that he reproves you and enters into judgment with you?" (Job 22:4). Eliphaz becomes extremely aggressive here because he believes that God, in his punishing providence, is rebuking Job and calling out his crimes: "Is not your evil abundant? There is no end to your iniquities" (v. 5). To call Job a sinner is one thing; to claim that his evil is abundant and his iniquities endless is a rather insensitive exaggeration. What crime has Job committed? The indictments are listed next:

> Is it for your fear of him that he reproves you
>   and enters into judgment with you?
> Is not your evil abundant?
>   There is no end to your iniquities.
> For you have exacted pledges of your brothers for nothing
>   and stripped the naked of their clothing.
> You have given no water to the weary to drink,
>   and you have withheld bread from the hungry.
> The man with power possessed the land,
>   and the favored man lived in it.
> You have sent widows away empty,
>   and the arms of the fatherless were crushed. (Job 22:4–9)

Notice here four appalling details. First, such a list is new. The friends have rarely made more than generalizations and guesses at Job's sins (e.g., impatience, pride). Now Eliphaz accuses Job of exploiting the needy (Job 22:6), letting the hungry starve (v. 7), and oppressing orphans and widows (vv. 8–9; cf. James 1:27; 2:1–7, 14–16; 5:1–6).[2] It's quite a list.

Second, as much as Eliphaz will talk about God in a moment, his focus here is on how Job has supposedly treated his fellow humans. Of course, as the apostle John points out, this is indeed a valid way to test a person's character: "If anyone says, 'I love God,' and hates his brother, he is a liar; for he who does not love his brother whom he has seen cannot love God whom he has not seen" (1 John 4:20).

Third, Eliphaz attacks Job directly and personally. As David Clines comments, "These are the most specific, most harsh, and most unjust words spoken against Job in the whole book, and it is strange to find them on the lips of Eliphaz, out of all his friends."[3] Here there is no third-person accusation (the

2. These crimes also relate to various Old Testament laws (cf. Ex. 22:22; Deut. 24:6, 17–18). Regarding Job 22:8, though it could be an additional charge, the verse could also be related to what comes either before it ("You gave no water to the weary and you withheld food from the hungry, though you were a powerful man, owning land—an honored man, living on it," 22:7–8 NIV) or after it ("Although you were a powerful man, owning land, an honored man living on it, you sent widows away empty-handed, and the arms of the orphans you crushed," 22:8–9 NET). I favor the second translation and interpretation.

3. David J. A. Clines, "The Arguments of Job's Three Friends," in *On the Way to the Postmodern: Old Testament Essays, 1967–1998*, 2 vols., JSOT Supplement Series (Sheffield Academic Press, 1998), 2:733.

wicked do this and that), as has been the friends' custom thus far, but rather, as Richard Belcher points out and describes: "Eliphaz accuses Job with direct statements using the second masculine singular form of the verb: You must have been taking pledges of your brothers for nothing. You must have been stripping the naked of their clothing. You must have been refusing water to the weary. You must have been denying bread to the hungry. You must have sent widows away empty."[4]

Fourth, Eliphaz is not only brutal, but brutally presumptuous. Without any evidence, he openly and unapologetically brands Job "The Biggest Sinner in the World!" and invents "an entire catalogue of transgressions."[5] Of course, as readers we know that such accusations are outrageous, but we also sense that Eliphaz realizes this too. During the months that he has spent with Job, has he witnessed Job's deceiving his own family or withholding food from the famished? Whatever the particular iniquities, the verdict is settled in Eliphaz's mind by the plain inference of Job's sufferings. The self-professed innocent man is guilty as charged. His punishment is just. Job is trapped and terrified by his sins ("Therefore snares are all around you, and sudden terror overwhelms you," Job 22:10). God's judgment is consuming him. His feet are ensnared, the lights are turned off ("darkness, so that you cannot see," v. 11a), and the waters of God's wrath start to fill his prison cell ("a flood of water covers you," v. 11b). All this is a friend's (or so-called friend's) "drastic attempt to bring Job face to face with his sin" and his God,[6] who obviously is severely judging his terrible transgressions.

Job's Theological Naiveté (Job 22:12–20)

Just as Eliphaz ended the last section with God's judgment depicted as "darkness" and a "flood of water" (Job 22:11), so he ends this section by speaking of the "fire" of God's wrath (v. 20). He begins, however, with a psalmlike statement about the exalted God. The psalmist sings, "For you, O Lord, are most high over all the earth; you are exalted far above all gods" (Ps. 97:9). Eliphaz echoes this lyric, with a rhetorical question: "Is not God

4. Richard P. Belcher Jr., *Job: The Mystery of Suffering and God's Sovereignty*, Focus on the Bible (Christian Focus, 2017), 146.

5. Thomas, *The Storm Breaks*, 183.

6. Francis I. Andersen, *Job*, Tyndale Old Testament Commentaries 13 (InterVarsity Press, 1976), 202.

high in the heavens? See the highest stars, how lofty they are!" (Job 22:12). The reason that Eliphaz returns to the theme of God's transcendence is to correct what he sees as Job's misperception of reality.

In Job 22:13–20, three characters speak and one acts. Job speaks ("you say," Job 22:13), the wicked speak ("They said to God," v. 17), and the righteous speak ("saying," v. 20); God acts ("he filled," v. 18). In verses 13–14, Eliphaz misinterprets—or "deliberately misquotes"[7]—Job's earlier statement (perhaps 7:17, "What is man, that you make so much of him, and that you set your heart on him?"), putting these words in his mouth:

> But you say, "What does God know?
> Can he judge through the deep darkness?
> Thick clouds veil him, so that he does not see,
> and he walks on the vault of heaven." (Job 22:13–14)

Eliphaz's accusation is that Job thinks God is so exalted ("he walks on the vault of heaven," Job 22:14b) that he cannot see through the clouds ("through the deep darkness," v. 13b; "thick clouds," v. 14a); and that because his perception is obstructed ("What does God know?," v. 13a; "he does not see," v. 14a; cf. 21:14; Ps. 73:11), so too is his justice ("Can he judge through the deep darkness?," Job 22:13b). In other words, Eliphaz claims that Job's belief in God's transcendence trumps God's omniscience and his care for the earth and all its inhabitants.

In verses 15–20 of Job 22, Eliphaz describes the way and words of the wicked and how God wipes out their way and makes them eat their words:

> Will you keep to the old way
> that wicked men have trod?
> They were snatched away before their time;
> their foundation was washed away.
> They said to God, "Depart from us,"
> and "What can the Almighty do to us?"
> Yet he filled their houses with good things—
> but the counsel of the wicked is far from me.
> The righteous see it and are glad;
> the innocent one mocks at them,

7. Thomas, *The Storm Breaks*, 184.

saying, "Surely our adversaries are cut off,
  and what they left the fire has consumed."

Later, in Job 22:21–30, Eliphaz encourages Job to repent so that he might reap the rewards of righteousness. Here, however, he warns him to escape the path of judgment: "Will you keep to the ancient path, which evildoers have trodden, who were shriveled up before their time, whose foundations were swept away by a flood" (Job 22:15–16, Cline's translation)?[8] The image is that of the wicked walking on the old and well-worn path of wickedness when suddenly the rain starts. Hours pass. Days. Soon enough, like the generation of Noah (cf. Gen. 6:5–7, 11–13; 7:4, 11–12, 17–23; Matt. 24:37–39), the wicked are washed away. Even the foundations of their homes are swept away in the flood (cf. Matt. 7:26–27). They thought they were untouchable, but their only relationship with their Creator was to mock his power: "They said to God, 'Depart from us,' and 'What can the Almighty do to us?'" (Job 22:17). They want to be left alone; but God will not leave them alone, and he has not let them alone. In fact, he has been good to them for so much of their lives ("he filled their houses with good things," v. 18; cf. Matt. 5:45). The way of the wicked, Eliphaz continues, makes no sense to him ("the counsel of the wicked is far from me," Job 22:18b). Or perhaps he is saying, in a more self-righteous tone, "Is not the plan of the wicked far from me?," as Tremper Longman believes,[9] or uttering "a sarcastic repetition (v. 18b) of Job's vehemently sincere line, 'But the counsel of the wicked is far from me' (21:16b)," as Gerald Janzen suggests.[10] Eliphaz cannot conceive of how anyone would want to walk right into God's wrath!

Next, Eliphaz steps back from the judgment scene—not to weep for the wicked but to rejoice over them. He sings his version of Revelation's Hallelujah Chorus (cf. Rev. 19:1–4). He joins the voices of the saints: "The righteous see and rejoice, The innocent deride them: 'Surely their substance is cut off, Their surplus the fire burns'" (Job 22:19–20, Pope's translation).[11]

8. David J. A. Clines, *Job 21–37*, Word Biblical Commentary 18A (Thomas Nelson, 2006), 539.

9. Tremper Longman III's translation; see *Job*, Baker Commentary on the Old Testament Wisdom and Psalms (Baker Academic, 2012), 288.

10. J. Gerald Janzen, *Job*, Interpretation: A Bible Commentary for Teaching and Preaching (John Knox, 1985), 162.

11. Marvin H. Pope, *Job: Introduction, Translation and Notes*, Anchor Bible 15 (Doubleday, 1973), 164.

The wicked and their wealth have been consumed by the fire of God, and the godly ("the righteous"/"the innocent," v. 19) rejoice as they taunt the proud and foolish ways of their "adversaries" (v. 20a). In Eliphaz's view, the downfall of the wicked serves as a vindication for the righteous, reinforcing the divine justice that ultimately prevails and brings joy to the faithful.

Repentance and Restoration (Job 22:21–30)

Eliphaz's belief that Job is theologically naive and has acted unethically (Job 22:2–20) leads him to end his final speech with a plea for repentance and a promise of restoration (vv. 21–30). In Job 22:21, Eliphaz summarizes his message by urging Job to "agree with God" and find "peace" and goodness ("good will come to you"), with the implication that agreeing with Eliphaz is equivalent to agreeing with God. Furthermore, in verse 22, Eliphaz urges Job to "receive instruction from his mouth" (and its parallel line—"and lay up his words in your heart," v. 22), effectively suggesting that listening to Eliphaz is the same as listening to God (cf. 4:15; 15:11). How arrogant! Later, Eliphaz will envision Job as agreeing with God's assessment of him (22:21) and in humility admitting his arrogance (v. 29a). How blind! By claiming to be God's spokesperson and placing Job "in the role of the ignorant student" and himself in "the role of the learned teacher,"[12] Eliphaz oozes arrogance. His vanity is shown in how he takes the Lord's name in vain.

Let us learn a lesson here. "One of the ways we can tell that we have read the book of Job rightly," notes Eric Ortlund, "is if we finish the book with a greater caution in how we speak to others—a deeper humility, an unwillingness to assume we understand what God is doing in the midst of suffering, and a deeper hesitancy to blame others."[13] Amen! May we never speak to others about God, as Eliphaz did, from "a condescending position of superiority."[14]

12. Daniel J. Estes, *Job*, Teach the Text (Baker, 2013), 94. "In 13:2 Job insisted that he is not inferior to his friends in his knowledge, but that he knows what they know. Eliphaz now exaggerates what Job said, as he inquires sarcastically not about Job's supposedly *equal* knowledge but about his purported *superior* knowledge. Actually, all of the characters seem to pride themselves in what they know, or think they know, with none of them evidencing an excess of humility in this regard" (94).

13. Eric Ortlund, *Suffering Wisely and Well: The Grief of Job and the Grace of God* (Crossway, 2022), 81.

14. Ortlund, 80.

Next, Eliphaz brings the unbending logic of the retribution principle to bear:

> If you return to the Almighty [then] you will be built up;
> if you remove injustice far from your tents,
> if you lay gold in the dust,
> and gold of Ophir among the stones of the torrent-bed,
> then the Almighty will be your gold
> and your precious silver. (Job 22:23–25)

Above (and "note the rhetorical rhythm of Eliphaz's argument"!)[15] he gives two *if/then* exhortations. First, *if* Job repents of his sins ("If you return to the Almighty"), *then* God will renew Job's status and fortunes ("you will be built up," Job 22:23a, or "healed").[16] Good things happen to those who go to God! Second, *if* Job ousts from his life all his ethical iniquities ("if you remove injustice far from your tents," v. 23b; cf. vv. 6–9) and returns his ill-gotten gain and idolatrous wealth ("if you lay gold in the dust, and gold of Ophir among the stones of the torrent-bed," v. 24),[17] *then* his relationship with God will revive ("then the Almighty will be your gold and your precious silver," v. 25). Put differently, "If he will forsake his own claims and make the Almighty his gold—ally himself unquestioningly and subserviently to God in the latter's divine rule and judgment—then all will be well."[18]

In Job 22:26–28, Eliphaz expands on this second *if/then* exhortation, emphasizing three aspects of that renewed relationship. First, Job will find the former happiness that he has been craving: "For then you will delight yourself in the Almighty and lift up your face to God" (Job 22:26). Second, instead of silence, God will hear and answer Job's prayers ("You will make your prayer to him, and he will hear you"), even helping Job to keep his word concerning following God's ways ("and you will pay your vows," v. 27). Third, rather than deep darkness blinding the way forward, Job will be given light to see which direction to go: "You will decide on a matter, and it will be established for you, and light will shine on your ways" (v. 28).

15. Janzen, *Job*, 163.

16. Pope's translation (*Job*, 164).

17. Andersen, *Job*, 205, notes that "Ophir" is the "legendary source of the best gold" and that "its location is not known (*cf.* Gn. 10:29)."

18. Janzen, *Job*, 163.

Eliphaz concludes his plea to Job with a reminder of the pattern of God's salvation of sinners ("he saves," Job 22:29b; "he delivers," v. 30a):

> For when they are humbled you say, "It is because of pride";
> but he saves the lowly.
> He delivers even the one who is not innocent,
> who will be delivered through the cleanness of your hands. (Job 22:29–30)

Eliphaz envisions Job as agreeing with the Almighty (Job 22:21) and in humility admitting his arrogance: "It is because of pride" (v. 29a). He then envisions God as saving this sinner who is now submissive (v. 29b). While Eliphaz will not speak of God's *grace* ("God opposes the proud but *gives grace* to the humble," 1 Peter 5:5), he does count on God's *generosity* ("He delivers even the one who is not innocent," Job 22:30a).

The meaning of the final phrase in this chapter ("who will be delivered through the cleanness of your hands," Job 22:30b) is difficult to determine. If we consider the word "your" to refer to God (maybe unlikely, since God has consistently been referred to as "he" throughout), then the implication is that the sinner is rescued through the purity of God. But if we interpret "your" as symbolizing the repentant sinner, now restored as a saint, then the sense is that this transformed sinner-saint has become an instrument in God's hands for the deliverance of this other now-righteous individual (as in v. 30b). If the second interpretation is accurate, it carries an ironic allusion to Job's future role in delivering his friends. A vindicated Job will mediate through sacrifice and intercede through prayer on behalf of Eliphaz's sins of the tongue ("the Lord said to Eliphaz the Temanite: 'My anger burns against you and against your two friends, for you have not spoken of me what is right,'" 42:7). Ironically, "Job does not need to repent of any sin that has caused his suffering but Eliphaz will need to repent of speaking falsely concerning God."[19]

Agree with the Almighty

Once again, as we conclude a chapter on the broken record of the friends' advice to Job, we wonder, "How do we read and apply the three friends'

19. Belcher, *Job*, 149.

advice?" While John Calvin is surely correct to say that "there is nothing in their remarks that we can discount, as if the Holy Spirit had declared it,"[20] we must balance a high view of Scripture with God's low view of the friends' counsel (see Job 42:7–9). We must side with God that they "have not spoken" about him (and his ways) "what is right" (v. 7). Yet we must also recognize that in most contexts (not Job's!), their advice is scriptural, that is, their ideas "echo ideas that are fully in accord with other parts of the Bible."[21] Therefore, since that is the case, there is value in echoing parts of their orthodox anthropology (e.g., Eliphaz in 4:17; 15:14–16; Bildad in 25:4) and components of their God-saturated and God-centered theology (e.g., Zophar in 11:5–7). Even though their understanding of God is ultimately corrected by God himself in Job chapter 42, we can still learn from what they say about God's incomprehensible nature, manifold wisdom, and great works, as well as his love for the righteous, punishment of the wicked, and corrective discipline toward his people. There are reasons that Paul quotes Eliphaz (Job 5:13 in 1 Cor. 3:19) and that his words of counsel are alluded to in six other places in the New Testament. This fool has some wise things to say. If we carefully mine the heap of rubble (their speeches in Job 4–5; 8; 11; 15; 18; 20; 22; 25), we can find gold. Additionally, what Job might have overlooked or disregarded as unimportant could be valuable to others. Think about how applicable this last speech would be to Zacchaeus, for example (see Luke 19:1–10)!

To illustrate this point, let's take a closer look at Job 22:6–9, where Eliphaz lists Job's supposed sins. Although his list may not match our own personal transgressions, it reminds us that we all have a list of the sins with which we struggle—whether it is expressing sexual interest toward someone we shouldn't, coveting our neighbor's possession, or spreading gossip about our coworkers. Furthermore, Eliphaz's final plea to Job in verses 21–30 can be deconstructed and reconstructed to make a solid and scriptural sermon. The title "Agree with the Almighty" would be catchy enough, and his admonitions to repent of pride (Job 22:29) and of loving mammon more than God (v. 24; cf. 28:12–19; Matt. 6:33; Luke 16:13) and his admonishments to listen

20. John Calvin, "Sermon 1," in *Sermons on Job*, facsimile ed. of the 1574 ed. (Banner of Truth, 1993), 3.

21. Roland E. Murphy, *The Tree of Life: An Exploration of Biblical Wisdom Literature*, Anchor Bible Reference Library (Doubleday, 1990), 38.

to God's Word (Job 22:22; John 3:31–36) and to delight in the Lord (Job 22:26; Phil. 3:1) are words that we all need to hear and heed. Moreover, his reminder of the promises of answered prayer (Job 22:27; James 5:13–18), guidance (Job 22:28; John 16:13), present and future blessings (Job 22:21; Matt. 5:3–12), and intimacy with the Almighty (Job 22:25; Rev. 21:1–4) for those who are in right relationship with him are encouraging and uplifting. Indeed, even from Job's jaded friend—with misconceptions about God and misunderstanding of Job's situation—we can celebrate the gospel, that we are saved from God by God through the cleanness of Jesus' hands (cf. Job 22:28b–30).

What to Avoid

Admittedly, these are lessons to learn only if we apply Eliphaz's well-intended, earnest, orthodox, and evangelistic appeal in the right context. The sole flaw (a major flaw!) in his admonition is its total irrelevance to Job's situation. If Eliphaz didn't completely misinterpret Job's situation ("Is not your evil abundant? There is no end to your iniquities," Job 22:5), his sermon on "salvation through forgiveness of the penitent would have been the brightest word that any of the friends have said."[22] But there are also lessons to learn about distancing ourselves from Eliphaz's attitude and actions. Eric Ortlund explains why:

> As we wade through chapter after chapter of bombastic, moralistic condemnation, their speeches quickly become very frustrating to read. My sense is, however, that this is exactly what the Joban poet intends and that he records the friends' speeches to show us what *not* to say to suffering brothers and sisters. Furthermore, I suspect that one of the reasons that the poet lets the debate go on for so long is to provoke such disgust at the friends that we resolve never to speak to a modern-day Job in the same way. The author is trying to inoculate us against this way of thinking and speaking.[23]

The main lesson in the what-not-to-say-and-do category, as it relates to Job 22, can be summarized as follows: Don't be an impersonal friend who promotes an impersonal God. Not only is Eliphaz arrogant, as pointed out

22. Andersen, *Job*, 204.
23. Ortlund, *Suffering Wisely and Well*, 63.

above, but he is so zealous to prove himself right that he overplays his argument, blurs facts into fantasy, and forgets that Job is a mere man[24]—an old friend who is desperate for a personal word of comfort and likely a physical touch of compassion. Let us not emulate his merciless method!

Then, from treating Job like a point in a debate to be won, rather than a friend to be cherished, Eliphaz makes the next move that we ought never to follow. He offers Job an impersonal God devoid of a true gospel. That is, while he offers some valuable expressions of God's transcendence and self-sufficiency (his version of Acts 17:24–25a),[25] he speaks wrongly about God ("you have not spoken of me what is right," Job 42:7) in that he misapplies those divine attributes to say that such a lofty God finds Job's claims of innocence inconsequential and, worse, that God doesn't care. Eliphaz's doctrine of God has become more important than God. His doctrine of God has obscured his view of the true and living God. He has become "a deist with a depersonalized God,"[26] a god who is entirely removed "from the sphere of compassionate involvement with humanity" and "too abstractly pure to be involved in anything except his own perfection."[27] His God is truncated.

Of course, Job hasn't bought into this lie, and neither should we. He hasn't understood the mystery of God's sovereignty, but he has pressed on: he has offered personal pleas to a personal God and continued to pursue God both for answers and, more foundationally, for a renewed relationship. He has held out hope to a personal God whom he knows and cares for and who knows and cares for him. Unlike the Eastern religions, such as Buddhism, Christianity does not offer a God who is removed from suffering, or who seeks to lift people "from their messy emotional lives . . . up onto the higher plane of divinely dispassionate existence."[28] Rather, it heralds a God who "so loved the world, that he gave his only Son, that whoever believes in him should not perish but have eternal life" (John 3:16). Our God is the Father who gives in love; the Son who lovingly dies; the Spirit who binds the love of the Godhead together and breathes it into the depths of our souls.

24. See Thomas, *The Storm Breaks*, 182.

25. "The God who made the world and everything in it, being Lord of heaven and earth, does not live in temples made by man, nor is he served by human hands, as though he needed anything."

26. Belcher, *Job*, 149.

27. Mike Mason, *The Gospel According to Job: An Honest Look at Pain and Doubt from the Life of One Who Lost Everything* (Crossway, 1994), 239.

28. Mason, 239.

Our gospel is indeed good news from a good God. It is not, as Mike Mason explains, "sterile stoicism [that] has no divine Person behind it, no real God at all[, and that] . . . cannot begin to embrace the God who loved the world so much that he gave his only begotten Son to be murdered for its sake." Mason continues, and I conclude, with this word on the gospel of Jesus:

> Contrary to what Eliphaz says, then, it is of the utmost importance to God whether or not people are righteous. That is why he died, and why he continues both to rejoice with us in our righteousness and to agonize with us in our sin. This is "how wide and long and high and deep is the love of Christ" (Eph. 3:18). Eliphaz apparently has no idea of what is really at stake here, not merely in Job's trial, but in the whole human project in the broadest sense. He seems to have no concept of how infinitely precious humanity is to God, and how much God's own honor is at risk in everything that happens on earth.[29]

29. Mason, 239–40.

20

Job: Why Aren't Times of Judgment Kept by the Almighty?

Job 23:1–24:25

Why are not times of judgment kept by the Almighty, and why do those who know him never see his days? (Job 24:1)

I remember preaching an evangelistic message to a group of college students in Africa when a student in the balcony stood up and shouted something at me. I paused for a second, looked up at the heckler, and kept speaking. Job's response to Eliphaz in Job 23:1–24:25 is less of a response and more of a continuation of where he left off at the conclusion of chapter 21. It's as if Job pauses for a second, looks at his friend, acknowledges and ignores him, and continues on. In fact, Job speaks quite a lot in the next nine chapters (Job 23–31). Excluding Bildad's brief barb (25:1–6), Job delivers a total of 203 verses! This is not because he has silenced his accusers but because his friends regard him as being so deluded by self-righteousness ("he was righteous in his own eyes," 32:1) that they deem further counsel to be pointless. Job deems their counsel pointless as well. Therefore, in Job 23:1–24:25 he turns his attention heavenward.

In Job chapter 23, Job focuses on his relationship with God, wondering why, despite being "an upright man," he cannot find God so that he may be acquitted ("I would be acquitted forever by my judge," Job 23:7). In chapter 24, Job contemplates God's relationship with "the wicked," whom he describes as those who oppress the poor (24:2–12) and "rebel against the light" (v. 13), and he wonders why they are not suffering in the place of the innocent righteous. This paradox is his problem. He again presents it to God, and yet heaven remains silent. But as we will see, Job expresses faith in God, even though God is silent, and in so doing he teaches us a number of important lessons about honesty in prayer, longing for God's coming judgment and his justification, and more!

A New Beginning; an Old Complaint (Job 23:1–2)

These two opening verses of Job 23 can be labeled as "A New Beginning; an Old Complaint." The new aspect is that Job refrains from verbally attacking his friends. He does not reiterate his previous snarky retorts, such as "No doubt you are the people, and wisdom will die with you" (Job 12:2), "miserable comforters are you all" (16:2; cf. 13:4), "How long will you torment me . . . ?" (19:2), and "mock on" (21:3). Instead, he returns to the tone he set at the beginning of the whole discussion. His opening words—"Today also my complaint is bitter; my hand is heavy on account of my groaning" (23:2)—more closely resemble 6:2–3a: "Oh that my vexation were weighed, and all my calamity laid in the balances! For then it would be heavier than the sand of the sea." Is this a sign of progress, a return to his earlier civility? Or has he given up on his friends, knowing that only God can speak for God? Likely the latter.

Looking for the Judge (Job 23:3–7)

Rather than turning on his three friends, Job directs his attention toward God for the remainder of the chapter (Job 23:3–17). In each verse, except the last (v. 17), Job mentions God as his primary focus. Yet Job's vision of God is out of focus. He knows that his "Redeemer lives" (19:25), but he doesn't know where to locate him: "Oh, that I knew where I might find him" (23:3a; cf. v. 8). Job wants to locate God so that God might hear his case (vv. 3b–7), and he yearns to come before the judgment seat, saying, "Oh, . . . that I might come even to his seat!" (v. 3). In that grand audience, he envisions that the following would take place:

> I would lay my case before him
> and fill my mouth with arguments.
> I would know what he would answer me
> and understand what he would say to me.
> Would he contend with me in the greatness of his power?
> No; he would pay attention to me.
> There an upright man could argue with him,
> and I would be acquitted forever by my judge. (Job 23:4–7)

As he had stated earlier (Job 9:33–35), here Job expresses a deep desire for God to serve as his "judge" (Job 23:7b) and hear his defense ("arguments"): "I would lay my case before him" (v. 4). The phrase "before him" can be literally translated "to his face" (*lepanayw*), indicating direct and intimate access to God. Because of such access, God's opened ear, and expected equity, Job envisions that God will listen to and side with him. Instead of contending against a mere mortal by using the "greatness of his power" (v. 6a), God "would pay attention" and, in paying attention, surely acquit the "upright" (vv. 6b–7).[1] Of course, when God finally responds to Job, Job is both silent and penitent, actions that suggest that when the moment comes he is "not so anxious to prove his innocence" by beating God in a debate as he is interested "to renew communion with God."[2] Like Abraham and Moses, he wants to hear from God. That said, he also wants justice!

Terrified About a Possible Encounter (Job 23:8–17)

Verse 8 of Job 23 echoes and expands on verse 3. This court case sounds great. The problem, as verse 9 points out, is that Job still cannot find God to plead his case. It is as though God were "playing a cosmic game of hide-and-seek":[3]

1. Job 23:3–7 marks another favorable transformation, since in the last instance when Job employed such legal terminology (cf. Job 9:3, 16, 19), he firmly believed that God would disregard and condemn him.

2. John E. Hartley, *The Book of Job*, NICOT (Eerdmans, 1988), 338.

3. David L. Allen, *Exalting Jesus in Job*, Christ-Centered Exposition (Holman Reference, 2022), 119.

Behold, I go forward, but he is not there,
 and backward, but I do not perceive him;
on the left hand when he is working, I do not behold him;
 he turns to the right hand, but I do not see him. (Job 23:8–9)

As Job continues in his search to find God ("Oh, that I knew where I might find him," Job 23:3), his quest, as stated above and reiterated now, "is not so much now a quest for understanding as a deep yearning for fellowship from the depths of his heart. . . . Job knows in his heart that his problem will be relieved not by theological dispute, nor by penitence for sins which he has not committed, nor by pulling his socks up, *but by the gift of communion with God*. It is *this* on which he now rests his hope."[4] Thus far, however, his quest has been in vain, as he expresses in verses 8–9 of Job 23. He has covered all directions of a compass—"forward" (east) and "backward" (west) and "on the left hand" (north) and "to the right hand" (south)[5]—but God remains elusive.

The problem is that Job still cannot find God to plead his case. Job is relieved, however, to know that God knows where to find him ("But he knows the way that I take") and knows what he is doing.[6] Further, Job is confident that when God finally does hear the case ("when he has tried me"), Job will be found innocent ("I shall come out as gold," Job 23:10). Job knows that his life is pure life (as pure as "gold" refined by fire; cf. Rev. 3:18), and in light of this fact he trusts that God will eventually see, vindicate, and even reward such righteousness. Like the psalmist of Psalm 119, Job has followed God's Word and delighted in his words:

My foot has held fast to his steps;
 I have kept his way and have not turned aside.
I have not departed from the commandment of his lips;
 I have treasured the words of his mouth more than my portion of food.
  (Job 23:11–12)

Perhaps it is good to pause here, before we read about Job's descent back into despair, to embrace what Job envisions—that is, to look forward to God's

4. David Atkinson, *The Message of Job*, The Bible Speaks Today (InterVarsity Press, 1991), 102.
5. See August H. Konkel, *Job*, Cornerstone Biblical Commentary 6 (Tyndale House, 2006), 152–53.
6. Daniel J. Estes, *Job*, Teach the Text (Baker, 2013), 142.

coming judgment. As Mike Mason observes: "Unlike most people Job sees the judgment-seat of God as a place of refuge, not of condemnation. In fact, what he longs for more than anything else is to be judged by God."[7] Job trusts that in the end, and in Abraham's words to God, "the Judge of all the earth" will "do what is just" and not make "the righteous fare as the wicked" (Gen. 18:25). Job's faith—what David Atkinson calls Job's "depths of faith"[8]—is most evident in Job 23:10 when he declares, "But he knows the way that I take; when he has tried me, I shall come out as gold." In this statement, Job affirms his belief that God, despite his silence, is observant. God has been meticulously scrutinizing every detail of Job's distressing situation. He will recognize his purity—how Job has steadfastly followed God's path ("My foot has held fast to his steps," Job 23:11a) and remained devoted to his teachings ("I have not departed from the commandment of his lips," v. 12a). Job even takes delight in God's Word more than in his daily bread ("I have treasured the words of his mouth more than my portion of food," v. 12b).

Like Job, we can look forward to the judgment day, when we too as Christians will be proved to be in the right. Of course, we believe, as Job himself believed, that God will judge us to be righteous not on the basis of our perfectly sinless lives, but on that of our Redeemer-Who-Lives; it is this faith that when tested as through fire ("the tested genuineness of [our] faith—more precious than gold that perishes though it is tested by fire") not only will result one day "in praise and glory and honor at the revelation of Jesus Christ" (1 Peter 1:7), but results even now in sure signs of our acceptance with God. The apostle John dwells on a similar theme when he writes:

> So we have come to know and to believe the love that God has for us. God is love, and whoever abides in love abides in God, and God abides in him. By this is love perfected with us, so that we may have confidence for the day of judgment, because as he is so also are we in this world. There is no fear in love, but perfect love casts out fear. For fear has to do with punishment, and whoever fears has not been perfected in love. (1 John 4:16–18)

God's love for us in Jesus has reached its perfection! Just as Jesus has a relationship of love and acceptance with the Father ("as he is"), so we

7. Mike Mason, *The Gospel According to Job: An Honest Look at Pain and Doubt from the Life of One Who Lost Everything* (Crossway, 1994), 245.

8. Atkinson, *Message of Job*, 102.

also who are living in this world now enter into that same relationship through faith. If we "believe the love that God has for us" (1 John 4:16) in "his Son" (3:23; cf. 4:14–15) and our "Savior" (4:14) and if we love others, then God reassures our heart (3:19–21) and casts out fear of God's judgment (4:17–18).[9]

With this New Testament theology in mind, we return to our Old Testament figure of Job, who serves as a reminder to Christians that we should eagerly anticipate God's impending judgment. We should envision the end—our vindication, when we encounter God's presence and experience eternal and enduring communion, righteousness, justice, and love.

While Job is assured when he envisions a positive outcome in the end (Job 23:8–12), in Job 23:13 he loses focus on the positive possibilities. His hope is deferred; his trust dissipates. Speaking about God, he says:

> But he is unchangeable, and who can turn him back?
>   What he desires, that he does.
> For he will complete what he appoints for me,
>   and many such things are in his mind. (Job 23:13–14)

The problem here is not Job's *innocence* but God's *sovereignty.* God's sovereignty should be a comfort to him, but instead it makes him fear for the future. Because of God's immutability ("he is unchangeable"),[10] omnipotence ("and who can turn him back?"), and absolute and autonomous authority and sovereignty ("what he desires, that he does," Job 23:13), Job dreads that he will have no say in *when* his case will be heard or *what* the outcome will be. He is totally in God's hands, for God "will complete what he appoints" or "decrees" for Job, doing whatever else he has planned for Job ("and many such things are in his mind," v. 14). Job expresses his fear of the unknown and his trepidation at actually meeting God in this way:

> Therefore I am terrified at his presence;
>   when I consider, I am in dread of him.

9. See Douglas Sean O'Donnell, *1–3 John: A Gospel-Transformed Life*, Reformed Expository Commentary (P&R Publishing, 2015), 141.

10. The ESV's "unchangeable" in Job 23:13 is literally "he is the one," which is a possible "allusion to one of Israel's epithets for Yahweh" and "a Yahwistic affirmation" that is comparable with Isaiah 43:13: "*I am he*; . . . I work, and *who can turn it back*?" J. Gerald Janzen, *Job*, Interpretation: A Bible Commentary for Teaching and Preaching (John Knox, 1985), 167.

God has made my heart faint;
the Almighty has terrified me. (Job 23:15–16)

Job is terrified to meet God,[11] and God's very presence is the cause of such trepidation. Nevertheless, Job presses on. He does the only thing that he now knows to do. He returns to lament. While he is blind to God's purposes, such "darkness" will not tie his tongue: "yet I am not silenced because of the darkness, nor because thick darkness covers my face" (Job 23:17). And speak he will! Job has another chapter to go before Bildad's quick interruption.

What the Wicked Do; What God Does Not Do (Job 24:1–12)

Like the psalmist, Job wonders: "How long, O Lord? Will you forget me forever? How long will you hide your face from me?" Job begs God to "consider and answer" him and do something to remove the "sorrow in [his] heart all the day" (Ps. 13:1–3). He feels this not only because of his losses, but also because of the prosperity of the wicked.

In Job chapter 24, Job shifts his focus from addressing God's unresponsive relationship with him to addressing God's apathetic association with evildoers. Unlike Eliphaz's untruthful and concise list of Job's sins (Job 22:6–9), the wicked have a genuine and lengthy list of sins against humanity (24:2–11, 13–16). Job employs the same categories as Eliphaz to outline these crimes: exploiting the needy (22:6), letting the hungry starve (v. 7), and oppressing orphans and widows (vv. 8–9). Job expounds on these categories, however, adding details such as murder and adultery in verses 13–16 of Job 24 and more directly addressing the theft of land and flocks in verse 2. Additionally, Job highlights the effects of these unjust crimes on the poor:

Some move landmarks;
they seize flocks and pasture them.
They drive away the donkey of the fatherless;
they take the widow's ox for a pledge.
They thrust the poor off the road;
the poor of the earth all hide themselves. (Job 24:2–4)

11. The word "terrified" in Job 23:15, 16 captures well the sense of the Hebrew (*bahal*), because this is not the fear (*yare'*) used to describe Job's "fear" (Job 1:1, 8, 9; 2:3) "of the Lord" (28:28).

Here Job explains how the disadvantaged suffer in two ways. First, the wicked "move landmarks" or boundary markers (Job 24:2a)—"among the most insidious of evils," according to Old Testament law[12]—and claim the poor man's land and animals ("they seize flocks," v. 2b), leaving the now-destitute with no place to go. Even the orphans' and widows' livestock are stolen. Second, when the wicked become violent, they push the destitute into a ditch ("thrust the poor off the road," v. 4a), causing the poor to seek to escape their malice: "the poor . . . hide themselves" (v. 4b) out of fear for their safety.

What happens next is vividly described:

> Behold, like wild donkeys in the desert
> the poor go out to their toil, seeking game;
> the wasteland yields food for their children.
> They gather their fodder in the field,
> and they glean the vineyard of the wicked man.
> They lie all night naked, without clothing,
> and have no covering in the cold.
> They are wet with the rain of the mountains
> and cling to the rock for lack of shelter.
> (There are those who snatch the fatherless child from the breast,
> and they take a pledge against the poor.)
> They go about naked, without clothing;
> hungry, they carry the sheaves;
> among the olive rows of the wicked they make oil;
> they tread the winepresses, but suffer thirst. (Job 24:5–11)

Like the plight of tens of millions of global refugees today, the poor (back in Job's day), stripped of their land, belongings, and dignity, become scavengers, "like wild donkeys in the desert" (Job 24:5a), who roam in search of scraps. They go out into "the wasteland," looking for "food for their children" ("go out to their toil, seeking game," v. 5b–c), but they must settle for whatever they can find. The sense, as we arrive at Job 24:6, is that these wanderers in the wilderness have wandered back to town to seek employment, but the only work available is with the landowners who have exploited and oppressed them. They work tirelessly for "the wicked man," gathering animal feed

12. Konkel, *Job*, 156. "Moving boundary markers was a cardinal sin in the biblical law (Deut. 19:14; 27:17; Prov. 22–28; 23:10)" (156).

("fodder in the field") and harvesting grapes ("glean the vineyard," v. 6), but they receive little compensation in return. They are deprived of basic human needs such as "shelter" (vv. 7b, 8) and "clothing" (vv. 7a, 10a), causing them to suffer in the cold and rain without proper cover or protection. The landless become the homeless.[13] They are forced to cling to rocks for shelter ("They are wet with the rain of the mountains and cling to the rock for lack of shelter," v. 8) and "lie all night naked, without clothing, and have no covering in the cold" (v. 7). They are also divested of the most absolute essentials—food and water ("They go about . . . hungry," v. 10, and "suffer thirst," v. 11b)—even though they work with food ("the sheaves" of wheat, v. 10b; rows of "olive[s]" for olive "oil," vv. 11a) and drink (the wine of "the winepresses," v. 11b).

In the midst of the great suffering described in Job 24:6–11, Job expresses his despair through a poetic aside in verse 9, a gross and graphic image of how bad times have become: "There are those who snatch the fatherless child from the breast, and they take a pledge against the poor." The "those" are the wicked who have reached a new low: kidnapping a baby from the mother who is nursing him and selling the child to pay off a debt or using him as collateral for a debt that the poor owe them ("they take a pledge against the poor," Job 24:9b).[14] The situation is so bleak that it resembles the darkest point in Israel's exile. Job is left questioning where God is amid such misery.

As previously mentioned, the sins of the wicked all revolve around oppressing the poor, which is emphasized by the repeated reference to "the poor" (Job 24:4, 5, 9) and related pronouns throughout Job 24:4–11 ("they" [vv. 6 (2×), 7, 8, 10 (2×), 11 (2×)]; "their" [vv. 5 (2×), 6]; "themselves" [v. 4]). This leads Job to grapple with the problem of evil, as he summarizes what the wicked *do* in verses 2–11 and what God *does not do* in verses 1 and 12. Job questions why, if God allows evil for a time, he doesn't seem to bring justice to the oppressed: "Why are not times of judgment kept by the Almighty, and why do those who know him never see his days?" (v. 1). He wonders why the cries of the poor go unanswered ("From out of the city the dying groan," v. 12a), though they plead with God from the very depths of their hearts ("the soul of the wounded," v. 12b). They cry for help, but heaven hears not and helps not. God "charges no one with wrong" (v. 12c). He fails to execute

13. See Konkel, 157.
14. Konkel, 157.

justice. "God leaves the oppressor 'undisturbed and unpunished.'"[15] We might also, as we seek to make sense of the evils we encounter today, ask similar questions and think similar thoughts as Job. Why does God seem so silent about the plight of the aborted baby, the hungry orphan, the sex-trafficked teen, the lonely refugee, and the violently displaced and exploited?

Two More Hideous Sins to Add to the List (Job 24:13–17)

Just as every line in Job 23:3–16 features God, so every line in Job 24:2–24 features the wicked. Verses 13–17 continue to focus on "those who rebel against the light" (Job 24:13) by featuring two notorious sinners: the "murderer" (v. 14) and the "adulterer" (v. 15). Job has moved from civil to criminal injustice:[16]

> There are those who rebel against the light,
>   who are not acquainted with its ways,
>   and do not stay in its paths.
> The murderer rises before it is light,
>   that he may kill the poor and needy,
>   and in the night he is like a thief.
> The eye of the adulterer also waits for the twilight,
>   saying, "No eye will see me";
>   and he veils his face.
> In the dark they dig through houses;
>   by day they shut themselves up;
>   they do not know the light.
> For deep darkness is morning to all of them;
>   for they are friends with the terrors of deep darkness. (Job 24:13–17)

The "light" likely represents God (cf. Isa. 60:19), specifically his light of revelation. Therefore, to "rebel against the light" is to refuse to hear God's Word (these rebels "are not acquainted with [God's] ways," Job 24:13b) or to heed his directions (they "do not stay in [God's] paths," v. 13c).

The murderer rebels against obeying God's Word. He wakes up around 2:00 a.m. ("rises before it is light," Job 24:14a). He has a premeditated plan

15. Gleason L. Archer Jr., *The Book of Job: God's Answer to the Problem of Undeserved Suffering* (Baker, 1982), 81.

16. See Allen, *Exalting Jesus in Job*, 120.

to senselessly slaughter the already oppressed ("that he may kill the poor and needy," v. 14b). He takes their possessions and their land as easily as he takes their lives ("in the night he is like a thief," v. 14c). In the morning, it is as though nothing has happened; he has gotten away with this horrific crime. In a similar manner and with a similar outcome, the adulterer rebels. After midnight ("The eye of the adulterer also waits for the twilight," v. 15a), trusting that he will not be seen ("saying, 'No eye will see me,'" v. 15b)—both because of the time and because of his disguise ("he veils his face," v. 15c)—he gets into the house, or many houses ("they dig through houses," v. 16a),[17] and *into* another man's wife (they "take [their] fill of love till morning," Prov. 7:18). The two adulterers continue their illicit affair until the next twilight ("by day they shut themselves up; they do not know the light," Job 24:16b–c) and part ways when the coast is clear. And unlike the adulterers in Proverbs 6:20–7:27, where the "twilight" rendezvous (7:9) is met with a husband's rage and "revenge" (6:34), the sinners in Job 24 manage to escape unnoticed and unpunished.

The two sinners, the murderer and the adulterer, both choose to commit their sins under the cover of darkness ("before it is light," Job 24:14a; "in the night," v. 14c; "waits for the twilight," v. 15a; "they do not know the light," v. 16c). In the words of Jesus, these rebels "loved the darkness rather than the light because their works were evil" (John 3:19; cf. 1 Thess. 5:4–8). In Job's rendition: "deep darkness is morning to all of them; for they are friends with the terrors of deep darkness" (Job 24:17). Innocent Job has experienced the "deep darkness" (16:16) of God's silence and not hearing from God; to the guilty ungodly, however, the "deep darkness" (24:17) safeguards their sin. It hides them, so it seems to Job, from God's inspecting and adjudicating eye. Job states that God, to whom Eliphaz has just attributed the ability to "see the highest stars" and "judge through the deep darkness" (22:12, 13), does not choose to "detect the skulking crimes which the wicked perpetrate whether in the night *or* in the day."[18] Of course, Job means that God does not see only in the sense that he chooses to remain indifferent to and inactive

17. "The summary of the covenant, or Ten Commandments, begins with a commitment to God himself, requires honor for those who gave us earthly life, and then in three staccato sentences summarizes how the lives of others must be respected: do not kill, do not commit adultery, do not steal. It is these three most direct violations of life that summarize the activities of the wicked at night (24:13–17)." Konkel, *Job*, 157.

18. Janzen, *Job*, 168–69.

in a world "full of miserable and weak people, suffering at the hands of the wicked who carry on unpunished."[19]

THE FORTUNE AND FATE OF THE WICKED (JOB 24:18–25)

Rather than being exposed and condemned for their transgressions, evildoers often experience the opposite outcome: they prosper! Similar to his argument in Job 21:7–21, here in 24:18–20 Job opposes his friends' perspective ("You say," Job 24:18a) and provides a concise critique of their flawed theology:

> You say, "Swift are they on the face of the waters;
> their portion is cursed in the land;
> no treader turns toward their vineyards.
> Drought and heat snatch away the snow waters;
> so does Sheol those who have sinned.
> The womb forgets them;
> the worm finds them sweet;
> they are no longer remembered,
> so wickedness is broken like a tree." (Job 24:18–20)

Job's old friends claim that the wicked do not get away with anything but experience a threefold fall into disgrace. First, whatever prosperity they might experience is very short-lived. They are pushed down the river and off a waterfall like driftwood ("Swift are they on the face of the waters," Job 24:18a), unnoticed, unimportant, unremembered. Their grapes are blighted ("their portion is cursed in the land," v. 18b), so their business deals fall through ("no treader turns toward their vineyards," v. 18c) and the family winery goes bankrupt. Then, second, comes death ("Sheol") to snatch "those who have sinned" away, as "snow waters" are soaked up on a 100-degree day or by a seven-month "drought" (v. 19). Third, they are forgotten. As they are buried in the ground, only the worm eyes and enjoys them ("the worm finds them sweet," v. 20b). No one else will remember them ("they are no longer remembered," v. 20c), not even their own mothers ("The womb forgets them," v. 20a). In the end, they have been judged by God and rendered useless—"so wickedness is broken like a tree" (v. 20d; cf. Ezek. 17:24).

19. Konkel, *Job*, 152, 156.

In summary, the friends claim that the wicked do not prosper, suffer quick deaths, and are soon forgotten. Job agrees with one point of his friends' analysis, namely, that the wicked will die and be forgotten:

> They are exalted a little while, and then are gone;
> they are brought low and gathered up like all others;
> they are cut off like the heads of grain. (Job 24:24)

But he cannot concede their other points, for he still struggles with his observation of life. He remains convinced ("If it is not so, who will prove me a liar and show that there is nothing in what I say?," Job 24:25) of the absolute truth of his observations in Job 24:1–17. Despite the wicked's committing the most atrocious acts ("They wrong the barren, childless woman, and do no good to the widow," v. 21; cf. Ex. 22:21–27; Deut. 24:17–22), swift justice is not served. They do not suffer immediate death or experience God's prompt judgment. Instead, it seems to Job that they experience his helping hand: God "prolongs the life of the mighty by his power; they rise up when they despair of life" (Job 24:22). He not only helps them up when they fall, but also provides them with security and support ("He gives them security, and they are supported," v. 23a). His eye is guarding their way ("and his eyes are upon their ways," v. 23b), rather than condemning it.

The Most Crucial Response

There are several ways to respond to these two chapters. One way is to ponder the depravity of sin and the wickedness that springs from the human heart—out of which comes murder and adultery and oppression of the innocent! As our Lord taught, "For from within, out of the heart of man, come evil thoughts, sexual immorality, theft, murder, adultery, coveting, wickedness, deceit, sensuality, envy, slander, pride, foolishness" (Mark 7:21–22). Another way to respond is to contemplate the importance of honesty in prayer and how Job once again teaches us to express the troubles we face and the complexities we cannot grasp, and to speak directly to God about our sense of his silence and abandonment. We could also respond by delving into the theological and ethical issues that Job raises. We could address the plight of the poor and how to fight injustice in this world to make sure that those in our neighborhoods and around the globe do not suffer the same atrocities described in Job 24:2–11. Do we "remember the poor," and are we "eager" to provide for their needs (Gal. 2:10)? Do we love the "least" among us (Matt. 25:40, 45)? Indeed, do we take seriously the warnings and blessings of the parable of the sheep and the goats (vv. 31–46)? Alternatively, we could respond by discussing the attributes of the Almighty—such as immutability and sovereignty—and how such attributes bring both assurance and confusion. We could even consider the pervasive presence of Satan, who is featured only in the prologue of Job but is undeniably active in the world then and now. It is evident that Satan, who is described as "the ruler of this world" (John 14:30) and "the god of this world" (2 Cor. 4:4), obstructs the righteous from instantly receiving their reward and prevents the wicked from facing immediate and complete punishment in this world.

Yet the most crucial response to these chapters is the Bible's solution to the problem of evil, the issue that Job struggles with most extensively. What is the Bible's answer to Job's question, "Why are not times of judgment kept by the Almighty?" (Job 24:1)? The Bible's ultimate answer is found in the first coming (Christ's incarnation and crucifixion) and the second coming (Christ's final judgment and vindication).

There is a time for everything under the sun (Eccl. 3:1), including a time for the Son "to be born, and . . . to die" (v. 2). Paul writes of the incarnation in this way: "when the fullness of time had come, God sent forth his Son, born of woman, . . . to redeem" (Gal. 4:4–5). God's answer to Eliphaz's question in Job 15:14—"What is man, that he can be pure? Or he who is born of a woman, that he can be righteous?"—is found in the pure and holy Son of God come in the flesh. Paul also writes about the crucifixion in a way that highlights its timelessness:

> In him we have redemption through his blood, the forgiveness of our trespasses, according to the riches of his grace, which he lavished upon us, in all wisdom and insight making known to us the mystery of his will, according to his purpose, which he set forth in Christ as a plan for the fullness of time, to unite all things in him, things in heaven and things on earth. (Eph. 1:7–10)

The crucifixion of Christ was wisdom ("Christ crucified" is "the wisdom of God," 1 Cor. 1:23, 24)! It revealed to us the mystery of God's inscrutable will. It demonstrated to us that God had a well-timed plan, whereby he conquered the wicked through the wicked men's plan of nailing his Son to a tree.

Moreover, the second coming of Christ makes clear that the times of judgment are indeed kept by the Almighty (see Job 24:1). Jesus will return soon, judge evil people and every evil angelic being, save the righteous (those who trust in his righteousness!), defeat death and sin, and make all things new—a new heaven and a new earth wherein God himself will dwell with his people forever and ever. An old Puritan prayer beautifully summarizes God's plan for dealing with evil once and for all, beginning with this praise for Christ's work and pledge:

> O Son of God and Son of Man,
> Thou wast incarnate, didst suffer, rise, ascend
> for my sake;
> Thy departure was not a token of separation
> but a pledge of return;
> Thy Word, promises, sacraments, show thy death
> until thou come again.
> That day is no horror to me,
> for thy death has redeemed me,
> thy Spirit fills me,
> thy love animates me,
> thy Word governs me.

The prayer concludes by summoning us to rejoicing:

> Every event and circumstance of my life will be
> dealt with—
> the sins of my youth, my secret sins,
> the sins of abusing thee, of disobeying thy Word,
> the sins of neglecting ministers' admonitions,
> the sins of violating my conscience—
> all will be judged;
> And after judgment, peace and rest, life and service,
> employment and enjoyment, for thine elect.
> O God, keep me in this faith,
> and ever looking for Christ's return.[20]

20. Arthur Bennett, ed., *The Valley of Vision: A Collection of Puritan Prayers and Devotions* (Banner of Truth, 2006), 48–49.

21

Bildad; Job: Job's Last Bout with Bildad

Job 25:1–27:23

Behold, these are but the outskirts of his ways, and how small a whisper do we hear of him! But the thunder of his power who can understand? (Job 26:14)

As we turn the page from Job chapter 24 to chapter 25, we perhaps want to know more about what Job thinks about God's incomprehensible sovereignty, the topic that he has waxed eloquent on in chapters 23–24. Instead, we have another interruption. We are not surprised by this, since Job's friends have repeatedly interrupted him. What is surprising, however, is how short the interruption is. Bildad belts out what amounts to only five verses (Job 25:2–6), fewer than forty words in the Hebrew. "This brevity," John Walton claims, "is defensible in light of his entrenched traditionalism, which, at this point in the dialogue, has reduced him to platitudinous reiteration of his major salient points." Those points? "God is unimaginably great; humans are intrinsically flawed and, in the grand scheme of things, are of little consequence. He believes in an ordered world, and as we have seen previously, that order is founded on the RP [retribution principle]."[1] Fair enough. But any sermon on the greatness of God and sinfulness of man, however flawed and brief, is worth listening to. Moreover, any final word from the friends that is not "caustic and critical"[2] is curious, to say the least. Elihu will foreshadow what God has to say out of the whirlwind. Might bumbling Bildad do so as well? As Robert Alden notes: "It is a welcome change to hear him begin with this lofty and worshipful theological statement. God rules."[3] That noted, in what seems like a straightforward lecture on systematic theology—God is good and great; man is bad and not so great—Bildad is actually mocking Job's outrageous idea that he can stand before God, present his case, and be found wholly spotless by the Holy One. Job will undoubtedly have something to say about that!

Bildad's Brief Barb (Job 25:1–6)

The first part of Bildad's rebuttal (Job 25:1–3) is that God is good and great, or, in more theological terms, majestic, mighty, and holy. He begins:

> Dominion and fear are with God;
>   he makes peace in his high heaven.
> Is there any number to his armies?
>   Upon whom does his light not arise? (Job 25:2–3)

Bildad attributes absolute authority ("dominion"), awe ("fear," or "reverence,"[4] Job 25:2a), and "peace" to God's reign over the loftiest realms of the cosmos ("his high heaven," v. 2b)—the seventy-times-seventy heights. Despite his being transcendent, there is no corner of the world where God's presence is absent ("Upon whom does his light not arise?," v. 3b); his rule extends everywhere ("Is there any number to his armies?," v. 3a). Do not underestimate this flawed theologian's observation: our Lord Jesus himself spoke of the 72,000-plus angels ("twelve legions") that could have come to his aid (Matt. 26:53), as well as of how the sun rises on both the evil and the good (5:45).

1. John H. Walton, *Job*, NIVAC (Zondervan, 2012), 249.
2. Robert L. Alden, *Job*, New American Commentary 11 (Broadman & Holman, 1993), 255.
3. Alden, 255–56.
4. Marvin H. Pope, *Job: Introduction, Translation and Notes*, Anchor Bible 15 (Doubleday, 1973), 180.

Recognizing God's absolute dominion and pervasive presence should deepen our reverence for him and our trust in his sovereign rule over our lives.

The second part of the rebuttal (Job 25:4–6) is in the form of an *a fortiori* argument (from the stronger to the weaker): if the bright celestial lights (the stronger) are not perfectly pure in God's eyes, then how can mere mortals (the weaker) be found right before his sight? Man is too bad and too small to stand before a good and great God. Returning to a foundational question in the dialogue—"asked originally by Eliphaz (4:17), recast and used by Job in his second speech (9:2), repeated and reinforced by Eliphaz (15:14)"[5]—Bildad makes the same inquiry in two different ways: "How then can man be in the right before God? How can he who is born of woman be pure?" (25:4). The question, along with its implied answer (that no individual can be blameless before God), is not a general theological assertion—something that we might find in a systematics textbook. Instead, it serves as a direct response (v. 1) to Job's assertions. By substituting the terms "man" and "he who is born of woman" with *Job*, we can discern Bildad's intended meaning: in his perspective, there are no exceptions to the retribution principle. "I'm sorry, Job, but your aspiration to be declared innocent before a divine Judge will never happen. The chasm between the creature and the Creator is simply too vast."

As usual, Bildad has overstepped his bounds. He seems to have neglected a thorough examination of the facts at hand, and in doing so, he undermines his own aspirations for a meaningful relationship with God. Instead of concluding his short speech by refuting Job's assertions that God permits wickedness to go unpunished (as seen in Job 24), Bildad draws a sharp contrast between God and man. To God, even the brightest and purest of the heavenly lights ("Behold, even the moon . . . and the stars") are "not bright, and . . . not pure in his eyes" (25:5). Consequently, one can only imagine what God makes of earthlings: "how much less man, who is a maggot, and the son of man, who is a worm!" (v. 6). In light of this, Job's situation appears utterly bleak. Bildad wants Job to picture an insignificant and repulsive creature—a "maggot" or a "worm"—standing before the exalted judgment "seat" of God (23:3b) and to contemplate whether such a great God would really "pay attention" to such a creature's "arguments" (Job's arguments!) and acquit him (vv. 4–7). Of course not!

5. Kenneth Laing Harris and August Konkel, "Job," in *ESV Study Bible* (Crossway, 2008), 907.

Right Lesson; Wrong Audience

Once again, we have the right lesson given to the wrong audience. Bildad's assertion about the greatness of God and the inherent depravity of man and conclusion that we all are therefore guilty and not innocent in his eyes is true (Ps. 14:1–3; Rom. 3:10–12). What Job needs to hear, however, is the hope of vindication for the righteous. He needs the assurance not only that God is just but also that he will administer justice. We might also add that he needs to hear more about the possibility of restoration with God through an advocate. In other words, Job needs to hear the gospel! As Blaise Pascal put it: "Knowing God without knowing our own wretchedness makes for pride. Knowing our own wretchedness without knowing God makes for despair. Knowing Jesus Christ strikes the balance because he shows us both God and our own wretchedness."[6]

So once more, from the friends' counsel we learn the danger of saying the right thing to the wrong person. We need prudence and discernment when applying biblical principles; it's not merely about what we say but also about who receives our message. Additionally, there's another valuable lesson to be gleaned: the danger of pressing a biblical truth too far. What do we make of "Bildad's maggot theology," as Tremper Longman cleverly labels it?[7] Are we really maggots and worms in God's sight and according to his design? Is it right, for example, to sing the last line of the first verse of a favorite hymn?

Alas! and did my Savior bleed,
 and did my Sovereign die!
Would he devote that sacred head
 for such a worm as I![8]

While God's people can act wormlike (Israel is called "you worm" in Isaiah 41:14) and feel like a worm ("I am a worm and not a man, scorned by mankind," Ps. 22:6), we must remember, as Longman points out, that God created human beings with unique grandeur, with "a special and dignified

6. Blaise Pascal, *Pensées*, trans. A. J. Krailsheimer, rev. ed. (Penguin, 1995), 57.

7. Tremper Longman III, *Job*, Baker Commentary on the Old Testament Wisdom and Psalms (Baker Academic, 2012), 309.

8. Isaac Watts, "Alas! and Did My Savior Bleed" (1707).

relationship with God."[9] Read Genesis 1–2; meditate on Psalm 8. We are the highest achievement of creation: made in God's image, made to rule over the rest of creation, made good, and crowned with glory and honor. We have been promised that one day we will "become partakers of the divine nature" (2 Peter 1:4), and more importantly, we know that the Son of God himself partook (and forever partakes!) of our human nature: "the second person of the Trinity didn't become a stone, a plant, or a donkey. He didn't become a penguin or a petunia. He didn't become wind or water. He didn't become the North Star or a black hole. He became a man."[10] Praise God for the incarnation! Praise God for our future glorification! Praise God that he created humans! But Bildad seems to have forgotten all this, if he ever believed it in the first place.

Job: A Last Bout with Bildad

Bildad finishes his short sermon on the maggot-ness of man. Will Job respond to Bildad or ignore him? Job is, after all, in the middle of an interesting and important monologue about God's work in the world. He decides to respond. Thus ends the third cycle of the friends' speeches; but Job has more to say, first to them and then beyond them. After he speaks eloquently about his awesome God (Job 26:5–14) and boldly reiterates his own innocence (27:2–6), he curses his enemies—his three *friends*—lumping them in with the wicked and reminding them of the frightful fate awaiting them (vv. 7–23).

Some Sarcasm to Start (Job 26:1–4)

Both Job (in Job 23:1–2) and Bildad (in 25:1–6) have briefly refrained from direct insults. That ceasefire comes to an end here. Job's response ("Then Job answered and said," 26:1) targets Bildad for his lack of help and sound counsel to "him" (vv. 2, 3) in his weak condition: "How you have helped him who has *no power*! How you have saved the arm that has *no strength*!" (v. 2). The ESV's exclamation points rightly enhance the sarcasm. The sarcasm continues in Job 26:3: "How you have counseled him who has

9. Longman, *Job*, 310.

10. Douglas Sean O'Donnell, *The Song of Solomon: An Invitation to Intimacy*, Preaching the Word (Crossway, 2012), 102–3.

no wisdom, and plentifully declared sound knowledge!" Job, who has "no wisdom" in Bildad's eyes, has been "counseled," given plentiful "sound knowledge." The scent of sarcasm, added to what Job says in verse 4, can be smelled a mile away. "With whose help have you uttered words?" (Surely God is whispering in your ear these prophetic rebukes, for they are out of this world!) "And whose breath has come out from you?" (Surely it is the Spirit of God himself, for you speak not like a mere wormlike man but like a god.) Job's biting sarcasm underscores his frustration with Bildad's empty rhetoric, highlighting the futility of his friends' attempts to provide genuine comfort or wisdom.

The Outskirts of God's Awesome Power (Job 26:5–14)

At this point, it appears that Job has completed his opening sarcastic rebuke, transitioning from addressing Bildad (the "you" of Job 26:2–4) to focusing on the "dead" (v. 5). Curiously, these "dead" beings appear to be in a state of eerie existence; they "tremble" despite their supposed demise: "The dead tremble under the waters and their inhabitants" (v. 5). It is as if these departed souls are continually submerged, grappling with the enigmatic aquatic creatures (referred to as the "inhabitants" of the waters) that roam the depths of the dark sea. But Job's primary focus is not on these aquatic zombies. Once again (see esp. 23:3–16; 24:1, 12, 22–23), it is "God" who is named in Job 26:6 and mentioned in every verse thereafter (26:7–14). With one of the most remarkable parallelisms in the book of Job, Job declares, "Sheol is naked before God, and Abaddon has no covering" (v. 6). "Sheol" (the place of death) and "Abaddon" (the place of destruction; "the bottomless pit," Rev. 9:11) are seen by God even though the sun ("his light," Job 25:3) cannot possibly penetrate the depths of the lowest point of the earth.

Job is on an *inspired* theological roll. He is talking about God, and he is doing so in the right way. Everything that follows makes us say, "Amen, preach it!" Next, God's actions are listed: "He stretches" (Job 26:7a), he "hangs" (v. 7b), "he binds up" (v. 8a), "he covers" (v. 9a), he "spreads" (v. 9b), "he has inscribed" (v. 10a), he rebukes (v. 11b), "he stilled" (v. 12a), "he shattered" (v. 12b), and "his hand pierced" (v. 13b). God has created the universe, stretching out the northern skies over emptiness ("He stretches out the north," v. 7a; cf. 9:8) and suspending the earth in the middle of immense blackness (he "hangs the earth on nothing," 26:7b). How did he do it? Without any help from some other so-called deity or his own created angel, "he binds up the waters in his thick clouds, and the cloud is not split open under them" (v. 8). In other words, as he stretched out the universe, so he stretched out what is above the earth ("the heavens," Gen. 1:1; "God called the expanse Heaven," v. 8) so that the clouds would make a natural barrier between heaven and earth. And with the moon, that great light for the earth that reflects the light of the sun, he can create the remarkable eclipse, covering "the face of the full moon" with darkness, as a "cloud" might cover the earth: "He covers the face of the full moon and spreads over it his cloud" (Job 26:9). It is awe-inspiring to watch "his cloud" (what we know to be the earth's shadow) doing its divinely ordained duty!

Job is not finished; he adds four more verses to his ode to an awesome God. Wherever he has been in his relationship with God, he has returned to the fear of the Lord. He is on his knees before his Creator, as we should be. Verse 10 of Job 26 picks up the theme of the God of Genesis: "He has inscribed a circle on the face of the waters at the boundary between light and darkness." Put differently: "God separated the light from the darkness. God called the light Day, and the darkness he called Night. And there was evening and there was morning, the first day" (Gen. 1:4b–5). Job rejoices in the fact that God in his wisdom drew a horizon over the waters, setting a daily boundary between the day and the night.

In Job 26:11–13, the protagonist recounts the power of God not *in* creation but *over* creation:

> The pillars of heaven tremble
>   and are astounded at his rebuke.
> By his power he stilled the sea;
>   by his understanding he shattered Rahab.
> By his wind the heavens were made fair;
>   his hand pierced the fleeing serpent.

Verse 11 of Job 26 likely speaks of a thunderstorm ("The pillars of heaven tremble and are astounded at his rebuke"). Martin Luther famously turned toward God in a thunderstorm. Who of us, when rightly meditating on God's power, is not taken aback by a crash in the heavens during a summer storm that makes us shake in our boots, or fear even for our lives? Even more, God demonstrates his power by taming the untamable: the ocean ("By his power he stilled the sea"/"By his wind the heavens were made fair," Job 26:12a, 13a) and its greatest monsters ("he shattered Rahab"/"his hand pierced the fleeing serpent," vv. 12b, 13b). Here, as Christians, we might think of Jesus' taming the wind and waves (Matt. 8:23–27) and Revelation 21:1—"the sea was no more"—where the point of those two texts, as is the point of this section of Job, is that God has absolute control over the uncontrollable!

Job's conclusion to his ode "The Outskirts of God's Awesome Power" (Job 26:5–14) offers arguably the three most profound lines within the thousand or so award-winning lines in the book of Job: "Behold, these are but the outskirts of his ways, and how small a whisper do we hear of him! But the thunder of his power who can understand?" (v. 14). This "behold" stands out as the most significant among the twenty-six occurrences in the book, fifteen of which come from Job himself. "Job is so far from thinking," as John Gill well summarizes, "that he had taken notice of all of them [the wonderful works of God], or even of the chief and principal ones, that what he observed were only the extremities, the edges, the borders, and outlines of the ways and works of God in creation and providence." Gill concludes with a question for us to ponder: "If these were so great and marvelous, what must the rest be which were out of the reach of people to point out and describe?"[11]

The Stubborn Innocent (Job 27:1–6)

At the start of Job chapter 27, Job pauses in his praise. Why? Is he used to interruptions? It is, after all, Zophar's turn to trounce him. We do not know. What we do know is that "without Zophar's third speech the third cycle is incomplete"[12] and that the narrator also notices the unusual pause. We read, "And Job again took up his discourse, and said" (Job 27:1), not "Then Job answered and said" (6:1; 9:1; 12:1; 16:1; 19:1; 21:1; 23:1; 26:1). While what follows is a continuation of Job's God-theme ("As God lives" is his first line, 27:2; also through this chapter he names "God" as *'el* or *'eloah* seven times

11. John Gill, "An Exposition of the Old Testament," in *ESV Church History Study Bible: Voices from the Past, Wisdom for the Present* (Crossway, 2023), 735.

12. The third cycle's incompleteness "demonstrates that the debate has collapsed." Richard P. Belcher Jr., *Job: The Mystery of Suffering and God's Sovereignty*, Focus on the Bible (Christian Focus, 2017), 41.

[with an eighth assumed instance in v. 8a], and four times as "the Almighty" [*shadday*]), the focus is first on Job's innocence (vv. 2–6) and second on his "enemy": the "wicked" (v. 7a; cf. v. 13a), the "unrighteous" (v. 7b), or the "godless" (v. 8a), as he calls them. Every line but one (v. 12, the second and only other "behold" of chaps. 26–27) speaks of the wicked. The pronouns "he," "his," and "him" reverberate in the chambers of Job's heart. He wants his friends to feel the weight of a later wise man's beatitude: "Blessed are you when others revile you and persecute you and utter all kinds of evil against you falsely" (Matt. 5:11).

In Job 27:2–6, the protagonist once again asserts his innocence. He opens with one of the most intriguing parallelisms in the book: "As God lives, who has taken away my right, and the Almighty, who has made my soul bitter" (Job 27:2). Is Job insinuating that the "Almighty," the living God ("as God lives") that he just paid homage to (see 26:6–14), is involved in some unjust activity? It is a possibility, since Job is known for his honesty and he has already expressed this view. But as he revisits the folly of his friends in 27:3–5—with particular emphasis in verse 5—and mentions God's "spirit" within (in 27:3), it appears that Job's primary targets are Eliphaz, Zophar, and Bildad. Notice the word "you" in what follows:

> As long as my breath is in me,
>   and the spirit of God is in my nostrils,
> my lips will not speak falsehood,
>   and my tongue will not utter deceit.
> Far be it from me to say that you are right;
>   till I die I will not put away my integrity from me.
> I hold fast my righteousness and will not let it go;
>   my heart does not reproach me for any of my days. (Job 27:3–6)

As long as Job lives ("as long as breath is in me, and the spirit of God is in my nostrils," Job 27:3), he is committed to upholding his purity. He will refrain from speaking "falsehood" or uttering "deceit" (v. 4) and will never concede that his misguided friends are correct ("Far be it from me to say that you are right," v. 5). Instead, he will steadfastly maintain his "integrity" and "righteousness" (vv. 5b, 6a). Despite many attacks against his character, his conscience remains clear ("my heart does not reproach me," v. 6b), spanning as far back as his memory allows ("for any of my days," v. 6b).

The Stupid Wicked (Job 27:7–23)

In Job 27:7–23, Job continues to focus on his three close friends (the "you" is plural in Job 27:11–12):

Let my enemy be as the wicked,
  and let him who rises up against me be as the unrighteous.
For what is the hope of the godless when God cuts him off,
  when God takes away his life?
Will God hear his cry
  when distress comes upon him?
Will he take delight in the Almighty?
  Will he call upon God at all times?
I will teach you concerning the hand of God;
  what is with the Almighty I will not conceal.
Behold, all of you have seen it yourselves;
  why then have you become altogether vain?

This is the portion of a wicked man with God,
  and the heritage that oppressors receive from the Almighty:
If his children are multiplied, it is for the sword,
  and his descendants have not enough bread.
Those who survive him the pestilence buries,
  and his widows do not weep.
Though he heap up silver like dust,
  and pile up clothing like clay,
he may pile it up, but the righteous will wear it,
  and the innocent will divide the silver.
He builds his house like a moth's,
  like a booth that a watchman makes.
He goes to bed rich, but will do so no more;
  he opens his eyes, and his wealth is gone.
Terrors overtake him like a flood;
  in the night a whirlwind carries him off.
The east wind lifts him up and he is gone;
  it sweeps him out of his place.
It hurls at him without pity;
  he flees from its power in headlong flight.
It claps its hands at him
  and hisses at him from its place.

Job desires his "enemy" (Job 27:7a) and "oppressors" (v. 13b) to suffer the fate of "the wicked" (v. 7a) because of their opposition against him (v. 7b), branding him as a wicked man under God's judgment for his supposed wickedness. While he eventually forgives his adversaries, at this moment he invokes curses on them, wishing that they were dead and gone, stopped, and punished!

In contrast to his previous speech on the destiny of the wicked (which I labeled "The Inexplicable Blessedness of the Wicked," Job 21) and, ironically, akin to Zophar's final speech (Job 20), Job recounts the fate of the wicked. He commences with the bleak demise of the "wicked," also called the "unrighteous" and the "godless" (27:7–8). When the godless man dies ("when God cuts him off"/"when God takes away his life," v. 8), there is no glimmer of hope. God will neither hear him in the grave nor rescue him from his misery ("Will God hear his cry when distress comes upon him?," v. 9). The wicked man can neither pray to God nor praise him from the grave. Thus Job asks, rhetorically: "Will he take delight in the Almighty? Will he call upon God at all times?" (v. 10).

Next, in verses 11–12 of Job 27, Job interjects to clarify for his friends the purpose of his imprecatory homily: he wants to teach them ("I will teach you"/"I will not conceal") about God's omnipotence ("concerning the hand of God"/"the Almighty," Job 27:11). While both he and his friends believe in God's judgment on the wicked, their counsel to Job has proved as insubstantial as smoke dissipating in the air ("altogether vain," v. 12). Their verdict has been totally off. Job is not the wicked one; they are. They are deemed the wicked because they are falsely accusing Job of wickedness. Thus, verses 13–23 serve as a reminder of what happens when God, in his good time, rectifies wrongs.

What does the wicked man receive ("the portion"/"the heritage") from God (Job 27:13)? First, after his death (vv. 8–10, 15), his family's fortune takes a dismal turn. If he happens to have numerous offspring ("If his children are multiplied"), it serves only to increase the likelihood of more of them meeting a violent end ("it is for the sword") or to strain their resources further by having too many mouths to feed ("have not enough bread," v. 14). Whether it is the sword or the deadly plague that claims them, death ("the pestilence buries," v. 15a) will have the last laugh. No one will care when the wicked man is gone, not even his former wives ("his widows do not weep,"

v. 15b). Second, the wealth of the wicked man will vanish with him. Despite his considerable bank account ("Though he heap up silver like dust") and extensive wardrobe (he piles "up clothing like clay," v. 16), it will be the righteous, not his children, who will inherit it: "but the righteous will wear it, and the innocent will divide the silver" (v. 17).

The wicked man might mistakenly believe that his stone house is indestructible, but it is as fragile as a cocoon ("his house like a moth's") or a hunting shack ("like a booth that a watchman makes," Job 27:18). "He goes to bed rich" one night, but the next day he wakes up ("he opens his eyes") and everything—the house, the money, the clothing—has vanished ("his wealth is gone," v. 19). Instead of breakfast in bed, he gets the ride of his life! Like floodwaters ("like a flood," v. 20a) or a hurricane ("a whirlwind," v. 20b; "the east wind," v. 21a), "terrors overtake him" (v. 20a); he is lifted up, carried off, swept "out of his place" (vv. 20–21). The terrors ("it"), or perhaps God himself ("it" can be translated "he" in vv. 22–23), relentlessly prevail against him ("hurls at him without pity," v. 22a). The wicked man tries in vain to escape the judgment ("he flees from its power in headlong flight," v. 22b). The terrors of death and hell taunt him, jeering ("claps its hands at him") and deriding him ("hisses at him," v. 23). Job ends here with the wicked man's *end*. For now, he will turn his attention from the wicked man to calmer and loftier thoughts (see Job 28).

What to Make of Job's Words?

In Job 26:1–27:23, Job responds to Bildad's brief barb on human insignificance by sarcastically criticizing Bildad's lack of helpfulness and wisdom, underscoring his frustration with Bildad's empty rhetoric. Job then shifts focus to praise God's immense power and control over creation, illustrating God's sovereignty through vivid descriptions of his actions and the natural world. Despite his suffering, Job asserts his innocence and commitment to integrity, contrasting himself with the fate of the wicked. Job's discourse culminates in a powerful depiction of the inevitable downfall and judgment of the wicked, highlighting the futility of opposing God's justice.

No doubt we can appreciate and apply the theological import of Job's beautiful and uplifting hymn about God (Job 26:5–14): "Behold, these are but the outskirts of his ways" (v. 14). Yet how should we approach the remaining content of these chapters, notably Job's persistent declarations of innocence (27:4–6) and his imprecatory psalm (vv. 7–23)?

While Job's assertions of innocence may, at first, strike us as surprising (e.g., "I hold fast my righteousness," Job 27:6a), particularly in contrast to our daily confessions of sins ("forgive us our sins," Luke 11:4; "God, be merciful to me, a sinner!," 18:13) wherein we acknowledge just how far we fall short of the glory of God, we should not be overly astonished, for the Bible offers instances of "righteous" individuals. The two Josephs we meet in the first books of the Old Testament and the New Testament (see Gen. 37–50; Matt. 1–2) are two such examples. Job is undoubtedly presented to us as such a man. Moreover, we know that he is innocent of all the accusations against him because no known sin is the cause of his calamities. He is on death row for a crime that he did not commit. Thus, for him to say that his conscience is clear ("my heart does not reproach me," Job 27:6b) makes sense. "Job has no resentment in himself," as one ancient commentator puts it, "and his conscience does not reproach him for any shameful act that he might have committed."[13] Finally, there is something about this aspect of innocence that is crucial to the overarching drama. If Job were not innocent, then the book of Job would fail to challenge the retribution principle. Moreover, and possibly of utmost significance, this theme might hold special meaning if Job functions as a typological figure. It appears that the author of Job is emphasizing and reiterating this theme for a reason. Could it be that, under the inspiration of the Spirit, he is establishing an important paradigm, one that will ultimately find its fulfillment in the coming of Christ? I believe so, and hope to demonstrate so, especially when we come to Job 28, 31, and 42.

Concerning Job's denunciation (cursing!) of his friends, two important considerations come to mind. First, it is crucial to acknowledge that Job will eventually pardon Eliphaz, Bildad, and Zophar and even facilitate their reconciliation with God through offering a prayer and a sacrifice on their behalf (Job 42:9). Second, while we might have hoped for him to emulate our merciful Lord's words on the cross, "Forgive them, for they know not what they do" (Luke 23:34)—what a perfect prayer that would be for Job's friends!—God's Word does reveal divine approval of human imprecations. Psalm 137 and Revelation 19, for instance, are songs that Christians can and

13. Isho'dad of Merv, "Commentary on Job," in *Job*, ed. Manlio Simonetti and Marco Conti, Ancient Christian Commentary on Scripture 6 (InterVarsity Press, 2006), 138.

should sing. Why? Because we yearn for justice, and if we yearn for justice, we must also yearn for God's righteous wrath to come upon the wicked. As I have expressed in my hymn lyrics based on Habakkuk 3, especially the third verse, we can and should sing:

O Lord, I know your mighty acts,
and on these works I dwell in awe.
And so I cry to you these days,
these darkest days, "Remember love."

For once your splendor filled the earth,
as it does fill the heavens above,
from lowest to the highest height,
your light did shine,
your strength unveiled.

So now we wait, O Lord, we wait,
and walk by faith until you come
to conquer all whose god is might,
with your right hand, your glory shown.

For though the fig tree blossoms not;
and field and vine, they yield no fruit;
Yet I will sing with joy of heart,
with heart so full, O Lord, my strength.[14]

That which God has done in past salvation history we trust him to do again in future salvation history. Through the injustices and trials, we wait for God's wrath because we know that God will save the righteous through the judgment of the wicked; we know that as "the righteous judge," he will bestow "the crown of righteousness" on "all who have loved his appearing" (2 Tim. 4:8).

14. Douglas Sean O'Donnell, "Though the Fig Tree Blossoms Not," a hymn based on Habakkuk 3, set to the tune O WALY WALY, in Douglas Sean O'Donnell, *God's Lyrics: Rediscovering Worship through Old Testament Songs* (P&R Publishing, 2010), 186.

Job's Final Speech

22

Job: Where Shall Wisdom Be Found?

Job 28:1–28

And he said to man, "Behold, the fear of the Lord, that is wisdom, and to turn away from evil is understanding."
(Job 28:28)

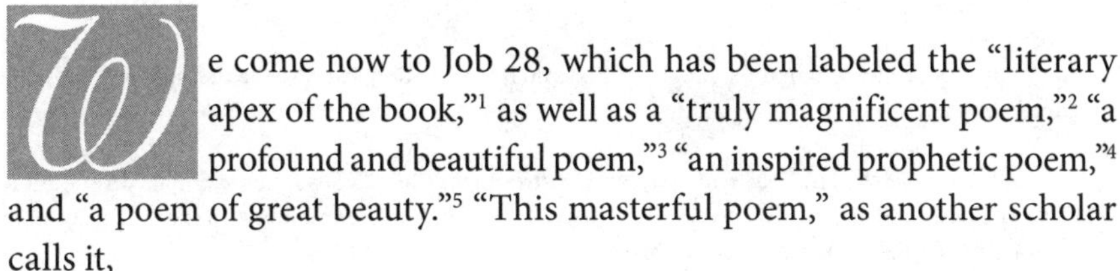

We come now to Job 28, which has been labeled the "literary apex of the book,"[1] as well as a "truly magnificent poem,"[2] "a profound and beautiful poem,"[3] "an inspired prophetic poem,"[4] and "a poem of great beauty."[5] "This masterful poem," as another scholar calls it,

> functions in two significant ways. First, it marks the end of the disturbing discussion between Job and his three friends, Eliphaz, Bildad, and Zophar,

1. Elmer B. Smick, "Job," in *The Expositor's Bible Commentary—Abridged Edition: Two-Volume Set*, ed. Kenneth L. Barker and John R. Kohlenberger III (Zondervan, 1988), 1:975.
2. C. Hassell Bullock, *An Introduction to the Old Testament: Poetic Books*, rev. and expanded ed. (Moody, 1988), 122.
3. Christopher Ash, *Job: The Wisdom of the Cross*, Preaching the Word (Crossway, 2014), 278.
4. Ash, 278.
5. David Atkinson, *The Message of Job*, The Bible Speaks Today (InterVarsity Press, 1991), 119.

> and thus serves as a transition or bridge to the more sanctified reflections of Elihu (in chapters 32–37)[6] and, more importantly, of God (in chapters 38–41). This chapter anticipates the climax of the story when God will present himself as the answer to the mystery Job and his friends have sought to fathom.[7]

It also functions to highlight the idea that wisdom (the poem's theme) is yet to be found. Indeed, the God-inspired author of this great, beautiful, magnificent, profound, masterful, and prophetic poem about wisdom "comes to the realization that there is no help available for him except from God himself," and because of that, he understands that "the fear of the Lord is still the beginning of wisdom."[8]

But who is this inspired speaker? On the one hand, this chapter might contain the narrator's voice, for the topic (the place where wisdom is found) is new and the language is very different from the "highly temperamental" and angry, accusatory language of Job and his friends in the previous twenty-five chapters. Where is the passion, the heated debate, the complaints? Here in Job chapter 28, we listen to a "quieter tone of voice,"[9] someone who seems to "stand outside" the disruptive dialogue,[10] a voice of serenity and tranquility, a voice of almost clinical objectivity, a voice that dwells on the topic that Job and his friends (and everyone else) need most: the wisdom of God found in the fear of God (Job 28:28).[11] Moreover, there are no direct addresses to the friends or God, nor is there mention of the preceding debate or rebuttal of accusations.[12] If the author is the Joban compiler, then like the director of

6. In my view, Elihu will make some sanctified and not-so-sanctified statements. See my discussion in later chapters.

7. Smick, "Job," 1:975.

8. Richard P. Belcher Jr., *Job: The Mystery of Suffering and God's Sovereignty*, Focus on the Bible (Christian Focus, 2017), 191. Cf. Tremper Longman III, *Job*, Baker Commentary on the Old Testament Wisdom and Psalms (Baker Academic, 2012), 333.

9. Christopher Ash, *Trusting God in the Darkness: A Guide to Understanding the Book of Job* (Crossway, 2021), 84.

10. John E. Hartley, *The Book of Job*, NICOT (Eerdmans, 1988), 384.

11. Francis I. Andersen, *Job*, Tyndale Old Testament Commentaries 13 (InterVarsity Press, 1976), 223–34.

12. Although "Delitzsch understood the poem to be a confirmation of the assertion in [Job] 27:13–23 that evildoers will have their punishment," Bullock explains, "By the discourse on wisdom and his final declaration that the fear of the Lord is wisdom (28:28), Job taught that although he could not see through the mystery of his suffering, he had to still hold fast to the fear of the Lord, and that those who fear him had to be judged by a difficult principle than the cause-effect principle that the friends had used." Bullock, *Introduction to the Old Testament*, 92. Cf. Franz Delitzsch, *Commentary on the Book of Job*, trans. Francis Bolton, 2 vols., Clark's Foreign Theological Library (T&T Clark, 1869), 2:116.

a play or actor in it (think of Shakespeare's *The Winter's Tale*), he stops the drama and addresses the audience, reminding everyone of the path that Job and his friends need to take.

On the other hand, the voice might be Job's, for he has had his moments (think especially of Job 9:4–10),[13] even quite recently (cf. 26:6–14), of deep reflection on the attributes and actions of God. He has also spoken specifically of "thick darkness" (3:6; 10:22 [2×]; 23:17), valuable metals ("gold," 3:15a; 23:10; "silver," 3:15b; 27:16–17; "iron," 19:24), "Abaddon" (26:6), "death" (3:21; 7:15; 9:23), and "wisdom," including: "With God are wisdom and might" (12:13a); "With him are strength and sound wisdom" (12:16a). Furthermore, it appears that Job deliberately transitions between familiar topics in his final speech (Job 26–31). He discusses God's unsearchable majesty (26:6–14), Job's own personal integrity (27:1–6), the judgment awaiting the wicked (27:7–23), the pursuit of wisdom (28:1–28), reminiscences of the good old days (29:1–25), the unbearable present circumstances (30:1–31), and his integrity once again (31:1–40). In this way, chapter 28 is not out of place. In fact, if Job is indeed the speaker, the hymn signals to the reader something of Job's spiritual growth, steadfastness, and wisdom—his fearing God (28:28a; cf. 26:6–14) by turning away from evil (28:8b; cf. 27:4–6; 31:1–40). The identification of Job as the speaker also coheres with God's commendation of Job's words in Job 42:7–8 ("spoken of me what is right"). Surely Job 28:1–28 tops the list of speaking right about God! It is also possible, as C. J. Williams argues, that "the uniqueness" of Job 28 makes a typological connection between Job "as a preacher of wisdom" and "the Messiah, who has 'the spirit of wisdom' upon him (Isa 11:2), and 'in whom are hidden all the treasures of wisdom and knowledge' (Col 2:3)."[14]

The Wisdom of Man (Job 28:1–11)

The structural outline of this wisdom hymn is straightforward. Job (whom I take to be the speaker) begins by dwelling on the wisdom of "man" (*'adam*) when compared to the rest of creation. Job does not speak of man's unique impulse and aptitude to create art (to draw, paint, sculpt, weave, etc.), which

13. In Job 9:4–10, Job moves from his legal language to an impressive ode on God's awesome authority.

14. C. J. Williams, *The Shadow of Christ in the Book of Job* (Wipf & Stock, 2017), 75.

is the "signature of man," as G. K. Chesterton puts it in *The Everlasting Man*.[15] Instead, Job illustrates human ingenuity and greatness through man's unique ability to mine precious stones, metals, and jewels from the earth:

> Surely there is a mine for silver,
> and a place for gold that they refine.
> Iron is taken out of the earth,
> and copper is smelted from the ore.
> Man puts an end to darkness
> and searches out to the farthest limit
> the ore in gloom and deep darkness.
> He opens shafts in a valley away from where anyone lives;
> they are forgotten by travelers;
> they hang in the air, far away from mankind; they swing to and fro.
> As for the earth, out of it comes bread,
> but underneath it is turned up as by fire.
> Its stones are the place of sapphires,
> and it has dust of gold.
>
> That path no bird of prey knows,
> and the falcon's eye has not seen it.
> The proud beasts have not trodden it;
> the lion has not passed over it.
>
> Man puts his hand to the flinty rock
> and overturns mountains by the roots.
> He cuts out channels in the rocks,
> and his eye sees every precious thing.
> He dams up the streams so that they do not trickle,
> and the thing that is hidden he brings out to light. (Job 28:1–11)

Because we live in a technologically advanced age, wherein most people do not view mining at the top of humanity's scientific accomplishments, we must nevertheless recognize that the feats of mining are, if carefully contemplated, still profound. Much like tales of the courageous and skilled men who, in the late 1850s, carved the core of the Rocky Mountains in their quest for treasures, this ancient poem vividly portrays a group of like-

15. G. K. Chesterton, *The Everlasting Man* (1925; repr., Ignatius Press, 1993), 34.

minded men who strip the mountains of their precious possessions: of the noble elements of "gold" (Job 28:1b, 6b) and "silver" (v. 1a) as well as the functional ones, "iron" and "copper" (v. 2) and "ore" (v. 3).[16] In fact, similar to excavators from the nineteenth century,[17] these ancient miners harness the power of "fire" (v. 5) and water to extract from the earth its abundant riches, including valuable "sapphires" (or "lapis lazuli," v. 6a ESV footnote).

The process of searching for these objects of abundant worth, described in Job 28:3–5 and 9–11, went something like this. After setting a large fire in a hand-dug shaft, miners poured water on the hot rock, causing it to crack: "As for the earth, out of it comes bread, but underneath it is turned up as by fire" (Job 28:5). Then they gathered the fallen stones and carried them to the surface. Next, they "[cut] out channels in the rocks" (v. 10a; cf. "shafts," v. 4a) and controlled any nearby rivers that might cause flooding ("He dams up the streams so that they do not trickle," v. 11a). Then, lowered down by ropes ("they hang in the air," v. 4c), they would enter the cavern they had created in the mountain ("puts an end to darkness," v. 3a) and go as deep as they could go ("searches out to the farthest limit," v. 3b). Once they had scraped up the fallen stones ("Man puts his hand to the flinty rock," v. 9a), they would carry them to the surface ("the thing that is hidden he brings out to light," v. 11b). Slowly but surely, through this tedious process, the earth would open itself to the hand of men, like a flower opening to the sunlight of spring. "Man . . . overturns mountains by the roots" (v. 9b)! Man's "eye" *alone* "sees every precious thing" (v. 10b): silver, gold, iron, copper, ore, sapphires.

In the poet's estimation, this amazing accomplishment highlights the greatness of man—an intelligence and an industry unsurpassed in all creation. "That path" to these precious materials even the king of the jungle and queen of the sky cannot find: "no bird of prey knows, and the falcon's eye has not seen it. The proud beasts have not trodden it; the lion has not passed over it" (Job 28:7–8). As John Hartley points out:

> Amazingly none of the animals with all their prowess can discover the path to such beautiful gems. The falcon and the lion, two magnificent creatures that dominate the sky and the land respectively, are representative of all animals. The falcon is known for its keen eyesight. From lofty heights it surveys the

16. Robert L. Alden, *Job*, New American Commentary 11 (Broadman & Holman, 1993), 271.
17. Alden, 270–71.

> land, spots its prey, and swoops down on it. But it never detects the hidden path to these minerals.[18]

Finally, on the earth's surface, we encounter the majestic lion, a creature that gracefully prowls, seizing whatever prey it wants. It is called "proud" because of "its unusual strength and its lack of fear."[19] Yet even though it reigns as the king of the jungle, it holds no dominion over the mines, unable to command or wield power over the very treasures concealed in the earth's depths. So we will not find falcons adorned with silver necklaces or lions sporting gold earrings to complement their golden manes. The falcon, celebrated for its vision, and the lion, celebrated for its courage, cannot compare to the vision and courage of "man" (*'adam*).[20]

The Inaccessibility of Wisdom (Job 28:12–22)

At this point in the poem, we might be glad to be far removed from Bildad's "Requiem to Man the Maggot and Worm" (Job 25:4–6); and in fact, we might feel fairly good about ourselves—our humanness. We are "man"—watch us roar and soar, or at least explore. Watch us, unlike any other creature on earth, explore the recesses of the deep! But before our pride soars higher than a falcon and our courage becomes as dangerous as a pride of lions on the prowl, Job 28:12–22 puts us in our place:

> But where shall wisdom be found?
> And where is the place of understanding?
> Man does not know its worth,
> and it is not found in the land of the living.
> The deep says, "It is not in me,"
> and the sea says, "It is not with me."
> It cannot be bought for gold,
> and silver cannot be weighed as its price.
> It cannot be valued in the gold of Ophir,
> in precious onyx or sapphire.
> Gold and glass cannot equal it,
> nor can it be exchanged for jewels of fine gold.

18. Hartley, *Job*, 377.
19. Hartley, 377.
20. See Andersen, *Job*, 226.

> No mention shall be made of coral or of crystal;
> the price of wisdom is above pearls.
> The topaz of Ethiopia cannot equal it,
> nor can it be valued in pure gold.
>
> From where, then, does wisdom come?
> And where is the place of understanding?
> It is hidden from the eyes of all living
> and concealed from the birds of the air.
> Abaddon and Death say,
> "We have heard a rumor of it with our ears." (Job 28:12–22)

While humans above all creatures can probe the mysteries of our earthly domain, we cannot probe the mysteries of the heavenly domain. With ingenuity and determination, we can "penetrate into the foreboding darkness of the earth's interior, the underworld, the abode of the dead in search of treasures,"[21] and we can search the extremities and limits of the earth's surface, but we cannot scratch the surface of wisdom. Man can bring to light all hidden material things, but he cannot unearth wisdom, which is the true light of the world.

The key to understanding this section is noticing the beautiful symmetry used to express the limits of human knowledge. The refrain of Job 28:12–14 is parallel in form and meaning to the refrain of verses 20–22. Both refrains ask the same question, "the main theological question of the book of Job":[22] "But where shall wisdom be found? And where is the place of understanding?" (Job 28:12; cf. v. 20). And both refrains give the same reply in slightly different ways, namely, that the world itself does not know where to find wisdom. All the eyes of the living, both "man" (v. 13) and the "birds of the air" (v. 21), cannot find it. The depths of the earth ("the deep," v. 14) and even the depths of the underworld ("Abaddon and Death," v. 22) cannot find it. Christopher Ash illustrates:

> And even were we to go to the guardians of the most desperate extremities of the cosmos, Destruction (Abaddon, the angel of the bottomless pit; see Rev. 9:11) and Death, even these terrible personified powers would have to shrug their shoulders and say, "Well, yes, if you press me, I think I did once

21. Hartley, *Job*, 376.
22. Atkinson, *Message of Job*, 119.

hear a third-hand rumor that somewhere Wisdom exists. But I have no idea where to find it."[23]

The best that this world can offer to aid humanity in its search for wisdom is merely a "rumor of it" (Job 28:22b). On, in, and above the earth, wisdom cannot be found. With the living and with the dead, wisdom cannot be found. That is the message of the bookends of this middle section (vv. 12–14, 20–22). While man can extract precious metals from the earth, the acquisition of wisdom from "the land of the living" (v. 13b) is an impossibility.

Within these two bookends lies the unaffordable price of wisdom (Job 28:15–19). Man falls short of attaining wisdom not only through his ingenuity but also through his wealth. One might assume that the "inquisitive nature and technological ability that enable [us] to find the riches of the earth no matter how difficult they are to obtain,"[24] coupled with the immense wealth derived from such mining operations, would afford us the means to purchase anything we wanted, including wisdom. But we do not know, as Job 28:13 calls it, the "worth" of wisdom. "If any search is worth pursuing," as Ash notes, "surely this is it. For Wisdom lies, as it were, at the root of the whole created order, underpinning it, set in place before the world was made (see Prov. 8:22–31)."[25] Wisdom is scarcer than a flawless ten-carat diamond. On God's scale, wisdom outweighs the earth's greatest treasures. Precious gems such as onyx, sapphire, coral, crystal, pearl, and topaz are "worthless in the marketplace of wisdom,"[26] and even gold and silver, the most precious of metals, are "unacceptable as tender for wisdom."[27] Just as money cannot buy love, it likewise cannot buy wisdom.

The Wisdom of God (Job 28:23–28)

After mining (pun intended) twenty-two verses of this twenty-eight-verse poem, we are still left without an answer to the key question, "Where shall wisdom be found?" (Job 28:12). If wisdom can be neither found in the depths of the earth nor bought by the deepest pockets, where shall we find this rare commodity?

23. Ash, *Trusting God in the Darkness*, 90–91.
24. Smick, "Job," 1:975.
25. Ash, *Trusting God in the Darkness*, 90.
26. Hartley, *Job*, 280.
27. Alden, *Job*, 274.

Thankfully, in the third stanza (Job 28:23–28)—what constitutes the "beautiful literary climax"[28] and the summary of the inspired author's worldview—wisdom gives up the secret of its location:

> God understands the way to it,
>   and he knows its place.
> For he looks to the ends of the earth
>   and sees everything under the heavens.
> When he gave to the wind its weight
>   and apportioned the waters by measure,
> when he made a decree for the rain
>   and a way for the lightning of the thunder,
> then he saw it and declared it;
>   he established it, and searched it out.
> And he said to man,
> "Behold, the fear of the Lord, that is wisdom,
>   and to turn away from evil is understanding."

The solution to the search for wisdom is "God" (Job 28:23) and "the fear of the Lord" (v. 28). While human ingenuity cannot find wisdom, and human wealth cannot buy wisdom, "God understands the way to it, and he knows its place" (v. 23). God alone knows where wisdom is to be found because he alone is omniscient ("he looks to the ends of the earth and sees everything under the heavens," v. 24). He also knows where wisdom ("it") is to be found because God ("he") is wisdom and used wisdom (see Prov. 8:22–23) to establish and govern the world. God

- "gave to the wind its weight" (told it when to blow hard and when soft)
- "apportioned the waters by measure" (told the flood and river waters and seas to go here but not there, to stop at this point; see Job 38:8–11)
- "made a decree for the rain" (telling it when, where, and how much to fall)
- "made . . . a way for the lightning of the thunder" (controlled every rumble of thunder and each lightning flash).[29]

28. Bullock, *Introduction to the Old Testament*, 122.
29. Ash, *Trusting God in the Darkness*, 92.

Beyond noticing how God governs the world, notice five more details about this profound final stanza. First, notice how countercultural is the solution offered, namely, that the search for wisdom is found only in "God" (Job 28:23) and accessed through "the fear of" the one and only God—Yahweh (v. 28). Many people wouldn't even have "God" as any part of the answer to the question "Where is wisdom found?" Instead, they might say that wisdom is found through innate intelligence, accumulated knowledge, or life experiences. The man with the high IQ, the woman with the top-tier education, the kid with street smarts—they can surely find wisdom. But the Bible says no! It contends that such worldly wisdom is inadequate—it is not the kind of wisdom essential for genuine living, and certainly not the kind of wisdom that Job needs to navigate through his inexplicable suffering. Proverbs, Ecclesiastes, and Job are not God's version of Ben Franklin's *Poor Richard's Almanack* ("Early to bed and early to rise, makes a man healthy, wealthy, and wise") or the ancient Chinese sayings of Confucius ("Silence is a friend who will never betray"). They are not simply a less humorous version of the aphorism "Never argue with a fool; people might not know the difference." What distinguishes the content of books such as Job from the rest of the world's wisdom literature are declarations like the one found in Job 28:28. True wisdom is indexed to Yahweh (Job 12:9; Prov. 1:7) and acquired through a proper relationship with Yahweh, coupled with a fitting attitude and actions toward him.

Speaking of that relationship, that attitude, and those actions, notice, second, that to fear God (as the poem's parallel line indicates) involves turning away from evil (Job 28:28b)—an expression that embodies the idea of both knowing and obeying God's ways (cf. Prov. 1:7; Eccl. 12:13). "It is to walk in obedience to what God has revealed: both in the natural revelation of the created world, and in God's Word written and infallibly inspired."[30] To fear God also involves humble faith, or "trembling trust," as I have expressed elsewhere.[31] Such faith shows itself through the attitude of bowing in awe and humility before the mystery of God's sovereign rule, trusting that he is working for our good even through our perplexing pains (see Rom. 8; Eph. 3:13) and that he will give us the strength to sustain us. We may not understand why God has brought such troubles into our lives, but we learn

30. Derek Thomas, *The Storm Breaks: Job Simply Explained*, Welwyn Commentary Series (repr., Evangelical Press, 2005), 221–22.

31. Douglas Sean O'Donnell, *Ecclesiastes: Enjoyment East of Eden*, Reformed Expository Commentary (P&R Publishing, 2014), 9, 78–79, 110, 143, 217.

to accept both that it is from his hand and that the heart behind that hand is wise and good and just. Thus, we refuse to blame God, resent him, demand explanations from him, or think that we could run the world better than he does.[32] Like Habakkuk (and Job!), we live by faith.

Third, notice that this is the first time since the prologue that we hear the voice of God. The fact that God reveals the place and way to wisdom shows that divine wisdom is a divine gift. As David Atkinson states:

> True wisdom is accessible to God alone—which means that it can come from him alone. The wisdom which will contain an answer to Job can come only from God. Chapter 28 thus stands in the book of Job as a warning that any further speculations along the lines of the three friends will be fruitless. The way out of the impasse will not be from below, upwards, but from above, downwards. It will not come as part of the belief system of mankind, but only as a gift of God. The starting-point for true knowledge of God is God himself in his own self-disclosure. We need to meet the Lord as he comes to us in grace. We need to begin with the fear of the Lord, in communion with him as he chooses to make himself known.[33]

Note also that the divine instruction echoes the narrator's description of God's approval of Job in the prologue (Job 1:1, 8; 2:3), and that, in doing so, "this poem ultimately affirms that the friends are wrong and Job is right in the sense that wisdom is found in a fear of God that depends on a righteousness that turns away from evil, rather than on one that relies on piety and appeasement and results in divine favor and prosperity."[34]

Fourth, notice that this heaven-gifted teaching counsels us not to seek first wisdom, but to seek after God, for wisdom is found in finding God and walking in his ways. As Ash well summarizes:

> In a saying crucial to the whole book, God directs our attention away from our agonized questions and toward himself. He does not take us by the hand and lead us to the answers; rather, he beckons us to bow before the Lord himself,

32. See John H. Walton, *Job*, NIVAC (Zondervan, 2012), 304.

33. Atkinson, *Message of Job*, 120–21.

34. Walton, *Job*, 294. Scott C. Jones argues that Job 28 "is in fact a parody of the approach of wisdom that the friends proffer. Rather than praising wisdom, Jones contends, the poem offers 'a critique of the modes by which "sages" like Job's friends seek out wisdom.'" *Rumors of Wisdom: Job 28 as Poetry*, Beihefte zur Zeitschrift für die Alttestamentliche Wissenschaft 398 (de Gruyter, 2009), as summarized by Choon-Leong Seow, "Elihu's Revelation," *Theology Today* 68, no. 3 (2011): 253–71.

> who knows the answers but chooses not to tell us. Our eyes are directed away from the search for the architecture and toward the person of the architect. We ask, "Why doesn't God answer my question?" to which he replies, "Turn your gaze and your enquiry away from the answer you want and toward the God you must seek. If you want to live in this world as a Wise person, a man or woman of understanding, rather than a fool, do not seek Wisdom for its own sake. For if you were to find it, you would become a puffed-up know-it-all (see 1 Cor. 8:1). So do not seek Wisdom; seek the Lord."[35]

But fifth and finally, as Christians, we read this poem in light of Jesus, the one whom Paul calls "wisdom from God" (1 Cor. 1:30), "the image of the invisible God" and the one in whom "all the fullness of God was pleased to dwell" (Col. 1:15, 19). In this one, God himself has drawn near to us to make himself known. Knowing Jesus to be "wisdom from God," we can specify more particularly the identity of the "Lord" (Job 28:28) in whose fear we find wisdom. While it is true that in creation and providence God manifests his wisdom, it is likewise true, as taught throughout the New Testament, that God most perfectly and more fully manifests his wisdom in the person and work of his Son, our Lord Jesus Christ. In his incarnation, Jesus brought "wisdom from above"—God's peaceable, gentle, merciful wisdom (James 3:17)—down to earth. This he demonstrated through his growth in wisdom, teaching of wisdom, life of wisdom (his perfect, God-fearing, sin-renouncing life), and, ultimately, sacrificial death. The apostle Paul speaks in Ephesians 3:8–11 of the "manifold wisdom of God" revealed or "realized" in our Lord Jesus Christ, and in Colossians 2:3 he explains how "all the treasures of wisdom and knowledge" are "hidden" in Christ. Finally, in 1 Corinthians 1:18–24, he claims that the preaching of "Christ" and him "crucified" is the "wisdom of God":

> For the word of the cross is folly to those who are perishing, but to us who are being saved it is the power of God. For it is written,
>
> "I will destroy the *wisdom* of the wise,
> and the discernment of the discerning I will thwart."
>
> Where is the one who is wise? Where is the scribe? Where is the debater of this age? Has not God made foolish the *wisdom* of the world? For since, in

35. Ash, *Trusting God in the Darkness*, 93–94.

> the *wisdom* of God, the world did not know God through *wisdom*, it pleased God through the folly of what we preach to save those who believe. For Jews demand signs and Greeks seek *wisdom*, but we preach Christ crucified, a stumbling block to Jews and folly to Gentiles, but to those who are called, both Jews and Greeks, Christ the power of God and the *wisdom* of God.

Christians are "fools." This is Paul's argument to the Corinthians. That is, Christians are those who trust that God through the crucifixion made Christ, "who became to us wisdom from God, righteousness and sanctification and redemption" (1 Cor. 1:30), appear foolish to the unwise—to the overly-wise-in-its-own-eyes—world. Yet he is no fool who abandons human pride and power to find the "secret and hidden wisdom of God" (2:7) now revealed in "Christ and him crucified" (v. 2). The seeming folly of a crucified God is God's wisdom perfected—the place where wisdom is ultimately found.[36]

So the New Testament does more than teach that all wisdom comes to us from God through Christ; it likewise teaches the surprising truth that the wisdom of God is most fully displayed in the death of Christ. Paradoxically, through Christ's death we attain eternal life; similarly, only through the crucifixion of Christ do we gain access to wisdom. When we read and reread the story of Job, we have the wonderful benefit of placing our knowledge of Jesus Christ, and of him crucified, as a transparent grid over this Old Testament text. Unlike the characters in the book of Job, we can easily connect the dots between the wisdom displayed in the sufferings of innocent Job and the wisdom displayed in the sufferings of innocent Jesus. The New Testament sheds clear light on the story of Job and on this grand theme of wisdom.

36. Douglas Sean O'Donnell, *The Beginning and End of Wisdom: Preaching Christ from the First and Last Chapters of Proverbs, Ecclesiastes, and Job* (Crossway, 2011), 29.

23

Job: I Waited for Light; Darkness Came

Job 29:1–30:31

But when I hoped for good, evil came, and when I waited for light, darkness came. (Job 30:26)

A man's last words often summarize what was first in his heart. The influential nineteenth-century clergyman Henry Ward Beecher, brother of the famous author Harriet Beecher Stowe, became a national figure for his sensational adultery trial, his acceptance of Darwinism, and his rejection of the divinity of Jesus. Beecher's final words expressed well his growing religious skepticism. Before he breathed his last breath, he said, "Now comes the mystery." The last words of Wilhelm Hegel, the German philosopher whose writings are notorious for their obscurity, highlighted both his arrogance and his incomprehensibility when he said: "Only one man ever understood me. And he really didn't understand me." Voltaire, the French Enlightenment thinker, had no love for Christ and Christianity. Of Christ he said, "Curse the wretch!" He also boasted: "In twenty years Christianity will be no more. My single hand shall destroy the edifice it took twelve apostles to rear." Voltaire was wrong about both. Shortly after his death, his house became the depot for the Geneva Bible

Society, and today Christianity is the largest religion in the world. It is reported that when Voltaire was asked on his deathbed to renounce Satan, he jested, "This is no time to make new enemies."[1]

Job's final soliloquy (Job 29–31), which we will cover in three chapters, does not give us his dying words—although he may feel that he is near death and certainly desires it. But like the carefully crafted examples above, Job's last long breath, so to speak, provides us with both a summary of his sorrows and a snapshot of his only hope.

Six words are of great importance in this last long speech: "days," "now," "if," "then," "oh," "let." The word "day" (*yom*, always in the plural construct, translated as "days" in these chapters) sets the scene for the contrast between two seasons in Job's life. First, Job recounts the good old days, the "days when God watched over" him (Job 29:2) as a friend (v. 4)—the days when he was respected by all in the city (vv. 7–24), living "like a king" (v. 25). Second, Job speaks of the "days of affliction" (30:16, 27; *yeme-'oni*). These "days" stretch from that dreadful day ("Now there was a day," 1:13) when Job lost his children to the present day, in which he still suffers in every imaginable way ("My inward parts are in turmoil and never still," 30:27; cf. 30:16a). Subsumed under the phrase "days of affliction" is the contrast between *then* and *now*, with the phrase "and now" (*we'attah*) repeated three times: "But now they laugh at me" (30:1a); "And now I have become their song" (v. 9a); "And now my soul is poured out within me" (v. 16a).

The word "if" (*'im*, 18×) and the implied "then" (5×) dominate Job 31. This *if-then* pattern commences after Job poses four questions (Job 31:1–4) and concludes only when Job stops speaking ("The words of Job are ended," v. 40c). Its purpose is to catalogue Job's innocence in a variety of ethical areas. Such a catalogue is intended by Job not to reassure himself of his utter blamelessness but rather to *present to God* what God should see and respond to. This catalogue is where the words "oh" and "let" (both rightly conveying the sense of the Hebrew) also come into play. In 31:6a, Job says, "Let me be weighed in a just balance." He wants God to know that he is innocent ("let God know my integrity!," v. 6b) and to judge accordingly. Job longs for God both to answer him ("Oh, that I had one to hear me! . . . Let the Almighty answer me!," v. 35) and to vindicate him ("Oh, that I were as

1. For the second scenario, see R. Kent Hughes, *Hebrews*, Preaching the Word (Crossway, 1993), 2:41–42. For aspects of this introduction, see Douglas Sean O'Donnell, *God's Lyrics: Rediscovering Worship through Old Testament Songs* (P&R Publishing, 2010), 27–28.

in the months of old," 29:2). These three chapters foreshadow precisely what unfolds later: God answers him (38:1; 40:6) and vindicates him (42:7–9), ultimately restoring his former prosperity and happiness (vv. 10–17). At this moment, however, Job lacks any sense that the "days of affliction" will ever come to an end.

Back in the Days of Friendship with God (Job 29:1–6)

Even though God has not granted Job a hearing, chapters 29–31 can be seen as the closing argument of Job's defense. Job begins with a personal testimony:

> And Job again took up his discourse, and said:
>
> "Oh, that I were as in the months of old,
> as in the days when God watched over me,
> when his lamp shone upon my head,
> and by his light I walked through darkness,
> as I was in my prime,
> when the friendship of God was upon my tent,
> when the Almighty was yet with me,
> when my children were all around me,
> when my steps were washed with butter,
> and the rock poured out for me streams of oil!" (Job 29:1–6)

Job's hyperbolic reminiscence takes on a nostalgic tone as he remembers what life was like before the events recorded in Job 1 ("the months of old," Job 29:2a). Thinking back on those days, he reflects on two blessings (or, we might say, what "the Lord gave," 1:21): Yahweh's warm company and bountiful provision. First, God was present with Job. Although God is the "Almighty," yet he was "with" Job (29:5a).[2] This close "friendship" (v. 4b) benefited his whole household (vv. 4b, 5b) and offered protection ("God watched over me," v. 2b)[3] and guidance for Job ("his lamp shone upon my head, and by his light I walked through darkness," v. 3). Second, God generously provided for Job with the blessings of offspring ("my children were all around me," v. 5b)

2. The "withness" of God is an important theological theme in both the Old Testament (e.g., Gen. 39:2–3, 21, 23; Isa. 8:10; Zech. 8:23) and the New Testament (Matt. 1:23; 20:28; Col. 2:13).

3. Compare this positive depiction of God's watching Job with what Job says in Job 10:14 and 13:27.

and of riches. The odd expression that ends this introduction—"when my steps were washed with butter, and the rock poured out for me streams of oil!" (v. 6)—describes an unusual abundance. As he walked through his rich pastures, it was as if the plentiful cream and butter produced by his livestock was beneath his every step, and as if the harvest from his olive trees was so bounteous that the oil poured out of the stones around them. Back in "the good old days," as we might put it, everything that Job touched (or that *God* touched for Job) "turned to gold." He had the Midas touch.

Judge Job (Job 29:7–17)

Verses 7–10 of Job 29 record the respect that Job received from all ages ("young men," "the aged," Job 29:8) and from every rank (even "princes," "nobles," vv. 9–10) at "the gate of the city" (v. 7a)[4] when he sat to adjudicate and educate:

> When I went out to the gate of the city,
>   when I prepared my seat in the square,
> the young men saw me and withdrew,
>   and the aged rose and stood;
> the princes refrained from talking
>   and laid their hand on their mouth;
> the voice of the nobles was hushed,
>   and their tongue stuck to the roof of their mouth. (Job 29:7–10)

In Job 29:7, Job mentions "the gate of the city." In the ancient near East, the city gate was "the center of community life"; it "combined the activities of the commercial marketplace (2 Kings 7:17–18), the legal court (Deut. 21:19; Ruth 4:1), and the intellectual interchange of ideas (cf. Ps. 127:5)." And as Daniel Estes notes, "To have a seat in the gate is to enjoy a privilege reserved for the most prominent citizens (Gen. 19:1; Prov. 31:23)."[5] The scene that Job paints in these verses is of his walking to the city gate to hear an important matter. As he reaches his destination (Job 29:7), teenagers respectfully step to the side (v. 8a), elderly gentlemen rise as a gesture of honor (v. 8b), and even princes and nobles fall silent. Their hushed conversations cease because

4. Daniel J. Estes, *Job*, Teach the Text (Baker, 2013), 176.
5. Estes, 176.

someone more important than they ("the greatest of all the people of the east," 1:3) has arrived (29:9–10).

In Job 29:11–17, Job recounts the reasons behind the respect he garnered (note the "because" in Job 29:12). Perhaps seeking to defend himself specifically from Eliphaz's false testimony (cf. 22:6–9) and to reiterate what he really believes about wickedness (cf. 24:3–4, 21), Job depicts himself as a merciful and righteous judge-king. The expression "When the ear heard, it called me blessed" and its parallel "and when the eye saw, it approved" (29:11) likely allude to his role in legal proceedings, underscoring that his judgments were not only equitable but also acclaimed (as evidenced in v. 14). What follows in verses 12–17, then, are the various reasons why people rejoiced in Job's rulings. First, he displayed mercy toward the vulnerable—the poor, the orphan, the widow:

> because I delivered the poor who cried for help,
> and the fatherless who had none to help him.
> The blessing of him who was about to perish came upon me,
> and I caused the widow's heart to sing for joy. (Job 29:12–13)

Job provided relief to those in dire need, possibly through his own actions (perhaps from his own wealth or through personal service) or, at the very least, through his legal judgments:

> I put on righteousness, and it clothed me;
> my justice was like a robe and a turban.
> I was eyes to the blind
> and feet to the lame.
> I was a father to the needy,
> and I searched out the cause of him whom I did not know. (Job 29:14–16)

If that were not enough, Judge Job disarmed those who sought to exploit the weak and destitute: "I broke the fangs of the unrighteous and made him drop his prey from his teeth" (Job 29:17). Despite his self-description as a heroic figure, the striking imagery need not be read as self-promotion. We are aware of the narrator's depiction of Job, God's perspective on him, and the future events that will transpire in Job's life. Therefore, sympathetic readers, as well as the theologically knowledgeable ones, might find themselves standing alongside the elders, deeply impressed by such a remarkable man. Furthermore, the biblically informed and canonically conscientious readers "cannot read this memory of Job without . . . remembering the one whom Job foreshadowed, who walked through this world in perfect harmony with his Father among men, causing the widow's heart to sing for joy (29:13; see Luke 7:11–17), giving eyes to the blind and feet to the lame."[6]

Friend of God (Job 29:18–20)

Similar to Abraham, Job enjoyed a friendship with God (Job 29:4; cf. Isa. 41:8), and fully anticipated dying as the patriarch had (Gen. 25:8–9). He envisioned himself as drawing his final breath in his own house ("in my nest," Job 29:18a), reaching a ripe old age ("I shall multiply my days as the sand," v. 18b), and being surrounded by his beloved family. In fact, when we read Genesis 25:8–9, it evokes a sense of sorrow for Job, especially when considering the lines describing Abraham's children's burying him. It is only natural for a father to mourn the prospect of not being interred by his own offspring. Yet Job has now experienced the heartbreaking loss of all ten of his children. This is a tragic reality that we, as readers, should not forget. Job also held the belief that he would enjoy robust health until his last hour, flourishing like a towering tree with deep roots ("my roots spread out to the waters, with the dew all night on my branches," Job 29:19). He presumed that the respect and honor he depicted in verses 8–10 and 21–25 would remain with him until the very end ("my glory fresh with me," v. 20a; cf. 19:9) and that he would continue to advocate for justice in the world even on his deathbed ("and my bow ever new in my hand," 29:20b). Sadly, none of this would even happen. Job has lost a lot! That is the point of all this. The man has lost his children, health, glory, and reputation.

Days of Old (Job 29:21–25)

In these concluding verses, Job once more reflects on the days gone by, when his words were not met with ridicule but earnestly heeded ("Men listened to me and waited," Job 29:21a). A hush would fall on the listeners

6. Christopher Ash, *Trusting God in the Darkness: A Guide to Understanding the Book of Job* (Crossway, 2021), 99.

as he spoke ("[men] kept silence for my counsel," v. 21b), and this quietude persisted afterward ("they did not speak again," v. 22a), so convinced were they of the truth of his pronouncements. His instructions were beneficial ("my word dropped upon them," v. 22b), like the life-giving spring rain following a long winter drought ("They waited for me as for the rain, and they opened their mouths as for the spring rain," v. 23). These experiences stand in stark contrast to what Job has endured from chapter 4 until this point in the story. His friends have not believed, listened to, or found any sustenance in his words. Instead, they have repeatedly chastised him for the folly of his speeches.

Job 29:24–25 encapsulates the utter honor that Job once enjoyed. He did not even have to open his mouth for people to feel blessed by his presence. To the hopeless, his warm smile and cheerful countenance brought the confidence they needed to lift their spirits ("I smiled on them when they had no confidence, and the light of my face they did not cast down," Job 29:24), and his leadership ("I . . . sat as chief"/"like a king") brought both wise guidance ("I chose their way") and compassionate consolation ("like one who comforts mourners," v. 25).

But Now . . . (Job 30:1–15)

The words "But now" at the beginning of Job chapter 30 stand in ominous contrast to the idyllic days of Job 29:2. As Job dreams about the past, he awakens in the present to the sounds of laughter: "But now they laugh at me" (Job 30:1a). The word "laugh" in verse 1 is the same word for "smiled" in 29:24 (*sachaq*). But this is not the genial laughter that follows a polite joke; it is mocking laughter toward Job as the butt of a cruel joke. The word "they" (repeated twenty times in 30:1–15) introduces us to Job's opposition, whom he characterizes as young ("men who are younger than I," v. 1b) and of the lowest social reputation ("whose fathers I would have disdained to set with the dogs of my flock," v. 1c–d). A gang of teenage thugs, whose fathers Job would not have hired as lowly shepherds (or even as sheepdogs!), are barking after him.

In verses 2–8 of Job 30, Job describes in vivid color the class and character of his new enemies:

> What could I gain from the strength of their hands,
>   men whose vigor is gone?

Through want and hard hunger
  they gnaw the dry ground by night in waste and desolation;
they pick saltwort and the leaves of bushes,
  and the roots of the broom tree for their food.
They are driven out from human company;
  they shout after them as after a thief.
In the gullies of the torrents they must dwell,
  in holes of the earth and of the rocks.
Among the bushes they bray;
  under the nettles they huddle together.
A senseless, a nameless brood,
  they have been whipped out of the land.

Job's enemies are weak (Job 30:2), homeless (vv. 6–7), and hungry scavengers who eat whatever they can find (vv. 3–4) and who have been ousted from honorable society (v. 5). They look, smell, and act like wild dogs. They are, in Job's summary estimation, "a senseless, a nameless brood" that has been expelled from any human community ("whipped out of the land," v. 8). *That* is who "they" are! And yet "they" join Eliphaz, Bildad, and Zophar (which hardly reflects well on their character) in destroying Job's reputation with their mockery: "now I have become their song; I am a byword to them" (v. 9).

Job's adversaries harbor such intense animosity toward him ("They abhor me," Job 30:10a) that mere verbal taunts no longer suffice. Not content with composing pub songs that revel in his downfall or crafting catchy proverbs about his poverty (cf. v. 9), they inflict psychological torment on him as well. They hold him in utter contempt, keeping their distance ("they keep aloof from me") to the extent that they even resort to spitting in the dirt before him ("they . . . spit at the sight of me," v. 10). This gesture of spitting might signify spitting in his face, as suggested in the NIV translation. Either way, the act of spitting moves their torment beyond the psychological realm to the physical, or blends psychological intimidation with an ugly physical act. In view of their relentless harassment, Job feels utterly defenseless. In his eyes, he believes that God has forsaken him ("God . . . loosed my cord"), allowing him to plummet into the abyss of ignominy ("and humbled me"). This abandonment by God serves as an invitation for this hostile street gang to ruthlessly assail him ("they have cast off restraint in my presence," v. 11). Anything goes. We cannot help thinking of our Lord Jesus, who, as the climax of a barrage of mockeries, suffered abuse and scorn by the two men beside him: "Those who were crucified with him also reviled him" (Mark 15:32).

Job next, in verses 12–15 of Job 30, describes what his mockers do to him with a mix of metaphors, ranging from a street brawl to the siege of a city. First, he is blindsided ("On my right hand the rabble rise," Job 30:12a) and knocked to the ground ("they push away my feet," v. 12b). Then, as he lies incapacitated on the ground, they subject him to further bodily harm ("they promote my calamity," v. 13b). In his own eyes, he is a vulnerable victim, an easy target ("they need no one to help them," v. 13c). In their eyes, however, he is a mighty fortress to be conquered. They blow up any bridges over which he might escape ("They break up my path," v. 13a) and construct siege ramps against him ("they cast up against me their ways of destruction," v. 12c). They batter down the wall, creating a gaping hole ("As through a wide breach they come," v. 14a) through which their forces, wave upon wave, flood through ("amid the crash they roll on," v. 14b).[7] Job lives in constant fear for his life ("Terrors are turned upon me," v. 15), and he despairs of his former glory ever being restored to him: "my honor is pursued as by the wind, and my prosperity has passed away like a cloud" (v. 15b–c).

The Days of Affliction (Job 30:16–23)

Where are the aged, the princes, and the nobles to defend Job (cf. Job 29:8–10)? Worse than that, where is God to champion the cause of the innocent and exalt the honorable? How can honorable Job be so dishonored by the least honorable? How can the just judge be sentenced by unrighteous criminals? How can the father to the needy be mocked and beaten by teenage thugs from among the poorest strata of society? Job expresses his anguish this way:

> And now my soul is poured out within me;
>   days of affliction have taken hold of me.
> The night racks my bones,
>   and the pain that gnaws me takes no rest.
> With great force my garment is disfigured;
>   it binds me about like the collar of my tunic.
> God has cast me into the mire,
>   and I have become like dust and ashes.

7. See Robert L. Alden, *Job*, New American Commentary 11 (Broadman & Holman, 1993), 291.

I cry to you for help and you do not answer me;
  I stand, and you only look at me.
You have turned cruel to me;
  with the might of your hand you persecute me.
You lift me up on the wind; you make me ride on it,
  and you toss me about in the roar of the storm.
For I know that you will bring me to death
  and to the house appointed for all living. (Job 30:16–23)

In Job 30:16, Job introduces the key phrase "days of affliction," which he will later use in verse 27, both times describing the unimaginable sufferings of his soul. Verse 16 also begins with the phrase "and now" (*we'attah*), repeated twice earlier: "But now they laugh at me" (Job 30:1); "And now I have become their song" (v. 9). This final "and now" accentuates the greatest contrast between *then* and *now*. *Then* Job walked on prosperous paths ("washed with butter," 29:6), bringing joy upon the joyless (v. 13b); *but now* he sits in the mud or dung (30:19a) with a soul that is poured on the floor like spoiled milk (v. 16a). More than that, his pain is eleven on a scale of ten! The relentless pain is so excruciating that it robs him of sleep ("The night racks my bones, and the pain that gnaws me takes no rest," v. 17). His own protective clothing becomes a strangling noose ("With great force my garment is disfigured," v. 18a), slowly constricting around his neck ("it binds me about like the collar of my tunic," v. 18b). Next, the cord snaps, as it did for Judas, and he falls to the ground. The cause of his descent is not gravity, however, but God: he "has cast me into the mire" (v. 19a).

If Job was helpless against the assaults of the street gang, how will he fare against almighty God? He is as good as dead: "I have become like dust and ashes" (Job 30:19b). Job recognizes that his only hope for restoration lies in God's decision to act on his behalf rather than against him. Yet here again (cf. 23:16), with each reference to God, Job loses a little more hope:

- "You do not answer me" (Job 30:20a).
- "You only look at me" (v. 20b).
- "You persecute me" (v. 21b).
- "You toss me about in the roar of the storm" (v. 22b).
- "You will bring me to death" (v. 23a).

God will not answer his prayers ("I cry to you for help and you do not answer me," Job 30:20a). Even though God sees Job and knows of his plight, he stands idly by ("you only look at me," v. 20b). Then when God does lift a hand, it is only to torment ("You have turned cruel to me; with the might of your hand you persecute me," v. 21). The persecuting pain comes because God lifts him from the ground ("You lift me up on the wind"), makes him ride the fast and furious wind for a while ("you make me ride on it"), and then tosses him into the thunder ("and you toss me about in the roar of the storm," v. 22). The ride is not yet over. The last leg of the ride, Job can only imagine, will end in death. Eventually God will drop him to the dust ("For I know that you will bring me to death"), for that is where every person eventually resides ("to the house appointed for all [the] living," v. 23). Job is a lot closer to where he began in Job chapter 3, where he cursed the day of his birth, than where he was in 26:6–14, where he praised God's power. A deep darkness is slowly covering the stage of this great drama.

In *A Grace Disguised*, Jerry Sittser describes a dream he had after the loss of his mother, wife, and child in a car accident. He writes:

> I dreamed of a setting sun. I was frantically running west, trying desperately to catch it and remain in its fiery warmth and light. But I was losing the race. The sun was beating me to the horizon and was soon gone. I suddenly found myself in the twilight. Exhausted, I stopped running and glanced with foreboding over my shoulder to the east. I saw a vast darkness closing in on me. I was terrified by that darkness. I wanted to keep running after the sun, though I knew it was futile, for it had already proven itself faster than I was. So I lost all hope, collapsed to the ground, and fell into despair. I thought at that moment that I would live in darkness forever. I felt absolute terror in my soul.[8]

Sittser goes on to recount how he shared the dream with a cousin and that "he mentioned a poem by John Donne that turns on the point that, though east and west seem farthest removed on a map, they eventually meet on a globe. What therefore appear as opposites—east and west—in time come together, if we follow one or the other long enough and far enough." Sittser also recalls his sister Diane's counsel that "the quickest way for anyone to reach the sun and the light of day is not to run west, chasing after the setting

8. Jerry Sittser, *A Grace Disguised: How the Soul Grows Through Loss* (Zondervan, 2021), 21–22.

sun, but to head east, plunging into the darkness until one comes to the sunrise." It was "*in* the darkness," he concludes, that he experienced life:

> I did not go through pain and come out the other side; instead, I lived in it and found within that pain the grace to survive and eventually grow. I did not get over the loss of my loved ones; rather, I absorbed the loss into my life, like soil receives decaying matter, until it became a part of who I am. Sorrow took up permanent residence in my soul and enlarged it. I learned gradually that the deeper we plunge into suffering, the deeper we can enter into a new, a different life—a life no worse than before and sometimes better.[9]

A Self-Lament (Job 30:24–31)

Job is not running west in Job 30:24–31, nor is he facing upward. God is not mentioned in these verses, and the chapter ends with neither an accusation against heaven nor a petition to it. Instead, Job offers a "self-lament,"[10] mourning the fact that no one—not even God—has extended him a helping hand: "Yet does not one in a heap of ruins stretch out his hand, and in his disaster cry for help?" (Job 30:24). Job has been left stranded, to struggle alone. This makes no sense to him, because he has lived his life extending an empathetic hand to rescue. He "delivered the poor who cried for help" (29:12a) and lifted the lame (29:15b). Or, as he puts it here with two rhetorical questions: "Did not I weep for him whose day was hard? Was not my soul grieved for the needy?" (30:25).

Here the retribution principle is busted. Lady Justice's blindfold is pulled over her mouth. And thus Job's world has been turned upside down. He had lived by another Sage's later beatitude, "Blessed are the merciful, for they shall receive mercy" (Matt. 5:7). What happened instead? "But when I hoped for good, evil came, and when I waited for light, darkness came" (Job 30:26).

Job cannot cope. His spiritual struggles affect his physical person:

> My inward parts are in turmoil and never still;
>   days of affliction come to meet me.
> I go about darkened, but not by the sun;
>   I stand up in the assembly and cry for help.

9. Sittser, 26.
10. John E. Hartley, *The Book of Job*, NICOT (Eerdmans, 1988), 404.

I am a brother of jackals
  and a companion of ostriches.
My skin turns black and falls from me,
  and my bones burn with heat.
My lyre is turned to mourning,
  and my pipe to the voice of those who weep. (Job 30:27–31)

Like Jeremiah, Job writhes in pain within the walls of his heart (cf. Jer. 4:19). His bowels boil! His skin is blackened "not by the sun" (Job 30:28a), but by his spiritual sickness and social sorrow. His inner darkness is even changing his complexion! He suffers both outwardly ("My skin turns black and falls from me") and inwardly ("and my bones burn with heat," v. 30). Since God is silent, his only hope is to appeal to those who once esteemed him at the city gate (cf. 29:7–11). "I stand up in the assembly," he says, "and cry for help" (30:28b). But that too is useless. His only family fellowship is with ugly and obnoxious animals: "I am a brother of jackals and a companion of ostriches" (v. 29). This verse, along with the final one (below), depicts Job on the ash heap, making mournful music ("My lyre is turned to mourning, and my pipe to the voice of those who weep," v. 31),[11] howling like a jackal, and hissing like an ostrich. As John Hartley explains: "The jackal's howl is a doleful, mourning sound, said to sound like the wailing of a child, while the ostrich gives out a hissing moan. Their moaning cries convey the stark loneliness of the steppe. Job feels so lonely that he senses that his only companions are these animals in their doleful crying."[12] There is a time, of course, for God's people to cry out to their God in such a fashion. Think of the mournful and honest laments of so many slave spirituals ("a theology in a minor key" that embraces "the harshness and fragility of life, the presence of evil, the shortcomings and limitations of humanity")[13] and traditional African-American prayers and songs, such as the following lines from Robert Nathaniel Dett, "Keep Me from Sinkin' Down" (1927):

O Lord, O my Lord
O my Lord, keep me from sinking down
I shall tell you what I mean to do

11. See also the use of the "flute" in Jeremiah 48:36; Matthew 9:23.

12. Hartley, *Job*, 406.

13. Stephen J. Nichols, *Getting the Blues: What Blues Music Teaches Us About Suffering and Salvation* (Brazos, 2008), 29.

Keep me from sinking down
I mean to get to heaven too
Keep me from sinking down.[14]

REFLECTION AND RESPONSE

With this long section of Job's final speech, many thoughts of reflection and response might come to mind. Let us consider four possible avenues of application.

First, it is difficult to read Job's portrayal of himself as a just judge in Job 29:11–17 and not yearn for justice in our present world. As much as we long for the coming Judge and his final and perfect justice, we should pray now for godly rulers and judges. What a difference it makes when those in high office are clothed with righteousness and justice (Job 29:14). How the world is changed for the better when godly laws that protect the vulnerable and poor are established and enforced. And what a difference it makes when the rich act righteously and generously with their time, treasures, and talents, being eyes to the blind, feet to the lame, and fathers to the needy (vv. 15–16). When those of high society look out for the lowly, the kingdom of God is at hand.

Second, Job's memories in chapter 29 of Job might nauseate some people if they think his nostalgia is an exercise in self-love. Instead, the point might be, as Estes indicates, that "when adversity comes, memories of God's past faithfulness can sustain us."[15] As followers of Yahweh, we are to remember what God has done for us, a command found in both the Old Testament (e.g., "you shall remember what the LORD your God did to Pharaoh and to all Egypt," Deut. 7:18) and the New Testament (e.g., "This is my body, which is given for you. Do this in remembrance of me," Luke 22:19), trusting that sometimes such memories can be healing for the soul.

Third, building on the preceding points (and potentially serving as a necessary corrective for some Christians), it is crucial for us not to confuse gratitude for God's generosity—expressed in his blessings of health and wealth—with the gospel. The gospel of Jesus Christ does not promise us the happiness of a pain-free existence or extravagant lifestyle, awed esteem when we enter a room, and a Job-like bank account. Instead, as our Lord

14. Dett, quoted in *Conversations with God: Two Centuries of Prayers by African Americans*, ed. James Melvin Washington (HarperPerennial, 1994), 144.

15. Estes, *Job*, 180.

Jesus makes clear, discipleship is a call to die to self: "If anyone would come after me, let him deny himself and take up his cross and follow me" (Mark 8:34). The apostle Paul not only followed this pattern but proclaimed it. As Tremper Longman well summarizes:

> Paul tells Christians that they are an afflicted people. Indeed, Paul speaks of the necessity of sharing in the sufferings of Christ and thereby "attaining to the resurrection from the dead" (Phil. 3:10–11 NIV). However, in their present affliction, they experience God's comfort (2 Cor. 1:3–11). Indeed, in spite of all of his troubles, Paul could still experience joy (2 Cor. 7:4). The absence of pain and the experience of unalloyed joy come not in this life but the next. Christians must endure the hardships of a fallen world today but can anticipate the joys of the future, when God will wipe away every tear (Rev. 7:17).[16]

Fourth, Job's accusations against God and his self-laments expressed in Job 30 are difficult to apply. But before we condemn Job or say, "I would never say that to God!" we must sit with him for a day. Job is totally distraught. His "days of affliction" (Job 30:16, 27) have stricken his body and soul. He is black on the outside (vv. 28, 30) and blue on the inside (vv. 16a, 27a). He is isolated, slandered, mistreated, bewildered, and ashamed. His shame, however, is not as a result of some sin. Therefore, it is not appropriate to expect him to pray his version of Psalm 32 or Psalm 51. And while I do not endorse employing each word from this chapter in our own conversations with God or interactions with others, I do recommend that, like Job, we take whatever shame we might feel—whether it arises from undeserved derision (as in Job's case) or unrepentant sin (usually in our case)—and use that shame as a catalyst to take us to God for answers or forgiveness.[17]

16. Tremper Longman III, *Job*, Baker Commentary on the Old Testament Wisdom and Psalms (Baker Academic, 2012), 343.

17. See Longman on this topic (352–53). "Shame can be redemptive when it drives a person to God" (353).

24

Job: Let God Know My Integrity and Answer Me! Part 1

Job 31:1–23

Let me be weighed in a just balance, and let God know my integrity! (Job 31:6)

The final line of Job 31 is "The words of Job are ended" (Job 31:40). Of course, Job will have a few more words (very few words!) to say in response to God's words in chapters 38–41. Job 31 records, then, Job's final words in the debate with his friends. We might wonder, at the start of this end, whether he will make a disingenuous admission of his guilt to his friends just to appease them or give a final diatribe to remind them that they are in the wrong. Job utters neither an admission nor a tirade. Instead, he puts down his flute and the score to the *Jackals' Requiem* (see 30:29) and takes up his old legal brief. He once again denies the allegations against him, calling on the Almighty to render a righteous judgment. He denies the libelous charges that his friends have leveled against him—e.g., dishonesty (22:6; 31:5–8) and neglecting the needy (22:7–9), as well as other common sins, such as idolatry, covetousness, sexual lust, and adultery. Job makes what many commentators call an "oath of innocence," and what Meredith Kline calls "the climax of his peroration [speeches]," Job's retrospective or "retroactive oath of covenant allegiance."[1] Daniel Estes explains how and why Job uses this "ancient legal strategy of negative confession":

> Several times, Job uses the form, "If I have done this crime, then let God punish me with this horrible consequence." Other times, Job states the condition, but he leaves the consequence undefined. By this means, Job as the defendant calls on God as judge either to condemn him to the full extent of the law or else to clear him of the erroneous charge. If Job is guilty, then he has invited God to strike him with horrific penalties. If God does not exact the punishment, then his failure to do so will tacitly acquit Job of the charges against him. By this legal procedure, even the silence of God the judge can exonerate Job.[2]

Job will deny or disavow committing eleven sins: lust (Job 31:1–4), dishonesty (vv. 5–8), adultery (vv. 9–12), oppression (vv. 13–15), neglect of the needy (vv. 16–23), materialism (vv. 24–25), paganism (vv. 26–28), vindictiveness (vv. 29–30), inhospitality (vv. 31–32), duplicity (vv. 33–34), and exploitation (vv. 38–40).[3]

Job Disavows Lust (Job 31:1–4)

Job begins with his disavowal of *lust*: "I have made a covenant with my eyes; how then could I gaze at a virgin?" (Job 31:1). To use the idiom of his day, Job has cut a covenant (*berit karatti*) with his eyes. In other words, he has pledged to himself, as a man who fears the Lord and turns away from evil, that he will control his eyes. He will not "gaze" on a young woman (a "virgin"), whether such a gaze would involve looking to add another woman

1. Meredith Kline, "Job," in *Wycliffe Bible Commentary*, ed. Charles F. Pfeiffer and Everett F. Harrison (Moody, 1963), 481.

2. Daniel J. Estes, *Job*, Teach the Text (Baker, 2013), 188.

3. Robert Gordis lists fourteen sins that Job denied, viewing this "double heptad" or "twice-seven" as symbolizing a complete adherence to moral law. *The Book of Job: Commentary, New Translation, Special Studies* (1978; repr., Jewish Theological Seminary of America, 2011), 542. Cf. John E. Hartley, *The Book of Job*, NICOT (Eerdmans, 1988), 409. With some slight alterations, I have followed Derek Thomas's list in *The Storm Breaks: Job Simply Explained*, Welwyn Commentary Series (repr., Evangelical Press, 2005), 237.

as a wife or, more likely, looking on any woman with lustful intent. Perhaps Job starts with the sin of lust because it is a common temptation for men, as John Goldingay writes: "Job is a man, and it looks as if Job knows that men think about sex a lot. So sex is the concrete starting point for understanding 'wrongdoing' and 'wickedness' and for a recognition that without a commitment to sexual propriety, he is liable to God's bringing disaster on his life."[4] Also, lust is something internal, a matter of the eyes and heart, so that it goes to the core of a man's character.

Job has been self-controlled in this vital area of sexual purity because he knows that God sees everything ("Does not he see my ways and number all my steps?," Job 31:4) and judges even the secret intentions of the heart. Job asks himself the question "What would be my portion from God above and my heritage from the Almighty on high?" (v. 2). In other words, what would God grant him if he indulged in sexual fantasies? His reply comes in verse 3—he should anticipate tragedy to come justly on him: "Is not calamity for the unrighteous, and disaster for the workers of iniquity?"

Concerning these opening verses that speak of Job's disavowal of sexual lust in particular but also his "knowledge of the power of temptation and his determination to overpower sin in his life" in general, Derek Thomas correctly notes that "if we are honest, there are at least two things that we should admit to in our lives: first, our failure to deal with our sin; and second, how inadequately we go about it."[5] Thomas is also right to note four elements of "Job's method" for handling sin that are applicable to us.

First, we must realize that our lives are lived in the light of God's presence. The fact that the all-knowing God sees our every step should help us step away from sin. Think about what Joseph said to Potiphar's wife when she tempted him to come to bed with her: "How then can I do this great wickedness and sin against God?" (Gen. 39:9). Joseph believed that God sees all. Second, we must believe that sin must be dealt with. Job is conscious of the danger associated with failing to scrutinize potential areas of sin, such as lusting after women. He knows that he could easily fall into this sin, and others like it, if he is not aware of the temptation and proactive in combating it. Third, we must guard our hearts and minds. Job knows that "his heart and mind

4. John Goldingay, *Job for Everyone*, Old Testament for Everyone (Westminster John Knox, 2013), 146.

5. Thomas, *The Storm Breaks*, 237.

are battlegrounds of the conflict between the flesh and the spirit,"[6] and he has determined to feed his spirit, not his flesh. "A gracious heart is as careful not to sin by evil thoughts as by evil acts."[7] Job understands what Jesus later taught, "that everyone who looks at a woman with lustful intent has already committed adultery with her in his heart" (Matt. 5:28). He also understands, fourth, that practical steps must be taken.[8] As John Owen famously phrased it, we must be killing sin or sin will be killing us.[9] Jesus gave the following hyperbolic metaphors for the mortification of the sinful flesh, followed by the sternest warnings: "If your right eye causes you to sin, tear it out and throw it away. For it is better that you lose one of your members than that your whole body be thrown into hell. And if your right hand causes you to sin, cut it off and throw it away. For it is better that you lose one of your members than that your whole body go into hell" (vv. 29–30). The Christian life is one of self-denial and self-mortification. Tearing out. Cutting off. Throwing away. May our lives as Christians be characterized by such actions.

Job Disavows Dishonesty (Job 31:5–8)

Next, Job disavows *dishonesty*:

> If I have walked with falsehood
>   and my foot has hastened to deceit;
> (Let me be weighed in a just balance,
>   and let God know my integrity!)
> if my step has turned aside from the way
>   and my heart has gone after my eyes,
>   and if any spot has stuck to my hands,
> then let me sow, and another eat,
>   and let what grows for me be rooted out. (Job 31:5–8)

Here Job uses three peripatetic metaphors for living dishonestly ("If I have walked with falsehood"/"my foot has hastened to deceit"/"my step has turned

6. Thomas, 238.

7. Joseph Caryl, "An Exposition upon Job," in *ESV Church History Study Bible: Voices from the Past, Wisdom for the Present* (Crossway, 2023), 740.

8. Thomas, *The Storm Breaks*, 238–40. I have reordered two of Thomas's four observations.

9. John Owen, "The Mortification of Sin," in *The Works of John Owen*, 16 vols. (Banner of Truth, 1965–68), 6:9.

aside," Job 31:5, 7a). He denies that he has walked this way. He also claims that both his heart and his hands are clean: his "heart" has not chased a profit for ill-gain (v. 7b), and there is no "damn'd spot," to use Lady Macbeth's language,[10] "stuck to [his] hands" (v. 7c) as the result of some shady deal. If his honesty were weighed on an honest scale ("Let me be weighed in a just balance"), it would prove to God that Job has been telling the truth ("know my integrity!," v. 6). If this is not so, Job continues, he will reap the consequence for not keeping covenant: someone else can eat from his fertile fields ("then let me sow, and another eat") and his land can fall forever barren after the stranger has been fed ("and let what grows for me be rooted out," v. 8).

As Christians, we must remember that we follow a God who cannot lie (Num. 23:19; Titus 1:2; Heb. 6:18) and who has clearly commanded us to honor honesty (Ex. 20:16; Lev. 19:11; Matt. 5:37). We must also remember that we live in a world under the power of Satan, "the father of lies" (John 8:44), and that judgment is coming to "everyone who loves and practices falsehood" (Rev. 22:15). Let us heed the Bible's warnings and also its encouragements. Like our truth-telling God, let us be known for telling the truth, the whole truth, and nothing but the truth.

Job Disavows Adultery (Job 31:9–12)

In these verses, Job returns to the theme of sexual immorality, perhaps bookending dishonesty as Jesus does in the Sermon on the Mount because sexual sin and deception go hand in hand:[11]

> If my heart has been enticed toward a woman,
> and I have lain in wait at my neighbor's door,
> then let my wife grind for another,
> and let others bow down on her.
> For that would be a heinous crime;
> that would be an iniquity to be punished by the judges;
> for that would be a fire that consumes as far as Abaddon,
> and it would burn to the root all my increase. (Job 31:9–12)

10. William Shakespeare, *Macbeth*, act 5, sc. 1.

11. Jesus similarly went from the topics of lust and adultery (Matt. 5:27–32) to the topics of honesty and oaths (vv. 33–37).

Here Job denies the sin of *adultery*, which he describes briefly in two lines. First, a man is smitten by another man's wife ("If my heart has been enticed toward a woman [or "wife"]," Job 31:9a). Second, he waits for the right occasion to seduce her ("and I have lain in wait at my neighbor's door," v. 9b). Third, and implied, he succeeds; he sleeps with her.

Job has never done this! Moreover, he is repulsed by the thought of it. A lustful glance (Job 31:1) is a sin against God and the girl, but adultery is a more grievous evil (a "heinous crime," v. 11) because it is premeditated and because it tears apart the very fabric of marriage and of society as a whole. Job lays out the consequences for such a crime in verses 10–12 of Job 31. First, he envisions his wife's leaving him for another man or, far worse, becoming like the town prostitute ("then let my wife grind for another, and let others bow down on her," v. 10). The verb "grind" (*tahan*) could refer to household labors, whatever such labors might have been for a wealthy woman (see Prov. 31:10–31)—in other words, "being reduced to menial slave labor (Ex. 11:5)."[12] Alternatively, it could mean that she would leave him for another man and make and bake that man's bread in a new home ("then may my wife grind another man's grain," Job 31:10 NIV; "then let my wife serve another man," NLT). Or the verb can take on a sexual connotation, namely, that various other men (perhaps her new master and his servants) from time to time are on top of her ("others bow down on her"), sexually abusing and taking advantage of her. The plural ("others," as in one after another man as though she is now relegated to a sex worker) is especially jarring and the whole concept seemingly cruel. But the point is that Job cannot imagine that this would ever happen because he is so certain of his steadfast loyalty to and love for his bride.[13] Thus, he is absolutely innocent of adultery!

Next, after detailing the horrific possibility of what would happen to his wife, he describes his own punishment: the elders of the city gate would stone him to death ("an iniquity to be punished by the judges," Job 31:11b)[14] and

12. Richard P. Belcher Jr., *Job: The Mystery of Suffering and God's Sovereignty*, Focus on the Bible (Christian Focus, 2017), 213.

13. "One should not conclude that Job is without feeling toward his wife and that he glibly offers her for the sexual pleasure of others. He is saying that if he has taken advantage of someone else's wife, then it is just punishment if someone else takes advantage of his wife." Belcher, 213.

14. "If a man commits adultery with the wife of his neighbor, both the adulterer and the adulteress shall surely be put to death" (Lev. 20:10).

set his property ablaze (adultery is a "fire that consumes as far as Abaddon, and it would burn to the root all my increase," v. 12).[15] A household and a society cannot survive when this sin from the pit of hell reigns!

Pastor R. Kent Hughes tells the story of the time he learned that his old college roommate decided that he was going to leave his wife of twenty-two years. As soon as Hughes heard the news, he got on the next plane—the red-eye special from Chicago to California. At 7:00 A.M., he was knocking on his friend's front door. The man had no choice but to let him in and talk to him. Kent spent that day trying to convince him of what the Bible had to say about marriage, that he had no grounds for leaving his wife whatsoever. He headed back to Chicago, optimistic that his friend was convicted of biblical truth. Yet several weeks later, his friend informed him that he was indeed leaving his wife. He gave this tenuous theological assumption: the unfaithful husband said that he knew that the Bible did not condone what he was doing, but that he was under grace and he was going to do it anyway and God was going to forgive him. What a hell-bent thought!

A year after this man left his wife, Kent received an invitation to attend his wedding. What audacity! According to the invitation, the wedding was to take place on the yacht *Mia Vita*, which means "my life." As Kent looked at the invitation, his mind turned to the lyrics of Frank Sinatra's song, in which the singer boasts of living a full life, traveling many highways, and doing everything *his* way. Well, Kent's friend did it his way. But what has he done?, Hughes went on to ask. This man quickly created a trail of broken relationships—with his wife, children, grandchildren, friends, and church. He sinned against God. He sinned against the leadership of his church. He sinned against his wife. He sinned against his children, and eventually his grandchildren (who were born long after the divorce). He broke what God had brought together, and the pieces of that separation were too many to pick up and put together. Hughes concludes by saying of this man's ungodly decision: "It's been devastating to his wife and it's been devastating to his now adult children. He thought that since his children were essentially raised, it wouldn't make any difference. What a mistake he made. It has devastated their lives. And so I say . . . that the primrose path to self-fulfillment that so many believers trip merrily down, is strewn with the bones of people who

15. Proverbs 6:27–29 speaks of the personal consequences to the man who carries "fire next to his chest" and "goes in to his neighbor's wife." Job 31:12 envisions adultery as a crime that burns the world!

have walked down that path and the bones of many of the people that they loved the most."[16]

How different that man's course is from that of my faithful in-laws. On a business trip to Hong Kong, my wife's father was convicted by the Holy Spirit. He confessed to his wife that he had been unfaithful for many years with many different women. She was devastated, as anyone would be. Indeed, she had biblical grounds for divorce. But she decided to forgive him. It was not an easy road. But he was truly repentant, and her attitude through it all was "I'm married to Christ first and my husband second. But because I'm married to a perfect heavenly Husband, I can forgive my imperfect earthly husband." They have been married over fifty years. What is their legacy? No broken relationships—with God, his people, and their family. Peace. Love. Forgiveness. The goodness of the gospel lived out.[17]

Adultery is like flirting with a deadly fire. If there are any flames or even the embers of adulterous thoughts in your mind, put them out completely. Vow to remain sexually pure. If you're married, recommit to your covenantal commitment, a "love" that "is strong as death" and whose "flashes are flashes of fire, the very flame of the Lord" (Song 8:5–6). Let only that God-fire warm your heart!

Job Disavows (or Denounces!) Oppression (Job 31:13–15)

If there is a pattern to Job's denials of sin, it emerges here. He moves from *seemingly* secret sins (lust, adultery) to societal sins (dishonesty in business, oppression of household slaves). This pattern seems to play out in the rest of the chapter, as illustrated in table 24.1:

Table 24.1. Pattern of Job's Denials in Job 31

Secret Sins	Societal Sins
Lust (vv. 1–4)	
Dishonesty (vv. 5–8)	

16. R. Kent Hughes, "The Sacredness of Marriage," sermon preached on February 14, 1988, available at The Gospel Coalition, https://resources.thegospelcoalition.org/library/the-sacredness-of-marriage, accessed July 9, 2019 and October 27, 2023.

17. This illustration was adapted from Douglas Sean O'Donnell, *Mark: Arise and Follow the Son*, Expository Reflections on the Gospels 3 (Crossway, 2024), 279–80.

Secret Sins	Societal Sins
Adultery (vv. 9–12)	
	Oppression (vv. 13–15)
	Neglect of the needy (vv. 16–23)
Materialism (vv. 24–25)	
Paganism (vv. 26–28)	
Vindictiveness (vv. 29–30)	
	Inhospitality (vv. 31–32)
	Exploitation (vv. 38–40)

Oppression is what Job denies in verses 13–15 of Job 31:

> If I have rejected the cause of my manservant or my maidservant,
> when they brought a complaint against me,
> what then shall I do when God rises up?
> When he makes inquiry, what shall I answer him?
> Did not he who made me in the womb make him?
> And did not one fashion us in the womb?

When we read about Job's servants, we should not think of the cruelties of American antebellum slavery as depicted in *Uncle Tom's Cabin* and *Roots*. Rather, we should think of the relationships depicted in *Pride and Prejudice* and *Downton Abbey*. Job's manservants and maidservants were beloved members of his large household. Remember that Job lost not only all his children but many of his servants as well (all but four died). Here Job states that he would never have treated one of his household servants without goodwill or liberality if they came to him with a grievance (Job 31:13). He knows that God judges inhumane masters (v. 14), and he also knows, far before Thomas Jefferson penned it, "that all men are created equal,"[18] that the same Creator made both his servants and Job himself: "Did not he who made me in the womb make him? And did not one fashion us in the womb?" (v. 15). Thus, Job confirms that he has always allowed his servants—both male and *female*—the right to take him to court.

Job models Paul's later exhortation to Christian masters, to treat those who are under their authority and part of their household with goodwill

18. Of course, ironically and tragically, Jefferson owned more than five hundred people of African descent during his lifetime, men, women, and children whom he did not view as his equals.

and without partiality (see Eph. 6:7, 9). He also offers an excellent lesson in anthropology: no matter their social status, every human being should be viewed with *equality* ("in that God shows no partiality in his treatment of those who he has made"),[19] deserves *dignity* ("in that every human being bears . . . the image of God [Gen. 1:26])," and is our *responsibility* ("in that it is our responsibility to be prepared to forego our rights for the sake of others").[20] Moreover, Paul urges Christians to emulate Jesus by humbly "count[ing] others more significant than [our]selves" and thus to "look . . . to the interests of others" (Phil. 2:3, 4) before we look to our own interests.

Job Disavows Neglecting the Needy (Job 31:16–23)

Job's longest denial is that he has not *neglected the needy.* Perhaps it is the longest because it is a specific charge that Eliphaz has brought against him (see Job 22:5–9), but Job has already offered a defense (see 24:1–13; 29:12–16). Or perhaps loving the least of his fellow humans is on the top of Job's list of living the God-fearing life.

> If I have withheld anything that the poor desired,
> or have caused the eyes of the widow to fail,
> or have eaten my morsel alone,
> and the fatherless has not eaten of it
> (for from my youth the fatherless grew up with me as with a father,
> and from my mother's womb I guided the widow),
> if I have seen anyone perish for lack of clothing,
> or the needy without covering,
> if his body has not blessed me,
> and if he was not warmed with the fleece of my sheep,
> if I have raised my hand against the fatherless,
> because I saw my help in the gate,
> then let my shoulder blade fall from my shoulder,
> and let my arm be broken from its socket.
> For I was in terror of calamity from God,
> and I could not have faced his majesty. (Job 31:16–23)

As with Paul (Gal. 2:10), remembering the poor is a big deal to Job. To use another New Testament text, Job will fare well come judgment day if judged

19. See Deut. 1:16–17; 10:17; 16:18–19.
20. Thomas, *The Storm Breaks*, 244.

on the basis of Jesus' teaching in the parable of the sheep and the goats (Matt. 25:31–46), for Job claims that he has cared for the least of God's people: the "poor" (Job 31:16a), the "widow" (v. 16b), the "fatherless" (vv. 17b, 21), and anyone in need of food, clothing, or shelter (vv. 17a, 18–20).

In one of the most personal lines in the book, Job recalls his childhood, when ostensibly orphans were a part of his parents' extended household, or a consistent ministry of his family ("from my youth the fatherless grew up with me as with a father," Job 31:18a). He also recalls, in hyperbolic terms, how the plight of widows has been his lifelong concern ("from my mother's womb I guided the widow," v. 18b). He has spent his entire life in the practice of true religion (see James 1:27; cf. Ex. 22:21–24). Job may be exaggerating, but if he is lying, he calls on God to rip off his arms ("then let my shoulder blade fall from my shoulder, and let my arm be broken from its socket," Job 31:22)! "Job's assertions of innocence," as Belcher comments with additional insight,

> may be alluding to the way he feels he has been treated by God, whose hand has oppressed and intimidated him (10:7; 12:9; 13:21; 19:21). The irony is that Job acted in justice toward the fatherless because he feared calamity from God. Even though he is innocent he has experienced calamity from the hand of God. Nonetheless, his acknowledgment of God's majesty gives him hope that God will do what is right in his situation. Job ultimately believes in the justice of God.[21]

Administer Justice

The word *justice* has fallen on hard times in the American evangelical church. For some, there is a fear that the liberal theology of the social-justice movement will subtly seduce and shift orthodox theological priorities and foundations. But political propaganda more than theological convictions may be the main reason why some Christians now fear speaking of justice. My wife works for Administer Justice, a ministry that helps people who can't afford a lawyer to receive legal help at an incredibly reasonable price. She works with churches to set up legal clinics where lawyers volunteer their time to give legal advice. Sadly, some churches won't give her the time of day simply because of the ministry's name. Some pastors have even asked her whether Administer Justice would consider changing its name. This is

21. Belcher, *Job*, 216.

laughable (but not so funny), since the name comes from the Bible! Twice (2 Sam. 8:15; 1 Chron. 18:14) we are told: "So David reigned over all Israel. And David *administered justice* and equity to all his people." Throughout God's Word, God's people, who worship "the God of justice" (Mal. 2:17), who loves "justice" (Isa. 61:8), "practices . . . justice" (Jer. 9:24), gives "justice to his elect" (Luke 18:7), and considers "justice," along with mercy and faithfulness, as one of "the weightier matters of the law" (Matt. 23:23), are commanded to "do justice" (Jer. 22:15), "execute justice" (2 Chron. 9:8), "seek justice" (Isa. 1:17), "bring justice" (v. 17), "give justice" (Ps. 82:3), "keep justice" (Isa. 56:1), "observe justice" (Ps. 106:3), "establish justice" (Amos 5:15), "hope for justice" (Isa. 59:11), and love "justice" (Pss. 33:5; 37:28). Oh, that we all would—like David, like Job, and like *Jesus*—administer such justice!

Consider Isaiah's summary of the Messiah's justice ministry from the lips of the Lord:

> Behold my servant, whom I uphold,
>   my chosen, in whom my soul delights;
> I have put my Spirit upon him;
>   he will bring forth justice to the nations. (Isa. 42:1)[22]

And bring forth justice Jesus did! When John the Baptist asked his disciples to ask Jesus, "Are you the one who is to come, or shall we look for another?," Jesus answered by saying, "Go and tell John what you hear and see: the blind receive their sight and the lame walk, lepers are cleansed and the deaf hear, and the dead are raised up, and the poor have good news preached to them" (Matt. 11:3–5). Elsewhere, Matthew summarizes Jesus' Galilean ministry in terms of mercy and justice:

> And Jesus went throughout all the cities and villages, teaching in their synagogues and proclaiming the gospel of the kingdom and healing every disease and every affliction. When he saw the crowds, he had compassion for them, because they were harassed and helpless, like sheep without a shepherd. (Matt. 9:35–36)

With compassion, our Lord lamented the lost and healed the afflicted in Galilee. In Jerusalem, with holy indignation, he ousted the money-changers and

22. Quoting Isaiah 42:1, Matthew writes of Jesus that "he will proclaim justice" (Matt. 12:18).

those who sold pigeons in the Court of the Gentiles, rebuking their oppressive behavior: "Is it not written, 'My house shall be called a house of prayer for all the nations'? But you have made it a den of robbers" (Mark 11:17). For the sake of expediency and with the goal of extortion, these "robbers" had turned the designated place of worship for the nations into the bizarre mix of a county fair and the pit of a stock exchange. As Jesus overturned their tables, he was *symbolically* overturning their "new, unlawful, unmerciful, and anti-Abrahamic-covenant temple traditions." But he was also *literally* offering the poor spiritual refuge. Indeed, as he was driving out the spiritual swindlers (those who squeezed the poor), the currency-exchange racketeers and the used-pigeon salesmen, he was opening the gates to the poor: those who "eked out their existence as beggars" outside the city gates,[23] namely, "the blind and the lame," who "came to him *in the temple*, and he healed them" (Matt. 21:14) free of charge. Jesus lets them in to him—his presence and healing touch. He brings justice to the Gentiles, good news to the poor![24]

Let us, likewise, bring justice to the world, or "do justice," as the prophet Micah puts it, and "love kindness" and "walk humbly with [our] God" (Mic. 6:8). Let us fervently pray, as Augustine prayed: "O Lord, who though you were rich yet for our sakes became poor, and [have] promised in your holy gospel that whatever is done for the least of your brethren you will receive as done to you: Give us grace, we humbly beseech you, to be always willing and ready to minister, as you enable us, to the needs of others, and to extend the blessings of your kingdom over all the world."[25]

23. Rudolf Schnackenburg, *The Gospel of Matthew*, trans. Robert R. Barr (Eerdmans, 2002), 203.

24. This paragraph is partly drawn from Douglas Sean O'Donnell, *Matthew: All Authority in Heaven and on Earth*, Preaching the Word (Crossway, 2013), 600–601.

25. Augustine, quoted in *Classic Christian Prayers: A Celebration of Praise and Glory*, ed. Owen Collins (Testament Books, 1999), 82.

25

Job: Let God Know My Integrity and Answer Me! Part 2

Job 31:24–40

Let me be weighed in a just balance, and let God know my integrity! (Job 31:6)

Because of the length of Job 31 and the highly applicable nature of Job's oath of innocence, we need to give separate attention to part 2 of Job's final speech. In part 1, we examined and applied Job's disavowal of the first five of eleven sins: lust (Job 31:1–4), dishonesty (vv. 5–8), adultery (vv. 9–12), oppression (vv. 13–15), and neglect of the needy (vv. 16–23); in part 2, we will examine and apply Job's disavowal of the sins of materialism (vv. 24–25), paganism (vv. 26–28), vindictiveness (vv. 29–30), inhospitality (vv. 31–32), duplicity (vv. 33–34), and exploitation (vv. 38–40).

Job Disavows Materialism and Idolatry (Job 31:24–28)

We begin with the way in which Job pairs *materialism* with *paganism*. This is an interesting, but not unexpected, combination, for as our Lord Jesus himself summarizes, the two vices go hand in hand: "No one can serve two masters, for either he will hate the one and love the other, or he will be devoted to the one and despise the other. You cannot serve God and money" (Matt. 6:24). Similarly, Paul tells us that "covetousness . . . is idolatry" (Col. 3:5). Job expresses it this way:

> If I have made gold my trust
> or called fine gold my confidence,
> if I have rejoiced because my wealth was abundant
> or because my hand had found much,
> if I have looked at the sun when it shone,
> or the moon moving in splendor,
> and my heart has been secretly enticed,
> and my mouth has kissed my hand,
> this also would be an iniquity to be punished by the judges,
> for I would have been false to God above. (Job 31:24–28)

Here Job asserts that he has not "made gold [his] trust" or, put differently, "called fine gold [his] confidence" (Job 31:24). His joy has not come from the fortune that he has made for himself (v. 25).

Money was not Job's god, and pagan deities were not his idols. The moon and the sun, natural candidates for worship in the ancient Near East, were not the objects of worship. He did not look at the sun when it rose (Job 31:26a) or the moon "moving in splendor" at night (v. 26b) and secretly pray that such celestial lights would prosper him (v. 27a). "He never threw a kiss [v. 27b] to them as a sign of affection and devotion, a widespread pagan practice,"[1] notably in Baal worship.[2] Why not? Because such sins are as evil as adultery ("this also would be an iniquity to be punished by the judges," v. 28a) and idolatry is a crime against Yahweh himself ("for I would have been false to God above," v. 28b; cf. Ex. 20:3–6).

While we may not be tempted to kiss a pagan idol in hopes of receiving a monetary blessing, we are daily tempted to treat wealth like an idol—something that we love, seek after, and live for. Some Christians today, especially those living in the West, must remind ourselves of Jesus' teachings on the

1. John E. Hartley, *The Book of Job*, NICOT (Eerdmans, 1988), 419.

2. Slightly paraphrasing, Hartley (418) translates the phrase as "and my hand threw a kiss from my mouth." It could be that the author of Job is referencing an activity that was part of Baal worship ("Yet I will leave seven thousand in Israel, all the knees that have not bowed to Baal, and every mouth that has not kissed him," 1 Kings 19:18; cf. Hos. 13:2).

dangers of wealth and heed his many warnings on the subject: "Do not lay up for yourselves treasures on earth, where moth and rust destroy and where thieves break in and steal, but lay up for yourselves treasures in heaven, where neither moth nor rust destroys and where thieves do not break in and steal" (Matt. 6:19–20); "Take care, and be on your guard against all covetousness, for one's life does not consist in the abundance of his possessions" (Luke 12:15); "Give to everyone who begs from you, and from one who takes away your goods do not demand them back" (6:30); "Sell your possessions, and give to the needy" (12:33). We are to be "rich toward God" (v. 21) by seeking first his kingdom and caring for the needs of others. The rich ruler walked away from Jesus "disheartened" and "sorrowful" because "he had great possessions" (Mark 10:22) or, we might say, because great possessions had him. Let us so treasure and trust God that none of our possessions entice our hearts and that "the deceitfulness of riches [does not] choke the word" (Matt. 13:22) that God has sown in our hearts.

Job Disavows Vindictiveness, Inhospitality, and Duplicity (Job 31:29–37)

In Job 31:29–37, the long-suffering protagonist disavows *vindictiveness*, *inhospitality*, and *duplicity*:

> If I have rejoiced at the ruin of him who hated me,
>   or exulted when evil overtook him
> (I have not let my mouth sin
>   by asking for his life with a curse),
> if the men of my tent have not said,
>   "Who is there that has not been filled with his meat?"
> (the sojourner has not lodged in the street;
>   I have opened my doors to the traveler),
> if I have concealed my transgressions as others do
>   by hiding my iniquity in my heart,
> because I stood in great fear of the multitude,
>   and the contempt of families terrified me,
>   so that I kept silence, and did not go out of doors—
> Oh, that I had one to hear me!
>   (Here is my signature! Let the Almighty answer me!)
>   Oh, that I had the indictment written by my adversary!

Surely I would carry it on my shoulder;
I would bind it on me as a crown;
I would give him an account of all my steps;
like a prince I would approach him.

Job states that he has not rejoiced over the ruin of his enemies, gloated over their misfortune, or prayed for their deaths (Job 31:29–30). Moreover, he has been gracious to all, extending hospitality to all, from his slaves to strangers (vv. 31–32). In showing hospitality, perhaps he has "entertained angels unawares" (Heb. 13:2) or even the preincarnate Christ (Dan. 3:24–25; cf. Gen. 18:1–8). Finally, with Job, what you see is what you get. He is not a hypocrite like the rich Pharisees whom Jesus denounced for cleaning the outside of their cups and plates while being "full of greed and self-indulgence," and being outwardly well dressed in pure white garments but within "full of hypocrisy and lawlessness" (Matt. 23:25, 28). Job does not curse his enemies under his breath, invite only the powerful to sup at table, or hide his sins ("concealed my transgressions"/"hiding my iniquity," Job 31:33) under the pretense of piety. When he has offended God or others, he has made it known. He has not kept silent, hiding in his house ("did not go out of doors," v. 34c) because he fears what people ("the multitude"/"families," v. 34a, b) might think if they only knew about all his sinful shortcomings.

What is unusual here, however, is that Job does not add the usual consequences of such sins, as he has done in Job 31:2–3, 8, 10–12, 14, 22, 28. Instead, he interrupts his disavowals (he has one more to go, Job 31:38–40) with a plea reminiscent of his earlier entreaties (most recently, v. 6b). In verses 35–37, Job again begs for a hearing ("Oh, that I had one to hear me!," v. 35a). He has already written (or wanted to write) his testimony in stone (cf. 19:23–24). Now he signs it ("here is my signature!," 31:35b).[3] He also demands an answer from God ("Let the Almighty answer me!" and write his own "indictment" against Job, v. 35b–c). Job is curious about what the charges from his "adversary" might be.[4] Like his sins (cf. vv. 33–34), he would take seriously and make public the charges against him ("Surely I would carry it on my shoulder; I would bind it on me as a crown," v. 36). He

3. "Interestingly, Job's word for 'signature' is, in fact, a letter *taw*, the last letter of the Hebrew alphabet. It is the equivalent of an illiterate person putting an 'X' on the dotted line." Derek Thomas, *The Storm Breaks: Job Simply Explained*, Welwyn Commentary Series (repr., Evangelical Press, 2005), 240.

4. For a similar statement about God, see Job 16:9.

needs an answer as soon as possible to the question of 13:23a, "How many are my iniquities and my sins?" He begs again, this time to God, "Make me know my transgression and my sin" (13:23b). Job is ready and eager to defend himself ("I would give him an account of all my steps," 31:37a); he is confident going into this court case ("like a prince" before a king "I would approach" God, v. 37b) because God is like a Father (the king) to him (the "prince"). He can approach God directly and without fear and with the honor due to his divine person and position.[5]

As Job models for us, we should be known for our hospitality. In 3 John 5, John commends Gaius's hospitality to traveling missionaries—those who went "out for the sake of the name" (3 John 5:7). He took in these "strangers" because they were "brothers" and "fellow workers for the truth" (vv. 5, 8). We too should provide housing, meals, prayer, and financial support to Christian missionaries today. Moreover, we should open our homes, as Job did, to anyone in need, especially unbelievers, as Rosaria Butterfield states: "Radically ordinary hospitality shows this skeptical, post-Christian world what authentic Christianity looks like." We "open doors, . . . seek out the underprivileged" because we "know that the gospel comes with a house key."[6]

Job also models for us how we can and should approach God. Job knows Yahweh through an act of special revelation (e.g., Job 38:1; 40:1, 3), similar to Abraham (e.g., Gen. 12:1, 7). Likewise, in Christ, God has made himself known to us: "Long ago, at many times and in many ways, God spoke to our fathers by the prophets, but in these last days he has spoken to us by his Son, whom he appointed the heir of all things, through whom also he created the world" (Heb. 1:1–2). We know, as the author of Hebrews also teaches us, that because "we have a great high priest who has passed through the heavens, Jesus, the Son of God," we should "then with confidence draw near to the throne of grace, that we may receive mercy and find grace to help in time of need" (4:14, 16). This continuity underscores

5. Contra Meredith Kline, who states that "with consummate arrogance," Job "declares how he will stand before God as a prince (v. 37b)." "Job," in *Wycliffe Bible Commentary*, ed. Charles F. Pfeiffer and Everett F. Harrison (Moody, 1963), 482. Job is not arrogant before God but intimate (or has been for so long!) with God.

6. Two quotes taken from "9 Notable Quotes from *The Gospel Comes with a House Key*," Crossway.org, May 22, 2020, https://www.crossway.org/articles/9-notable-quotes-from-the-gospel-comes-with-a-house-key/, accessed November 7, 2023.

how both Job's and our approaches to God are grounded in divine revelation, whether through a direct encounter with the Holy Spirit or through the mediation of Christ, enabling us to approach God with confidence and receive his grace.

Job Disavows Exploitation (Job 31:38–40)

Before we read the narrator's declaration that the "words of Job are ended" (Job 31:40c), Job ends with his final crime/consequence pairing ("if"-"let"), in which he disavows *exploitation*:

> If my land has cried out against me
> and its furrows have wept together,
> if I have eaten its yield without payment
> and made its owners breathe their last,
> let thorns grow instead of wheat,
> and foul weeds instead of barley.
>
> The words of Job are ended. (Job 31:38–40)

Not that Job was under the law of Moses, but the compiler of the book of Job certainly was, and the law has, as Thomas points out, "specific demands on landowners: the land was not to be sown with two kinds of seed (Lev. 19:19), it was to receive a rest every seventh year (Ex. 23:10–11; Lev. 25:2–7; 26:34–35), and in particular, no blood was to be shed on it, for if it was, the land would cry out for vengeance—as the death of Abel highlighted (Gen. 4:10–12; cf. Num. 35:33–34). Job has not been guilty of abusing these laws."[7] Job has not exploited his land (the "land" has not "cried out against" him//"its furrows" have not "wept together," Job 31:38), nor have the tenants who farm it (he has not "made its owners breathe their last," v. 39b). "Job denies benefiting from the harvest of the land without paying those who work it."[8] He has not underpaid or cheated the farmers (he has not "eaten its yield without payment," v. 39a). For if he has, the final curse (an echo of Adam's curse) should apply: "let thorns grow instead of wheat, and foul weeds instead of barley" (v. 40a–b).[9] Like any other believing person

7. Thomas, *The Storm Breaks*, 249.

8. Richard P. Belcher Jr., *Job: The Mystery of Suffering and God's Sovereignty*, Focus on the Bible (Christian Focus, 2017), 220.

9. "The 'primal imagery' of these verses is, specifically, the garden imagery of Genesis 2–3. . . . Even

suffering from extreme pain, Job has often shifted from loud lament to awe-filled worship, from strong defense to utter despair, from promises to plagues.

Iain Provan's description of "oppression" could apply to what I am labeling *exploitation*. Provan defines *oppression* as "accumulation—seeking after profit—without regard to the nature, needs, and rights of other people," and he illustrates this sin from Scripture as follows:

> In the Bible, oppression involves cheating one's neighbor of something (Lev. 6:2–5 associates it with expropriation, stealing, retaining lost property that has been found, and swearing falsely), defrauding him, and robbing him. It involves making an unjust gain, including the profit made from interest on loans (e.g., Ezek. 22:1–29, esp. vv. 12, 29). It is the abuse of power, financial and otherwise, perpetrated on those who are not so powerful and are indeed valuable—the poor, the widows, orphans, and strangers (e.g., Ezek. 22:7, 29; Amos 4:1; Mic. 2:1–2). Thus it is often associated with violence and bloodshed in the Old Testament and with the denial of rights and justice (e.g., Jer. 22:17; Ezek. 22:6–7, 12, 29; cf. also Prov. 1:10–19).[10]

We may not cheat our neighbors, employers, employees, coworkers, and clients by directly robbing them or physically harming them, but some of us are surely enticed to overcharge for labor, slack on fulfilling tasks, abuse time off, overindulge in charging the corporate card, and waste time by surfing the web on company time. Let us, like Job, vow to be honest, productive, hardworking, and loving (nonoppressive and nonexploitive!) citizens, bosses, employees, neighbors, consumers, and church members.

Responding to Job's Oath of Innocence

What should we make of Job's oath of innocence? Perhaps we find it off-putting because Job comes across to us as self-righteous (e.g., Job 31:31–33a) and self-promoting ("I" [31×], "me" [13×], "my" [44×]).[11] Or if we give his

in the very last word 'foul weeds,' in Hebrew *bosa*, we may hear an inverted echo, by a play on word sounds, of the garden story." J. Gerald Janzen, *Job*, Interpretation: A Bible Commentary for Teaching and Preaching (John Knox, 1985), 215–16.

10. Iain Provan, *Ecclesiastes/Song of Songs*, NIVAC (Zondervan, 2001), 103–4.

11. This is certainly how some commentators view Job, namely, that his oath expresses "a remarkable depth of self-righteousness in him." Kline, "Job," 482.

words a more generous reading (that Job is simply claiming that "there was no fault to be found in him" related to the specific charges against him not related to all sin),[12] we still might think it odd for a believer to make such a detailed inventory of sins followed by a disavowal of them. If we remember the historical and literary context, however, it makes sense that Job is offering a final defense. In this way, he is no different from any defendant offering self-representation in a criminal case (e.g., Paul before Agrippa in Acts 26). He is dismissing, one by one, the charges against him. "Job's oath of innocence," as Richard Belcher summarizes, "is not a statement of self-righteousness," but a claim "that he is innocent of all the charges the friends have brought against him."[13]

Beyond the original context, how might this chapter speak into our contemporary world? Do such self-evaluations deny the gospel of grace? They do not have to. In 2 Corinthians 13:5, Paul makes it clear that Christians should "examine [ourselves], to see whether [we] are in the faith," and in 2 Peter 1:10, Peter exhorts us to "confirm [our] calling and election." In context, Paul makes it clear that to "fail to meet [pass] the test" (2 Cor. 13:5) is to be found living in sin; specifically named are the sins of "quarreling, jealousy, anger, hostility, slander, gossip, conceit, and disorder" and practicing "impurity, sexual immorality, and sensuality" (12:20–21). Likewise, Peter writes of the other side of passing the test, namely, adding to saving faith sanctifying virtue, knowledge, self-control, steadfastness, godliness, brotherly affection, and love (2 Peter 1:5–7). These lists of vices and virtues can prove helpful for self-examination.

Likewise, walking through the Ten Commandments is beneficial. And if we pass the moral test, it is neither prideful nor untruthful to say so. Note how many of the Ten Commandments Job covers! Protestant Christian confessions and catechisms often use the Ten Commandments to remind us of our need for mercy *and* to show us how to live in a manner worthy of the gospel. For example, soon after we read in answer 44 of the Westminster Shorter Catechism that "we are bound to keep all his commandments," the catechism asks, "What is required in the first commandment?" (Q. 46). The answer: "The first commandment requireth us to know and acknowledge

12. John Calvin, "Sermon 118," in *Sermons on Job*, facsimile of the 1574 ed. (Banner of Truth, 1993), 555.

13. Belcher, *Job*, 230.

God to be the only true God, and our God; and to worship and glorify him accordingly." Question and answer 47 follows:

> **Q. What is forbidden in the first commandment?**
> A. The first commandment forbiddeth the denying, or not worshiping and glorifying, the true God as God, and our God; and the giving of that worship and glory to any other, which is due to him alone.

Do we affirm those words? Can we commit to live by them? Are we willing to give, like Job, an "oath of covenant allegiance"?[14]

Luther's Small Catechism similarly uses the Ten Commandments to train us in righteousness:

> **The Sixth Commandment**
> Thou shalt not commit adultery.
> *What does this mean?*
> Answer: We should fear and love God that we may lead a chaste and decent life in words and deeds, and each love and honor his spouse.
>
> **The Seventh Commandment**
> Thou shalt not steal.
> *What does this mean?*
> Answer: We should fear and love God that we may not take our neighbor's money or property, nor get them by false ware or dealing, but help him to improve and protect his property and business [that his means are preserved and his condition is improved].

The Heidelberg Catechism follows the same pattern:

> **Question 110.** What does God forbid in the eighth commandment?
> **Answer:** God forbids not only those thefts, and robberies, which are punishable by the magistrate; but he comprehends under the name of theft all wicked tricks and devices, whereby we design to appropriate to ourselves the goods which belong to our neighbor: whether it be by force, or under the appearance of right, as by unjust weights, ells, measures, fraudulent merchandise, false coins, usury, or by any other way forbidden by God; as also all covetousness, all abuse and waste of his gifts.

14. Kline, "Job," 481.

Question 111. But what does God require in this commandment?
Answer: That I promote the advantage of my neighbor in every instance I can or may; and deal with him as I desire to be dealt with by others: further also that I faithfully labor, so that I may be able to relieve the needy.

In a book called *The Beginning and End of Wisdom*, I offer five tips on how to preach Christ from Old Testament Wisdom Literature. The first tip I label "Gospel Ethics," and after I explain how seven direct quotes from the New Testament demonstrate that the early church used Wisdom Literature to reaffirm Old Testament ethics, I offer this admonition and exhortation:

> Christ-centered sermons should call us to holiness in light of Christ's incarnation (2 Peter 1:1–12, 17) and his second coming (3:11–12). Christ-centered sermons should promote the Great Commission's commission—"teaching them to observe all that I have commanded you" (Matt. 28:20a). Christ-centered sermons should make us wise in salvation through faith in Christ and train us in godliness (see 2 Tim. 3:16). Moreover, Christ-centered sermons should include Paul's confession of the work of the cross—"[Jesus] gave himself for us to redeem us from all lawlessness and to purify for himself a people . . . zealous for good works" (Titus 2:14; cf. Acts 3:26); the author of Hebrews's firm exhortations toward endurance in light of Jesus's high priesthood (e.g., 4:14); and our Lord Jesus's final words of warning (not consolation) in the Sermon on the Mount (Matt. 7:21–27).
>
> Christ-centered sermons can and should have an ethical edge to them; our messages should carry a moral weight. As we walk under the cross from Proverbs to Philippians, Ecclesiastes to Ephesians, or Job to James, we must not dull this edge or lessen this weight. Our Christ-centered sermons on the Wisdom Literature must impress upon us, on the one hand, the greatness of God and, on the other hand, our response of obedient gratitude to grace, for as Paul says: the purpose of being "filled with . . . all spiritual wisdom" is so we might "walk in a manner worthy of the Lord" (Col. 1:9–10).
>
> This requires we keep in mind various broader issues that are closely related to the gospel in the New Testament—(1) faith: the proper response to the gospel, and (2) ethics: life under the gospel.[15]

15. Douglas Sean O'Donnell, *The Beginning and End of Wisdom: Preaching Christ from the First and Last Chapters of Proverbs, Ecclesiastes, and Job* (Crossway, 2011), 122–23.

Both-And: Gospel Ethics and the Gospel

Belcher rightly argues that innocent Job models for us "what a person who fears God looks like (Job 28:28)," namely, that he is "blameless and upright" in both his inward attitudes and his outward actions (he turns "away from evil," 1:1; cf. 28:28), and thus that he is "a model of righteous behavior." But only to a point! As Belcher himself acknowledges, "And yet, in the total message of the book of Job, Job fails when he calls into question God's justice." This moral failure, along with his intellectual shortsightedness, reminds us that "whoever keeps the whole law but fails in one point has become guilty of all of it" (James 2:10) and that "none is righteous, no, not one" (Rom. 3:10). None is righteous, except, as Belcher says beautifully,

> the One who was blameless in every way, the One who kept the law in its entirety, the One who was tempted in all ways as we are yet without sin, the One who is fully righteous and can stand before God in his own righteousness. This One was also an innocent sufferer. He did not need a mediator because He is our mediator before a holy God. This is the One in whom we trust.[16]

Perfectly innocent Jesus is the antitype to innocent-of-all-charges-leveled-against-him Job. In fact, the very language of our text supports this connection. In Job 31:33, when Job claims that he has not "concealed [his] transgressions as others do by hiding [his] iniquity in [his] heart," the word "others" in the phrase "as others do" is literally *'adam*, and the ESV offers as its footnoted translation "Or *as Adam did*." Of course, the Hebrew word *'adam* can be "understood as a reference to Adam or a reference to human beings in general," but here "Adam" is best because it is clear in verse 40, with the language of "thorns" and "weeds," that Job is making a connection to Genesis, "to the sin of the first Adam that resulted in the curse of the earth,"[17] and the language in verse 33 itself (of the man's trying to hide his sin) points this way as well. The point, then, is for us to see that "Job is

16. Belcher, *Job*, 222.

17. Belcher, 220n42; cf. Norman C. Habel, *The Book of Job: A Commentary*, Old Testament Library (Westminster, 1985), 440. Job and his friends had a wealth of knowledge either through direct revelation ("in a dream, in a vision of the night," Job 33:15) or through the general spread of the word about the God of Abraham, Isaac, and Jacob.

claiming to have succeeded where Adam failed"[18] and to also see that Christ has succeeded where Job failed!

Let's flesh out this important truth by recalling what the New Testament says of Jesus. Judas admits to the chief priests and the elders, "I have sinned by betraying innocent blood" (Matt. 27:4); Pilate repeatedly declares both to the chief priests and to the crowds, "I find no guilt in this man" (Luke 23:4; cf. John 18:38; 19:4, 6), and the author of Hebrews speaks of Jesus as our High Priest who was and is "holy, innocent, unstained, separated from sinners" (Heb. 7:26). Job's innocence will get him acquitted in the end, but Jesus' innocence gets us acquitted unto the end of the ages. Job's oath offers a thorough defense, but God's oath is more enduring: "this one [Jesus] was made a priest with an oath by the one who said to him, 'The Lord has sworn and will not change his mind, "You [our Lord Jesus] are a priest forever"'" (v. 21). What are the implications of this vow? The implications are that Jesus is "the guarantor of a better covenant" (v. 22) than the covenant under Moses and the Aaronic priesthood, a new covenant under our forever Priest ("he holds his priesthood permanently," v. 24), who is "able to save to the uttermost those who draw near to God through him, since he always lives to make intercession for them [us!]" (v. 25). Yes, God who through "the word of the oath" accepted the once-and-for-all-time sacrifice of his Son, "a Son who has been made perfect" (v. 28), has made us—through his atoning blood—perfectly perfect (white as snow) and will one day make us unable to sin—to be morally perfect, innocent of all sin.

Our Savior wept that all our tears might be wiped from our eyes; he bore a thorny crown that we might have a glory-diadem; he bowed his head that we might lift up ours; he experienced reproach that we might receive welcome; he closed his eyes in death that we might gaze on unclouded brightness; he died that we might forever live;[19] and he became sin that we might become the righteousness of God—perfectly pure, wholly holy, absolutely innocent.

18. C. J. Williams, *The Shadow of Christ in the Book of Job* (Wipf & Stock, 2017), 79. I concur with Williams that Job's oath of innocence can be viewed typologically, with Christ as the antitype, but disagree with his assessment that this is "undoubtedly the crescendo of the typological imagery in the book of Job" (78) because, as I will argue, Job 42:7–9 is the cream of the typological crop.

19. Adapted from Arthur Bennett, ed., *The Valley of Vision: A Collection of Puritan Prayers and Devotions* (Banner of Truth, 2006), 77.

Enigmatic Elihu

26

Elihu: Burning with Anger

Job 32:1–33:33

Then Elihu the son of Barachel the Buzite, of the family of Ram, burned with anger. He burned with anger at Job because he justified himself rather than God. (Job 32:2)

In chapters 32–37 of Job, we are introduced to the enigmatic Elihu, "who inserts himself into the debate."[1] Richard Belcher says "inserts" because instead of waiting to see whether God will now respond to Job's oath of innocence (Job 31), "Elihu assumes that God will not answer Job because for God to appear before a human court is improper." So Elihu "steps forward to take charge of the case himself and to bring the case to an orderly close."[2] With this insertion, however, questions come to mind, such as "Is he an Israelite or Edomite?"[3] and "How

1. Richard P. Belcher Jr., *Job: The Mystery of Suffering and God's Sovereignty*, Focus on the Bible (Christian Focus, 2017), 225.

2. Belcher, 226.

3. Of all the characters, only Elihu's lineage is recorded (Job 32:2; cf. 1:1; 2:11). In Hebrew, the name Elihu is used of Israelites (1 Sam. 1:1; 1 Chron. 12:20; 26:7; 27:18), and it means "He is my God." For the view that Elihu is an Israelite, see Tremper Longman III, *Job*, Baker Commentary on the Old Testament Wisdom and Psalms (Baker Academic, 2012), 381; for the view that he is an Edomite, see Gerald H. Wilson, *Job*, Understanding the Bible Commentary 10 (Baker, 2007), 361.

long has he been listening in?" Evidently long enough to have an opinion on the matter. Elihu claims to speak for God ("I have yet something to say on God's behalf," 36:2), and the reader at this point, like Job, is longing for a word from God. But does Elihu truly speak for God?

It is difficult to know what to make of Elihu. After twenty-eight chapters of poetry, he receives a lengthy prose introduction (Job 32:1–5) and is allowed four unbroken speeches (more space than any of the other friends). In Job 42, when everything gets sorted out, God offers no rebuke to Elihu and Job offers no sacrifice on his behalf. Does this mean that God approves of his message[4] or ignores it as unimportant?[5] Does God look past this young man's offenses (i.e., he simply covers them as Job did his children's sins)? We are not told. All this leaves us to wonder whether none, some, much, or all of what Elihu says is wise and true. We wonder whether he is a long-winded, arrogant buffoon pushed onto the stage at the end of the drama for comic relief, a wise prophet whose word we should heed, or something in between those two extremes. While Elihu may want us to believe that he resembles a young Joseph (Gen. 41:38) or a young Daniel (Dan. 5:12, 14), in that he offers his inspired "wisdom" (Job 33:33) only after all the other "wise men" (34:2, 34; cf. 37:24) have offered their wisdom and failed, my view is that he is more like Jonah. That is, he is an angry young man who, in a fit of folly, misjudges the situation and the prophetic word it requires. Nevertheless, like Jonah, Elihu still speaks the word of the Lord. In other words, he is not a false prophet but a flawed one, a sometimes Spirit-inspired messenger (32:8, 18; 33:4).

Here, then, is the overview of Elihu's flawed, but at times truly prophetic, prophecy: after he introduces himself (Job 32:1–5) and gives a long apology for his need to speak (vv. 6–22), he gives the first of four speeches.[6] The first speech is a rebuke of Job (33:1–33). Elihu is like a voice crying in the wilderness (cf. Isa. 40:3)—no one is listening to him. His final three

4. Commenting on why there is no reply to Elihu, D. A. Carson writes, "If he is not praised, it is because his contribution is eclipsed by what God himself says; if he is not criticized, it is because he says nothing amiss." *How Long, O Lord? Reflections on Suffering and Evil*, 2nd ed. (Baker Academic, 2006), 148.

5. "The absence of a response," Longman suggests, "should be understood as a lack of interest" because "the bulk of Elihu's speech simply parrots what the three friends have said before." *Job*, 367.

6. Scholars divide the speeches into four sections because of the phrases "Elihu . . . answered and said" (Job 32:6), "Elihu answered and said" (34:1; 35:1), and "Elihu continued, and said" (36:1). Since his formal speech does not start until Job 33:1, I label it above "the first speech."

speeches, whatever their major and minor flaws, prepare the way of the Lord (namely, Yahweh's speeches in Job 38–41). In the second speech, Elihu asserts God's justice (34:1–37); in the third, he extols God's greatness (35:1–16); and in his brilliant and climactic fourth speech, he announces God's majesty (36:1–37:24). In this chapter, we will cover Job 32–33.

The Angry Young Man Who Must Speak (Job 32:1–22)

We are told in Job 32:1 why Eliphaz, Bildad, and Zophar "ceased to answer Job": it was because they deemed him "righteous in his own eyes." This phrase perhaps means "self-righteous," but certainly it includes the exasperating idea that Job will not admit guilt. Then we are introduced to Elihu. Unlike the record of the three friends, we are given reference to his father: he is the "son of Barachel the Buzite" (Job 32:2, 6). We also learn that he is "of the family of Ram" (v. 2) and that he "had waited to speak to Job because they were older than he" (v. 4). What is most important, however, is not his lineage, age, or respectful patience, but his emotional state:

> Then Elihu . . . *burned with anger.* He *burned with anger* at Job because he justified himself rather than God. He *burned with anger* also at Job's three friends because they had found no answer, although they had declared Job to be in the wrong. Now Elihu had waited to speak to Job because they were older than he. And when Elihu saw that there was no answer in the mouth of these three men, he *burned with anger.* (Job 32:2–5)

Burned with Anger (Job 32:1–5)

Such rage, unlike the Lord's fury in Job 42:7 ("my anger burns"), is a mix of righteous and unrighteous anger. Elihu is angry "at Job because he justified himself rather than God" (Job 32:2); that is, Job "maintained his innocence at the expense of God's own justice (33:9–12)."[7] The issue here, as Christopher Ash rightly points out, is God's honor. Elihu thinks that Job has dishonored God because he is more interested in clearing his own name than God's name. But that is a false dichotomy. What if clearing Job's name is tantamount to clearing God's name? Ash is incorrect, in my view, to state that Elihu's anger is "not an immature anger, but a defensible and

7. C. Hassell Bullock, *An Introduction to the Old Testament: Poetic Books*, rev. and expanded ed. (Moody, 1988), 93.

godly anger." Furthermore, it seems to me that Ash is also incorrect when he equates Job's self-defense with the self-righteous Pharisee in Jesus' parable (Luke 18:9–14).[8] Elihu's anger toward Job is all or mostly unrighteous anger. Yet his anger toward the three friends at least leans in the righteous-anger category. He is upset with them because they have accused Job of wrongdoing ("they had declared Job to be in the wrong," Job 32:3b) but have produced neither evidence of iniquity nor answers to his defenses ("they had found no answer," v. 3a; cf. v. 5). They were losing the debate with Job, in other words. Elihu is right that they are wrong, and he is right to be upset at their counsel.

Timid and Afraid? (Job 32:6–22)

In reaction to scholars who strongly suggest that Elihu is eccentric, angry, and arrogant (along with pompous, opinionated, brash, self-important, verbose, and banal),[9] some commentators today claim that Elihu can do no wrong,[10] or does little wrong.[11] Such a conclusion is unjustified, and some of the error of that interpretation is demonstrated in the wrongheadedness of Elihu's first words.

While Elihu might be honest in his opening statement (Job 32:6–7), his hesitancy to speak can also be read in the voice and tone of Charles Dickens's memorable character Uriah Heep. As Heep consistently talks about how humble (his "umble" below) he is, the reader senses that something is amiss:

> "When I was quite a young boy," said Uriah, "I got to know what umbleness did, and I took to it. I ate umble pie with an appetite. I stopped at the umble point of my learning, and says I, 'Hard hard!' When you offered to teach me Latin, I knew better. 'People like to be above you,' says father, 'keep yourself down.' I am very umble to the present moment, Master Copperfield, but I've got a little power!"[12]

8. Christopher Ash, *Trusting God in the Darkness: A Guide to Understanding the Book of Job* (Crossway, 2021), 107.

9. Belcher, *Job*, 226, describing "the negative view of Elihu."

10. See note 4.

11. See note 14. Cf. Choon-Leong Seow, "Elihu's Revelation," *Theology Today* 68, no. 3 (2011): 253–71. Seow lists medieval Jewish commentators who were "unanimously appreciative of Elihu" (254), along with the Protestant Reformer John Calvin, who "held Elihu in highest esteem," portraying him "as a mouthpiece of God, namely, an earthly transmitter of divine revelation" (255).

12. Charles Dickens, *David Copperfield*, in *The Works of Charles Dickens* (P. F. Collier, 1879), 272.

Elihu might have waited to talk, as he states, because young men should not interrupt their elders or speak out of turn ("I am young in years, and you are aged; therefore I was timid and afraid to declare my opinion to you. I said, 'Let days speak, and many years teach wisdom,'" Job 32:6–7). But I hold the view, based on what follows, that he is not as respectful of his elders or as "timid and afraid" as he suggests. The word "but" (*'aken*) at the start of verse 8 introduces a sharp move away from his stated humility:

> But it is the spirit in man,
> the breath of the Almighty, that makes him understand.
> It is not the old who are wise,
> nor the aged who understand what is right. (Job 32:8–9)

Elihu begins his long speech with a true statement about how wisdom comes from God (Job 32:8), not necessarily or automatically from life experience (v. 9; cf. Ps. 119:100). In light of this possibility, Elihu feels justified in opening his mouth: "Therefore I say, 'Listen to me; let me also declare my opinion'" (Job 32:10). With this contrast he is suggesting that the "breath of the Almighty" (v. 8) is breathing words into his ear that God has not breathed into the "old"/"aged" Eliphaz, Bildad, and Zophar (v. 9). "Thus he represents," as Tremper Longman states, "yet another human pretension to wisdom, a false kind of spirituality that leads to error rather than insight."[13]

Elihu seems to know that his claim could come across as overconfidence. So next, with a mixture of sureness in what he is about to say and apprehension about the one to whom he is about to say it, he feels the need to first justify himself further. It is not just that a young man, in principle, may know more than his elders; it is also that these three "wise" men have not said anything wise. "Listen," he says in effect, "I listened to your rebukes and arguments against Job ('I listened for your wise sayings,' Job 32:11b; 'I gave you my attention,' v. 12a)—quite patiently, I might add ('I waited for your words . . . while you searched out what to say,' v. 11a, c). The problem, however, is that all three of you failed to prove that Job was wrong in what he said or did ('there was none among you who refuted Job or who answered his words,' v. 12b–c). And now what do you do? Nothing! Your tongues are tied. It is no excuse to say that the wisest thing to do now ('We have found wisdom') is to hope for God to rise up

13. Longman, *Job*, 367–68.

and drive Job completely away from your presence ('God may vanquish him,' v. 13). You cannot wait for God to kill Job while you mutter: 'We did what we could. Our best shot was a good shot. Now it is time for God to shoot the target in the heart.' I will wait no longer ('And shall I wait, because they do not speak, because they stand there, and answer no more?,' v. 16). You might have grown weary and discouraged ('dismayed') from the war of words you have not won, so much so that you have nothing left to say ('they answer no more; they have not a word to say,' v. 15). But I am ready to go! Job has not yet been in the ring with me ('He has not directed his words against me,' v. 14a), and rest assured, he will not know what hit him when I use my left hook—some new and inspired logic ('I will not answer him with your speeches,' v. 14b)."

Elihu is indeed ready to go. He spends four verses telling everyone just how ready he is:

> I also will answer with my share;
>   I also will declare my opinion.
> For I am full of words;
>   the spirit within me constrains me.
> Behold, my belly is like wine that has no vent;
>   like new wineskins ready to burst.
> I must speak, that I may find relief;
>   I must open my lips and answer. (Job 32:17–20)

We find plenty of first-person personal pronouns on the lips of blameless Job, but the plethora of personal pronouns here is a bit over the top, especially since there is a melodramatic attitude from this young man attached to them. Does he need to add a third "behold" (Job 32:11, 12, now v. 19)? Is he really sure that God's spirit is within him, that what he is about to say will be purer than what Job and the three friends have said (v. 18; cf. v. 8)? Is he so constipated with amazing rebuttals to Job's speeches ("I am full of words," v. 18) that if he does not "find relief" (v. 20a) he will "burst" like unvented wine in "new wineskins" (v. 19)? Must he really speak ("I must speak"/"I must open my lips," v. 20)?

Elihu concludes his long-winded foreword to his forthcoming discourse by speaking more, a conclusion in which he assures the world that what he is about to say is pure: "I will not show partiality to any man or use flattery toward any person" (Job 32:21). Why will Elihu (presumably unlike the three friends) be impartial and abandon all obsequiousness? His answer is simple: he does not know how to do otherwise ("For I do not know how to flatter," v. 22a), and if he did know how to do such a wicked thing (which he does not!), he realizes that God would eradicate him instantaneously ("else my Maker would soon take me away," v. 22b). What a flair for drama!

Speech One: Job Rebuked (Job 33:1–33)

At long last, as we come to Job 33, we arrive at Elihu's actual first speech, a twofold rebuke to Job ("But now, hear my speech, O Job," Job 33:1; "Pay attention, O Job, listen to me," v. 31). Elihu rebukes Job, first, for claiming to be innocent (vv. 9–12) and second for not grasping that God has already spoken to Job (vv. 13–23). Both rebukes are ungrounded, but the second one adds a new idea to the debate.

In Job 32:18–20, Elihu spoke of needing to "find relief" (Job 32:20) from all the words fermenting inside him ("I am full of words," v. 18; "I must speak"/"I must open my lips," v. 20). In chapter 33, the wineskins crack (33:1–5) and then burst (vv. 6–33). In verses 1–5, as well as verses 31–33, Elihu speaks a lot about speaking: "hear my speech . . . and listen to all my words" (v. 1); "my words declare [and] . . . my lips . . . speak" (v. 3); "Pay attention, . . . listen to me; . . . I will speak. . . . Listen to me . . . , and I will teach you" (vv. 31–33). And some of his statements about speaking are so redundant that they almost overwhelm the simple beauty of the art of Hebrew poetry (e.g., "Behold, I open my mouth; the tongue in my mouth speaks," v. 2).

At both the top (Job 33:1–5) and the tail (vv. 31–33), Elihu calls on Job to listen to him, as shown in table 26.1:

Table 26.1. The Top and Tail of Job 33

But now, hear my speech, O Job, and listen to all my words. Behold, I open my mouth; the tongue in my mouth speaks. My words declare the uprightness of my heart, and what my lips know they speak sincerely. The Spirit of God has made me, and the breath of the Almighty gives me life. Answer me, if you can; set your words in order before me; take your stand. (33:1–5)	Pay attention, O Job, listen to me; be silent, and I will speak. If you have any words, answer me; speak, for I desire to justify you. If not, listen to me; be silent, and I will teach you wisdom. (33:31–33)

In these verses, Elihu provides three reasons why Job would be wise to listen. First, his words come from a pure heart and serious and sober thinking on the matter ("My words declare the uprightness of my heart, and what my lips know they speak sincerely," Job 33:3). Second, his basis for speaking is grounded in God. God has created him: "The Spirit of God has made me, and the breath of the Almighty gives me life" (v. 4). God has also, implied here (cf. 32:8, 18; 33:14), given him words to speak. Elihu talks only because God has given him wisdom. "God's own Spirit," as Barry Webb explains, has "enlivened" Elihu "for the task he is now undertaking. In other words, there is an implied claim to inspiration as the source of Elihu's boldness and authority. Job should pay particular attention to Elihu because his natural human faculties have been enhanced by the Spirit of God, giving him a wisdom greater than that of the three friends and of Job himself."[14] Thus, Elihu can confidently assert his purpose statement in the final line of his first speech: "Be silent, and I will teach you wisdom" (33:33), or as Gleason Archer charitably paraphrases: "If I have said anything so far that is unfair to you or inappropriate to your case, please tell me now. Otherwise let me continue and try to convey the wisdom the Lord has taught me in this matter."[15] Third, Elihu proposes a simple solution to Job's quandary: vindication! "I desire to justify you" (v. 32b). How? Easy! If Job would only admit his guilt (say, "I sinned," v. 27), then God would graciously "accept" (v. 26a), "deliver" (v. 24b), "ransom" (v. 24c), "redeem" (v. 28a), "bring back" (v. 30), and "restore" (v. 26c; cf. vv. 25, 28b, 30b). But notice this: while Elihu claims to have something new to say, these three reasons are no different from those offered by the three friends. The friends did not have some deep, dark ulterior motive (2:11). They too claimed to be God-made and God-inspired (e.g., 4:12–16). They offered Job justification through confession of sin, which would lead to redemption and restoration (22:21–30).

While Elihu offers no new rationale for listening to him, he does bring a few fresh arguments to the debate (Job 32:12–22). We will explore these soon. First, however, Elihu feels obliged to rebuke Job for asserting his innocence. Before this rebuke, Elihu seeks to level the playing field (33:6–7). We might imagine him as a high school principal who starts a conversation with a

14. Barry G. Webb, *Job*, Evangelical Biblical Theology Commentary (Lexham Academic, 2023), 367.

15. Gleason L. Archer Jr., *The Book of Job: God's Answer to the Problem of Undeserved Suffering* (Baker, 1982), 94.

student who is about to be expelled with gentle and affirming words before lowering the hammer of discipline. "Behold," Elihu states, "I am toward God as you are; I too was pinched off from a piece of clay" (Job 33:6). Put differently, "We are both humans whom God created out of the earth." "Elihu is so self-confident that he feels it necessary to tell Job that he is only a human like Job himself."[16] So there is no reason to be afraid of him ("no fear of me need terrify you"), for he will take it easy on Job ("my pressure will not be heavy upon you," v. 7). No, he won't, for not a second later, an elephant's weight of indictments falls on Job's boil-bleeding head. This is all that Job needs—a patronizing disclaimer followed by a personal pounding.

The personal pounding is no different from what Job has received thus far. Having listened carefully to the debate ("Surely you have spoken in my ears, and I have heard the sound of your words," Job 33:8), Elihu claims that Job's claim in Job 33:9–11 is false: "Behold, in this [see vv. 9–11] you are not right" (v. 12a). "You say, 'I am pure, without transgression; I am clean, and there is no iniquity in me. Behold, he finds occasions against me, he counts me as his enemy, he puts my feet in the stocks and watches all my paths'" (vv. 9–11). Here Elihu exaggerates Job's assertion of innocence (cf. 9:20). Job has never claimed sinless perfection (e.g., "my sin," 14:16), only that there was not a specific sin that caused his calamities. He is even open to some unknown sin, if God would only reveal it to him (7:20), or to some sin from his youth as the cause (13:26). He certainly longs for his "transgression" to "be sealed up in a bag" and buried (that God "would cover over [once and for all time!] my iniquity," 14:17). Yet Elihu does summarize well enough Job's claim that God has acted as his opponent by seeing (16:9; cf. 19:11) and seizing him. Back in chapter 13, Job said to God, "Why do you . . . count me as your enemy?" (13:24) and "You put my feet in the stocks and watch all my paths; you set a limit for the soles of my feet" (v. 27).

The basic reason why Elihu believes that Job is "not right" in claiming that he is innocent and God is guilty (Job 33:12a) is that Job has, in Elihu's estimation, reversed the roles ("God is greater than man," v. 12b), and because God is greater than man, a man such as Job cannot "contend against him" (v. 13a). God is not obliged in any way to answer Job's attestations of innocence or assertions against him ("He will answer none of man's words," v. 13b). Moreover, there is no need for God to say anything further when

16. Longman, *Job*, 368.

he has already spoken. In verses 14–22 of Job 33, Elihu lays out two ways in which God regularly speaks ("God speaks in one way, and in two"), ways that are often missed by man ("though man does not perceive it," v. 14).

First, says Elihu, God speaks through dreams ("In a dream, in a vision of the night, when deep sleep falls on men, while they slumber on their beds, then he opens the ears of men and terrifies them with warnings," Job 33:15–16). On this point, Elihu is right enough. Dreams from God are not uncommon in the Bible, occurring in the time of the patriarchs (Gen. 20:3), announcing the birth of Christ (Matt. 1:20), and even continuing into the first days of the Christian church (Acts 16:9). But Elihu imagines these dreams to be more like nightmares, the purpose of which is to suppress sin ("that he may turn man aside from his deed"), subdue pride ("conceal pride from a man," Job 33:17), and warn of the consequence of unconfessed sin: death (God, through the dreams, "keeps back his soul from the pit, his life from perishing by the sword," v. 18). Indeed, Job himself *has* experienced such nightmares ("you [God] scare me with dreams and terrify me with visions," 7:14). But he has not found them to be revelatory; certainly they have not made him aware of some sin underlying his current predicament, or provoked him to confession or repentance.

Second, Elihu says, God speaks through suffering: "Man is also rebuked with pain on his bed" (Job 33:19a). In verses 19b–22 of Job 33, Elihu details such pain. Man's body aches ("with continual strife in his bones," v. 19b); his appetite is suppressed and oppressed (he "loathes" both the basics, such as "bread," and delicacies, "the choicest food," v. 20); "his flesh" is so emaciated that he is practically see-through ("so wasted away that it cannot be seen"), and "bones" that are usually unseen—such as the rib cage and hips—now "stick out" (v. 21). According to Elihu, such suffering amounts to God's shouting, "Stop sinning before it is too late!" "His soul draws near the pit, and his life to those who bring death" (v. 22; cf. v. 18). Elihu is conveying the idea that Job should view his suffering not as an unwelcome intrusion, but as a companion sent by God to guide him toward repentance and safeguard him from death.

Of course, taken at its most general level, Elihu's insight—God speaks through suffering—is a crucial Christian concept. Indeed, he is ahead of his time! The cross of Christ is God's ultimate revelation. Our sinless God suffers on our behalf, and that suffering shouts like a bullhorn to wake up an indifferent world. But this isn't really what Elihu has in mind. Again,

Elihu is assuming that Job is guilty of not listening to God in the suffering and not grasping that the pain is not punitive or purgative but preventive.[17] But is Elihu right? Is God trying to prevent Job from sinning, as he does with Paul (2 Cor. 12:7)? Is this general principle—God speaks through suffering—true for Job? Is it "the reality . . . that Job has been deaf and not that God has been dumb"?[18] I do not believe so. Job chapters 3–31 depict Job as one who has been waiting to hear even the faintest whisper from God, and chapters 38–41 depict God as finally, and for the first time, speaking. Elihu's counsel, like that of Job's other friends, is somewhat wise, but not the counsel that Job needs in his situation.

Moreover, if there is one thing that Job certainly does *not* need to hear, it is yet another sermonette on his need for repentance and the guarantee of restoration for his definite mortal illness. But alas, that is exactly what he gets in the following verses:

> If there be for him an angel,
> a mediator, one of the thousand,
> to declare to man what is right for him,
> and he is merciful to him, and says,
> "Deliver him from going down into the pit;
> I have found a ransom;
> let his flesh become fresh with youth;
> let him return to the days of his youthful vigor";
> then man prays to God, and he accepts him;
> he sees his face with a shout of joy,
> and he restores to man his righteousness.
> He sings before men and says:
> "I sinned and perverted what was right,
> and it was not repaid to me.
> He has redeemed my soul from going down into the pit,
> and my life shall look upon the light."
>
> Behold, God does all these things,
> twice, three times, with a man,
> to bring back his soul from the pit,
> that he may be lighted with the light of life. (Job 33:23–30)

17. See Hywel R. Jones, *Job*, EP Study Commentary (Evangelical Press, 2007), 241.
18. As suggested and summarized by Jones, 240.

As stated above, Elihu offers a simple solution to Job's dilemma: if Job would only admit his guilt before God ("prays to God," Job 33:26a) and others ("He sings before men and says: 'I sinned and perverted what was right'")—if he would just recognize that the punishment he has received was more lenient than he deserved ("and it was not repaid to me," v. 27)—then "God" (v. 29) would graciously and joyously ("he sees his face with a shout of joy," v. 26b) restore his health and wealth. If he would just do these things, Elihu promises, Job's sad song will turn into a song of salvation: "He sings before men and says: '. . . He has redeemed my soul from going down into the pit, and my life shall look upon the light'" (vv. 27a, 28).

A similar *if-then* solution is offered by Eliphaz in his "Agree with God" sermon (Job 22:21–30). What is new here is that Elihu takes seriously Job's desire for a mediator (cf. 9:32–35; 16:19; 19:25). He proposes the possibility of a messenger ("an angel") who will speak on behalf of Job ("for him," 33:23a). If such a creature exists, he is rare ("a mediator, one of the thousand," v. 23b); and if he spoke for God to man, he would basically confirm Elihu's words. He would "declare to man what is right for him" (v. 23c), namely, to find God's mercy through confession of sin (v. 27). This confession will serve as man's "ransom" (v. 24c), one that will "deliver him from going down into the pit" (v. 24b, parallel with 30a) and restore his good old (young!) life: "his flesh [will] become fresh with youth"; he will "return to the days of his youthful vigor" (v. 25); he will be "lighted with the light of life" (v. 30b). Ultimately, however, Elihu has misjudged Job's situation and, consequently, mischaracterized God's dealings with man. Though God *can* shout to sinners in their suffering, and though repentance is the right response for one suffering the consequences of sin, in this case sin is not the source of Job's suffering. So Elihu's counsel that Job seek restoration through repentance comes dangerously close to treating God as a cosmic gumball machine—in goes the quarter, out comes the treat; in goes "repentance," out comes restoration.

A Bundle of Contradictions

Mike Mason labels Elihu "a bundle of contradictions—at once arrogant and sensitive, cold and passionate, brash and insecure, foolish and wise." Mason goes on to claim that Elihu is "in short exactly that sort of person whom God has often used throughout history as an instrument of revival."[19] That may or may not be true. What is certain is that Elihu's words fail to produce any stirrings of the Spirit in the heart of Job or the three friends. They are silent. This, of course, is not to say that God doesn't use Elihu for his purposes or that there is no wisdom in this otherwise arrogant, cold, brash, insecure, and foolish young man. In the next chapter, we will see something of his wisdom. But there are at least five flaws in Elihu's character and words. We will consider the first three here; the last two will come at the end of the next chapter.

He Speaks from Anger

Elihu's first flaw is that he speaks from anger. Righteous indignation is biblical. God burns in anger in Job 42:7; Jesus exhibits righteous wrath when he cleanses the temple (John 2:13–22). But this does not mean that when we read the threefold refrain in Job 32:1–5 ("He burned with anger"), Elihu's anger is also righteous. It is not. Speaking out of anger, he says things such as "What man is like Job, who drinks up scoffing like water, who travels in company with evildoers and walks with wicked men?" (Job 34:7–8). Not only are those allegations cruel, but they are also false. Job never mocks or derides God, and he certainly does not sit with scoffers. What is also cruel, arising as it does from unbridled anger, is Elihu's astringent statement to Job in 35:12–16. In those verses, he basically says "that there is simply no point of contact between Job and God. Job doesn't make any difference to God; God doesn't make any difference to Job."[20] How harsh! "The tongue is a fire," as James tells us; it is "a restless evil, full of deadly poison" (James 3:6, 8). Don't be like Elihu. Don't let your tongue burn your brothers!

His Pleading Is Annoying

Elihu's second flaw (a lesser sin) is that his pleading for a hearing is annoying. He is like the student who always raises his hand, and repeatedly says, "Oh, pick me. Pick me!" It is fine to raise a hand for every question. What is not fine is the continual "Oh, oh, oh." "I must speak," says Elihu, "that I may

19. Mike Mason, *The Gospel According to Job: An Honest Look at Pain and Doubt from the Life of One Who Lost Everything* (Crossway, 1994), 334.

20. John Goldingay, *Job for Everyone*, Old Testament for Everyone (Westminster John Knox, 2013), 173.

find relief; I must open my lips and answer" (Job 32:20). Must he? Later he will say, "If you have understanding, hear this; listen to what I say" (34:16). Yes, he likes saying words about his words: "Pay attention, O Job, listen to me" (33:31; cf. 32:10; 33:33). In fact, his preamble, which takes up a whole chapter, is a bit ridiculous. It is fine to say that one waits to speak because he is young, but when Elihu displays his "deference" with so many words, we suspect that something other than modesty is at work. He ought to get to the point, to stop saying things such as "I also will answer with my share; I also will declare my opinion" (32:17). Once we get to Job chapter 33, we expect to finally get to the meat of the matter, but first we have to hear "But now, hear my speech, O Job, and listen to all my words" (33:1), followed by "Behold, I open my mouth; the tongue in my mouth speaks" (v. 2). If Elihu has something to say, he should say it! Instead, he keeps saying that he has something to say without actually saying it.

Proverbs 25:11 declares, "A word fitly spoken is like apples of gold in a setting of silver." But with many words comes much sinning. People treat long-windedness as a genetic trait. It might be. Some of my family members must have swallowed the Blarney Stone! But excessive talking might also be a sin: "When words are many, transgression is not lacking, but whoever restrains his lips is prudent" (10:19). What D. L. Moody said of prayer, we might say of speech: "Some men's prayers need to be cut short on both ends and set on fire in the middle."[21] Elihu has more lines in the book of Job than Eliphaz, Bildad, and Zophar combined. Oh, that some of his words were set on fire! He is "full of words" (Job 32:18) but not full of wisdom! He would have done better to adhere to this proverb: "Whoever restrains his words has knowledge, and he who has a cool spirit is a man of understanding" (Prov. 17:27).

He Puts Himself Forth as a Mediator

Elihu's third flaw is that he presumes himself to be the mediator that Job has been waiting for. It is possible that when Elihu speaks of "an angel, a mediator, one of the thousand" (Job 33:23), he is speaking of an angel among

21. D. L. Moody, *Narrative of Messrs Moody and Sankey's Labors in Great Britain and Ireland*, Supplementary Issue 4 (Anson D. F. Randolph, 1895), 97–98, quoted in Nigel Scotland, *Apostles of the Spirit and Fire: American Revivalists and Victorian Britain*, Studies in Evangelical History and Thought (Wipf & Stock, 2009), 156.

the heavenly multitudes who intercedes on behalf of the man who is near death ("His soul draws near the pit," v. 22)—praying for him ("prays to God, and he [God] accepts him [the man under the judgment of death,"] v. 26) and offering a "ransom" (v. 24) that will restore this man ("his righteousness") before God (v. 26)—and who rescues the man by such intercession. Yet I side with those commentators who suggest that "Elihu himself is that messenger."[22] In Job 32:12, he said to Job, "I gave you my attention, and, behold, there was none among you who refuted Job or who answered his words." Furthermore, both here and in 33:6 and 33:23, Elihu brashly steps in to "fill this role, saying, 'Truly, I am as your spokesman before God" (33:6)."[23] If this is so, then Elihu is both "putting himself at the center of things" and displacing the need for God ("Elihu's ego is pushing through here and getting in the way of [his] giving full credit to the God whose honor he claims to be defending").[24] Williams goes so far as to call him an antichrist figure:

> By presuming to take on the role of mediator between God and man, he became an antichrist figure in the story of Job; a false mediator who would tempt Job to place his trust in man. Job knew better, and knew that he needed more than a mere man as a mediator, because the God with whom he needed to be reconciled is "not a man, as I am."[25]

While Elihu envisions a mediation that can flow through him, or some angelic figure, bringing restoration through repentance (the admission "I sinned and perverted what was right," Job 33:27), Job envisions a *heavenly* ally who would serve as a witness on his behalf without casting judgment on him or making him offer a confession of guilt. Not only are the *terms* for the mediator different—Elihu's "angel" versus Job's "arbiter" (9:33), "witness" (16:19), and "Redeemer" (19:25)—but so is the *theology*; that is, Job has in mind a divine heavenly helper (no mere man or angel) who would vindicate him—rescue him not from the pit but from false accusation. His "witness . . . in heaven" (16:19) would testify on his behalf ("he who testifies for me is on high," 16:18; "he would argue the case of a man with God," v. 21) and bring

22. Webb, *Job*, 371.
23. C. J. Williams, *The Shadow of Christ in the Book of Job* (Wipf & Stock, 2017), 66, his translations.
24. Webb, *Job*, 71.
25. Williams, *Shadow of Christ in the Book of Job*, 66.

both parties together—an "arbiter" between God and Job "who [would] lay his hand on" them "both" (9:33). In short, Job has in mind a divine Redeemer.

Elihu's third flaw is a deadly mistake, regarding both Job and everyone else who listens to his words. For to listen to Elihu is to listen to folly dressed up as conventional wisdom. Elihu can perhaps be forgiven for not foreseeing that God could take on flesh, but he is absolutely mistaken when he dismisses the possibility out of hand. Kelly Kapic writes:

> God will ultimately answer Job's questions by *becoming* Job's substitute. God will enter the human predicament. He who is Spirit will take on flesh and become fully human. He will not only see physical pain everywhere but experience it deeply himself, and he will defeat sin and all the chaos it brings about, both in the human heart and in all our relationships. The Son of God comes as God's great answer to Job's deepest questions and concerns. He comes silently, quietly, humbly. *But he comes.*[26]

Elihu can envision only a mediator who would "declare to man what is right for him" (Job 33:23); ultimately, however, the perfect Mediator would both declare what is right and make sinners right with God. Let us thank God for his plan of salvation, and let us thank God for our "arbiter," "witness," and "Redeemer"—our Lord Jesus Christ!

26. Kelly M. Kapic, *Embodied Hope: A Theological Meditation on Pain and Suffering* (IVP Academic, 2017), 69.

27

Elihu: Asserting God's Justice

Job 34:1—35:16

Therefore, hear me, you men of understanding: far be it from God that he should do wickedness, and from the Almighty that he should do wrong. (Job 34:10)

In the previous chapter, we saw how Elihu wanted his hearers to think of him as a young Joseph or Daniel—that is, as a young man who offers his inspired wisdom only after all the other wise men have offered their wisdom and failed. But he is more like the prophet Jonah in that he is an angry young man who in his arrogance wrongly assesses the prophetic situation that he has been placed into, but nevertheless, in due time, speaks the truth. He is also like Jonah, that flawed (but not false) prophet, in that he may be going the wrong way, but (unlike Jonah) only unwittingly. Moreover, he does make a few contributions to the conversation. He may be overly optimistic, however, as he pauses between Job 33:33 and 34:1 to see what Job will say. Will Job answer him ("answer me," Job 33:5, 32)?

Job for the first time gives no reply. Is his silence because he agrees with Elihu or because he has had enough fighting with fools? Likely there is a mix of both. Whatever his faults, Elihu is preparing the way for the Lord, and however bitter Job might feel after the start of the angry young man's long speech, he will listen in silence. Perhaps he is hoping for a treasure of truth, however small, to come from the misguided messenger. Yet in Elihu's second (Job 34:2–37) and third speeches (35:2–16), Job will hear only more oversimplifications from the novice theologian. Elihu, once again "confident that he has deciphered the puzzle that has baffled Job,"[1] invites the esteemed crowd to gather around him ("hear me, you men of understanding," 34:10), that they might learn how to put the pieces together.

Speech Two: Hear My Words (Job 34:1–37)

Elihu begins with a bold announcement:

Hear my words, you wise men,
  and give ear to me, you who know;
for the ear tests words
  as the palate tastes food.
Let us choose what is right;
  let us know among ourselves what is good. (Job 34:2–4)

The "wise men" here (Job 34:2), and in Job 34:10, 16, and 34 ("men of understanding"), are presumably Job, Eliphaz, Bildad, and Zophar. This sounds like mere flattery, however, since Elihu makes it clear that Eliphaz, Bildad, and Zophar are among those in whom he has found no wisdom (32:11–14), and that Job is to be counted among the wicked in that he "speaks without knowledge; his words are without insight," (34:35). Elihu wants these so-called "wise men" to learn a thing or two from him ("Hear my words"/"give ear to me," 34:2; "hear me," v. 10; "hear this"/"listen to what I say," v. 16) and to realize that understanding comes from him ("the wise man who hears me," v. 34b). The wise are those who can discern "what is right"/"what is good" (his words!) from what is wrong/bad (v. 4, their words!), just as a refined palate can taste the difference between a meal made by a master chef at La Rôtisserie d'Argent in Paris and one made by the first-day-in-the-kitchen cook at the Waffle House in Pearl River, Louisiana.

1. Daniel J. Estes, *Job*, Teach the Text (Baker, 2013), 204.

First Rebuke

The heart of this second speech is a defense of God's justice (esp. Job 34:10–30). The structure of Elihu's argument is as follows: it begins with what Job has supposedly said ("For Job has said," v. 5; "For he has said," v. 9) and should say ("For has anyone said," v. 31), followed by Elihu's own replies (vv. 7–8, 10–30, 33–37).

The first claim that Job has made, as interpreted by Elihu, is that God has unjustly denied justice to just Job:

> For Job has said, "I am in the right,
> and God has taken away my right;
> in spite of my right I am counted a liar;
> my wound is incurable, though I am without transgression."
> What man is like Job,
> who drinks up scoffing like water,
> who travels in company with evildoers
> and walks with wicked men?
> For he has said, "It profits a man nothing
> that he should take delight in God." (Job 34:5–9)

While it is true that Job has often asserted his innocence, questioned God's fairness, and seen God as warring against him, Elihu's representation is not completely accurate. Elihu glosses over the context that we, the reader, know: Job *is actually* an innocent sufferer! Moreover, Elihu leaves out a great deal of what Job has had to say. For example, where is Elihu's representation of Job's heartfelt and hope-filled cries to God and acknowledgments of God's wisdom and greatness?

In Job 34:9, Elihu advances Job's second claim: "For he has said, 'It profits a man nothing that he should take delight in God.'" Has Job ever said that it does not pay to please God? In 9:29–31, he admits to struggling with living righteously if it leads only to a condemnable existence, and in Job 21:15 he notes that the wicked say: "What is the Almighty, that we should serve him? And what profit do we get if we pray to him?" But again, Elihu has gone too far. His paraphrase of Job's position is a stretch, and it misses how Job has rebutted a similar accusation from Satan ("Does Job fear God for no reason?," 1:9). Job does not follow God merely for the perks. As Derek Thomas comments: "Elihu is unfair to Job, deeply unfair, for he makes Job out to have fallen to Satan's charge. . . . Had Job said this, the test would have been over and Satan would have been vindicated! For all Elihu's cleverness, he has, unwittingly, sided with Satan."[2] We too can side with Satan when we malign people's motives and falsely accuse them. Sadly, such ungodly behavior has become all too common a sin on social media, even among Christians. Let us be warned that God does not look down lightly on such serious transgressions.

Second Rebuke

Even more, Elihu's second rebuke (Job 34:10–30) is over the top and unnecessary. As much as he rejects and denounces the three friends, what he says here simply echoes and affirms what they themselves have said. Because of this, some commentators suggest that no one replies to Elihu's four speeches because they have all fallen asleep during the sermon! This is easy enough to do when the preacher is preaching the same three-point (make it four!) sermon that we have heard for nearly thirty chapters:

> Therefore, hear me, you men of understanding:
> far be it from God that he should do wickedness,
> and from the Almighty that he should do wrong.
> For according to the work of a man he will repay him,
> and according to his ways he will make it befall him.
> Of a truth, God will not do wickedly,
> and the Almighty will not pervert justice.
> Who gave him charge over the earth,
> and who laid on him the whole world?
> If he should set his heart to it
> and gather to himself his spirit and his breath,
> all flesh would perish together,
> and man would return to dust. (Job 34:10–15)

Point one is that God is good ("far be it from God that he should do wickedness, and from the Almighty that he should do wrong," Job 34:10b–c) and, consequently, just ("God will not do wickedly"; he "will not pervert

2. Derek Thomas, *The Storm Breaks: Job Simply Explained*, Welwyn Commentary Series (repr., Evangelical Press, 2005), 267. In "The Testament of Job," like Satan (Job 7:1), Elihu is labeled "the evil one." K. Kohler, trans., "The Testament of Job," in *Semitic Studies in Memory of Rev. Dr. Alexander Kohut* (S. Calvary & Co., 1897), 316, 333.

justice," v. 12). Point two is that God demonstrates such justice through enforcing the retribution principle: "For according to the work of a man he will repay him, and according to his ways he will make it befall him" (v. 11). Point three is that God is a self-sufficient Sovereign ("Who gave him charge over the earth, and who laid on him the whole world?," v. 13) who has such absolute power over creation that he can destroy people whenever he wants ("If he should set his heart to it and gather to himself his spirit and his breath, all flesh would perish together, and man would return to dust," vv. 14–15). "With these words," as Daniel Estes notes, "Elihu comes very close to affirming the deistic dogma that whatever is, is right."[3] Point four, based on the previous points, is that it is inappropriate to accuse a sovereign, good, and just God of acting unjustly. Comparing God to a just king, Elihu asks two rhetorical questions:

> If you have understanding, hear this;
> listen to what I say.
> Shall one who hates justice govern?
> Will you condemn him who is righteous and mighty,
> who says to a king, "Worthless one,"
> and to nobles, "Wicked man,"
> who shows no partiality to princes,
> nor regards the rich more than the poor,
> for they are all the work of his hands? (Job 34:16–19)

With the first question, Elihu assumes that the answer is obvious: God, like a righteous and mighty king, loves justice and thus governs by it. With the second question, Elihu emphasizes that God, like an impartial king, does not show favoritism: he never favors the powerful over the powerless or the rich over the poor:

> In a moment they die;
> at midnight the people are shaken and pass away,
> and the mighty are taken away by no human hand.
>
> For his eyes are on the ways of a man,
> and he sees all his steps.

3. Estes, *Job*, 207.

There is no gloom or deep darkness
    where evildoers may hide themselves.
For God has no need to consider a man further,
    that he should go before God in judgment.
He shatters the mighty without investigation
    and sets others in their place.
Thus, knowing their works,
    he overturns them in the night, and they are crushed.
He strikes them for their wickedness
    in a place for all to see,
because they turned aside from following him
    and had no regard for any of his ways,
so that they caused the cry of the poor to come to him,
    and he heard the cry of the afflicted—
When he is quiet, who can condemn?
    When he hides his face, who can behold him,
    whether it be a nation or a man?—
that a godless man should not reign,
    that he should not ensnare the people. (Job 34:20–30)

In these verses, Elihu moves beyond the analogy of God as a good earthly king and judge to his status as the almighty God who sees all ("his eyes are on the ways of a man, and he sees all his steps," Job 34:21; he knows "their works," v. 25a) and judges all without any need for a drawn-out court case ("God has no need to consider a man further. . . . He shatters the mighty without investigation," vv. 23–24). Even the seemingly invincible ("the mighty," vv. 20, 24), who think they have gotten away with evil, are soon found out ("There is no gloom or deep darkness where evildoers may hide themselves," v. 22), promptly punished ("in a moment they die; at midnight the people are shaken and pass away," v. 20a–b; "he overturns them in the night, and they are crushed," v. 25b) directly by God ("are taken away by no human hand," v. 20c; "he strikes them for their wickedness") for turning aside ("from following him" and "his ways") and for afflicting "the poor" (vv. 26–28), and replaced (God "sets others in their place," v. 24b). God acts justly! He makes sure that wicked rulers are deposed. He does not allow a "godless man" to "reign" and "ensnare the people" (v. 30). Thus, only a godless man (such as Job!) would ever condemn God for the way he rules the world. Job must learn the lesson of Job 34:29: if God chooses to be silent

("When he is quiet"/"When he hides his face"), there is no man or nation in a position to find him ("who can behold him?") and pass judgment on him ("who can condemn?"). God rules however he sees fit.

So if Job wants to say anything further ("For Job has said," Job 34:5; "he has said," v. 9), Elihu suggests, he should learn from God's disciplinary hand that his sins should be confessed, not God condemned. Job should say, "I have borne punishment; I will not offend any more" (v. 31b) and "teach me what I do not see; if I have done iniquity, I will do it no more" (v. 32). But it is rare for people to do so ("has anyone said" such things "to God?," v. 31a). Job certainly has not done so yet.

In Conclusion

Elihu ends his second speech by turning first to Job ("Will he then make repayment to suit you, because you reject it? For you must choose, and not I; therefore declare what you know," Job 34:33), then to what he assumes that the wise will say about his brilliant assessment (vv. 34–35), and finally to all who are sitting at his feet and awaiting his climactic conclusion (vv. 36–37). First, he says to Job (the "you" is singular in v. 33) in effect: "Let me make clear to you that you have rejected God's terms. God is not going to reward you ['make repayment to suit you']. You have a choice to make ['you must choose']. I look forward to your making a wise decision. Let me know what you decide ['declare what you know']." Then egocentric Elihu adds what will be the response of the wise:

> Men of understanding will say to *me*,
>   and the wise man who hears *me* will say:
> "Job speaks without knowledge;
>   his words are without insight." (Job 34:34–35)

It is not enough that Elihu calls Job an idiot ("Job is not only a sinner," but "stupid" too![4]) and does so through a pretend response to a sermon that is not yet finished. He must also end with a curse (hoping that Job will experience even further punishment: "Would that Job were tried to the end," Job 34:36a) and four unfeeling and ungrounded accusations (vv. 36b–37):

4. Thomas, *The Storm Breaks*, 269.

1. "He answers like wicked men."
2. "He adds rebellion to his sin."
3. "He claps his hands among us."
4. He "multiplies his words against God."

Perhaps it is true that Job is guilty of a sinful statement or two in his honest responses in the midst of his sufferings, but is it true to say, as Elihu does here, that Job is guilty not only of sin and stupidity, but "of sedition, of mutiny against God"?[5] That is hardly fitting, or fair!

Speech Three: Extolling God's Greatness (Job 35:1–16)

As we transition to Elihu's third speech, take note that his content and tone have changed dramatically from the first speech. Thomas points out that Elihu's words have been getting progressively darker. "All compassion is gone" by the time we get to the second speech. Whereas the first speech had "promising words about a mediator in the heavenly courts defending the cause of the likes of Job," all that promise is replaced in the second speech by "the sound of cold, analytical logic." Moreover, whereas "the first speech had closed with a note of joy," the second speech "closes in doom." Thomas suggests that these changes are due to pride (Elihu loves hearing "his own rhetoric") and that Elihu has "managed to gain the attention of the greybeards of wisdom," those men of understanding whom he beckoned to come closer to hear his words of wisdom.[6] Whatever the motives, the content and tone grow even colder. Elihu has the audacity to say to blameless and upright Job that his righteousness makes no difference to God. Of course, we know from the prologue what Elihu does not know, namely, that "God has a huge stake in Job's righteousness."[7]

Lowering the Hammer (Again!)

This shorter third speech begins with Elihu's answering ("And Elihu answered and said," Job 35:1) his own assertions. We might be surprised that he does not answer with self-congratulations, "Amen, preach it!" But in light

5. Thomas, 269.
6. Thomas, 266.
7. J. Gerald Janzen, *Job*, Interpretation: A Bible Commentary for Teaching and Preaching (John Knox, 1985), 220.

of the whole of the sermon, perhaps that would be the better option instead of once again lowering the hammer on poor Job. The multiple instances of the word "you" (14× in the ESV translation) in the singular (namely, you, Job) are the fourteen nails he uses to drive home his point that God is so great that he does not care about the superficial cries of sinners such as Job.

Elihu starts with a loaded question to Job: "Do you think this to be just?" (Job 35:2a). The "this" follows: Elihu wants to know whether Job thinks he is right in claiming, "It is my right before God" (v. 2b), the sense being "I am right and God is wrong," or perhaps "I am righteous before God." Elihu also wants to know whether Job really believes what he has supposedly stated before: "What advantage have I? How am I better off than if I had sinned?" (v. 3). These queries are twisted and exaggerated representations of Job's cries to God for help and pleas to his friends to bring true wisdom to his inexplicable situation. They are loosely based on overhearing Job's press conferences before a looking-for-a-sound-bite gotcha journalist: "[God,] you know that I am not guilty" (10:7a); "[God,] what profit do [I] get if [I] pray?" (21:15b); "[God,] far be it from me to say that you [in context: the friends, not God] are right; till I die I will not put away my" absolutely perfect "integrity" (27:5). These so-called press conferences, by the way, are given while Job is under extraordinary duress. He is living through unimaginable pain—financial bankruptcy, the loss of ten children, festering sores from top to toe, and the silence of his speaking God.

When Elihu asks Job, "Do you think this to be just?" (Job 35:2), he is not posing a serious question; it is a straw man that has been set up to push down and burn. The clause "I will answer you and your friends with you" (v. 4) is one of the most arrogant statements in the Bible. How condescending! After putting words in Job's mouth, now Elihu makes sure that his own words of "wisdom" are heard, because, after all, that is to him the only wisdom that can possibly shed light on this situation. Distorting Job's heartbreaking question "What is man, that you make so much of him?" (7:17a), Elihu orates:

> Look at the heavens, and see;
> and behold the clouds, which are higher than you.
> If you have sinned, what do you accomplish against him?
> And if your transgressions are multiplied, what do you do to him?
> If you are righteous, what do you give to him?
> Or what does he receive from your hand?

Your wickedness concerns a man like yourself,
and your righteousness a son of man. (Job 35:5–8)

The substance of this section of the third sermon is simple: it is merely an expansion of Eliphaz's earlier musings (Job 22:2–3). God is too big and Job is too small for God to pay attention to Job's puny pleas. Both Job's righteousness and his unrighteousness might affect other human beings, but they do not affect God. He is too far removed!

We have read the prologue to this book and Elihu has not, so we might be lenient on him here, or else we might be disgusted by this deistic-like view of God. The latter response is more appropriate. As Christians, we know that God is both transcendent and immanent. We also sense that this is how Job understood God and has spoken about him. To Job, the struggle is between his firm theological convictions (God is not a distant and detached deity but a near and involved friend) and his current experience (God seems distant and detached from his sufferings, so far removed and unfriendly).

It is worth noting here that while it is true that "God is neither hurt nor helped by our sin," it is absolutely false—according to the whole testimony of Scripture—that "whatever happens on earth is of little concern to God, even if it is wickedness."[8] A barrage of biblical texts come to mind, such as God's immediate and personal response to humanity's first sin. God descends into the garden, walks over to Adam and Eve, starts up a conversation, levies a just (and gracious!) punishment, but then promises the gospel to come while clothing their shame in the meantime (see Gen. 3:8–21). Other examples that God is both grieved by sin and abounding in steadfast love and mercy abound. Think of the language Moses uses to record Abraham's response to God's plan to destroy Sodom: "Then Abraham drew near [to God] and said, 'Will you indeed sweep away the righteous with the wicked?'" (18:23). Or think of similar words, from just a few chapters earlier, in the record of the flood narrative:

> *The* Lord *saw that the wickedness of man* was great in the earth, and that every intention of the thoughts of his heart was only evil continually. And the *Lord regretted* that he had made man on the earth, and *it grieved him to his heart.* So the Lord said, "I will blot out man whom I have created from the face of the land, man and animals and creeping things and birds of the

8. Thomas, *The Storm Breaks*, 271.

> heavens, for I am sorry that I have made them." But *Noah found favor in the eyes of the Lord*. (Gen. 6:5–8)

Of course, the greatest example of this principle is played out in Jesus' own death. "This is precisely the paradox of the gospel," writes Mike Mason, in that "there is an answer to Elihu's rhetorical question, 'If you sin, how does that affect [God]?' [35:6 NIV] and the answer is: it crucifies him." Mason continues: "Yes, there is a wall between God and man, but the cross breaks down that wall and so produces a common ground upon which man's sin *does* directly affect God, in order that God's righteousness might also directly affect man. It is the cross that brings God close, that literally pins his shoulders to the mat and holds him there until he blesses us [cf. Gen. 32:22–32]."[9]

The Second Half

As we return to the second half of Elihu's third speech, things only get worse for Job. Next, Elihu discounts Job's genuine lamentations as hypocritical defamations. When most people are in trouble because powerful tyrants are tyrannizing them ("Because of the multitude of oppressions people cry out; they call for help because of the arm of the mighty," Job 35:9), they ultimately implore God to do something: "Save us!" According to Elihu, Job is like these foxhole atheists. But Elihu asks, in effect, where the really righteous person is who wonders, "Where is God my Maker, who gives songs in the night, who teaches us more than the beasts of the earth and makes us wiser than the birds of the heavens?" (vv. 10–11). Elihu is a confused deist, for out of one side of his mouth he says, "The First Cause does not care about earthlings," but out of the other side he chides, "Why are there not more pious prayers from the pinnacle of creation (humans) to the glorious Creator, the one who provides for and protects his people?" We know that this young man must not have gone to seminary yet, but still there is something theologically amiss here.

This sort of confusion continues for the remainder of his speech. It will, however, find its resting place, as Jonah does in Nineveh, when Elihu finally speaks the word of the Lord (he does have some good things to say!). But first we come to Job 35:12–16:

9. Mike Mason, *The Gospel According to Job: An Honest Look at Pain and Doubt from the Life of One Who Lost Everything* (Crossway, 1994), 359–60.

> There they cry out, but he does not answer,
>   because of the pride of evil men.
> Surely God does not hear an empty cry,
>   nor does the Almighty regard it.
> How much less when you say that you do not see him,
>   that the case is before him, and you are waiting for him!
> And now, because his anger does not punish,
>   and he does not take much note of transgression,
> Job opens his mouth in empty talk;
>   he multiplies words without knowledge.

These words are nauseating; Job is being repeatedly stabbed in the soul. He has said that he cannot see what God is doing ("I do not perceive him," Job 9:11), that he wishes for some sort of legal hearing before his Judge (23:4; 31:35), that he hopes that God might rescue him (13:15; 14:14), and yet that it seems as though God is not playing fair (9:24; 12:6; 21:17). But what does Elihu do with these honest statements? He "takes Job's words and spins them so that they sound like an arrogant rejection of God."[10]

Elihu claims that Job and people like him "cry out" to God but that "he does not answer" or "regard" their petition because "the pride of evil men" makes God indifferent to their "empty cry" (Job 35:12–13). Elihu asserts that the more Job protests as he waits for some imaginary court case, the worse he makes matters ("How much less when you say that you do not see him, that the case is before him, and you are waiting for him!," v. 14). Because God is so distant and detached—"his anger does not punish" and "he does not take much note of transgression" (v. 15; Elihu is hoping to impress everyone with his high view of God)—Job's words are like dandelion fluff trying to stay on the stem through a hurricane. "Job opens his mouth" (v. 16a), and what comes out? "Empty talk" ("empty" in verse 16a is *hebel*)—mere breath, smoke curling up into the air. Job "multiplies words without knowledge" (v. 16b). Ouch! What an unfair criticism and cruel accusation. What would Elihu make, one wonders, of the Father's "no" to Jesus' threefold prayer in Gethsemane (Mark 14:32–42), or of God's "no" to Paul's plea to remove his thorn in the flesh (2 Cor. 12:1–10)? Elihu has no category for a God whose "no" is good, wise, and powerful enough to save the world and gentle enough to keep a powerful Christian preacher humble.

10. Estes, *Job*, 215. I also credit Estes for the references in the sentence above.

Two More Flaws to Avoid

Three down; one to go. We have listened alongside Job (poor man!) to three of the worst sermonettes in the Bible. Something positive will be said in the fourth sermon, and while we can admit that Elihu has an earnest zeal to defend the justice of God and offers a noble attempt to engage with Job's words and to rescue him, in the end (or, at least, the end of Job 35), we are left with little so far to admire and emulate. Following the conclusion of the previous sermon, where I summarized three flaws (Elihu speaks from anger, his pleading to be heard is annoying, and he puts himself forth as a mediator)—in the hope that we would be and do the opposite—here I offer two more.

He Is Arrogant

Elihu's fourth flaw is that he is arrogant or, as Mason states, "enormously conceited" and "an astonishingly pompous little windbag."[11] Not only does Elihu talk down to Job in front of others—such as when he says, "Job opens his mouth in empty talk; he multiplies words without knowledge" (Job 35:16)—he further follows that with "I have yet something to say on God's behalf" (36:2) and "I will get my knowledge from afar" (v. 3). Elihu claims to have heard from Yahweh—the God who has been silent to righteous Job. And what does the Lord say? He says what Elihu says! As Elihu puts it, "truly my words are not false; one who is perfect in knowledge is with you" (v. 4).

This proud flaw warns us to be careful in our God-talk (e.g., "God told me to say this to you"). It is so easy to hide our pride under the pretense of prophecy. For example, if someone is leaving a church because of a relational difficulty, dislike of the pastor's preaching, or a sense that the direction in which the church is going is unbiblical, he must not tell everyone that he is leaving because God told him to do so. We must not use the Lord's name in vain! In his book *Hope Beyond Cure*,[12] Dave McDonald writes about Christians who tell cancer patients that God will heal them if they just believe. In one instance, one false prophet had a word from the Lord that the cancer would be gone by the end of the week. Such counsel is devilish. We ought to be careful when we "speak for God," as Elihu claimed to do.

11. Mason, *Gospel According to Job*, 343.
12. David McDonald, *Hope Beyond Cure* (Matthias Media, 2018).

His Accusation Is Off

Elihu's fifth flaw is that his accusation is off. Eliphaz, Bildad, and Zophar have claimed that Job's suffering is caused by Job's sin. Elihu claims that "Job's greatest sin may not be something he said or did *before* the suffering started, but the rebellion he is displaying *in* the suffering."[13] In other words, Job has sinned in what he has said to God from his opening words in Job chapter 3 till Elihu arrived on the scene to offer saving wisdom. The distinction between his criticism and Job's friends' criticism is minor. Elihu's retribution theology echoes theirs. For example, in 34:11 he says, "For according to the work of a man [God] will repay him, and according to his ways he will make it [good or bad] befall him." In 34:36–37 he says: "Would that Job were tried to the end, because he answers like wicked men. For he adds rebellion to his sin; he claps his hands among us and multiplies his words against God." In 36:11 he promises blessing to those who listen to God's instruction: "If they listen and serve him, they complete their days in prosperity, and their years in pleasantness." He is just the B-side to the same broken record. As John Goldingay puts it: "For all his protestations that he has something new to say, Elihu's understanding of Job's position and of how life with God works is not so different from that of the friends. Job is suffering, so he must have sinned, and he needs to repent."[14] The B-side is a little better than the A-side, but it is just as scratched as the other, and its song is still distorted. Did Job sin before his suffering (as the first three friends claim) or during his suffering (as Elihu claims)? The answer to the first question is certainly "no," and the answer to the second, based on God's own final evaluation (that his "servant Job" has "spoken of [God] what is right," Job 42:7), appears to be "no" as well. Elihu's accusation is as far off as the accusations of Eliphaz, Bildad, and Zophar.

A Mouthpiece of God?

My assessment of Elihu thus far has been mostly negative. I do not view him as the esteemed exegete John Calvin did, namely, as the Spirit-inspired

13. D. A. Carson, *How Long, O Lord? Reflections on Suffering and Evil*, 2nd ed. (Baker Academic, 2006), 149–50.

14. John Goldingay, *Job for Everyone*, Old Testament for Everyone (Westminster John Knox, 2013), 166.

mouthpiece of God. But like the medieval manuscript from the Monastery of St. John in Patmos that pictures God in heaven and Elihu on earth, right below God, extending their right hands simultaneously toward Job as they speak to him (and thus symbolizing that God and Elihu are on the same page),[15] I do view what Elihu says next to be truly prophetic and divinely approved.

15. An illustration can be found in Choon-Leong Seow, "Elihu's Revelation," *Theology Today* 68, no. 3 (2011): 256.

28

Elihu: Announcing God's Majesty

Job 36:1–37:24

Hear this, O Job; stop and consider the wondrous works of God.
(Job 37:14)

Like the flawed prophet Jonah finally arriving at Nineveh to give his prophetic pronouncement, we as readers of Elihu's speeches are longing for a God-given message from the thus-far-often-pathetic prophet. We can celebrate that Elihu has proclaimed God's justice and extolled his greatness. But surely, when we come to his final two chapters—in which he preaches the good news of God's majesty—we realize that, however flawed a messenger he may be, there is something both profound and preparatory here. God is soon to speak—so let us listen.

Something to Say on God's Behalf (Job 36:1–25)

Before we hear his pure words, Elihu introduces his fourth speech ("And Elihu continued, and said," Job 36:1) with an arrogant assertion of his divine inspiration and Godlike knowledge:

> Bear with me a little, and I will show you,
>   for I have yet something to say on God's behalf.
> I will get my knowledge from afar
>   and ascribe righteousness to my Maker.
> For truly my words are not false;
>   one who is perfect in knowledge is with you. (Job 36:2–4)

The fact that Elihu describes God in his forthcoming speech as "perfect in knowledge" (Job 37:16) demonstrates that he is unwittingly destroying his own argument; that is, he is claiming that no one is like God, but here he starts by essentially saying, "Well, except me, I suppose." Tremper Longman thus labels him "narcissistic,"[1] and Eric Ortlund observes that "his self-importance does not generate much confidence in this theology."[2] Yet Elihu next rightly (and thankfully!) turns a theological corner and heads in the right direction. He exalts God's power. His favorite word, "behold," is used four times in Job chapter 36 to emphatically introduce this main point: "Behold, God is mighty, and does not despise any; he is mighty in strength of understanding" (36:5); "Behold, God is exalted in his power; who is a teacher like him?" (v. 22); "Behold, God is great, and we know him not; the number of his years is unsearchable" (v. 26); "Behold, he scatters his lightning about him and covers the roots of the sea" (v. 30). In these four verses, God's power is linked to his wisdom and his wisdom to his justice. Elihu asserts that God's cosmic authority ensures his wise governance and judgment of the world, themes that God himself will address in due time.

While Elihu's tone has softened, his theological position has not changed. In Job 36:5–25, the same broken record is played: *Retribution Principle's Greatest Hits*. Job has to sit and listen to more of this atrociously off-key album. Elihu's allegedly perfect knowledge is for Job personally ("you," "your," and "yourself," 20× in Job 35). What Job presumably needs to know is what he has already heard, namely, that God is using suffering to save him from his sin and that Job needs to be willing to submit to this discipline and

1. Tremper Longman III, *Job*, Baker Commentary on the Old Testament Wisdom and Psalms (Baker Academic, 2012), 367. Other scholars, such as Choon-Leong Seow, take Elihu's claim to be "perfect in knowledge" as a positive reflection that he is indeed "a divinely inspired intermediary," "an earthly reflex of the perfection of knowledge that is divine." See "Elihu's Revelation," *Theology Today* 68, no. 3 (2011): 264, 271. I side with Longman.

2. Eric Ortlund, *Piercing Leviathan: God's Defeat of Evil in the Book of Job*, New Studies in Biblical Theology (IVP Academic, 2021), 58.

allow God to correct him. The principle is plainly laid out in verses 5–15 of chapter 36 and the application in verses 16–25. Verses 5–15 focus mostly on God:

> Behold, God is mighty, and does not despise any;
> he is mighty in strength of understanding.
> He does not keep the wicked alive,
> but gives the afflicted their right.
> He does not withdraw his eyes from the righteous,
> but with kings on the throne
> he sets them forever, and they are exalted.
> And if they are bound in chains
> and caught in the cords of affliction,
> then he declares to them their work
> and their transgressions, that they are behaving arrogantly.
> He opens their ears to instruction
> and commands that they return from iniquity.
> If they listen and serve him,
> they complete their days in prosperity,
> and their years in pleasantness.
> But if they do not listen, they perish by the sword
> and die without knowledge.
>
> The godless in heart cherish anger;
> they do not cry for help when he binds them.
> They die in youth,
> and their life ends among the cult prostitutes.
> He delivers the afflicted by their affliction
> and opens their ear by adversity.

God is powerful, wise, and fair (Job 36:5). Evil men are judged ("He does not keep the wicked alive") and the oppressed are saved (he "gives the afflicted their right," v. 6). God's watchful protection ("He does not withdraw his eyes from the righteous") ensures that good people prosper and that the righteous are promoted as rulers ("but with kings on the throne he sets them forever, and they are exalted," v. 7; or the sense of v. 7b might be that God raises up good kings to rule over these good people). If these good people sin, however (God "declares to them their work and their transgressions, that they are behaving arrogantly," v. 9; "iniquity," v. 10b), God sends suffering to wake them up. It is when "they are bound in chains and caught in the cords of affliction" (v. 8) that God tells them where they have sinned. The godly hear God's voice in the pain and return to him: "they listen and serve him" (v. 11a). Then what happens? God rewards the righteous: "they complete their days in prosperity, and their years in pleasantness" (v. 11b–c). By contrast, what happens to those who will not listen—to "the godless in heart" who "cherish anger" or "harbor resentment" (NIV) toward God and "do not cry [to God] for help when he binds them" (v. 13)? Those who will not learn from the school of suffering will die an unexpected, violent, and disgraceful death—either by sword ("if they do not listen, they perish by the sword and die without knowledge," v. 12) or by some sexually transmitted disease ("They die in youth, and their life ends among the cult prostitutes," v. 14; "They die when they are young, after wasting their lives in immoral living," NLT).

Elihu wants Job to understand that this general principle—that God "delivers the afflicted by their affliction and opens their ear by adversity" (Job 36:15)—is good news for Job personally. Through the gift of punitive pain, God is wooing Job out of the slough of despond ("He also allured you out of distress"), seeking to move him to a safe place ("into a broad place"), where he will be free from suffering ("where there was no cramping"), with a feast awaiting him (a "table . . . full of fatness," v. 16). Basically, all that Job needs to do is to say what the psalmist says: "Before I was afflicted I went astray, but now I keep your word" (Ps. 119:67). But what has Job done instead? He has done the opposite, and for this Elihu lays into him: *But you!* "But you are full of the judgment on the wicked; judgment and justice seize you" (Job 36:17).

In verses 18–25 of Job 36, Elihu offers five admonitions, which we can trace by noticing the key verbs: "beware" (Job 36:18), "do not long for" (v. 20), "take care" (v. 21), "behold" (v. 22), and "remember" (v. 24):

> Beware lest wrath entice you into scoffing,
>   and let not the greatness of the ransom turn you aside.
> Will your cry for help avail to keep you from distress,
>   or all the force of your strength?
> Do not long for the night,
>   when peoples vanish in their place.

Take care; do not turn to iniquity,
for this you have chosen rather than affliction.
Behold, God is exalted in his power;
who is a teacher like him?
Who has prescribed for him his way,
or who can say, "You have done wrong"?

Remember to extol his work,
of which men have sung.
All mankind has looked on it;
man beholds it from afar.

First, Elihu warns Job that even though his loss has been great ("let not the greatness of the ransom"), he should still return to God (do not let the losses "turn you aside," Job 36:18b) and certainly should not allow his anger to lead to mocking God ("Beware lest wrath entice you into scoffing," v. 18a). The loud, angry cries need to stop, since they are not helping Job's cause: "Will your cry for help avail to keep you from distress, or all the force of your strength?" (v. 19). Second, Elihu warns Job not to "long for the night" (v. 20a; perhaps an allusion to death), because there is no safety even in sleep ("when peoples vanish in their place," v. 20b)—perhaps alluding to criminal activities that happen at night (cf. 24:14–17), including murder (v. 14; cf. 36:12). Third, Elihu accuses Job of choosing to sin in the pain rather than listening to the pain ("for this you have chosen rather than affliction," 36:21b), and he exhorts him to stop such wicked behavior ("Take care; do not turn to iniquity," v. 21a). Fourth, instead of touting his innocence and demanding his rights, Job needs to acknowledge God's power ("Behold, God is exalted in his power"), wisdom ("who is a teacher like him?," v. 22), sovereign freedom ("Who has prescribed for him his way"), and justice ("or who can say, 'You have done wrong'?," v. 23). Fifth, Job also needs to "remember to extol [God's] work" (v. 24a), joining all humankind in noticing God's justice (see Deut. 32:4, "his work is perfect, for all his ways are justice"), mighty deeds (see "work"/"mighty deeds" in Ps. 77:12), and creation (see Job 37:14, 16; "All mankind has looked on it; man beholds it from afar," 36:25) and even singing about it ("of which men have sung," v. 24b; cf. Ps. 77:6, "Let me remember my song in the night").

Behold, God Is Exalted in Power (Job 36:26–37:24)

While the admonitions above are excellent and would apply in many situations to many people, once again they do not fit Job's situation. Elihu's assessment is inaccurate. But an important shift has occurred in Job 36:22. When Elihu says, "Behold, God is exalted in his power," he moves the discussion beyond Job alone to everyone then listening and now reading. He wants us all to behold God! And as he "breaks into [his] hymn of praise to the God of creation"[3] (Job 36:26–37:24), we sense that Elihu might indeed "have yet something to say on God's behalf" (36:2) that is true even in Job's situation. The two key admonitions here are to (1) "stop and consider the wondrous works of God" (37:14) so as to (2) "fear him" (v. 24). Both these admonitions tie in to important ideas in chapters 1–2 and 28. They also connect closely with what God himself will ask Job to do in Job 38:1–40:2 and 40:6–41:34,[4] and what Job himself will do in Job 40:3–5 and 42:1–6. "Elihu's magnificent conclusion drives us on toward the climax of the whole magnificent book,"[5] and it serves "to set the stage for his divine successor."[6] And as a point of application for us, no matter what we wrestle with theologically and experientially, if we move toward God's majesty, we are moving in the right direction.

The First Admonition

The first admonition focuses on God's awesome power displayed throughout creation, from the sun (the "light," Job 37:21) to the "roots of the sea" (36:30b). Elihu especially focuses on God's control ("he draws up," v. 27a; "he covers," v. 32a; he "commands," v. 32b; "he says, 'Fall on the earth,'" 37:6a) of storms, including clouds, thunder, lightning, rain, snow, ice, and winds (see table 28.1).

3. Derek Thomas, *The Storm Breaks: Job Simply Explained*, Welwyn Commentary Series (repr., Evangelical Press, 2005), 281.

4. The latter part of Elihu's fourth speech (Job 36:24–37:24) connects to Yahweh's theophany "in form (as in the use of a series of rhetorical questions to establish the distance between the infinite God and the finite mortal) and in content (as in the appeal to meteorological phenomena)," and also in "the role that God will play in the speeches that follow: God as teacher without peer (36:22b) over whose conduct none has oversight (36:23a)." Seow, "Elihu's Revelation," 267–68.

5. Christopher Ash, *Trusting God in the Darkness: A Guide to Understanding the Book of Job* (Crossway, 2021), 112.

6. J. Gerald Janzen, *Job*, Interpretation: A Bible Commentary for Teaching and Preaching (John Knox, 1985), 224.

Table 28.1. God of the Storm

Clouds, thunder, and lightning	"Can anyone understand the spreading of the clouds, the thunderings of his pavilion? Behold, he scatters his lightning about him and covers the roots of the sea" (Job 36:29–30); "He covers his hands with the lightning and commands it to strike the mark. Its crashing declares his presence; the cattle also declare that he rises" (36:32–33); "Under the whole heaven he lets it go, and his lightning to the corners of the earth. After it his voice roars; he thunders with his majestic voice, and he does not restrain the lightnings when his voice is heard" (37:3–4); "He loads the thick cloud with moisture; the clouds scatter his lightning. They turn around and around by his guidance, to accomplish all that he commands them on the face of the habitable world" (37:11–12); "Do you know how God lays his command upon them and causes the lightning of his cloud to shine? Do you know the balancings of the clouds, the wondrous works of him who is perfect in knowledge?" (37:15–16).
Waters	"For he draws up the drops of water; they distill his mist in rain, which the skies pour down and drop on mankind abundantly" (36:27–28); "For to the snow he says, 'Fall on the earth,' likewise to the downpour, his mighty downpour" (37:6); "By the breath of God ice is given, and the broad waters are frozen fast" (37:10).
Winds	"From its chamber comes the whirlwind, and cold from the scattering winds" (37:9); "you whose garments are hot when the earth is still because of the south wind" (37:17); "And now no one looks on the light when it is bright in the skies, when the wind has passed and cleared them" (37:21).

In such storms, God speaks:

Keep listening to the thunder of his voice
  and the rumbling that comes from his mouth.
Under the whole heaven he lets it go,
  and his lightning to the corners of the earth.
After it his voice roars;
  he thunders with his majestic voice,
  and he does not restrain the lightnings when his voice is heard.
God thunders wondrously with his voice;
  he does great things that we cannot comprehend. (Job 37:2–5)

Both man and beast acknowledge God's power (Job 36:33; 37:7–8), but humans—uniquely among the rest of creation—are "wise in their own conceit" (37:24b) and presume to answer back to God's thundering voice (vv. 19–20). Instead, humanity is called to "fear him" (v. 24a), to stand before his light and his power in chastened humility.

The Second Admonition

The fear of God is Elihu's second main admonition. In context, to fear God is not only to be in awe of his awesomeness ("God is clothed with awesome majesty," Job 37:22b) or to shake before his presence ("my heart trembles and leaps out of its place," v. 1), but also to humbly acknowledge that God governs the world justly (with the same storm "he judges" some people and "gives food in abundance" to others, 36:31; "for correction . . . or for love," 37:13) and that human beings cannot teach God how to run the world ("Teach us what we shall say to him; we cannot draw up our case because of darkness. Shall it be told him that I would speak? Did a man ever wish that he would be swallowed up?," vv. 19–20), because we do not fully comprehend how he controls everything:

> Behold, God is great, and *we know him not*;
> the number of his years is unsearchable. (Job 36:26)
>
> *Can anyone understand* the spreading of the clouds,
> the thunderings of his pavilion? (36:29)
>
> God thunders wondrously with his voice;
> he does great things that *we cannot comprehend*. (37:5)
>
> *Do you know* how God lays his command upon them
> and causes the lightning of his cloud to shine?
> *Do you know* the balancings of the clouds,
> the wondrous works of him who is perfect in knowledge,
> you whose garments are hot
> when the earth is still because of the south wind? (37:15–17)
>
> The Almighty—*we cannot find him*;
> he is great in power;
> justice and abundant righteousness he will not violate. (37:23)

It is this kind of humility, therefore, that Elihu seeks to cultivate when he remarks that God "does not regard any who are wise in their own conceit" (Job 37:24b). Those who fear God know that they do not know what God knows, and they know that God has wise designs for the ways in which he rules his creation, whether or not we can perceive his purposes.

Elihu's expression of confidence in God's unseen purposes is another rebuke to Job ("Hear this, O Job," Job 37:14), but this time it is a right rebuke, since it aligns with what God himself will say next. God, whose voice thunders (40:9; cf. 37:2) as he speaks out of a whirlwind (38:1; 40:6; cf. 37:9), will refer to his rule of creation, including clouds (38:9, 34, 37), rain (vv. 25a, 28), snow (v. 22), lightning (vv. 25b, 35), ice (v. 30), and "springs of the sea" (v. 16).

Layton Talbert provides an excellent summary of five "thematic parallels [that] connect the speeches of Elihu and God." First, Elihu focuses more on Job's words than alleged actions. Second, he criticizes Job's defense of his own righteousness at the expense of upholding God's righteousness: "He alone underscores the sober implications of Job's insistence that if he is in the right, God must be in the wrong. The Lord, with conspicuous displeasure, levels this very indictment against Job ([Job] 40:2, 8)." Third, he emphasizes "the glory and incomprehensibility of God in creation (36:22–37:24)," which is "a major thrust of God's discourse (e.g., 40:9–14)." Fourth, he "questions Job's knowledge of God's ways in creation (37:14–18)," which is "the driving force propelling the Lord's interrogation of Job"—his "eighty questions . . . on this very point"! According to Talbert, "Elihu's preliminary interrogation is a miniature version of the full-scale interrogative assault Job is about to encounter, the first drops of rain before the hurricane hits," and his "charge that Job is speaking 'words without knowledge' (34:35; 35:16) becomes God's own opening keynote when he addresses Job (38:2)." Fifth, Elihu "hints at the condescending kindness of this sovereign and inscrutable God," mixing words on God's "purity and justice, glory and majesty, omniscience and omnipotence" with God's benevolence: "He is also compassionate and merciful (36:28, 31; 37:13), correcting and forgiving (33:17–18, 29–30), gracious (33:24–26) and attentive to the needy (34:28; 36:15)." God echoes "his more intimidating attributes . . . with subtle tokens of his tender mercy and compassionate nature (e.g., 38:25–27, 39–41; 39:1–4)."[7]

7. Layton Talbert, *Beyond Suffering: Discovering the Message of Job* (Bob Jones University Press, 2007), 172–74.

Some Positives in Elihu's Speech

Previous chapters have highlighted negative aspects of Elihu and his speeches. Elihu's first three flaws were explained and applied at the end of the chapter on Job 32–33 and his fourth and fifth flaws in the chapter on Job 34–35. To reiterate, the first flaw is that he speaks from anger. His second flaw is that his pleading to be heard is annoying. His third flaw is that he presumes himself to be the mediator that Job has been waiting for. His fourth flaw is that when he finally opens his mouth, he is not only long-winded but also arrogant. His fifth flaw is that his accusation is off the mark. Again, to quote John Goldingay: "For all his protestations that he has something new to say, Elihu's understanding of Job's position and of how life with God works is not so different from that of the friends. Job is suffering, so he must have sinned, and he needs to repent."[8] That said, we can also see Elihu as a Jonah-like character: not a false prophet but a flawed one. He is an angry young man who, in his arrogance, wrongly assesses the prophetic situation that he has been placed into but nevertheless, in the end, speaks some of God's truth.

With respect to divine truth, this young and aspiring theologian makes two admirable contributions. Put simply, here is what is true about Elihu's teaching.

First, what Elihu says about God's speaking through suffering is true. In Job 33:14, Elihu seeks to teach or remind Job that God speaks in many ways: "God speaks in one way, and in two, though man does not perceive it." How does God speak? He might speak in a prophecy or through the conscience. But he also might speak "in a dream," especially through a nightmare, because "then he opens the ears of men and terrifies them with warnings" (Job 33:15–16). How else might God speak? One other way is through suffering: "Man is also rebuked with pain on his bed and with continual strife in his bones" (v. 19). As Choon-Leong Seow summarizes:

> Suffering may not be punitive at all but purposive; it may be "to uncover human ears" (33:16a), that is, render one more open to the word of God. Elihu would later reiterate that God makes people more amenable to revelation (lit. "opens

8. John Goldingay, *Job for Everyone*, Old Testament for Everyone (Westminster John Knox, 2013), 166. "The bulk of Elihu's speech simply parrots what the three friends have said before." Longman, *Job*, 367.

> their ear") by *musar* and thus turns them away from trouble in the future (36:10). Even more poignantly, he adds that God "rescues the afflicted through their affliction" and "through distress" God "opens their ears" (36:15).[9]

Elihu wants Job to hear God's voice in his afflictions. He says in effect: "Job, God has not been silent. You keep saying, 'God is silent; God will not speak to me.' You are wrong. He speaks through the suffering. You are just not listening." What Elihu wants Job to hear from God is a rebuke. In the pain, God is disciplining Job—he is communicating his correction.

Setting aside the errors in Elihu's theory, we may still agree with what Elihu is saying here, especially as it relates to our personal histories. In *The Problem of Pain*, C. S. Lewis famously writes, "God whispers to us in our pleasures, speaks in our conscience, but shouts in our pains: it is his megaphone to rouse a deaf world."[10] Many of us come to a knowledge of sin and a need for a Savior through suffering. God wounded us before he healed us. This is my own testimony; I became a Christian in the pain. When I was nineteen years old, God took away everything I had worked for and wanted in life: my academics, athletics, and fiancée. I lost everything precious to me. But in that losing, I was found. I came to a knowledge of my sin and of my Savior through suffering.

We may also agree with Elihu that God speaks to us through suffering as it relates to salvation history. Hebrews begins, "Long ago, at many times and in many ways, God spoke to our fathers by the prophets, but in these last days he has spoken to us by his Son" (Heb. 1:1–2). And how has God spoken? In the cross of Christ! In "Jesus, the mediator of a new covenant"—his "blood that speaks a better word than the blood of Abel" (12:24). In the sufferings of the Son of God, we hear God's voice: "You are forgiven," "You have been granted eternal life," and "You are children of God."

Second, Elihu's closing argument (Job 36:22–37:24) is both correct and convicting. Elihu does not win the case, but what he says here is beautiful and brilliant: "Behold, God is exalted in his power; who is a teacher like him?" (36:22). "Behold, he scatters his lightning about him and covers the roots of the sea" (v. 30). "God thunders wondrously with his voice; he does great things that we cannot comprehend" (37:5). "Therefore men fear him" (v. 24).

9. Seow, "Elihu's Revelation," 266.

10. C. S. Lewis, *The Problem of Pain* (Macmillan, 1948), 81.

Elihu shifts the focus from Job's problem to God's power, demonstrated in creation. Here is how Goldingay simply summarizes his complex speech:

> Creation shows that God is too big for us to be able to tell God how to run the world, and it reminds us that we can hardly even appear before God to ask such questions and offer God such advice. If we cannot look the sun in the eye, we can hardly look God in the eye. Insightful people focus on revering and submitting to God rather than expecting to show up to see him.[11]

Exactly. So despite Elihu's false accusations against Job, and his arrogance and verbosity, we need to appreciate here that he does rightly exalt the justice of God (e.g., Job 37:23) as he leans us forward to the fear of God (v. 24) and the voice of God. Elihu prepares Job, as he also prepares the reader, to hear from God in Job chapters 38–41. For what does God talk about there? He talks about so much of what Elihu has talked about: his own majestic transcendence, his inexplicably mysterious providence, and his absolute moral freedom. In this way, Elihu is an Elijah-like figure who prepares the way for the Lord.[12] In a way, he is like a burning bush, signaling to Job that he should think about taking off his sandals because he is about to have a close encounter with the living God!

From Creation to the Creator

Many people have seen beautiful beaches, majestic mountains, exotic birds, colorful fish, and creatures nearly as frightening as Leviathan. In response, they praise Mother Nature and want to protect the environment. But how few people make the link that Elihu does, from creation to the Creator, from awe before a beautiful garden to awe before our glorious God?

Nineteenth-century Romanticism and twenty-first-century planet appreciation are not what Elihu is on about. No, he calls Job, as he calls us, to "stop and consider the wondrous works of God" (Job 37:14). Why? So that we might bow before our Maker. The "awe-inspiring impressiveness of creation" should generate in us an "awe-inspiring awareness of God's greatness."[13]

11. Goldingay, *Job for Everyone*, 183.

12. See Robert Gordis, *The Book of God and Man: A Study of Job* (University of Chicago Press, 1965), 116.

13. Goldingay, *Job for Everyone*, 182.

What is most true about Elihu's speeches is his theology of the cross and his theology of creation. Indeed, he anticipates the ultimate combination of these themes, namely, in the crucifixion of the Creator. As Paul put it, the one by whom "all things were created" and in whom "all things hold together" reconciled "to himself all things, whether on earth or in heaven, making peace by the blood of his cross" (Col. 1:16–20). We too should *long for* the day when the church will return to a robust theology of the cross and of creation: a "proper recovery" of an aesthetic theology, as Richard Hess notes, "lies in an appreciation of the incarnation and the ultimate exhibition of Christ on the cross—at once a terrible and horrifying spectacle and yet also the sacrifice of love that transcends all other forms as the most beautiful and desirable subject the world has ever known."[14] Moreover, we should *live for* the day when the world grasps something of the greatness of God!

14. Richard S. Hess, *Song of Songs*, Baker Commentary on the Old Testament (Baker Academic, 2005), 158.

Job's Unexpected Trial: God Prosecutes

29

God Calls His First Witnesses

Job 38:1–38

Where were you when I laid the foundation of the earth?
Tell me, if you have understanding. (Job 38:4)

Before we hear from the prosecution, let's answer three important questions.

First, who is the God of Job? The ESV uses "God" 127 times as its translation for *Shaddai*, *Eloah*, and *El*, and "LORD" 32 times for the tetragrammaton. The narrator uses the latter of these terms thirty of those times, and Job uses it twice (1:21; 12:9). This indicates that the author of this book (written in Hebrew) was likely an Israelite and that Job has knowledge of the covenant God of Israel.[1]

Second, how did Job and his friends know Yahweh? The book of Job implies that they knew him in two ways. First, "the knowledge of [God's] ways" (Job 21:14) and will ("the commandment of his lips; . . . the words

1. Moreover, Job, along with Elihu and his three friends, lives among pagans who worship many gods through idols ("who bring their god in their hand," Job 12:6), and yet these five, presumably, worship Yahweh and him alone (to them, those false gods are dead: "there is none to deliver out of your hand," 10:7).

of his mouth," 23:12) comes through direct divine revelation. Abram was outside of God's covenant people when God revealed himself to him, and in Job the main human characters—especially Job—appear to have a similar experience. For example, Job expects God to communicate with him, and he with God (13:3, 22), because that is how their relationship has worked in the past ("I, who called to God and he answered me," 12:4b). Job expects God to speak directly to him, and in the end, God does speak. This divine revelation could be audible and directly from God himself, as it is in God's speeches in Job 38–41, or it could be through a spirit (32:8b; 4:15–16) or dream or vision (7:14; 33:14–16).

Another way that Job and his friends came to know God was through other people. Elihu believes that he is such a selected intermediary,[2] and in some ways he does truly speak for God. Job took on this role as well, as Eliphaz notes: "Behold, you [Job] have instructed many" (Job 4:3). Job's instruction surely included what he learned from his elders and their elders before them ("For inquire, please, of bygone ages, and consider what the fathers have searched out. . . . Will they not teach you and tell you and utter words out of their understanding?," 8:8, 10), but nothing rules out, as Job himself expresses, the direct revelation that he personally received ("I will teach you concerning the hand of God; what is with the Almighty I will not conceal," 27:11). Moreover, it is not out of the question that other Israelites would have instructed them. If Jonah could share God's word with the Ninevites (over seven hundred miles north of Jerusalem), then it is surely possible that there was a connection between Israelites and people from Uz, a region some three hundred miles south of Jerusalem.

Having answered the questions "Who is the God of Job?" and "How did Job and his friends know Yahweh?," we come to our third question, "What do we learn about God from the book of Job?" The appendix ("God's Attributes and Actions in the Book of Job") offers an anthology of answers.[3] In short, as summarized here, the attributes of God most emphasized are his power,[4] wisdom, justice, holiness, and mystery; he is also presented as eternal, incomprehensible, majestic, omniscient, wrathful, and merciful. God's actions include creating the world and all in it, ruling and preserving his creation,

2. Choon-Leong Seow, "Elihu's Revelation," *Theology Today* 68, no. 3 (2011): 262.

3. The texts included in the appendix are a sample of a number of possible texts, for some (not all) of God's attributes and actions.

4. God is called "the Almighty" thirty-one times in Job and forty-eight times total in the Bible!

revealing himself to people and interacting with them, judging the wicked, redeeming and saving those who trust in him, and blessing, disciplining, testing, and forgiving them, prompting their desiring a relationship with him that manifests itself in fear, trust, delight, obedience, prayer, and hope. This data is taken from what has been said about God by the narrator and by various characters throughout the book of Job. Now, in Job 38:1–40:2 and 41:1–34, God speaks for himself!

God's power, wisdom, and justice as demonstrated in his rule in creation and over creation are especially emphasized, something that Job clearly and correctly acknowledges: "I know that you can do all things, and that no purpose of yours can be thwarted" (Job 42:2). Yet God's gracious accommodation is also on display. The almighty Creator speaks to a mere mortal—"even engages him in conversation."[5] He doesn't talk *down to* Job but directly *to* him.[6] What condescension! Moreover, in his speeches, God does not condemn Job in his wrath but offers, in love, "the immediacy and directness of divine presence."[7] What kindness! Yahweh—the same God who spoke to Moses and saved Israel from slavery (see Ex. 6:2–9), who has proved his presence to his people through steadfast love and faithfulness to his promises—speaks directly and personally to someone outside the covenant. God will not answer Job's question, "Why such suffering?" but I AM WHO I AM now announces, "Here I Am."[8] The almighty God, who Elihu claimed cannot be found (Job 37:23), is found—or, better, has found his servant Job.

What Did God Say? God Calls His First Witnesses (Job 38:1–40:2)

Before we look at what God said to Job, let us set God's first of two speeches in context. In Job 32–37, we have heard from Elihu. There we spoke of the flaws of his character and claims, but we also saw how some

5. Kelly M. Kapic, *Embodied Hope: A Theological Meditation on Pain and Suffering* (IVP Academic, 2017), 67.

6. "Like God's speech to Israel at Mount Sinai (Exodus 20:1, 19)," Job 38 records an "unmediated speech." Christopher Ash, *Job: The Wisdom of the Cross*, Preaching the Word (Crossway, 2014), 374.

7. Samuel L. Terrien, "The Yahweh Speeches and Job's Responses," *Review & Expositor* 68, no. 4 (December 1971): 498.

8. "A suffering person might exclaim, 'Why!' but the answer is rarely 'Because,' but 'Here I am'. . . . In the book of Job, it is YHWH who answers, 'Here I Am.'" T. C. Ham, "The Gentle Voice of God in Job 38," *Journal of Biblical Literature* 132, no. 3 (2013): 541.

of what he said prepared the way for the Lord. As we read Elihu's last line about fearing God, we wonder whether there is a pregnant pause, since we hear no response from Job or the friends. Is everyone who has been listening stunned to silence or just bored to death? Or might it be that God interrupts Elihu? Perhaps it is best to envision Yahweh ("Then the Lord answered," Job 38:1) as entering the stage right on cue ("Therefore . . . fear him," 37:24). Either way, the Lord now finally speaks; and in Job 38:1–40:2, the one who is "clothed with awesome majesty" (37:22) lives up to his label.

Job has been begging God to speak (Job 13:3; 23:4; 31:35). But he expected that when God spoke, it would mean that Job's vindication would finally come. That vindication *will* come (42:7–17), but first Job will wait, listen, and learn. He will learn that even someone who has been greatly humbled ("God has . . . humbled me," 30:11) can be further humbled, and that even the righteous (see 1:8; 42:7, 8) should repent (42:6). Job has asked honest questions and offered prayerful laments. But he will learn that he has asked one (or ten!) too many questions, and offered a few too many misguided accusations. He will learn that he should have been more concerned with defending God's justice and less concerned with his personal justification. He will learn that the clay should not have contended with the potter (see 40:2) and that the creature should not have overquestioned the Creator (v. 8; 38:3). He will learn that as great as the "Almighty" (40:2) is to Job, his vision of God is yet too small. Indeed, by the end of the second speech, Job will learn that the immense God who controls the stars (see 38:31–33), the seas (even the fierce Leviathan, 41:1–34), and the earth (even the incredibly powerful Behemoth, 40:15–24) can be trusted. Yahweh's ways might be, at times, incomprehensible, but he is always good and just; and this God of goodness and justice will in his time and for his purposes "do what is just" (Gen. 18:25) and wise.

A Strong Opening Statement (Job 38:1–3)

God's speech starts with a strong opening statement:

> Who is this that darkens counsel by words without knowledge?
> Dress for action like a man;
> I will question you, and you make it known to me. (Job 38:2–3)

Perhaps echoing the language of Exodus 19:16, Yahweh speaks from a storm ("out of the whirlwind," Job 38:1); here, the content of that speech concerns the mystery of God's rule of an exceedingly complex world. It might surprise us that our merciful Lord does not start with a consolation ("Sorry, friend. Hang in there. The testing is almost done") or an explanation ("Here is why I had you go through all this"). Instead, God makes an accusation ("Who is this that darkens counsel by words without knowledge?") followed by a challenge: "Dress for action like a man; I will question you, and you make it known to me" (vv. 2–3).

Earlier Job thought that if God heard his case, God would listen to him ("Would he contend with me in the greatness of his power? No; he would pay attention to me," Job 23:6). That prediction proves to be incorrect. Here the Almighty will showcase the greatness of his power by taking Job on a brief "tour of his creation (38:4–38) and the animals living within it (38:39–39:30)," including describing "at length the mysterious creatures Behemoth (40:15–24) and Leviathan (41:1–34)."[9] His goal will be not merely to silence Job, but to help Job better understand that God's complete control of creation is careful and caringly calculated. God's means of obtaining his goal is to overwhelm Job with eighty or so questions to which the answer for each is some version of "no," "who knows?," or "God and God alone!" The first question, however, Job should answer with the word "me." "Who is this that darkens counsel by words without knowledge?" (38:2). It is Job.

Job is a wise man and (as we have been arguing throughout) also a good man. But Job has questioned the wisdom of God's rule. Job does not have the necessary information to offer "knowledge" about how God runs the world, and in this sense God's counsel is "darken[ed]" (Job 38:2) by Job's questions. For example, Job has questioned God's governance, claiming that God "destroys both the blameless and the wicked" and even "mocks at the calamity of the innocent" and blindfolds "judges" so that "the earth is given into the hand of the wicked" (9:22–24; cf. 24:1–25). "Despite the foolish things Job has said," however, God does not remain silent; and he does not open his case against Job with a "crushing or berating or blasting" blow.[10] Instead, with the grace of his very presence and the "stern gentleness" of

9. Eric Ortlund, *Suffering Wisely and Well: The Grief of Job and the Grace of God* (Crossway, 2022), 119.

10. Ortlund, 124.

a fatherly rebuke,[11] he invites Job to wrestle mentally with him ("Dress for action like a man," lit. "gird up your loins") by putting Job in the dock for cross-examination ("I will question you, and you make it known to me," 38:3). As Daniel Estes summarizes, "Using the familiar biblical image of girding up one's garment by inserting it in the belt (cf. Ex. 12:11; 1 Kings 18:46; Jer. 1:17; 1 Peter 1:13 KJV), Yahweh exhorts Job to prepare himself for a formidable intellectual and theological challenge."[12]

Yahweh's case against Job has three parts. Job is confronted about cosmogony (Job 38:4–21),[13] meteorology (vv. 22–38), and zoology (38:39–39:30).[14] We will cover the first two parts in this chapter. Under each creation category, God asks a number of questions.

What Does Job Know of Cosmogony? (Job 38:4–21)

The first four questions, within the category of cosmogony, come in Job 38:4–11:

> Where were you when I laid the foundation of the earth?
>   Tell me, if you have understanding.
> Who determined its measurements—surely you know!
>   Or who stretched the line upon it?
> On what were its bases sunk,
>   or who laid its cornerstone,
> when the morning stars sang together
>   and all the sons of God [angels] shouted for joy?
>
> Or who shut in the sea with doors
>   when it burst out from the womb,
> when I made clouds its garment
>   and thick darkness its swaddling band,
> and prescribed limits for it
>   and set bars and doors,

11. Michael V. Fox, "Job 38 and God's Rhetoric," *Semeia* 19 (1981): 59. Ham goes a bit further than I am willing to go ("The tone of the YHWH speeches is closer to one of genuine compassion and comfort"). But his perspective is worth noting. "Gentle Voice of God in Job 38," 528.

12. Daniel J. Estes, *Job*, Teach the Text (Baker, 2013), 243–44.

13. Cosmogony explores the astrophysical aspects of the origin and development of the universe, the solar system, and the earth-moon system.

14. This helpful summary and division of the text comes from Robert Alter, *The Art of Biblical Poetry* (Basic Books, 1985), 94.

and said, "Thus far shall you come, and no farther,
and here shall your proud waves be stayed"?

Here, God calls Genesis to the witness stand, and the Bible's first chapter proves Job guilty of ignorance. Job was not alive when God designed the earth ("determined its measurements," Job 38:5), laid its "foundation" (v. 4), and set its "cornerstone" in place (v. 6). He wasn't there to hear the constellations cheer near the start and angels shout for joy at its completion (v. 7). God asks Job whether he has any idea who was in charge of the seven seas, making sure that the oceans, which first burst forth like a quickly delivered baby (v. 8), do not flood the land. God also asks how the clouds, which could flood the world completely in forty or so days, are restrained. The answer is *God alone* (the awesome I!)—"made . . . prescribed . . . set . . . said." Job did not witness how God in his wisdom (see Prov. 8:22–31) set the boundaries of the seas (Job 38:8) and restrained the clouds from flooding all the earth.

With all these opening questions ("Tell me, if you have understanding," Job 38:4b; and "Declare, if you know all this," v. 18b) and sarcastic statements ("surely you know!," v. 5a; cf. "You know, for you were born then," v. 21a), God is seeking to instruct Job that Job's understanding is insufficient. One is reminded of the sentence in Jonathan Edwards's treatise "Some Thoughts Concerning the Revival," where he wrote: "There is not so much difference, before God, between children and grown persons as we are ready to imagine; we are all poor, ignorant foolish babes in his sight: our adult age doesn't bring us so much near to God as we are apt to think."[15] How true for us, and how true even for Job, "the greatest [man] of all the people of the east" (1:3), and in God's own estimation, the most unusual man in the world ("there is none like him on the earth," v. 8). The distance between Job and his lowest servant's youngest child is far closer than the distance between Job and God; and the knowledge gap between that child and this patriarch is not far. Human beings, no matter how small or how great, know very little about our great God.

In his speeches, God revisits Job's beautiful poem on wisdom and reminds Job of what he already knows. We can dig deep into the recesses of human understanding and mine diamonds from the caverns of human existence,

15. Jonathan Edwards, "Some Thoughts on Revival," in *The Works of Jonathan Edwards*, ed. John E. Smith, vol. 4, *The Great Awakening*, ed. C. C. Goen (Yale University Press, 1972), 408.

experience, and observation, but we cannot find "wisdom from above" (James 3:17) from the one who is "above all" (John 3:31) unless the Lord of heaven and earth climbs down Jacob's ladder to give us a glimpse of his wisdom—a glimpse of his greatness that can be received only with opened eyes, soft hearts, and faces flat to the ground. Job had previously testified, "The fear of the Lord, that is [the only way one receives] wisdom" (Job 28:28a).

Again, with all these opening questions, God is seeking to instruct Job that his understanding is insufficient. In the next round of questions (Job 38:12–21), the goal is to teach him that God's lesson plan has not changed and that theology school is still in session:

> Have you [Job] commanded the morning since your days began,
> and caused the dawn to know its place,
> that it might take hold of the skirts of the earth,
> and the wicked be shaken out of it?
> It is changed like clay under the seal,
> and its features stand out like a garment.
> From the wicked their light is withheld,
> and their uplifted arm is broken. (Job 38:12–15)

Unlike God, Job has not ordered the sun to rise ("commanded the morning"/"caused the dawn," Job 38:12). Nor can he see what God sees. As the sun spreads across the earth, bringing everything to light and exposing the earth's various and diverse geological "features" (v. 14), God sees all wickedness ("From the wicked their light is withheld," v. 15a), in every imaginable hidden place on earth ("the skirts of the earth," v. 13a), and judges it ("the wicked [are] shaken out of" the earth, v. 13b; "their uplifted arm is broken," v. 15b). God's mercies are new every morning, but so too are his condemnations of the evildoers. Each day the wicked, who love "the darkness rather than the light" (John 3:19), are exposed and judged by God. Thus, every sunrise should be a reminder to Job, and to us as well, that God's wrath against evil occurs more often than we think and that each daily dose of his destruction of evildoers and their schemes is a down payment on his final eradication of evil. Each sunrise is also a reminder that even evil plays its role in the divine drama, and that where we see disorder, God sees purposeful planning. "The ugliness of evil," writes Christopher Ash, "is part of the creation of God and will ultimately serve the glory of God."[16]

Next, God moves Job's view from the sunrise on earth to eyeing (or trying to eye the impossible!) the depths of the ocean floor, followed by a visit to Sheol and the underworld. "Have you entered into the springs of the sea, or walked in the recesses of the deep?" (Job 38:16), God asks. Of course, Job has not swum to the bottom of the ocean ("entered into the springs of the sea") to explore ("walked in the recesses of the deep," v. 16) and see all the exotic creatures swimming there. Moreover, Job has talked a good deal about death, but to answer God's question, "Have the gates of death been revealed to you, or have you seen the gates of deep darkness?" (v. 17), Job knows that he knows little or nothing about Sheol—its location or its power. He also cannot "comprehend" the mysterious underworld—"the expanse of the earth" (v. 18). Beyond those places of deep darkness, Job knows nothing of the sources of light and darkness.

> Where is the way to the dwelling of light,
>   and where is the place of darkness,
> that you may take it to its territory
>   and that you may discern the paths to its home?
> You know, for you were born then,
>   and the number of your days is great! (Job 38:19–21)

Job was surely not there (the phrase "you were born then," Job 38:21, is sheer sarcasm) when God's voice pierced the "darkness . . . over the face of the deep" and said, "Let there be light" (Gen. 1:2, 3). Ken Taylor captures the sense of the sarcasm well: "Where does the light come from, and how do you get there? Or tell me about the darkness. Where does it come from? Can you find its boundaries, or go to its source? But of course you know all this! For you were born before it was all created, and you are so very experienced!" (TLB).

At this point, Job might be hoping for a question that he can actually answer. "What is your name?" Job. "Where are you from?" Uz. He might also be hoping for a brief recess from these legal proceedings. But God lobs him no softballs; Yahweh takes no break. Instead, the Lord unleashes the second and third volleys of interrogatives. As we get to this point in the text,

16. Ash, *Job*, 382.

we would do well to pause, stretch our exegetical legs, and add a simple but important application—one taken from Derek Thomas's commentary on Job: "There is a rule in the kingdom of God which runs counter to natural law: in order to grow up spiritually, we shall need to grow downwards, to grow *up* into Christ we shall need to grow *down* in lowliness, or humility. As Packer puts it: 'Christians . . . grow greater, by getting smaller.'"[17] When we feel the heavy hand of God upon us, as Job does now and in the days before now, we must remember that our Lord is pushing us down only so that we might grow up. Christians descend into greatness. It is cross-bearing before crown-wearing. Christianity is not a social club; it is a life course in cruciformity.

What Does Job Know of Meteorology? (Job 38:22–38)

Returning to the courtroom drama, in Job 38:22–38 Job is cross-examined with respect to his meteorological knowledge. He is asked to explain the effects of snow, hail, wind, thunder, and lightning on the earth. As Job cannot grasp the workings of the human mind ("Who has put wisdom in the inward parts or given understanding to the mind?," Job 38:36), so also he cannot grasp how God uses extreme weather to impact important events—such as the outcome of wars. God asks:

> Have you entered the storehouses of the snow,
>   or have you seen the storehouses of the hail,
> which I have reserved for the time of trouble,
>   for the day of battle and war?
> What is the way to the place where the light is distributed,
>   or where the east wind is scattered upon the earth?
>
> Who has cleft a channel for the torrents of rain
>   and a way for the thunderbolt,
> to bring rain on a land where no man is,
>   on the desert in which there is no man,
> to satisfy the waste and desolate land,
>   and to make the ground sprout with grass? (Job 38:22–27)

17. Derek Thomas, *The Storm Breaks: Job Simply Explained*, Welwyn Commentary Series (repr., Evangelical Press, 2005), 290. The J. I. Packer quote is from *A Passion for Holiness* (Crossway, 1992), 120.

The unpredictability of a heaven-wrought storm is beyond the greatest general's control.[18] Similarly, Job cannot see from where the storm starts ("where the light is distributed," Job 38:24a). He cannot guess the movements of the wind—"the east wind" that is "scattered upon the earth" (v. 24b). He does not know when the storm might hit ("a channel for the torrents of rain"/"a way for the thunderbolt," v. 25). Will it strike his command center? Will it strike the city gate of the enemy? Or might the wind blow and the rain fall in the middle of nowhere ("a land where no man is"/"on the desert in which there is no man," v. 26) for seemingly no purpose, military or otherwise, or for any benefit to anyone ("to satisfy the waste and desolate land, and to make the ground sprout with grass," v. 27)?

Today we have cellphones that within seconds can tell us what the weather is and what it will be anywhere in the world. But weather apps and meteorologists also make mistakes. We have all been surprised by the severity of a storm! When my family lived in Brisbane, Australia, we were told to stay inside because a severe storm was coming. So we did. But there was no warning that the wind and snowball-sized hail would smash, in an instant, all the windows on the west side of the house. Thankfully, no one in our family was hurt. But that storm did put the fear of God in us! Moreover, it reminded this theologian that "the wind blows where it wishes" (John 3:8) and that God controls the weather in the world and that he is powerful. Indeed, he is the Almighty!

After God questions Job about "the waters" (Job 38:30) in their different forms, he invites Job to move from street view to satellite view, and to ask the even bigger questions about the storm's source:

> Has the rain a father,
>   or who has begotten the drops of dew?
> From whose womb did the ice come forth,
>   and who has given birth to the frost of heaven?
> The waters become hard like stone,
>   and the face of the deep is frozen. (Job 38:28–30)

The rain and dew do not have a father to tell them to water the earth. Nor do the ice and frost have a mother who has birthed them ("from whose

18. For examples of God's using storms for military purposes, see Exodus 9:22–26, Joshua 10:11, and Isaiah 30:30.

womb . . . come forth," Job 38:28b–29). God is the source, and God alone is in charge of the storm. He determines the temperatures. He can do boiling hot. He can also do bitter cold ("The waters become hard like stone"/"the face of the deep is frozen," v. 30).

As the ice on the lake heeds his command, so do the heavenly constellations. Next, God turns Job's eyes and attention upward (higher than the clouds):

> Can you bind the chains of the Pleiades
> or loose the cords of Orion?
> Can you lead forth the Mazzaroth in their season,
> or can you guide the Bear with its children?
> Do you know the ordinances of the heavens?
> Can you establish their rule on the earth? (Job 38:31–33)

Of course, Job cannot "bind the chains of the Pleiades," "loose the cords of Orion" (Job 38:31), or lead and guide "the Mazzaroth," the Great "Bear," and the Little Bear ("with its children," v. 32 [i.e., Ursa Major and Ursa Minor]). But God can and God does! God alone orders "the ordinances of the heavens" (v. 33) and understands their effect on the earth.

In the final verses of Job 38, God descends from the stars to the clouds and returns again (cf. Job 38:22–27) to the theme of God's control of storms:

> Can you lift up your voice to the clouds,
> that a flood of waters may cover you?
> Can you send forth lightnings, that they may go
> and say to you, "Here we are"?
> Who has put wisdom in the inward parts
> or given understanding to the mind?
> Who can number the clouds by wisdom?
> Or who can tilt the waterskins of the heavens,
> when the dust runs into a mass
> and the clods stick fast together? (Job 38:34–38)

The countless clouds ("Who can number the clouds by wisdom?," Job 38:37a) God alone controls. During a drought ("when the dust runs into a mass" and "the clods stick fast together," v. 38), he can command the clouds to produce rain. He lifts his "voice to the clouds" (v. 34), and the floodwaters come. He tilts "the waterskins of the heavens" (v. 37b) and throws each unpredictable lightning bolt (v. 35). The God of the stars is also the God of the storms!

Acknowledging God's Infinite Power

In *The Daily Liturgical Devotional*,[19] I offer a collection of classic hymns, memory verses, short Bible readings, and biblical and ancient Christian prayers to help the reader offer adoration and gratitude to God, confess sins, and ask for help to read God's Word and live the Christian life. As I read through many traditional prayers from classic prayer books and liturgies, I found several prayers that focused on creation, praising God as Creator, and one prayer in particular that models so clearly what should be Job's response and our response to what God reveals in Job 38:

> Lord, in this world you have set before us many things whose cause we do not know, but whose effect we can clearly see. And where this kind of ignorance is part of who we are, reverence toward you brings about faith.
>
> When I raise my feeble eyes toward the skies, I know for certain that it is yours. I see in it the paths of the stars, how they move through the seasons: Pleiades and the Big Dipper and the morning star. Each have their appointed places. And I recognize your presence, Lord, in those things in which I cannot gain any clear understanding.
>
> When I watch the amazing movements of your oceans, I know I do not comprehend the origins of the waters, nor the changing currents. Yet I can grasp in faith a reasonable, intelligent cause, even if I cannot see it. I recognize you in these things, though I do not understand them.
>
> I think of the earth itself, which by some hidden power causes seeds to decay, then brings them to life and multiplies them in strength. In all these changes I find nothing my mind can understand, yet my ignorance helps me recognize you. Though I know nothing of nature, I recognize you when I experience these wonders.
>
> So even though I do not understand myself fully, I experience so much that I marvel at you even more because of that ignorance. Without understanding fully, my mind can still perceive stars in motion or growing things in the earth—and I owe this ability to you.

19. Douglas Sean O'Donnell, *The Daily Liturgical Devotional: 40 Days of Worship and Prayer* (Crossway, 2024).

> You have kept from me the ability to understand my first beginning, yet you still allow me to perceive the charms of nature. And since I recognize you as it concerns me, ignorant as I am, I will have faith in your infinite power. My lack of understanding will not lessen that faith.
>
> I will not attempt to grasp or master the origin of your only-begotten Son, and I will not strain to reach beyond the truth that he is my creator and my God.
>
> Amen.[20]

Hilary of Poitiers prays so well! As we eye creation—from the highest stars to the ocean's depths—we admit our ignorance, express awe and reverence for Yahweh's infinite power, ask for clearer understanding, and praise the only-begotten Son, our Creator God and loving Savior.

20. Hilary of Poitiers, quoted in *Fount of Heaven: Prayers of the Early Church*, ed. Robert Elmer (Lexham, 2022), 55–56.

30

God Calls Nine More Witnesses

Job 38:39—40:5

Shall a faultfinder contend with the Almighty? He who argues with God, let him answer it. (Job 40:2)

rticle 2 of the Belgic Confession (1561) correctly summarizes the "two means" by which we know God:

> First, by the creation, preservation and government of the universe; which is before our eyes as a most elegant book, wherein all creatures, great and small, are as so many characters leading us to contemplate the invisible things of God, namely, his power and divinity, as the apostle Paul saith, Romans 1:20. All which things are sufficient to convince men, and leave them without excuse. Secondly, he makes himself more clearly and fully known to us by his holy and divine Word, that is to say, as far as is necessary for us to know in this life, to his glory and our salvation.

In Job 38–42, Job comes to know God through another means (direct revelation from God!), along with the first means listed above. Thus far in Yahweh's case against Job, God has opened before Job's eyes the "most elegant book" of the revelation of himself through his creation—confronting Job about cosmogony (Job 38:4–21) and meteorology (vv. 22–38). He concludes with questions on zoology (38:39–39:30; cf. 40:6–41:34), lining up eleven animals—"creatures, great and small," who offer yet more insights into "the invisible things of God, namely, his power and divinity," or specifically—in keeping with the attributes most emphasized in the book of Job—God's wisdom and might.[1]

What Does Job Know of Zoology? (Job 38:39–39:30)

The zoology lesson begins with a consideration of nine animals: the lion, the raven, the mountain goat, the wild donkey, the wild ox, the ostrich, the warhorse, the hawk, and the eagle. What unites this sampling is that man cannot fully comprehend and/or tame these creatures. Other creatures could surely be added to the list,[2] but these few examples will suffice to reiterate the lesson that "there is not a single square inch of God's world, not a single animal living in it (whether easily domesticated, dangerous, or just plain weird) that does not witness to God's unstinting care and goodness"[3] and that man's understanding and authority cannot compare with the Creator of these creatures. God's wisdom and power are unsurpassable.

The Lion and the Raven

The King of the Universe begins this round of questioning by reflecting on the king of the jungle:

> Can you hunt the prey for the lion,
>   or satisfy the appetite of the young lions,
> when they crouch in their dens
>   or lie in wait in their thicket?
> Who provides for the raven its prey,

1. "He is wise in heart and mighty in strength" (Job 9:4); "With God are wisdom and might; he has counsel and understanding" (12:13); "With him are strength and sound wisdom" (v. 16); "By his power he stilled the sea; by his understanding he shattered Rahab" (26:12).

2. With the number ten representing completeness in Job (see Job 1:2; 19:3; 42:13; cf. 1:3; 42:12b), the number nine (or eleven, if we include Behemoth and Leviathan) might symbolize that this list is intentionally "incomplete."

3. Eric Ortlund, *Suffering Wisely and Well: The Grief of Job and the Grace of God* (Crossway, 2022), 135.

> when its young ones cry to God for help,
> and wander about for lack of food? (Job 38:39–41)

Again, we can hear Job, with question after question, muttering under his breath, "No." "Can you provide lunch for the proud lion ('hunt the prey for the lion,' Job 38:39)?" No. "How about the unclean and clever raven (v. 41a)?" No again. "How then will their children survive?" Job's answer to this question is not "no" but "God"! For their young who "cry to God for help" because of their "lack of food" (v. 41b–c), God will provide. God will "satisfy the appetite of the young lions" (v. 39b) and the raven's "young ones" (v. 41b). Our Lord Jesus offers a similar insight into God's provision for all his creatures in the Sermon on the Mount: "Look at the birds of the air: they neither sow nor reap nor gather into barns, and yet your heavenly Father feeds them" (Matt. 6:26a).

The Mountain Goat

From the lion and the raven, Yahweh turns to the lofty mountain goat:

> Do you know when the mountain goats give birth?
> Do you observe the calving of the does?
> Can you number the months that they fulfill,
> and do you know the time when they give birth,
> when they crouch, bring forth their offspring,
> and are delivered of their young?
> Their young ones become strong; they grow up in the open;
> they go out and do not return to them. (Job 39:1–4)

Daniel Estes notes: "The mountain goat here is the ibex that today can be seen in the En Gedi area of Israel. It is an elusive animal that can be observed only from a distance, and it resists domestication by humans. With telephoto lenses humans can now learn some of the habits of animals like the ibex, but until recent times little was known of its patterns of life."[4] Yet Job does not have a telephoto lens on hand. He cannot see when they give birth ("Do you know when the mountain goats give birth?," Job 39:1a), how they give birth ("Do you observe the calving of the does?," v. 1b), how long they are pregnant ("Can you number the months that they fulfill?," v. 2a), when they go into labor ("do you know the time when they give birth?," v. 2b), how

4. Daniel J. Estes, *Job*, Teach the Text (Baker, 2013), 236.

they give birth ("when they crouch, bring forth their offspring," v. 3a), or what happens to their young soon after birth ("Their young ones become strong; they grow up in the open; they go out and do not return to them," v. 4). Job is too shortsighted to see what God sees.

The Wild Donkey

Then there is the wild donkey:

> Who has let the wild donkey go free?
> Who has loosed the bonds of the swift donkey,
> to whom I have given the arid plain for his home
> and the salt land for his dwelling place?
> He scorns the tumult of the city;
> he hears not the shouts of the driver.
> He ranges the mountains as his pasture,
> and he searches after every green thing. (Job 39:5–8)

If Job cannot see the movement of the ibex, neither can he domesticate the fast and free-moving donkey of the wasteland ("the arid plain" is "his home"/"the salt land . . . his dwelling place," Job 39:6; this refers to the salt flats by the Salt Sea; cf. Gen. 14:3). This creature is a loner and a roamer. He roams the hills for food ("He ranges the mountains as his pasture" and he searches "after every green thing," Job 39:8). He does not need man to feed him, and he will not let man master him ("He scorns the tumult of the city" and "he hears not the shouts of the driver," v. 7).

This donkey reminds me of the wild horses I saw on my hike up the Great Sugar Loaf Mountain in Ireland. When I came down, the "great" (but actually small) hill, there they were! The horses grazed a bit, looked up at me, and then ran off to wherever their wild hearts desired. I didn't try to run after them.

The Wild Ox[5]

The wild ox is just as wild:

> Is the wild ox willing to serve you?
> Will he spend the night at your manger?

5. On an interesting historical note, the KJV, following the Geneva Bible, renders the Vulgate's *rinoceros* and LXX's *monokerōs* as "unicorn"! The Hebrew [*rym*] is clearly "ox."

Can you bind him in the furrow with ropes,
  or will he harrow the valleys after you?
Will you depend on him because his strength is great,
  and will you leave to him your labor?
Do you have faith in him that he will return your grain
  and gather it to your threshing floor? (Job 39:9–12)

The major difference between the donkey and the ox is the ox's strength ("his strength is great," Job 39:11). Such strength could be useful for humans. This ox could till the fields ("harrow the valleys") and move the heavy harvest to the "threshing floor" (vv. 10–12). This particular ox, however, is no one's slave. Good luck getting this beast to "spend the night at your manger" (v. 9). Again, the point here, as it has been with all the animals, is to reiterate to Job that "Job is not in charge or control of the created order"[6]—including powerful, unclean, wild, and unusual animals.

The Ostrich

The ostrich adds further proof of God's creative power. Among the nine animals, the ostrich receives special attention. Not only does it receive six verses, compared with the usual four (for the mountain goat, wild donkey, and wild ox),[7] it is also described to Job with fewer questions (only one!). Having heard question after question from Job 38:2 to 39:12, we note that the lack of questions in Job 39:13–18 stands out:

The wings of the ostrich wave proudly,
  but are they the pinions and plumage of love?
For she leaves her eggs to the earth
  and lets them be warmed on the ground,
forgetting that a foot may crush them
  and that the wild beast may trample them.
She deals cruelly with her young, as if they were not hers;
  though her labor be in vain, yet she has no fear,

6. Tremper Longman III, *Job*, Baker Commentary on the Old Testament Wisdom and Psalms (Baker Academic, 2012), 436.

7. Among the animals in Job, only the warhorse (Job 39:19–25) receives more verses, and only one more. Yet "the ostrich makes sport of the fearless warhorse [see Job 39:18]. As it flees, the ostrich reaches a height of over 8 feet (2.4 m), strides of over 15 feet in length (4.6 m), and speeds of more than 40 miles (64 km) an hour." Kenneth Laing Harris and August Konkel, "Job," in *ESV Study Bible* (Crossway, 2008), 929.

because God has made her forget wisdom
　and given her no share in understanding.
When she rouses herself to flee,
　she laughs at the horse and his rider.

God stops to give a short three-point sermon on this odd animal. Point one is about a seemingly useless feature. Why does the ostrich have massive "wings" that "wave proudly" (Job 39:13a) but cannot lift the bird off the ground? It cannot fly! Its feathers are all for show, used only as aphrodisiacs ("the pinions and plumage of love," v. 13b). The male ostrich has a strange mating dance. To allure the ladies, he struts around in circles, bobs his head up and down, and erects his "stubby wings," fluffing and flapping his "dull and mottled feathers."[8] It looks ridiculous, but it works!

Point two focuses on the ostrich's stupidity, now concentrating on the female mother. "God has made her forget wisdom" and he has "given her no share in understanding" (Job 39:17). This stupidity is shown in how she treats her young. Since she cannot fly, she is not like the eagle, who leaves her offspring in a safe high place. Instead, she "leaves her eggs [on] the earth" (v. 14a) or slightly buried in the sand. This, of course, makes them extremely vulnerable. A large animal might step on them ("a foot may crush them"/"the wild beast may trample them," v. 15), or a human hunter could grab them or a beastly predator devour them. This seems both cruel ("She deals cruelly with her young, as if they were not hers," v. 16) and stupid. How will her species survive? But her ignorance is bliss ("though her labor be in vain, yet she has no fear," v. 16b). God has made her this way (v. 17); furthermore, God has made the ostrich shell extremely tough to crack. Her species survives, even thrives.

The third point is the ostrich's unique (and humorous!) maneuverability and uncanny ability to escape her enemies. This tall (up to ten feet high) and bulky (about three hundred pounds) bird, "when she rouses herself to flee, . . . laughs at the horse and his rider" (Job 39:18). While the ostrich cannot dive at the speed of an eagle (100 mph), it can run at almost half that speed,[9] faster than anything else on two legs. It can even outrun some

8. Robert L. Alden, *Job*, New American Commentary 11 (Broadman & Holman, 1993), 386.

9. It can run up to 40 mph and is able to "run for hours at sustained speeds of 32 mph." Hugh Ross, *Hidden Treasures in the Book of Job: How the Oldest Book in the Bible Answers Today's Scientific Questions* (Baker, 2011), 160.

incredibly fast four-legged creatures, such as the horse and the lion, and even the antelope. It certainly would leave the mountain goat, wild donkey, and wild ox in the dust. This is why the ostrich "laughs" when a man on a horse tries to hunt her down. We might also wonder whether this ignorant animal is laughing at the theologies of Eliphaz, Zophar, Bildad, Elihu, and, even in part, Job. Whether she laughs or stands there looking stupid, the existence of the awkward, ugly, and odd ostrich is a visual reminder that God's ways are mysterious.[10] It is also a rebuttal of the retribution principle's tidy system of theology. There is nothing sensible about this tall, fast, and powerful (but silly) bird. "If Job cannot even understand ostriches," writes Eric Ortlund, "what makes him so confident he can penetrate God's plan for guiding the entire universe and demonstrate that God is not a fair ruler?"[11]

The Warhorse

From the ostrich eluding a fast horse, next the Lord has Job look at the horse itself. Again, the divine questions return:

> Do you give the horse his might?
>   Do you clothe his neck with a mane?
> Do you make him leap like the locust?
>   His majestic snorting is terrifying.
> He paws in the valley and exults in his strength;
>   he goes out to meet the weapons.
> He laughs at fear and is not dismayed;
>   he does not turn back from the sword.
> Upon him rattle the quiver,
>   the flashing spear, and the javelin.
> With fierceness and rage he swallows the ground;
>   he cannot stand still at the sound of the trumpet.
> When the trumpet sounds, he says "Aha!"
>   He smells the battle from afar,
>   the thunder of the captains, and the shouting. (Job 39:19–25)

10. God "does great things and unsearchable, marvelous things without number" (Job 5:9), and "great things beyond searching out, and marvelous things beyond number" (9:10). He holds "the secrets of wisdom" (11:6), truths that are inaccessible to us ("Can you find out the deep things of God?," v. 7). We grasp only "the outskirts of his ways" (26:14).

11. Ortlund, *Suffering Wisely and Well*, 133.

God asks Job whether Job is responsible for giving such an amazing creature its "might" (Job 39:19a), its "mane" (v. 19b), its ability to jump ("leap like the locust," v. 20a), and its imposing and fearsome sounds ("His majestic snorting is terrifying," v. 20b). The implied answer is "Of course not." Job has not created, and cannot control, the fury of this ferocious beast. When the warhorse is ready, with his hoofs digging in the ground ("He paws in the valley," v. 21a), he rushes into battle ("he goes out to meet the weapons," v. 21b; "charges into the fray," NIV). With each step he "exults in his strength" (v. 21a). He is fearless ("He laughs at fear and is not dismayed") of the fight ahead ("he does not turn back from the sword," v. 22). He is armed for war ("Upon him rattle the quiver, the flashing spear, and the javelin," v. 23). When he arrives at the battlefield, he awaits the horn. Once he hears the battle cry ("the trumpet sounds"), he says to himself, "Aha!" (v. 25a), and he races ahead, with an almost reckless courage.[12] "With fierceness and rage he swallows the ground; he cannot stand still at the sound of the trumpet" (v. 24). Snorting, he kicks up the dust. He hears the captains' orders ("the thunder of the captains, and the shouting," v. 25c), sniffs the violence ahead ("He smells the battle from afar," v. 25b), and races right into it. A soldier might ride him, but who can control him? He is like the wind or the waves, an uncontrollable force. As the prophet Jeremiah warned: when "plunging headlong into battle," the horse will steer "his own course" (Jer. 8:6). Only the Almighty could create such an awesome animal and know how to rein it in.

The Hawk and the Eagle

Yahweh continues and concludes, for now, his zoological inventory with the hawk and the eagle (Job 39:26–30), symbolizing "the epitome of avian animals":[13]

> Is it by your understanding that the hawk soars
>   and spreads his wings toward the south?
> Is it at your command that the eagle mounts up
>   and makes his nest on high?
> On the rock he dwells and makes his home,
>   on the rocky crag and stronghold.

12. See Alden, *Job*, 389.
13. Alden, 390.

From there he spies out the prey;
his eyes behold it from far away.
His young ones suck up blood,
and where the slain are, there is he.

God returns Job's vision to the sky (cf. Job 38:9–38). Look up! Regarding both birds, Yahweh asks two rhetorical questions followed by a description that fits them both. The point again is Godward. Job is to see that it is only by God's "understanding that the hawk soars and spreads his wings toward the south" (39:26) and by his "command that the eagle mounts up and makes his nest on high" (v. 27). Job has not given and cannot give these birds flying lessons. Neither can he reach them. The eagle "makes his home . . . on the rocky crag" (v. 28). Job cannot fly or climb to such inaccessible mountaintop heights to pet the eagle's offspring.[14] Their "stronghold" (v. 28b) is stalwart; their nest is safe from every predator. But other animals are not safe from the eagle. "From there he spies out the prey; his eyes behold it from far away" (v. 29). This bird of prey can see his quarry from nearly three miles away; once the eagle dives, the poor rabbit or rodent doesn't have a chance. Going a hundred miles an hour, this big and burly bird grabs its main course, uses its sharp beak to kill, and returns home to feed the whole family ("His young ones suck up blood," v. 30a). Other times, roadkill will do for dinner ("and where the slain are, there is he," v. 30; cf. Matt. 24:28//Luke 17:37).

Again, why does God bring these birds before Job's eyes? Estes summarizes the point perfectly: "The hawk and the eagle demonstrate that there is much in Yahweh's design for the world that humans do not know or control."[15] Moreover, the eagle dovetails (pun intended) with the first creature named, a lion. As Job cannot stake out a meal for the king of the jungle (Job 38:39), so he cannot tell the monarch of the sky where to find food. It is an inclusio of ignorance. Job is not God. Job cannot fathom even a few behaviors of some of the amazing and mysterious creatures of the earth and sky. (How will he fare with the enormous animal of the earth and the mysterious monster of the sea that are still to come?)

14. "The 'eagle' is the most common bird in the Bible. . . . Most references to it are figurative with points made about its strength (Exod 19:4; Isa 40:31), speed (2 Sam 1:23; Jer 4:13), grandeur in flight (Prov 30:19; Jer 48:40), or ability to take prey (Job 9:26; Hab 1:8) or find carrion (Prov 30:17; Matt 24:28). Here, as in Jer 49:16 and Obad 4, the point is the 'soaring' and 'nesting' in high, craggy, inaccessible places." Alden, 390.

15. Estes, *Job*, 239.

God's Rebuke; Job's Reaction (Job 40:1–5)

In William Blake's painting *Behemoth and Leviathan* from his *Book of Job* (c. 1793), God is depicted as pointing to (nearly touching!) the biggest and baddest beast he ever created (Behemoth), while Job, who is depicted right below God and above the creatures, offers four physical reactions. First, he is on his knees. Second, his right hand is beneath his chin. He looks like the man in Auguste Rodin's bronze sculpture *The Thinker*, and indeed he is thinking. Third, he has an inquisitive look; his eyes seem to be opening. Fourth, with his right hand he is pointing at God's pointing finger.

Before Job beholds Behemoth and looks upon Leviathan, however, God's finger turns toward him. God concludes his first speech as he began it (Job 38:2), with a rebuke: "And the Lord said to Job: Shall a faultfinder contend with the Almighty? He who argues with God, let him answer it" (40:1–2). Job has repeatedly hoped to enter the courtroom with God. He wanted to put his case both to God and against God. He wanted vindication from God. But God reminds him here that it is not wise to contend with the Almighty. Yahweh should not be subpoenaed, for his testimony may not prove our case. Nor should he be accused, because he cannot be condemned for folly or schooled in wisdom.

Job gets this, or the gist of it. After the swirl of scattered dust and ashes settles after God speaks from the whirlwind, Job confesses his ignorance and repents of his presumption:

> Then Job answered the Lord and said:
>
> "Behold, I am of small account; what shall I answer you?
> I lay my hand on my mouth.
> I have spoken once, and I will not answer;
> twice, but I will proceed no further." (Job 40:3–5)

Imagine two kindergarteners attending a graduate lecture at Cambridge University. If the professor turned to Tommy, age five, and asked, "What do you think of Hawkins's theory of black holes?" what would the boy say? If the professor then asked Lily to explain to the class what Hawkins meant when he said, "There is no escape from a black hole in classical theory, but quantum theory enables energy and information to escape," what would she say? Both children would be dumbfounded. If they were smart, they'd say nothing.

Likewise, in his first response to God's barrage of complex questions, Job is smart. Here "the greatest of all the people of the east" (Job 1:3) grasps that he is not so great ("Behold,[16] I am of small account," 40:4a), at least when compared to God. He speaks of his smallness before God followed by an admission of ignorance ("what shall I answer you?," v. 4a)[17] and silence ("I lay my hand on my mouth. I have spoken once, and I will not answer; twice, but I will proceed no further," vv. 4b–5). With his silence, Job is not pleading the Fifth; he is admitting defeat. He is also taking off his sandals, for he is on holy ground. He realizes that he has said more than he should have said. He will listen now, if God desires to speak more. Smallness and silence are the appropriate responses.

Smallness and Silence

Job's first response to God's first speech was right; we should follow his lead. We must recognize our smallness compared with God's greatness. We must be silent before his sovereignty. We do not and cannot know everything there is to know about even nine (soon, eleven!) animals. What makes us think, therefore, that we can tell God how to run the universe? The way God works might seem as unpredictable as a thunderstorm or as silly as an ostrich. We must trust, however, that if God can tame a tsunami and supervise the stars, he can and will deal with our problems in a wise way. Our right response, then, is to worship. We worship a God that we can know, a God who has revealed himself to us. But we also worship a God that we cannot completely know, and who has revealed only something of himself to us.

But the "something" of himself that God has made known to us is no small thing. In fact, God has made himself known to us in the fullness of a

16. Following Elihu's sixteen previous "beholds," Job adds his own for emphasis here.

17. After all of God's rhetorical questions, here Job answers with one of his own. In doing so, Job drops his lawsuit against God, admitting that he is unable to answer even one of God's questions. It is as if Job recognizes that hearing from God has provided him with an understanding of a different kind than he had sought. Thus, as John J. Murray writes, "It was when Job was willing not to understand that he began to understand." *Behind a Frowning Providence* (Banner of Truth, 1990), 22, quoted in Jackie Gibson, *You Are Still a Mother: Hope for Women Grieving a Stillbirth or Miscarriage* (New Growth Press, 2023), 31.

person who is "the radiance of the glory of God and the exact imprint of his nature," as the author of Hebrews writes in the opening verses of his letter (Heb. 1:3). The apostle John tells us that "the Word became flesh and dwelt among us" (John 1:14). God the Son became a man, not an ox or ostrich. So however small and insignificant we are, the incarnation reminds us that we are not too small or insignificant. Our Redeemer *is* one of us. He died for us. Thus, we know that God loves us. "In this the love of God was made manifest among us, that God sent his only Son into the world, so that we might live through him. In this is love, . . . that he loved us and sent his Son to be the propitiation for our sins" (1 John 4:9–10). God might provide eaglets with rabbit stew, but he has provided salvation for me and you. So then, let us join "every creature in heaven [the eagle] and on earth [the lion] and under the earth [Behemoth, or at least in the marsh] and in the sea [Leviathan]" in saying, "To him who sits on the throne and to the Lamb be blessing and honor and glory and might forever and ever!" (Rev. 5:13).

31

God Calls His Final Two Witnesses

Job 40:6—42:6

I had heard of you by the hearing of the ear, but now my eye sees you; therefore I despise myself, and repent in dust and ashes.
(Job 42:5–6)

Once more (see Job 38:1), "out of the whirlwind," God speaks ("the Lord answered Job . . . and said," 40:6). Also, as in Job 38:3, God begins with the same command to Job ("Dress for action like a man") and declaration ("I will question you, and you make it known to me," 40:7). What is different in the short forewords to these two speeches is that God's first question in the second speech comes after, not before (as in 38:2, "Who is this that darkens counsel by words without knowledge?"), that command and that declaration. In Job 40:8–9, God asks Job three penetrating questions:

Will you even put me in the wrong?
  Will you condemn me that you may be in the right?
Have you an arm like God,
  and can you thunder with a voice like his?

Again, these rhetorical questions imply negative answers. To the first two we can imagine Job as saying, "Not anymore," and to the third, "No." Job is learning both that he is not as powerful as God (he does not have as strong an "arm" or as thunderous a "voice," Job 40:9; cf. Ps. 44:1–3) and that he has been wrong to put God "in the wrong" (Job 40:8a)—to defame God's name ("Will you condemn me"; cf. 9:24; 27:2) in order to clear his own ("that you may be in the right?," 40:8b). Job wrongly "was more concerned with his own reputation for righteousness than he was with God's reputation for justice."[1]

Next, with eight imperatives God challenges Job to act as only God can:

> Adorn yourself with majesty and dignity;
>   clothe yourself with glory and splendor.
> Pour out the overflowings of your anger,
>   and look on everyone who is proud and abase him.
> Look on everyone who is proud and bring him low
>   and tread down the wicked where they stand.
> Hide them all in the dust together;
>   bind their faces in the world below.
> Then will I also acknowledge to you
>   that your own right hand can save you. (Job 40:10–14)

First, Yahweh calls Job to exist like God: to "adorn" himself "with majesty [*ga'on*] and dignity [*gobah*]," to "clothe" himself "with glory [*hod*] and splendor [*hadar*]" (Job 40:10; cf. Elihu's "God is clothed with awesome majesty," 37:22). Second, God repeatedly challenges Job to judge justly like God—to condemn the proud ("Pour out . . . your anger," 40:11a; "abase him," v. 11b; "bring him low," v. 12a; "tread down the wicked," v. 12b; "hide them all in the dust," v. 13a; "bind their faces in the world below," v. 13b). If Job were able to exist and act like God, then God would be glad to let Job go on with his suggestion of a court trial in which God hears all his defenses and answers all his questions. God will even acknowledge that he is not needed. Job can save himself! "Then will I also acknowledge to you that your own right hand can save you" (v. 14). (More sarcasm!) Of course, the point is that Job needs to realize afresh that God alone can save him. Although as a man made in God's image he is called to be Godlike, he is unable to fulfill divine prerogatives.

1. Tremper Longman III, *Job*, Baker Commentary on the Old Testament Wisdom and Psalms (Baker Academic, 2012), 440.

Behold, Behemoth (Job 40:15–24)

In Job chapters 38 and 39, God paraded the lion, raven, mountain goat, wild donkey, wild ox, ostrich, warhorse, hawk, and eagle. In Job 40:15–41:34, he brings Job face-to-face (as in a vision) with two of the fiercest creatures in the world—on the land and in the sea. He begins, "Behold, Behemoth" (Job 40:15a). What is this creature? Who has heard of "Behemoth"?[2] On the one hand, it is possible that this is a hippopotamus, since the following description seems to fit that magnificent creature (esp. Job 40:20–24), and hippopotamuses were known to have existed in the ancient Near East,[3] especially in lower Egypt.[4] On the other hand, Behemoth could be a mythical beast.[5] But the opening line, in which God speaks of creating this animal as he did man ("I made as I made you," v. 15b) and which follows nine literal animals in chapters 38–39, strongly favors the interpretation that a hippopotamus is in view.[6]

At first glance, the hippopotamus merely resembles the ox. "He eats grass like an ox" (Job 40:15c). He is extremely strong. Not only is his backside formidable ("his strength in his loins"), so too is his stomach ("his power in the muscles of his belly," v. 16), and his massive legs look indestructible ("the sinews of his thighs are knit together," v. 17b). Even his tail as it arises in the waters appears powerful ("He makes his tail stiff like a cedar," v. 17a),[7] and his rump poses a serious threat to humans and watercraft in its territory. Both on the outside (vv. 16–17) and the inside he is formidable: "His bones are tubes of bronze, his limbs like bars of iron" (v. 18). The animal has, metaphorically speaking, muscles of steel and bones of bronze. Who,

2. On the Hebrew as plural (*behemot*), Christopher Ash notes, "Here the plural seems to be a plural of majesty, conveying something like 'The Superbeast.'" *Job: The Wisdom of the Cross*, Preaching the Word (Crossway, 2014), 410.

3. See Robert L. Alden, *Job*, New American Commentary 11 (Broadman & Holman, 1993), 396n87.

4. See John E. Hartley, *The Book of Job*, NICOT (Eerdmans, 1988), 524.

5. See Marvin H. Pope, *Job: Introduction, Translation and Notes*, Anchor Bible 15 (Doubleday, 1973), 320–22.

6. For further support of Behemoth and Leviathan as real creatures, see David J. A. Clines, *Job 38–42*, Word Biblical Commentary 18B (Thomas Nelson, 2011), 1183–1201; Robert Gordis, *The Book of Job: Commentary, New Translation, Special Studies* (1978; repr., Jewish Theological Seminary of America, 2011), 569–72; Longman, *Job*, 441–45.

7. The hippopotamus's tail, while it is thick and strong at the base, is short and curly. Thus some scholars think that an elephant and its trunk are being described, others the hippopotamus's stiffened penis. The best solution might be that the poet is using hyperbole, the sense being "just try to find a weak spot."

then, could conquer such a beast? Humans cannot hurt him.[8] He ranks "first" among the "works of God" (v. 19a, i.e., the greatest among the great beasts of the land); only Yahweh, who brought him to life, has the power to take his life ("let him who made him bring near his sword!," v. 19b). Behemoth is strong, but not stronger than God! "Unafraid, Yahweh *can approach* Behemoth *with his sword*," thus symbolizing "his complete mastery of this beast."[9] Only God is his King.

But God does not slay the fearsome hippopotamus; rather, he provides for him. Even the hillsides bring him his meals ("the mountains yield food for him," Job 40:20a). The sense is that this enormous beast climbs the riverbanks in search of a late-night gorge. His midnight playground is "where all the wild beasts play" (v. 20b). But he fears them not. What can they do to him? This nocturnal herbivore spends part of the day relaxing riverside ("Under the [Zizyphus] lotus plants he lies," v. 21a) but most of the day submerged in the swamp waters ("in the shelter of the reeds and in the marsh. For his shade the lotus trees cover him; the willows of the brook surround him," vv. 21b–22).

This three-ton beast does not sink.[10] The *Hippopotamus amphibius* does not feed on aquatic plants or animals, but only grass! How does he remain so strong? How does he maintain his weight? How does he ensure that his body armor stays indestructible? Strangest of all (this command receives a "behold"!), how on earth does he swim? "Behold, if the river is turbulent he is not frightened; he is confident though Jordan rushes against his mouth" (Job 40:23). He is not afraid of the wild beasts at night. During the day, he is not afraid of any raging river (even the "Jordan" River or the Nile River when it floods). By running underwater, he can actually swim (!), and this plump, round giant can swim faster than any svelte and successful Olympian ever dreamed (30-mph bursts, compared with 6 mph!). Like the big

8. "One creature seems to fit best with this cluster of details—an herbivore (in the *nepesh* category) that spends its time in marshes, streams, and rivers, lies hidden in its watery habitat, possesses indomitable strength, vigorously defends its territory, and poses severe threat to humans, but only if they venture into its vicinity—and that's the hippopotamus." Hugh Ross, *Hidden Treasures in the Book of Job: How the Oldest Book in the Bible Answers Today's Scientific Questions* (Baker, 2011), 179. Note that both Behemoth and Leviathan are God-made creatures (Job 40:15; 41:33), not mythical embodiments of evil or "symbols of chaotic power that rebel against God." Contra Eric Ortlund, *Suffering Wisely and Well: The Grief of Job and the Grace of God* (Crossway, 2022), 155.

9. Hartley, *Job*, 525, emphasis his.

10. Unless he wants to! Hippos can float or sink by controlling their breathing and body positions.

bird in the sky (the eagle), the fat mammal in the marsh can do what man could never do.

A comparison with man concludes the portrait of Behemoth. Man cannot capture him with some bait on a hook: "Can one take him by his eyes, or pierce his nose with a snare?" (Job 40:24), God asks. We might picture the huge and heavy hippopotamus smiling with his twenty-inch teeth as some man tries to catch him like a trout. Preposterous! Again (see v. 19), the point is that only God could capture him as a man catches a fish, if he wanted to do so. But why would he even want to? Such a beast boasts of God's greatness!

Look at Leviathan! (Job 41:1–34)

Equally boastful is Leviathan (also called "Rahab," Job 9:13; 26:12)—a mighty "sea monster" (Ps. 74:13–14) that Job describes as a "fleeing serpent" (Job 26:13b; cf. "the dragon that is in the sea," Isa. 27:1). The Bible speaks of this great beast as being under God's *control* (God "formed" Leviathan "to play" in the sea, Ps. 104:26) and, when needed, under God's *condemnation* (God "shattered Rahab," Job 26:12b; "his hand pierced," v. 13b; "he will slay the dragon that is in the sea," Isa. 27:1). The purpose of putting Behemoth and Leviathan on parade is to help Job "realize that Yahweh totally controls all threats to his order" and that "compared with the Lord, Job has paltry knowledge and feeble power."[11] In Yahweh's own words, it is to teach Job that "whatever is under the whole heaven is mine" (Job 41:11b), and that even the fierce, powerful, and seemingly uncontrollable and unconquerable Leviathan cannot "stand before" him (v. 10b). Leviathan might be the king *of* all creatures (v. 34b), but God is King *over* all creatures.[12]

As with Behemoth, it is difficult to know whether Leviathan is some real or mythical creature. But because it is likely that Behemoth is a hippopotamus, it is also possible that Leviathan is a crocodile. While there is some evidence for this claim, it is less easy to prove. The point that God has

11. Daniel J. Estes, *Job*, Teach the Text (Baker, 2013), 242, 247. This reading also fits the other mentions of Leviathan in the Old Testament. God has formed the ocean for the Leviathan to "play in" (Ps. 104:26), and God alone can destroy this beast ("crushed the heads," 74:14), using his "strong sword" (cf. Job 40:19) to "punish . . . the twisting serpent, . . . the dragon that is in the sea" (Isa. 27:1).

12. Contrary to many contemporary commentators, I neither take Behemoth and Leviathan to be supernatural wonders nor agree that the purpose, as they claim, is that God is able to control not only the nine natural animals of creation but the two supernatural wonders as well.

been making since Job 38:39, however, depends on the eleven animals listed being real and not mythical creatures (e.g., Leviathan is like the Canaanite's seven-headed Lotan)[13] or mere symbols (e.g., the "embodiment of cosmic evil itself"[14] or of "chaotic forces of evil"[15]). In what ways is a fanciful sea creature more symbolic of "evil" than the eagle devouring its innocent prey, or the violent warhorse loving the smell of the blood in battle?[16]

The Leviathan is special, however. Thus, Yahweh saves him for last, offers him the longest description of any creature (thirty-four verses), and concludes climactically with two statements about this sea monster: "On earth there is not his like" (Job 41:33a) and "he is king over all the sons of pride" (v. 34b). Perhaps it is best to read Job 41:1–34 and imagine someone in Job's time and day who has never seen such a ferocious creature as a twenty-foot-long saltwater crocodile.

The description of Leviathan begins with the humorous idea of men's trying to fish him out of the waters and raise him as a pet. Imagine baiting a "fishhook" with some small mammal ("Can you draw out Leviathan with a fishhook?," Job 41:1a). Then, as the mighty monster jumps out of the water and devours the bait, the hook lodges inside its mouth and its tongue is "pressed down by the rope tied to the hook"[17] ("press down his tongue with a cord," v. 1b). Finally, via a "rope" through "his nose" and a "hook" through "his jaw," he is dragged to the shore: "Can you put a rope in his nose or pierce his jaw with a hook?" (v. 2). This feat is as unlikely as a boy's catching a killer whale with a plastic toy fishing rod. It is also foolish. Who

13. "Mesopotamian myth identifies the primeval seas with the god Mumu-Tiamat, in particular, who rises up and then is vanquished by the god Marduk, who then divides her body to create the protective environment in which the ordered world is made possible. . . . Some biblical texts seem to reflect a similar idea of conflict between God and the sea serpent, Leviathan (see, e.g., Isa. 27:1). In other passages Leviathan appears to be a sea creature . . . that humans might be expected to encounter on the sea (41:1–2; Ps. 104:26)." Gerald H. Wilson, *Job*, Understanding the Bible Commentary 10 (Baker, 2007), 70.

14. Robert S. Fyall, *Now My Eyes Have Seen You: Images of Creation and Evil in the Book of Job*, New Studies in Biblical Theology 12 (InterVarsity Press, 2002), 157. Fyall also argues that Behemoth symbolizes death (137).

15. Hartley, *Job*, 530. Cf. Eric Ortlund, *Piercing Leviathan: God's Defeat of Evil in the Book of Job*, New Studies in Biblical Theology (IVP Academic, 2021).

16. It is curious that commentators who view Behemoth and Leviathan symbolically do not do the same for other unclean animals previously mentioned: "the detestable: the eagle, . . . every raven of any kind, the ostrich, . . . the hawk of any kind" (Lev. 11:13–16). It is also curious that commentators do not see the warhorse as an embodiment of evil, connecting it to the red, black, and pale horses of Revelation 6.

17. Hartley, *Job*, 530.

in the world is brave enough to hunt him so as to adopt him as a pet ("No one is so fierce that he dares to stir him up," v. 10a)?

If we play along, though, we can next imagine man's relationship with this captured beast. Will Leviathan beg for mercy: "Will he make many pleas to you? Will he speak to you soft words?" (Job 41:3)? No! Will he admit defeat and offer himself as a bondslave for life: "Will he make a covenant with you to take him for your servant forever?" (v. 4)? No! Will he eventually become domesticated like a dove or a collie: "Will you play with him as with a bird, or will you put him on a leash for your girls?" (v. 5)? Of course not!

God is leading Job from one absurd idea to another:

> Will traders bargain over him?
>   Will they divide him up among the merchants?
> Can you fill his skin with harpoons
>   or his head with fishing spears?
> Lay your hands on him;
>   remember the battle—you will not do it again!
> Behold, the hope of a man is false;
>   he is laid low even at the sight of him.
> No one is so fierce that he dares to stir him up.
>   Who then is he who can stand before me? (Job 41:6–10)

In Job 41:6, another humorous picture comes into view. Who can imagine merchants in the afternoon fish market bargaining over Leviathan ("Will traders bargain over him?") or trying to cut up ("Will they divide him up?," Job 41:6) his indestructible flesh (see vv. 13, 15–17, 23, 26–30) into little pieces for sushi? Taking us back to the opening scene (vv. 1–2), God calls the whole scenario that he has depicted in verses 1–6 absurd. Can one really fish for Leviathan: "fill his skin with harpoons or his head with fishing spears" (v. 7)? If you try to get him out of the water and "lay your hands on him," you might not have any hands left! It will be a day that you will not forget ("remember the battle") and an act of such stupidity that "you will not do it again!" (v. 8). The idea of even bringing this creature out of the waters (let alone to the market!) is an optimism of idiocy ("the hope of a man is false," v. 9a). The mere sight of the crocodile raising his head in the waters ("When he raises himself up, the mighty are afraid," v. 25a) or of his wake in the waters (v. 32) is enough to make even the boldest hunter shake in his boots ("he is laid low even at the sight of him," v. 9b). Leviathan is "so fierce that" no one is foolish enough to fish for him, let alone come near him ("dares to stir him up," v. 10a).

In verses 10b–11 of Job 41, God gives the reason for this imaginary fishing expedition: it is to remind Job that he should not be stirring up God and that he is not in a position to stand toe to toe with the Almighty ("Who then is he who can stand before me?," Job 41:10b), whether it be in some court of law or face-to-face. Two reasons are given. First, God is the Creator and Sustainer of the world ("Who has first given to me, that I should repay him?," v. 11a). Second, God is sovereign over all creation ("Whatever is under the whole heaven"—white tigers, brown snakes, black widows, the nearly invisible box jellyfish, and so on—"is mine," v. 11b). God cannot be challenged. God has no equal. Even the deadliest animals are his pets!

In Job 41:12–24, Yahweh provides an extended inventory of Leviathan's anatomy (cf. the short description of Behemoth, Job 40:16–18). "I will not keep silence concerning his limbs, or his mighty strength, or his goodly frame" (41:12). The inventory of his strong body begins with his skin and mouth (vv. 13–17). His skin is like a double coat of mail armor ("Who can strip off his outer garment?," v. 13a; also later, "the folds of his flesh stick together, firmly cast on him and immovable," v. 23), with a thousand or so tile-like pieces of impenetrable metal interlocking together, sealed with inseparable super glue: "His back is made of rows of shields ['His scales are his pride,' KJV], shut up closely as with a seal. One is so near to another that no air can come between them. They are joined one to another; they clasp each other and cannot be separated" (vv. 15–17).

The only opening is his mouth. But that is not the safest place to attempt an attack! No one would dare try to put a bridle around his head ("Who would come near him with a bridle?," Job 41:13b). He is not a docile pony. He is not even a half-tamed warhorse. Moreover, how would one even open this beast's mighty jaws to set the mask in place ("Who can open the doors of his face?," v. 14a)? Moreover, if some man could open them, watch out! Leviathan's greatest weapon awaits: "Around his teeth is terror" (v. 14b).[18]

18. According to the ESV, Job 41:14 contains the twelfth and final question (there are no more questions in 41:15–34) that God asks Job about Leviathan. The two questions in verses 10–11 are about God. Thus, there are fourteen questions total. The final questions center on the terror that Job would experience if he were face-to-face with this seemingly invincible crocodile and also relate back to the two questions about God in verses 10–11. As John Hartley summarizes: "In contemplating taking up

His seventy-plus sharp and strong teeth can kill incredibly large animals, fish, and birds. That is not all:

> His sneezings flash forth light,
>   and his eyes are like the eyelids of the dawn.
> Out of his mouth go flaming torches;
>   sparks of fire leap forth.
> Out of his nostrils comes forth smoke,
>   as from a boiling pot and burning rushes.
> His breath kindles coals,
>   and a flame comes forth from his mouth. (Job 41:18–21)

It is likely that these verses are metaphors for the way in which a crocodile roams the water, as Hywel Jones suggests ("Its nostrils squirt spray that becomes translucent in the light [Job 41:18]. . . . Spray from its mouth looks like fire in the sunshine [v. 19]"[19]), as well as John Hartley ("When this creature sneezes, the water spray sparkles in the sunlight like flashes of light," and "when this creature emerges from the water, it spews out its pent-up breath in a steaming spray that appears like *sparks of fire* or like *smoke from a boiling pot*"[20]). Verses 20–21 describe the aftermath of a crocodile killing its prey. As he descends back into the waters, a captured bird or mammal is totally *incinerated* (i.e., devoured, without a trace) within seconds!

A metaphorical reading also fits the context. The parallel line to "His sneezings flash forth light" (Job 41:18a) is a metaphor for his thin, black pupils set against reddish-green eyes resembling the morning sun peeking over the horizon ("and his eyes are like the eyelids of the dawn," v. 18b). Moreover, there is hardly a line that is not a metaphor in Job 41:12–32.[21] For example, verses 18–21 are followed by verse 22, where "terror dances

---

his case with God, Job has been concerned with being overcome by terror (cf. 9:32–35; 13:20–21). Now Yahweh is showing Job that his apprehensions were on target. If he would have to retreat in terror before Leviathan, surely he could not stand before God at court." *Job*, 534.

19. Hywel R. Jones, *Job*, EP Study Commentary (Evangelical Press, 2007), 278.

20. Hartley, *Job*, 532, emphasis his.

21. For example, "his face" is like "doors" (Job 41:14a), "terror" hangs around his teeth (v. 14b), "his back is made of rows of shields" (v. 15a), "he counts iron as straw, and bronze as rotten wood" (v. 27), "sling stones are turned to stubble" (v. 28b), "clubs are counted as stubble" (v. 29a), "he laughs at the rattle of javelins" (v. 29b), "his underparts are like sharp potsherds" (v. 30a), "he spreads himself like a threshing sledge" (v. 30b), and the sea is turned "white-haired" in his wake (v. 32b). See also Job 4:9, where God is possibly depicted metaphorically as a fire-breather.

before him" (this is as metaphorical as it gets!) as his neck breaks the prey into pieces ("In his neck abides strength," v. 22). Also, in verse 24 this cold-blooded and hard-hearted killer ("His heart is hard as a stone, hard as the lower millstone")[22] with his safely protected chest does not care if he is consuming his own children or a man's wife.

In verses 25–32 of Job 41, Yahweh returns to the crazy notion of humans' trying to attack the super creature of the sea:

> When he raises himself up, the mighty are afraid;
> at the crashing they are beside themselves.
> Though the sword reaches him, it does not avail,
> nor the spear, the dart, or the javelin.
> He counts iron as straw,
> and bronze as rotten wood.
> The arrow cannot make him flee;
> for him, sling stones are turned to stubble.
> Clubs are counted as stubble;
> he laughs at the rattle of javelins.
> His underparts are like sharp potsherds;
> he spreads himself like a threshing sledge on the mire.
> He makes the deep boil like a pot;
> he makes the sea like a pot of ointment.
> Behind him he leaves a shining wake;
> one would think the deep to be white-haired.

In Job 41:1–2, we had a depiction of a man using fishing gear to catch this beast, which is a futile enterprise. In verses 25–32, man employs weapons of war: the sword, spear, dart, javelin, arrow, sling stones, and clubs. Better idea, but same results. Not only is Leviathan's back covered in bone (osteoderms) that looks like spears, but his belly is also like hard and jagged stones ("his underparts are like sharp potsherds," Job 41:30; "sharp stones are under him," KJV). The "spear" can reach him under the waters, but "it does not avail" against his thick skin (v. 26). The sword, then? Chop off his head when he raises it above the waters? A sword might easily cut off a man's head, but not Leviathan's. His neck is massive and strong (v. 22a). Can something be thrown from a distance? Sure. But why lose valuable iron and bronze spears,

22. These metaphors are also hyperbole. The idea is that even if a hunter could get through Leviathan's invincible body, he would be met with a surprise. This creature's heart is as hard as his hide!

darts, javelins, and arrows? They bounce off him like "straw" and "rotten wood" (v. 27). "He laughs at the rattle of javelins" (v. 29b).[23] How about King David's slingshot? This may work against Goliath of the Canaanites, but not against Samson of the Deep. When stones strike his body, they turn to nothing—"stubble" (the short and stiff stumps of grain left after harvesting) (v. 28b). A baseball bat or a macuahuitl would yield similarly disappointing results ("Clubs are counted as stubble," v. 29a).

What can conquer Leviathan? Nothing. Even the mightiest men tremble when they see him ("When he raises himself up, the mighty are afraid"); they turn green and yellow when he splashes beside the boat ("at the crashing they are beside themselves," Job 41:25). Watch him laugh in the mire, crying his crocodile tears, and rubbing his belly against the mud of the earth's rivers and seas ("he spreads himself like a threshing sledge on the mire," v. 30b). As his "fire" shows itself on the surface (vv. 19–21), so he makes the underbelly of the sea shake, rattle, roll, and boil (!) when he swims by ("He makes the deep boil" like a pot of tea, or like someone brewing the newest fragrance [a "pot of ointment," v. 31]). He leaves a boastful wake above the surface ("Behind him he leaves a shining wake," v. 32a) and turns the dark sea white as he speeds through the waters ("one would think the deep to be white-haired," v. 32b).

Among all creatures, none is as inimitable ("On earth there is not his like") or intrepid ("a creature without fear," Job 41:33). What Martin Luther said of the devil in his hymn "A Mighty Fortress Is Our God" we might say of Leviathan: "on earth is not his equal." Indeed, this beast is like the beast of Revelation 13:4 ("Who is like the beast, and who can fight against it?"). Every arrogant creature, from the blue peafowl of Sri Lanka to the Siamese cat to fallen *Homo sapiens*, knows that Leviathan is the "king over all the sons of pride" (Job 41:34b). "He sees everything that is high" (v. 34a)!

Repentance of the Righteous (Job 42:1–6)

The only appropriate response of Job to this amazing creature is to fear its awesome Creator. Job should stop complaining, stay the avowals of innocence,

23. Hartley summarizes Habel's insight on laughter being a "thread that runs through the animal portraits." He writes: "The wild ass laughs at the noise in the city ([Job] 39:7), the ostrich laughs at the horse and its rider (39:18), the horse laughs at fear (39:22), the wild animals play (laughingly) near Behemoth (40:20), and no one can play (laughingly) with Leviathan (40:29) [Eng. 41:5])." *Job*, 533, citing Norman C. Habel, *The Book of Job: A Commentary*, Old Testament Library (Westminster, 1985), 573.

submit. Job's final answer ("Job answered the Lord," Job 42:1, with the context of his answer in vv. 2–6) is as remarkable as his first (1:20–21). He trusts God atop the garbage dump.

As Christopher Ash summarizes: "Job's response is in three parts. He speaks of something he now knows, of things he did not know, and supremely of one he has now seen."[24] First, he states how he now knows, or knows afresh, that God "can do all things" or, put differently, that "no purpose of yours can be thwarted" (Job 42:2). Job has acknowledged God as "the Almighty" many times.[25] Now he acknowledges that Yahweh really is all-mighty. He indeed grasps that every verse about two great monsters helps him "see God as even more gloriously and unsurpassably indomitable."[26]

Second, Job acknowledges that there is a major knowledge gap between himself and God. To God's question "Who is this that darkens counsel by words without knowledge?" (Job 38:2, repeated here by Job in 42:3a, with two slight variations), Job speaks of speaking sophomorically. He has "uttered what" he "did not understand"/"know"—concepts beyond his comprehension ("things too wonderful for me," 42:3).

Third, having heard clearly God's challenges to him ("Hear, and I will speak; I will question you, and you make it known to me," Job 42:4, echoing 38:3; 40:7), Job speaks of seeing what God wants him to see, or really seeing God for more of who God is. God is bigger than Job imagined. He is greater than the traditions he has heard. Yahweh makes Leviathan look little and Behemoth brittle. This perception of created reality and aural vision of the Divine Reality causes him to tremble, tremble, tremble and to change his mind and turn away from previous thoughts and postures:

> I had heard of you by the hearing of the ear,
>   but now my eye sees you;
> therefore I despise myself,
>   and repent in dust and ashes. (Job 42:5–6)

Here we have the repentance of the righteous. In these verses Job pours out his heart, contritely confessing that he has spoken beyond his knowl-

24. Ash, *Job*, 416.
25. See Job 6:4, 14; 13:3; 21:15, 20; 23:16; 24:1; 27:2, 10, 11, 13; 29:5; 31:2.
26. Ortlund, *Suffering Wisely and Well*, 149.

edge. Job has misjudged God, and for this he recants his accusations. In self-humiliation, he retracts his case against God and despises himself for the abusive words that he foolishly hurled at God.[27] Job never questioned God's power, but he did challenge God's seeming indifference. Now Job submits himself to the God who has appeared to him by acknowledging that God is lovingly involved in the operations of an exceedingly complex universe. Job admits that compared with the omniscience of God, he has drawn his conclusions from a limited examination of life. What Job now comprehends is that God and his mysterious providence are too wonderful to comprehend and that human perceptions of justice are not the scales on which the righteousness of God is weighed. He finally grasps that "God has an inescapable purpose in whatever he does,"[28] even if that inescapable purpose is never revealed to the creatures it affects. Job finally sees clearly that he cannot see clearly!

Through God's two speeches, Job has been given neither a bill of indictment nor a verdict of innocence; rather, he has been given eyes to see the greatness of God. He sees now "with, not through, the eye"[29] in such a way that the apparent madness of God becomes his only sanity. In the presence of God, all his complaints against God now seem insignificant. His intellectual problem remains unsolved but unimportant.[30] Still in the midst of extreme pain, Job is spiritually healed by the revelation of God. He sings upon the ashes that his Redeemer lives!

A Clearer Vision of God

It may surprise us that in God's two speeches we find no superficial niceness, no artificial comfort, no tickling of ears. We might think that God has a poor bedside manner. If we are searching for the answer to the question why there is suffering in the world, we will find no answer here. God gives no answer to the source of Job's misery or the reason for it. In fact, he makes no mention of Job's sufferings at all. Instead, Yahweh gives Job the one thing he needs: a clearer vision of God. God in essence says to him: "Job, all that you need to know about your suffering is that I am God. I am still

27. See Clines, *Job 38–42*, 1204–24.
28. Hartley, *Job*, 537.
29. William Blake, "The Everlasting Gospel" (1818).
30. See H. H. Rowley, *Job*, New Century Bible Commentary (repr., Eerdmans, 1980), 266.

in control. I still care about you. And I am always just in everything I do." God demonstrates this by asking Job to "stop and consider the wondrous works of God" (Job 37:14), for the wondrous works of God's creation are the visible attestation of his "abundant righteousness" (v. 23).

In Job 38–41, God offers no extravagant philosophical argument in defense of his character. Rather, he argues that the existence and maintenance and operation of the earth, stars, waters, and animals confirm his just rule and also "testify against human arrogance, ignorance, and ingratitude."[31] God calls creation to the witness stand, when creation's respectable, valid testimony renders all human beings morally inexcusable and intellectually incapable of criticizing God's character. God's control, constraint, and care, clearly portrayed every day, ought to silence all accusations against his goodness.

Through questioning Job in this manner, God in essence says to all of us: "If you understood but a fraction of the details of my creation and of my detailed interaction with it, you would never open your mouth to accuse me of injustice. For even the mightiest of creatures I hold tight on a leash. So who are you, O man, to place me under the lens of your judgment, to talk back to the Creator of the universe?" A mere observation of nature should be enough to acquit God of any charge of injustice. If we considered the beauty and order of creation, we would conclude that God is no cosmic bully. He is not "making sport" of us with his providential power.[32] God's "rule of human history," as Susan Schreiner summarizes John Calvin, "is inexplicable, incomprehensible, and beyond human reason. And yet nature points beyond itself and promises that the same God who brought the beauty and order of creation into being is wise and powerful enough to bring order out of what appears to be present confusion."[33] The world is the theater of God's glory. Before the vast panorama of the heavens and earth, the majestic face of God shines.

By the start of Job chapter 42, Job finally realizes that even in the worst of life's storms, the sun does not fail to warm or sustain the earth. From the whirlwind God speaks, and in the swirl of scattered dust and ashes Job confesses his ignorance and repents of his presumption. To his credit, Job

31. John H. Eaton, *Job*, Old Testament Guides (JSOT Press, 1985), 141.

32. John Calvin, *Institutes*, 1.71.1, quoted in Susan E. Schreiner, *Where Shall Wisdom Be Found? Calvin's Exegesis of Job from Medieval and Modern Perspectives* (University of Chicago Press, 1994), 93.

33. Schreiner, *Where Shall Wisdom Be Found?*, 152.

does not suffer from our obsession with the question *why*;[34] neither does he suffer from our obsession with having felt needs met. God does not offer Job healing, and he certainly does not offer Job a restored self-esteem. There is no therapeutic babble from the tongue of God; there is no healing here from the hand of God; and the beautiful result is that Job is not concerned about those things anymore. Job does not want anything but God. That is what God offers. And that is what Job takes.

Job takes God for who he is, no more questions asked. Job has come to the point in his struggles that he finally gets it. He *sees* God's point. He agrees with God and finds true comfort in the character of God. Oh, that we would do the same, no matter our sad or happy situation.[35] In the grand design of the universe, God's wisdom and justice surpass human understanding, and through Job's story, we are reminded of our limited perspective. This realization should inspire us to have a deeper trust in God's sovereign plan, acknowledging that his ways are higher than our ways and his thoughts higher than our thoughts.

34. Job and his friends have been asking the question *why*. God asks the question *who* (Job 38:5, 36, 41; 39:5; 41:13–14), as well as *have you* (38:12, 16, 17, 18, 22; 40:9), *can you* (38:31, 32, 33b, 34, 35, 39; 39:2, 10; 40:9; 41:1, 2, 7), and *do you* (38:33; 39:1, 2b, 12, 19, 20). All these questions are designed to move Job and his friends to admit that God is God and man is not. God alone has the wisdom required to create and govern the world.

35. Parts of the final paragraphs are taken, or adapted, from Douglas Sean O'Donnell, *The Beginning and End of Wisdom: Preaching Christ from the First and Last Chapters of Proverbs, Ecclesiastes, and Job* (Crossway, 2011), 112–13.

Epilogue

32

Job's Vindication and Restoration

Job 42:7–17

And the LORD restored the fortunes of Job, when he had prayed for his friends. And the LORD gave Job twice as much as he had before. (Job 42:10)

I used to think that the book of Job was the Bible's answer to the philosophical questions of the origins of evil and the problem of pain. But then I read it. That is, I carefully read through each and every sentence, realizing forty-two chapters later that the question "Why suffering?" was more my question than the book's question. In other words, I realized that the book answers questions related to the issues of life's incomprehensible cruelties, but that it does not specifically address the question *why*.

Some churches today design their sermon series based on *our* questions:

- How can we mend a broken marriage?
- What are seven keys to financial success?
- Why does a good God allow good people to suffer so badly?

Interestingly, although God's Word answers these questions, it does so only indirectly. Sometimes the questions that *feel* so crucial to us turn out to be different from the questions that we most *need* God to answer. It is not that our felt needs are unimportant; rather, it is that they aren't always our greatest actual needs. In God's great wisdom, his Word addresses our deepest actual needs.

In Job, our Lord asks and answers four key questions through a diverse cast of characters. First, there is Satan's question, "Does Job fear God for no reason?" (Job 1:9). In broader terms, Satan asks whether it is possible to love God not only in times of plenty but also in times of want. Job, through three tough tests—the loss of his possessions and children, his health, and his friends' comfort and respect—answers in the affirmative. Yes, it is possible![1]

The next two key questions center on the topics of the righteousness of man and the righteousness of God. "Do the righteous ever suffer?" This is the question that Job's friends are addressing. The answer is obvious to us. Of course! Job is righteous and yet he suffers. "Is God righteous in all he does, even when he allows or *ordains* suffering?" This is the question that Job is struggling with. God answers that question in the affirmative with his speeches to Job. Yes! In his often-inexplicable sovereignty, God always does what is wise and just.

The fourth question, which is another of Job's questions, is "Will the righteous be vindicated?" Job 42:7–17 answers with another resounding "yes"! The epilogue offers a happy—and surprising—ending. I say "surprising" because we might have expected after God's barrage of questions and Job's own admission of shortsightedness and irreverence that the Lord would vindictively "declare that Job was a blasphemous and wicked man deserving of everything that happened."[2] But (surprise!) this is not what happens, and that, of course, is not the God we worship. Instead, Job is publicly vindicated (Job 42:7–9). The Lord rebukes the three friends for their reckless words. Then the Lord restores Job's former blessings twofold (vv. 10–17). These blessings, it should be noted, are not bestowed out of some obligation that God has to prosper the righteous. They are a gift, one that can be given or taken away. In

1. Part of this introduction and part of the "Connection with Christ" section are taken from Douglas Sean O'Donnell, *The Beginning and End of Wisdom: Preaching Christ from the First and Last Chapters of Proverbs, Ecclesiastes, and Job* (Crossway, 2011), 105–6, 114–17.

2. David R. Jackson, *Crying Out for Vindication: The Gospel According to Job*, Gospel According to the Old Testament (P&R Publishing, 2007), 164.

fact, Job had no idea that vindication and restoration would follow his repentance. So once again, he demonstrates that he fears God not because of God's blessings (see 1:9–11) but because God is God and worthy to be worshiped.

The epilogue, which records Job's vindication, is divided into two parts: the Lord's rebuke of Job's friends (Job 42:7–9) and the Lord's restoration of Job (vv. 10–17).

The Lord's Rebuke (Job 42:7–9)

We start with the Lord's rebuke. "After the Lord had spoken these words to Job,"[3] he turns to talk to "Eliphaz," the representative for Bildad and Zophar ("your two friends," Job 42:7), and says:

> My anger burns against you and against your two friends, for you have not spoken of me what is right, as my servant Job has. Now therefore take seven bulls and seven rams and go to my servant Job and offer up a burnt offering for yourselves. And my servant Job shall pray for you, for I will accept his prayer not to deal with you according to your folly. For you have not spoken of me what is right, as my servant Job has. (Job 42:7b–8)

First, Yahweh describes his "anger" as burning (*harah 'appi*) against Job's friends. Second, he explains what has stirred up his anger. It is because the three friends "have not spoken of me what is right, as my servant Job has." They have accused God of inflicting suffering on Job to punish him for his sin. This is not true. So God is right to tell Job's friends that they are in the wrong. But what of Job? What does God mean when he says that Job has "spoken of me what is right"?

An Important Aside on the Nature of Job's Words

It is possible that God is stating that Job has spoken rightly only in his two humble responses to God's speeches (Job 40:3–5; 42:1–6), since it is difficult to categorize everything that Job has said throughout this book under the phrase "what is right." Aren't "many of his harsh criticisms of God," as Eric Ortlund contends, "simply sinful to utter," and thus not right to say, along with some of his more outrageous claims, such as that "God laughs when innocent

3. Job 38:1–40:1; 40:6–41:34.

lives are ruined (9:22–24)"?[4] Perhaps. But we can be certain that what Job said about God's redemptive plan is also right. As Hugh Ross points out, Job discerned that his Creator exists (9:8; 10:8; 12:10), possesses limitless power and wisdom (9:4, 10), cares for him (10:12), and is good and has perfection as his standard (7:18; 10:14; 23:10). Job also discerned that he falls hopelessly short of the Creator's goodness (9:2, 14, 28–29; 14:4; 15:14), but that because the Creator is powerful, wise, and loving, he formed a plan to redeem him (14:14–15; 16:19–21), and if Job entrusts his life to the Redeemer, he will be rescued by him (9:15; 13:15; 14:17; 17:3), and if he receives the Creator's offer, his rescue is assured (19:25–27; 23:10).[5] Moreover, because the friends are judged for what they have said within the dialogues (chaps. 4–25), the more natural reading is to assume that the same is true for Job. Put differently, if Job has sinned with his lips, God would compel him to make restitution. Instead, Job offers sacrifices for his friends but not for himself.

Thus, Derek Kidner rightly concludes that "we are forcibly reminded that God, for all his rough handling of his servant's rude demands, reads between the lines and listens to the heart."[6] That God "reads between the lines" is another way of saying that he mercifully chooses to overlook offenses, or, to use Job's own imagery, to take all of Job's sins, bundle them in a big bag, bury them in the depths of the earth, and completely cover them over (see Job 14:17). Kidner's line that God "listens to the heart" is also significant. Like David, who was labeled "a man after [God's] own heart" (1 Sam. 13:14), Job's heart is in line with God in earnestly desiring his whole life to obey God's will ("I have found in David the son of Jesse a man after my heart, *who will do all my will*," Acts 13:22) and, when he falls short, in going to God for forgiveness and restoration (in Job's case, his repentance after God's speeches; in David's case, his repentance reflected in Psalms 32 and 51). Moreover, as Christopher Ash suggests, "While the friends want a system, Job wants God"—that is, "Job cannot be satisfied with any system: he must know God and speak to the living God. He must, for nothing else will satisfy him. This heart-longing of Job is the core reason why the Lord says Job has spoken rightly of him."[7]

4. Eric Ortlund, *Piercing Leviathan: God's Defeat of Evil in the Book of Job*, New Studies in Biblical Theology (IVP Academic, 2021), 59.

5. See Hugh Ross, *Hidden Treasures in the Book of Job: How the Oldest Book in the Bible Answers Today's Scientific Questions* (Baker, 2011), 206–7.

6. Derek Kidner, *Wisdom to Live By* (Inter-Varsity Press, 1985), 73.

7. Christopher Ash, *Trusting God in the Darkness: A Guide to Understanding the Book of Job* (Crossway, 2021), 131.

If the evaluation above of God's line that Job has "spoken of me what is right" (Job 42:7, 8) is accurate, then "the surprising divine evaluation of the tortured hero at the end of the book . . . requires the reader to approve of what Job says—though his bold speeches must have regularly shocked the reader."[8] Indeed, the divine decree teaches us how to reread Job's speeches, not only with an open mind but also with open ears and eyes to hear and see what God would teach us through Job's speeches about him. Thus, it is good to go back and consider what Job said to and about God in Job chapters 3–31. Here is my summary of the so-called negative data:

- Job openly complains: "I will not restrain my mouth; I will speak in the anguish of my spirit; I will complain in the bitterness of my soul" (Job 7:11).
- He curses the day he was born (3:1) and wants God to kill him: "Oh . . . that he would let loose his hand and cut me off" (6:8–9).
- He claims, in extremely provocative language, that God is against him: "The arrows of the Almighty are in me" (6:4); "You have turned cruel to me; with the might of your hand you persecute me" (30:21); "Why do you . . . count me as your enemy?" (13:24). Indeed, he directly questions God's goodness and justice in the world ("Why is light given to him who is in misery?," 3:20) and especially in his own situation ("although you know that I am not guilty, and there is none to deliver out of your hand," 10:7).
- Job thinks that if he were allowed a hearing before God, the Lord would decline to challenge him: "Would he contend with me in the greatness of his power? No; he would pay attention to me. There an upright man could argue with him ["argue my ways to his face," 13:15], and [as a result] I would be acquitted forever by my judge" (23:6–7).

In all this, Job does not *see* right. But this is not the same as Job's not *speaking* right. Is it a sin to question God? Not always. "My God, my God, why have you forsaken me?" (Matt. 27:46). Remember who asked that! Is it a sin to complain against God? Not always. "How long?" the persecuted saints call out in Revelation 6:10. Is it a sin for Job to say that God is against him without cause (Job 9:17)? No, because Job has not been given the cause, and

8. Andreas J. Köstenberger and Gregory Goswell, *Biblical Theology: A Canonical Thematic and Ethical Approach* (Crossway, 2023), 287.

because God is actually against him in one sense. Reread the prologue: the Lord has given and the Lord has taken away. Is it wrong to ask for personal vindication? No. Is it wrong to ask God to act justly? No. What, then, is wrong with Job's speeches? It is not clear in the context of Scripture, as well as the divine declaration in Job 42, that there is anything terribly wrong with what he says to and about God. Even though Job cannot find God (23:8–9), this does not mean that he does not know where wisdom can be found (28:28). Even though Job despairs of life (3:3–10), this does not mean that he has denied the Holy One (6:10). Even though Job thinks God is acting unjustly in his situation (9:22), this does not mean that he does not recognize his human limitations: "If it is a contest of strength, behold, he is mighty! If it is a matter of justice, who can summon him?" (9:19); "For he is not a man, as I am, that I might answer him, that we should come to trial together" (9:32); "Will any teach God knowledge, seeing that he judges those who are on high?" (21:22). Furthermore, even though Job sometimes sounds hopeless (7:6), this does not mean that he cannot also cry out, "Though he slay me, I will hope in him" (13:15).

In summary, Job has spoken rightly in this respect: even in his laments, questions, complaints, and accusations, he has expressed a heart desirous to be restored with God and to grow in their relationship. He never stopped pursuing God, even though he sensed that God was in wrathful pursuit of him. He still saw God as his only salvation from God.

Returning to the Three Points

Returning, then, to the three points, let us review the first two and add a third. First, Yahweh describes his anger as stirred up. Second, God gives the rationale for that stirring up. He is upset because the three friends "have not spoken of me what is right, as my servant Job has" (Job 42:7, 8). Third, God extends restoration to the friends through Job. They are to "take seven bulls and seven rams and go to my servant Job and offer up a burnt offering for yourselves. And my servant Job shall pray for you, for I will accept his prayer not to deal with you according to your folly" (v. 8).

In one of the most important turning points in the book, we read that the two warring parties obey God: "Eliphaz the Temanite and Bildad the Shuhite and Zophar the Naamathite" presumably repent because they "went and did what the Lord had told them" (Job 42:9a). They offered their sacrifices through Job; and Job presumably prayed for them, and through his prayer and the burnt offering, the three friends are reconciled both to God ("the Lord accepted Job's prayer," v. 9b) and to Job. For the three friends to humble themselves in this way, offering an incredibly expensive, costly, complete (7 + 7), and bloody substitutionary sin sacrifice ("seven bulls and seven rams," v. 8)[9] through righteous Job's mediation,[10] is a great act of submission to God. Moreover, for Job to pray for his enemies is remarkable as well. Together they model what Jesus would later teach ("Love your enemies," Matt. 5:44; cf. 6:12, 14–15) and also embody ("Father, forgive them, for they know not what they do," Luke 23:34). We might hope that this ironic ending was not lost on Job's friends, since they had long expected the opposite to occur, namely, for them as the righteous men to offer a prayer that would avail on Job's behalf. Instead, the long-but-wrongly-accused sinner restores them to God through the power of prayer, and with this act, as Ash points out, it becomes clear that "it is Job who is righteous, justified, vindicated, in right relation with the Lord."[11]

Connection with Christ

There is more to this sacrifice than a picture of Job's mediation and vindication. The scene also points to Christ's sacrifice. Job's blood sacrifices for his few foolish friends from the east foreshadow the ultimate sacrifice scene in the Bible, where Jesus offers his own blood sacrifice for "a great multitude that no one could number, from every nation" (Rev. 7:9)—north, south, east, and west—"the many" who are "made righteous" through his "obedience" (Rom. 5:19; cf. Mark 10:45). Further, at least four more typological connections can be made between Job (the type) and Jesus (the antitype).

9. On this as a substitutionary sin offering, see Numbers 23:1, 29; 1 Chronicles 15:26; 29:21; Hebrews 10:4. As Derek Thomas writes: "As part of the ritual, hands were laid on the animal's head, firstly to identify the victim with the worshipper, but also, and more importantly, to signify a representative and substitutionary significance in the act that followed. Of all the sacrifices offered, the burnt offering demonstrated most clearly God's anger poured out against sin in that the victim of the sacrifice was totally consumed. The offering, which represented and was a substitute for the offerer, quite literally went up in smoke!" *The Storm Breaks: Job Simply Explained*, Welwyn Commentary Series (repr., Evangelical Press, 2005), 316.

10. "The intercession of Job for his friends is the best proof of his righteousness," according to Dariusz Ivanski, *The Dynamics of Job's Intercession*, Analecta Biblica 161 (Pontifical Biblical Institute, 2006), 357, as quoted in Tremper Longman III, *Job*, Baker Commentary on the Old Testament Wisdom and Psalms (Baker Academic, 2012), 459. On Job's delivering through his righteousness, see Ezekiel 14:14, 20.

11. Ash, *Trusting God in the Darkness*, 135.

First, the gospel answers the book's two key questions: "Do the righteous suffer?" and "Is God righteous when the righteous suffer?" God's mercy and justice are on full display when sinless Jesus dies the death of a criminal. Consider the Morning Prayer for the *Book of Common Prayer*, which begins with an acknowledgment of our depravity, followed by a confession of sin. But then, around the midpoint, the first Bible reading comes. It is from Romans 3, where Paul transitions from his declaration that "none is righteous" (Rom. 3:10) to the manifestation of "the righteousness of God through faith in Jesus Christ" (v. 22). Hear afresh the good news:

> All have sinned and fall short of the glory of God, and [all] are justified by his grace as a gift, through the redemption that is in Christ Jesus, whom God put forward as a propitiation by his blood, to be received by faith. This was to show God's righteousness, because in his divine forbearance he had passed over former sins. It was to show his righteousness at the present time, so that he might be just and the justifier of the one who has faith in Jesus. (Rom. 3:23–26)

Second, the narrative of Job 42:7–9 reads like a gospel tract:

- Man has sinned against God. While Job's friends thought themselves to be in the right, they were very much in the wrong.
- God is angry at sin, and rightfully so. It is an assault on his name and glory.
- Yet in his mercy, God does not deal with these sinners according to their folly. It is through a blood sacrifice and a blameless and upright man's mediation that their sins are forgiven.

Third, the full narrative of Job prefigures the metanarrative of the Bible's story of our ultimate salvation in Christ. Here's the story of Job in summary:

- There was a righteous man.
- This man, by God's set purpose, was handed over to satanic-inflicted sufferings.
- This man in his sufferings was mocked and mistreated.
- This man prayed for his enemies, for those who persecuted him.
- This man, after a costly, perfect, substitutionary, blood sacrifice, became a priestly mediator between God and sinners.

- This man was fully and publicly vindicated by God.
- This man, in the end, was exalted, receiving honor and glory and power and wealth, even (seemingly) to a greater extent than that which he first had.

Sound familiar? I am not saying that Job is Jesus. Job was a sinner (as he admits he is, and as all people are except the sinless Son of God), and he is to blame for certain aspects of his weak-sighted perception of God. Yet it is difficult to deny that the story of Job (a story written many hundreds of years before the incarnation) prepares us in an extraordinary way for the story of Jesus—of what to expect in the Messiah. To put it plainly: the narrative of Job prepares us mentally and spiritually for the master narrative, or metanarrative, of Jesus. To put it more boldly: the primary purpose of the book of Job is to prepare us for Jesus (cf. Luke 24:26, 46)!

The fourth typological connection between Job and Jesus comes through the title "my servant," which Yahweh uses for Job twice in the prologue (Job 1:8; 2:3) and four times in the sacrifice scene of the epilogue ("my servant Job" has "spoken of me what is right," 42:7, 8; "go to my servant Job and offer up [through his priestly mediation] a burnt offering," v. 8a; and "my servant Job shall pray for you, for I will accept his prayer not to deal with you according to your folly," v. 8b). The title "servant" itself evinces a typological connection with Christ. In addition, the title (*'abdi*, used 62×) is used almost exclusively for key figures in salvation history,[12] most prominently of Israel/Jacob (as a nation, 12×),[13] Moses (6×),[14] David (22×),[15] and the Servant in Isaiah (5×).[16] Of course, the New Testament makes it clear that Jesus is the new Israel and new Moses, the Son of David, and the Suffering Servant.[17]

The fourfold repetition in the climactic atonement section of the book of Job (42:7–8, an echo of 1:5) is too thematically similar to be coincidental. To be clear, Job's sufferings were not vicarious—his *sufferings* did not atone

12. The title is also used of Abraham (Gen. 26:24), Israel and/or Jacob as a nation (Isa. 41:8; 44:1, 2, 21; 45:4; 49:3; Jer. 30:10; 33:26; 46:27, 28; Ezek. 28:25), Caleb (Num. 14:24), Naaman (2 Kings 5:6), Isaiah (Isa. 20:3), Eliakim (Isa. 22:20), and the king of Babylon (Jer. 25:9; 27:6; 43:10).

13. Isa. 41:8; 44:1, 2, 21; 45:4; 49:3; Jer. 30:10; 33:26; 46:27, 28; Ezek. 28:25; 37:25.

14. Num. 12:7, 8; Josh. 1:2, 7; 2 Kings 21:8; Mal. 4:4.

15. 2 Sam. 3:18; 7:5, 8; 1 Kings 11:13, 32, 34, 36, 38; 14:8; 2 Kings 19:34; 20:6; 1 Chron. 17:4, 7; Ps. 89:3, 20; Isa. 37:35; Jer. 33:21, 26; Ezek. 34:23, 24; 37:24, 25.

16. Isa. 42:1; 43:10; 49:6; 52:13; 53:11.

17. See Matt. 8:17; 12:18; Luke 22:37; Acts 8:32–35; 1 Peter 2:22–25; cf. Jesus as the "holy servant" (Acts 4:27, 30).

for his friends' sins. But both Job and Jesus, as God's servants, suffered and interceded through blood sacrifice. In other words, the fourfold repetition of "my servant Job" is ultimately intended to make us think of the cross of Christ, where the Suffering Servant would suffer and die for God's people.

So Job's friends were not too far removed from those who cried out to our suffering Savior, "If you are the Son of God, come down from the cross" (Matt. 27:40). The last picture they could imagine was of a suffering servant. How could a suffering servant demonstrate the blessing of God? How could a suffering servant bring peace between God and man? How could a suffering servant defeat Satan and his schemes? How could a suffering servant be perfectly innocent and yet God perfectly just? The story of Job contains the seed of God's answer to this conundrum.

Jesus once declared to the Pharisees, "You search the Scriptures because you think that in them you have eternal life; and it is they [the Hebrew Scriptures, including Job!] that bear witness about me, yet you refuse to come to me that you may have life" (John 5:39–40). Jesus was upset at the Pharisees' suppression of the truth because they were the ones who knew the Scriptures and therefore should have known better. They should have understood, as the prophet Isaiah so clearly foretold and as Job so perfectly illustrates, that it is quite possible for an innocent man to suffer and yet for God—in it and through it—to show forth his justice.

The Lord's Restoration (Job 42:10–17)

After the Lord's rebuke of Job's friends (Job 42:7–9), which serves also as Job's vindication before them (and makes compelling Christological connections), comes the Lord's restoration of Job (vv. 10–17). In these final verses, we learn that more is restored to Job than his relationship with his friends. Immediately after Job offers prayer "for his friends" (v. 10a), God honors the man who has honored him:

> And the Lord restored the fortunes of Job, when he had prayed for his friends. And the Lord gave Job twice as much as he had before. Then came to him all his brothers and sisters and all who had known him before, and ate bread with him in his house. And they showed him sympathy and comforted him for all the evil [or "disaster"] that the Lord had brought upon him. And each of them gave him a piece of money and a ring of gold.

> And the Lord blessed the latter days of Job more than his beginning. And he had 14,000 sheep, 6,000 camels, 1,000 yoke of oxen, and 1,000 female donkeys. He had also seven sons and three daughters. And he called the name of the first daughter Jemimah, and the name of the second Keziah, and the name of the third Keren-happuch. And in all the land there were no women so beautiful as Job's daughters. And their father gave them an inheritance among their brothers. And after this Job lived 140 years, and saw his sons, and his sons' sons, four generations. And Job died, an old man, and full of days. (Job 42:10–17)

God's restorative blessings come in three ways. First, God gives wealth. When Job's siblings, old friends, and good acquaintances arrive, they each give him "a piece of money and a ring of gold" (Job 42:11c), and his livestock is doubled ("And he had 14,000 sheep, 6,000 camels, 1,000 yoke of oxen, and 1,000 female donkeys," v. 12; cf. 1:3).

Second, God gives family. Job has a renewed relationship with "all his brothers and sisters" and with his community ("all who had known him before"), and together they feast at table ("and ate bread with him in his house," Job 42:11). Those who maligned him (cf. 19:13–22) now dine with him. He has a renewed (and repeatedly intimate) relationship with his wife; together they have ten more children ("seven sons and three daughters," 42:13; cf. 1:2).[18] Moreover, the wholesomeness, harmony, and happiness of the home is expressed in Job's naming his "beautiful" (42:15a)[19] daughters ("Jemimah," "Keziah," and "Keren-happuch," v. 14), whom he includes in his inheritance ("And their father gave them an inheritance among their brothers," v. 15b), an unusual act, especially in the patriarchal period. Job remains involved in his children's, grandchildren's, and great-grandchildren's lives: "and [Job] saw his sons, and his sons' sons, four generations" (v. 16b). How blessed!

Third, God gives long life. "Job lived 140 years" (Job 42:16a), a perfect or complete number of years (70 × 2) and double the norm ("The years of our life are seventy," Ps. 90:10). These 140 years are on top of what he has

18. Note that the number of children is not doubled. This might be to symbolize that the original ten are not forgotten, as cattle would be, for example. It might also be that ten is a perfect number, as opposed to twenty.

19. The point of mentioning their beauty ("no women so beautiful," Job 42:15a) is to say that these doubly endowed virgins (they have good looks and a rich inheritance) will not have any trouble finding husbands, an important concern for a caring father.

already lived ("after this," Job 42:16a). Does he live to two hundred? Who knows? However old he is when he dies, he certainly does so as "an old man, and full of days" (v. 17). Like Abraham and Isaac, Job is depicted as living a long life ("full of years," Gen. 25:8; and "full of days," 35:29) and, like David, as someone dying at "a good age, full of days, riches, and honor" (1 Chron. 29:28).[20]

The important insight to obtain from Job's blessings is that "God is not mocked, for whatever one sows, that will he also reap" (Gal. 6:7). In context, Paul is talking about the big picture of our salvation, not the possible blessings that might come our way if we live God's way. Yet the principle still stands whether we receive blessings now, after a season of suffering, or in heaven ("reap eternal life," v. 8). The application from that insight is, as Paul put it to the Galatians, "And let us not grow weary of doing good, for in due season we will reap, if we do not give up" (v. 9).

At times, Job gave up on life and hope for restoration. But he never gave up on God, and he never gave up on being and doing good. Like Job, we too will reap the benefits of integrity and faithfulness; and like Job, we need to understand, or come to understand, that we rarely reap what we sow "in the immediate, obvious, domino-like fashion that Eliphaz and his friends imagine."[21] We play the long game because we believe that trusting and following God is "really worth it in the end, no matter what suffering it costs us along the way."[22] The Jesus pattern is our pattern: cross in life; crown in paradise. The promises of God are our hope: that if "we suffer with him" we will "be glorified with him" (Rom. 8:17; cf. 1 Peter 5:10); that "this light momentary affliction is preparing for us an eternal weight of glory beyond all comparison" (2 Cor. 4:17); that our "reward is great in heaven" (Matt. 5:12). We will be comforted, be satisfied, receive mercy, see God, be called sons of God, and inherit the earth, if we are humble, meek, mournful, pure

20. All that was earlier, and ironically, predicted by Eliphaz comes to fruition. See table 6.2, "Echoes of Job 5:19–26 in Job 42:7–17," on page 68.

21. Eric Ortlund, *Suffering Wisely and Well: The Grief of Job and the Grace of God* (Crossway, 2022), 71: "It is true that you reap what you sow, but it is not true to say that you reap only what you sow. Suffering and loss can meet God's imperfect but sincere saints in such a way that cannot be explained with reference to their past sins and failures. Sometimes suffering meets us, but not because we have sown it. The pattern of retribution ultimately holds true in God's universe—but not in a quick or automatic way." Cf. Mark Talbot, *Give Me Understanding That I May Live: Sustaining Our Suffering Within God's Redemptive Plan*, vol. 2, *Suffering and the Christian Life* (Crossway, 2022), 18–19.

22. Ortlund, *Suffering Wisely and Well*, 71.

in heart, peaceful, and merciful, hunger and thirst for righteousness, and are persecuted for righteousness' sake (see Matt. 5:3–12). We believe the certain promise that "those who by patience in well-doing seek [now on earth] for [future] glory and honor and immortality" will be granted just that (God "will give eternal life," Rom. 2:6–7).

Two More Important Insights

What a happy ending! Or almost-happy ending. The final line "and full of days" is happy, but the phrase (one word in Hebrew, *wayyamat*) that comes before it is not: "And Job died" (Job 42:17). Job does not live happily *ever* after. He too experiences the results of the curse: "you shall surely die" (Gen. 2:17). He thus joins in the sad chorus of Genesis 5, where the phrase "and he died" is repeated eight times.

In one of the church's ancient hymns, Ephrem the Syrian (c. 306–73) sings of Job's conquering Satan, but not death, and of "Christ conquer[ing] Death where Job could not."[23] Amen! Ephrem also writes of Job's suffering being only on his own behalf, and of Christ's being on behalf of all his people.[24] Amen, again! These are two important insights. As Christians, thanks to Christ's sufferings and conquering of the grave, we can be glad that our stories will not end with merely a final "and he/she died." We have the hope of heaven. We have the hope of the resurrection and the return of Christ. Amen?

In James 5:11, the apostle writes, "You have heard of the steadfastness of Job, and you have seen the purpose of the Lord, how the Lord is compassionate and merciful." The example of Job is set within the context of the admonition to "be patient, therefore, brothers, until the coming of the Lord" (James 5:7). On these texts—James 5:7, 11 and Job 42:7–17—Ash writes these beautiful words:

> The purpose of the Lord to show mercy and compassion will be seen finally only when the Lord Jesus returns in glory. Job 42 anticipates the return of the Lord Jesus. . . . The blessings God will pour out on the believer at the end will be every bit as *real* as the blessings of Job. Job knew real prosperity, real joy

23. Nisibene Hymns 53.14, summarized by C. L. Seow, *Job 1–21: Interpretation and Commentary*, Illuminations (Eerdmans, 2013), 179.

24. See Hymns on Nativity 13.34; Hymns on Epiphany 2.34.

> and celebration, real fruitfulness, and real beauty (his dazzling daughters!). The blessings of the new heavens and new earth will be rock-solid real; we look forward to beauty that makes the most beautiful woman in the world seem dull; we look forward to fruitfulness that will make the most abundant family in the world seem barren; we look forward to prosperity that will make Bill Gates seem poor; and we look forward to celebration that will make the best party in the world seem like a quiet glass of apple juice.[25]

More than any other passage in this tragic and triumphant book, Job 42:7–17 offers the most clear and valuable connections with Christ. Moreover, as Ash points out above, this text can also serve as a great impetus for Job-like perseverance in view of the coming of Christ. As we look for the end—our vindication, the crown of life, the paradise of God, the marriage supper of the Lamb, the defeat of Satan, and the new heaven and new earth wherein eternal righteousness, happiness, beauty, and prosperity dwell (Rev. 19–22)—let us model patient endurance, holding fast to Jesus' name, as we long for our resurrection (and he lives!) and our Lord's return (and we will live with him forever and ever, Amen).

25. Ash, *Trusting God in the Darkness*, 136–37.

Appendix

God's Attributes and Actions in the Book of Job

Attribute	Verses
Almighty	"God is mighty" (36:5 [2×]); "he is mighty" (9:19); "his power" (24:22); "Behold, God is exalted in his power" (36:22); "I know that you can do all things, and that no purpose of yours can be thwarted" (42:2)
Eternal	"Behold, God is great, and we know him not; the number of his years is unsearchable" (36:26)
Holy	"Can mortal man be in the right before God? Can a man be pure before his Maker? Even in his servants he puts no trust, and his angels he charges with error; how much more those who dwell in houses of clay, whose foundation is in the dust, who are crushed like the moth" (4:17–19); "Behold, God puts no trust in his holy ones, and the heavens are not pure in his sight" (15:15)
Incomprehensible	"he does great things that we cannot comprehend" (37:5b); "we cannot find him" (37:23)
Just	"Does God pervert justice? Or does the Almighty pervert the right?" (8:3); "Behold, God will not reject a blameless man, nor take the hand of evildoers" (8:20); "If it is a matter of justice, who can summon him?" (9:19); "For according to the work of a man he will repay him, and according to his ways he will make it befall him. Of a truth, God will not do wickedly, and the Almighty will not pervert justice" (34:11–12); "he does not regard any who are wise in their own conceit" (37:24)

Attribute	Verses
Living	"God lives" (27:2)
Loving	"Whether for correction or for his land or for love, he causes it to happen" (37:13)
Majestic	"clothed with awesome majesty" (37:22)
Merciful	"If you will seek God and plead with the Almighty for mercy" (8:5); "my transgression would be sealed up in a bag, and you would cover over my iniquity" (14:17)
Mysterious	"who does great things and unsearchable, marvelous things without number" (5:9); "who does great things beyond searching out, and marvelous things beyond number" (9:10); "and that he would tell you the secrets of wisdom! For he is manifold in understanding. Know then that God exacts of you less than your guilt deserves. Can you find out the deep things of God? Can you find out the limit of the Almighty?" (11:6–7); "Behold, these are but the outskirts of his ways, and how small a whisper do we hear of him! But the thunder of his power who can understand?" (26:14)
Omniscient	"you watcher of mankind" (7:20); "For he looks to the ends of the earth and sees everything under the heavens" (28:24)
Unchanging	"he is unchangeable" (23:13)
Wise	"Will any teach God knowledge, seeing that he judges those who are on high?" (21:22); "perfect in knowledge" (37:16b)
Wrathful	"The possessions of his house will be carried away, dragged off in the day of God's wrath. This is the wicked man's portion from God, the heritage decreed for him by God" (20:28–29); "Let their own eyes see their destruction, and let them drink of the wrath of the Almighty" (21:20)

Action	Verses
Creates	"Your hands fashioned and made me" (10:8a); "You clothed me with skin and flesh, and knit me together with bones and sinews. You have granted me life and steadfast love, and your care has preserved my spirit" (vv. 11–12); "My Maker" (32:22; 35:10; 36:3); "The Spirit of God has made me, and the breath of the Almighty gives me life" (33:4); "I laid the foundation of the earth" (38:4a)
Preserves	"he gives rain on the earth and sends water on the fields" (5:10); "In his hand is the life of every living thing and the breath of all mankind" (12:10); "gives food in abundance" (36:31a); "provides for the raven its prey" (38:41)
Gives revelation	"But I would speak to the Almighty" (13:3); "Then call, and I [Job] will answer; or let me speak, and you reply to me" (13:22)
Mediates rule through the "sons of God"	"Now there was a day when the sons of God came to present themselves before the LORD, and Satan also came among them. The LORD said to Satan, 'From where have you come?' Satan answered the LORD and said, 'From going to and fro on the earth, and from walking up and down on it.' And the LORD said to Satan, 'Have you considered my servant Job, that there is none like him on the earth, a blameless and upright man, who fears God and turns away from evil?' Then Satan answered the LORD and said, 'Does Job fear God for no reason? Have you not put a hedge around him and his house and all that he has, on every side? You have blessed the work of his hands, and his possessions have increased in the land. But stretch out your hand and touch all that he has, and he will curse you to your face.' And the LORD said to Satan, 'Behold, all that he has is in your hand. Only against him do not stretch out your hand.' So Satan went out from the presence of the LORD" (1:6–12); "Again there was a day when the sons of God came to present themselves before the LORD, and Satan also came among them to present himself before the LORD. And the LORD said to Satan, (continued on next page)

Action	Verses
	'From where have you come?' Satan answered the LORD and said, 'From going to and fro on the earth, and from walking up and down on it.' And the LORD said to Satan, 'Have you considered my servant Job, that there is none like him on the earth, a blameless and upright man, who fears God and turns away from evil? He still holds fast his integrity, although you incited me against him to destroy him without reason.' Then Satan answered the LORD and said, 'Skin for skin! All that a man has he will give for his life. But stretch out your hand and touch his bone and his flesh, and he will curse you to your face.' And the LORD said to Satan, 'Behold, he is in your hand; only spare his life.' So Satan went out from the presence of the LORD and struck Job with loathsome sores from the sole of his foot to the crown of his head" (2:1–7)
Interacts with his creation, including angels, people, and animals	"What is man, that you make so much of him, and that you set your heart on him, visit him every morning and test him every moment?" (7:17–18); "Can you lift up your voice to the clouds, that a flood of waters may cover you? Can you send forth lightnings, that they may go and say to you, 'Here we are'?" (38:34–35); "Who provides for the raven its prey, when its young ones cry to God for help, and wander about for lack of food?" (38:41)
Allows people to be tested	See chaps. 1–2; "But he knows the way that I take; when he has tried me, I shall come out as gold" (23:10)
Can be, for a season, silent to human prayer	See chaps. 3–37
Desires people to have a relationship with him that manifests itself in fear, trust, delight, obedience, prayer, hope, and animal sacrifices	Fear ("feared God," 1:1; "fear of God," 4:6; "He who withholds kindness from a friend forsakes the fear of the Almighty," 6:14; "the fear of the Lord," 28:28; "fear him," 37:24), trust (see both 19:25 and 42:8), delight ("delight yourself in the Almighty," 22:26; also 27:10; 33:26b), obedience (1:1, 8, 21; 2:10; 42:2), prayer (22:27; 27:10a; 33:26), hope (13:15; 14:13; 19:24–27), and animal sacrifices (1:5; 42:8–9; "pay your vows," 22:27b)

Action	Verses
Judges and blesses	"fire of God fell from heaven" (1:16); gives and takes away (1:21); humans receive "good from God" and they "receive evil" (2:10); "those who plow iniquity and sow trouble reap the same. By the breath of God they perish, and by the blast of his anger they are consumed" (4:8–9; cf. 38:12–15; 40:11–12); God also blesses (e.g., 29:2–4; 42:10–17)
Corrects/disciplines	"Behold, blessed is the one whom God reproves; therefore despise not the discipline of the Almighty" (5:17; also 37:13)
Rules over all people	"He makes nations great, and he destroys them; he enlarges nations, and leads them away" (12:23)
Forgives sin	"pardon my transgression and take away my iniquity" (7:21); "plead with the Almighty for mercy" (8:5); "bring back his soul from the pit" (33:30)
Brings comfort to people	"the comforts of God" (15:11)
Redeems and saves	"But he saves the needy from the sword of their mouth and from the hand of the mighty" (5:15; also 5:19); Job knows God to be a "Redeemer" (19:25); "he saves the lowly. He delivers even the one who is not innocent" (22:29–30); "How you have helped him who has no power! How you have saved the arm that has no strength!" (26:2)
Can be "with" people	"when the Almighty was yet with me" (29:5)
Can be sought and turned to for help	"As for me, I would seek God, and to God would I commit my cause" (5:8)

Select Bibliography

Alden, Robert L. *Job*. New American Commentary 11. Broadman & Holman, 1993.

Allen, David L. *Exalting Jesus in Job*. Christ-Centered Exposition. Holman Reference, 2022.

Alter, Robert. *The Art of Biblical Poetry*. Basic Books, 1985.

———. *The Wisdom Books: Job, Proverbs, and Ecclesiastes*. W. W. Norton & Company, 2010.

Andersen, Francis I. *Job*. Tyndale Old Testament Commentaries 13. InterVarsity Press, 1976.

Aquinas, Thomas. *The Literal Exposition of Job: A Scriptural Commentary Concerning Providence*. Translated by Anthony Damico. Classics in Religious Studies 7. Scholars Press, 1989.

Archer, Gleason L., Jr. *The Book of Job: God's Answer to the Problem of Undeserved Suffering*. Baker, 1982.

Ash, Christopher. *Job: The Wisdom of the Cross*. Preaching the Word. Crossway, 2014.

———. *Out of the Storm: Grappling with God in the Book of Job*. Regent College Publishing, 2004.

———. *Trusting God in the Darkness: A Guide to Understanding the Book of Job*. Crossway, 2021.

Atkinson, David. *The Message of Job*. The Bible Speaks Today. InterVarsity Press, 1991.

Belcher, Richard P., Jr. "Job." In *A Biblical-Theological Introduction to the Old Testament: The Gospel Promised*, edited by Miles V. Van Pelt. Crossway, 2016.

———. *Job: The Mystery of Suffering and God's Sovereignty*. Focus on the Bible. Christian Focus, 2017.

Blake, William. *Illustrations of the Book of Job*. D. Appleton, 1903.

Boadt, Lawrence. *The Book of Job: Why Do the Innocent Suffer?* Classic Bible Series. St. Martin's Press, 1997.

Brownback, Lydia. *Job: Trusting God When Suffering Comes*. Flourish Bible Study. Crossway, 2023.

Bullock, C. Hassell. *An Introduction to the Old Testament: Poetic Books*. Rev. and expanded ed. Moody, 1988.

Calvin, John. *Sermons on Job*. Translated by Rob Roy McGregor. 3 vols. Banner of Truth, 2022.

Carson, D. A. *How Long, O Lord? Reflections on Suffering and Evil*. 2nd ed. Baker Academic, 2006.

Clines, David J. A. "Job." In *New Bible Commentary*, edited by G. J. Wenham, J. A. Motyer, D. A. Carson, and R. T. France. 4th ed. Inter-Varsity Press, 1994.

———. *Job 1–20*. Word Biblical Commentary 17. Word, 1989.

———. *Job 21–37*. Word Biblical Commentary 18A. Thomas Nelson, 2006.

———. *Job 38–42*. Word Biblical Commentary 18B. Thomas Nelson, 2011.

Dhorme, Edouard. *A Commentary on the Book of Job*. Translated by H. Knight. Nelson, 1967.

Eaton, John H. *Job*. Old Testament Study Guides. JSOT Press, 1985.

Estes, Daniel J. *Job*. Teach the Text. Baker, 2013.

Fyall, Robert S. *How Does God Treat His Friends?* Christian Focus, 1995.

———. *Now My Eyes Have Seen You: Images of Creation and Evil in the Book of Job*. New Studies in Biblical Theology 12. InterVarsity Press, 2002.

Gatiss, Lee. "Job." In *ESV Gospel Transformation Study Bible*. Crossway, 2018.

Goldingay, John. *Job for Everyone*. Old Testament for Everyone. Westminster John Knox, 2013.

Gordis, Robert. *The Book of God and Man: A Study of Job*. University of Chicago Press, 1965.

———. *The Book of Job: Commentary, New Translation, Special Studies*. 1978. Reprint, Jewish Theological Seminary of America, 2011.

Green, William Henry. *The Argument of the Book of Job Unfolded*. 1873. Reprint, James & Klock, 1977.

Gregory the Great. *Moral Reflections on the Book of Job*. Translated by Brian Kerns. 6 vols. Cistercian Studies. Liturgical Press, 2014–22.

Greidanus, Sidney. *Preaching Christ from the Old Testament: A Contemporary Hermeneutical Method*. Eerdmans, 1999.

Habel, Norman C. *The Book of Job: A Commentary*. Old Testament Library. Westminster, 1985.

Hartley, John E. *The Book of Job*. NICOT. Eerdmans, 1988.

Holbert, John C. *Preaching Job*. Preaching Classic Texts. Chalice, 1999.

Jackson, David R. *Crying Out for Vindication: The Gospel According to Job*. Gospel According to the Old Testament. P&R Publishing, 2007.

Janzen, J. Gerald. *Job*. Interpretation: A Bible Commentary for Teaching and Preaching. John Knox, 1985.

Jones, Hywel R. *Job*. EP Study Commentary. Evangelical Press, 2007.

Kidner, Derek. *The Wisdom of Proverbs, Job, and Ecclesiastes: An Introduction to Wisdom Literature*. InterVarsity Press, 1985.

Kline, Meredith. "Job." In *Wycliffe Bible Commentary*, edited by Charles F. Pfeiffer and Everett F. Harrison. Moody, 1963.

Konkel, August H. *Job*. Cornerstone Biblical Commentary 6. Tyndale House, 2006.

Kynes, Bill, and Will Kynes. *Wrestling with God: Defiant Faith in the Face of Suffering*. IVP Academic, 2022.

Longman, Tremper, III. *Job*. Baker Commentary on the Old Testament Wisdom and Psalms. Baker Academic, 2012.

MacKenzie, R. A. F., and Roland E. Murphy. "Job." In *New Jerome Biblical Commentary*, edited by Raymond E. Brown et al. Prentice Hall, 1990.

Mason, Mike. *The Gospel According to Job: An Honest Look at Pain and Doubt from the Life of One Who Lost Everything*. Crossway, 1994.

Murphy, Roland E. *The Tree of Life: An Exploration of Biblical Wisdom Literature*. Anchor Bible Reference Library. Doubleday, 1990.

O'Donnell, Douglas Sean. *The Beginning and End of Wisdom: Preaching Christ from the First and Last Chapters of Proverbs, Ecclesiastes, and Job*. Crossway, 2011.

———. "Job." In *Ezra–Job*. Vol. 4 of *ESV Expository Commentary*, edited by Iain M. Duguid, James M. Hamilton Jr., and Jay Sklar. Crossway, 2020.

Ortlund, Eric. *Job: A 12-Week Study*. Knowing the Bible. Crossway, 2017.

———. *Piercing Leviathan: God's Defeat of Evil in the Book of Job*. New Studies in Biblical Theology. IVP Academic, 2021.

———. *Suffering Wisely and Well: The Grief of Job and the Grace of God*. Crossway, 2022.

Pope, Marvin H. *Job: Introduction, Translation and Notes*. Anchor Bible 15. Doubleday, 1973.

Robinson, H. Wheeler. *The Cross in the Old Testament*. SCM, 1955.

Rowley, H. H. *Job*. New Century Bible Commentary. Reprint, Eerdmans, 1980.

Schultz, Carl. "Job." In *Evangelical Commentary on the Bible*, edited by Walter A. Elwell. Baker, 1989.

Seow, C. L. *Job 1–21: Interpretation and Commentary*. Illuminations. Eerdmans, 2013.

Simonetti, Manlio, and Marco Conti, eds. *Job*. Ancient Christian Commentary on Scripture 6. InterVarsity Press, 2006.

Smick, Elmer B. "Job." In *The Expositor's Bible Commentary*, edited by Frank E. Gaebelein. Vol. 4. Zondervan, 1988.

Thomas, Derek. *The Storm Breaks: Job Simply Explained*. Welwyn Commentary Series. Reprint, Evangelical Press, 2005.

Vicchio, Stephen J. *The Book of Job: A History of Interpretation and a Commentary*. Wipf & Stock, 2020.

———. *Job in the Ancient World*. Wipf & Stock, 2006.

Walton, John H. *Job*. NIVAC. Zondervan, 2012.

Walton, John H., and Tremper Longman III. *How to Read Job*. IVP Academic, 2015.

Webb, Barry G. *Job*. Evangelical Biblical Theology Commentary. Lexham Academic, 2023.

Whybray, R. N. *Job*. Readings: A New Biblical Commentary. Sheffield Phoenix Press, 1998.

Williams, C. J. *The Shadow of Christ in the Book of Job*. Wipf & Stock, 2017.

Wilson, Gerald H. *Job*. Understanding the Bible Commentary 10. Baker, 2007.

Index of Scripture

Jeremiah

Lamentations

Ezekiel

Daniel

Hosea

Joel

Amos

Index of Subjects and Names

Available in the Reformed Expository Commentary Series

Old Testament

Genesis, by Richard D. Phillips
Deuteronomy, by Trent Casto
1 Samuel, by Richard D. Phillips
2 Samuel, by Richard D. Phillips
1 Kings, by Philip Graham Ryken
2 Kings, by Philip Graham Ryken
Ezra & Nehemiah, by Derek W. H. Thomas
Esther & Ruth, by Iain M. Duguid
Job, by Douglas Sean O'Donnell
Psalms 42–72, by Richard D. Phillips
Psalms 73–106, by Richard D. Phillips
Ecclesiastes, by Douglas Sean O'Donnell
Song of Songs, by Iain M. Duguid
Daniel, by Iain M. Duguid
Hosea, by Richard D. Phillips
Jonah & Micah, by Richard D. Phillips
Zephaniah, Haggai, and Malachi, by Iain M. Duguid and Matthew P. Harmon
Zechariah, by Richard D. Phillips

Forthcoming

1 Chronicles, by Andy Palmer
2 Chronicles, by Richard D. Phillips
Psalms 1–41, by Iain M. Duguid and James C. Duguid

Available in the Reformed Expository Commentary Series

New Testament

The Incarnation in the Gospels, by Daniel M. Doriani, Philip Graham Ryken, and Richard D. Phillips
Matthew, by Daniel M. Doriani
Luke, by Philip Graham Ryken
John, by Richard D. Phillips
Romans, by Daniel M. Doriani
2 Corinthians, by Trent Casto
Galatians, by Philip Graham Ryken
Ephesians, by Bryan Chapell
Philippians, by Dennis E. Johnson
Colossians & Philemon, by Richard D. Phillips
1 & 2 Thessalonians, by Richard D. Phillips
1 Timothy, by Philip Graham Ryken
2 Timothy & Titus, by Daniel M. Doriani and Richard D. Phillips
Hebrews, by Richard D. Phillips
James, by Daniel M. Doriani
1 Peter, by Daniel M. Doriani
1–3 John, by Douglas Sean O'Donnell
Revelation, by Richard D. Phillips

Forthcoming

1 Corinthians, by Daniel M. Doriani and Bradley J. Matthews
2 Peter & Jude, by Richard D. Phillips